BUYING *and* SELLING *a* HOME *in* CALIFORNIA

For *Allan*—again

DIAN HYMER

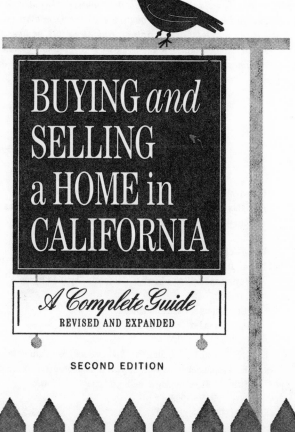

BUYING *and*
SELLING
a HOME in
CALIFORNIA

A Complete Guide
REVISED AND EXPANDED

SECOND EDITION

CHRONICLE BOOKS
SAN FRANCISCO

All the forms reproduced in this book are reprinted with permission from the California Association of Realtors®. Endorsement not implied.

The comments, observations, and recommendations in this book are the opinions of the author, and are based on over 16 years of experience in the residential real estate field. However, the author is not qualified to render legal, accounting, engineering, or other professional advice. Consult the appropriate expert for legal, tax, or other professional recommendations, and be aware that real estate practices and customs are constantly changing and differ from one area to the next.

Library of Congress Cataloging in Publication Data:
Hymer, Dian Davis.
    Buying and selling a home in California / by Dian Hymer.
        p.   cm.
    "Completely revised and updated."
    Includes index.
    ISBN 0-8118-0433-X
    1. House buying—California. 2. House selling—California.
    3. Real estate business—California. 4. Real property—California.
    I. Title. II. Title: Buying & selling a home in California.
HD266.C2H95   1993
333.33'09794—dc20   93-27347
                                                 CIP

Design/Illustration: Karen Smidth
Composition: Words & Deeds

Printed in the United States.

Distributed in Canada by Raincoast Books, 112 East Third Ave., Vancouver, B.C. V5T 1C8

10 9 8 7 6 5 4 3 2 1

Chronicle Books
275 Fifth Street
San Francisco, CA 94103

CONTENTS

INTRODUCTION

There are few certainties in life. One thing you can count on, though, is a constantly changing real estate market. For instance, look at the past 15 years or so. At the end of the 1970s, the residential real estate market was booming, financing was easy, and buyers bought with reckless abandon. In contrast, the 1980s began with a whimper. Interest rates soared to unprecedented heights in 1981, ushering in the worst real estate recession since World War II. The market recovered in the mid-1980s, and the decade finished with a huge run-up in California home prices. In 1989, many communities in the state saw home prices increase a whopping 20 to 30 percent in just one year. Buyers couldn't buy fast enough in a market characterized by the lowest inventory of homes available for sale on record. Financing big ticket purchases was easy in a lax lending environment that ultimately led to the savings and loan crisis. A credit tightening regime set in as lenders reacted with stiffer loan qualification procedures. The real estate market took a downturn in 1990 and home prices dropped in California. By 1993, interest rates were at their lowest level in 20 years. The combination of decreased home prices and low interest rates improved affordability so that first-time buyers, who were virtually shut out of the 1989 market, became vital players again and accounted for nearly half of the state's home sales in 1992.

Simultaneous with this roller-coaster real estate market, a strong climate of consumer awareness flourished in California, resulting in new laws relating to residential real estate sales. "Buyer beware," formerly a tenet of the industry, was cast aside in favor of a far more explicit approach to maximizing consumer protection. Sellers must now disclose property defects to buyers when they sell. Agents are required to disclose who they'll represent in a real estate transaction: buyer, seller, or both. In fact, the disclosure business has exploded in California. Disclosures relating to fire areas, environmental hazards, a death on the property in the last three years, the existence of smoke detectors, and even earthquake weaknesses, to name a few, must be made to California home buyers before they complete a purchase. Purchase contracts have been expanded and revised to provide more consumer protection.

What do these developments portend for the California home buyer and seller? An increasing level of care will be necessary in order to make solid buying and selling decisions. This is not just because of a cyclical real estate market, new disclosure requirements, and an increasingly litigious society—although these are important considerations. Buying a home is also a large investment, especially in California where home prices remain high despite recent price deflation. In 1992, the median price of existing homes sold statewide was $197,900. In comparison, the median price of existing homes sold nationally in January 1993 was only $103,700. The stakes are high if you play the home ownership game in California, and the rules by which you play the game have changed. A home is the biggest investment most people make in a lifetime, and few of us can afford to make such a costly mistake.

Buying and Selling a Home in California is designed to provide you with the tools you need to ensure that your real estate purchase or sale is a success story, not a tale of woe. After reading this book you won't worry about qualifying for a loan because you'll know how to prequalify yourself, and you'll understand how the loan qualification process works. You'll learn how to decide when is the best time to buy and to sell, how to select the agent who'll best serve your needs, how the tax laws will affect your move, and what disclosures you need to make to protect yourself. You'll also know how to find your dream home, how to fix up your current home and sell it for top dollar, how to negotiate the purchase contract, and when to order a further inspection.

Whether you're a first-time buyer, a homeowner trading up to a larger home, or a retiree who needs to sell the family home to trade down to a smaller one, you'll find valuable tips on how to structure your purchase or sale. Anyone considering an adjustable rate mortgage will find the list of questions to ask adjustable rate lenders a must. Real estate topics that are rarely discussed are dealt with here, such as termite reports, environmental hazards, and what to do if you're dissatisfied with your real estate agent. Real estate agents, too, particularly those new in the business, will find the book useful. Agents become good agents through years of hard work; benefiting from another agent's knowledge acquired through years of experience will help to increase your level of professionalism.

The book also provides copies of the actual real estate forms you'll be likely to use in your California real estate transaction: the listing agreement, purchase contract, counteroffer, and various disclosure forms required by law. Buyers and sellers will reduce their anxiety by reading this book since they will understand in advance how the process works, and they will be able to monitor their real estate transactions to successful completion.

Keep in mind that this book is based on the opinions of the author and does not represent the standard of care of any individual realty company. Be sure to read all contracts and forms carefully, front and back. Read the fine print, too, even if you think it's a waste of time or the print's too small. If you have any questions during the course of a purchase or sale transaction, call your agent, escrow officer, accountant, attorney, or building inspector for the answer. Ask a lot of questions; the answers will save you plenty.

CHAPTER 1

STARTING OUT

Determining Your Price Range

The first thing you should do, even before starting to look at houses, is find out what price you can afford. Whether you're considering a condominium or single-family home, a new home or a resale, whether you're a first-time buyer or a homeowner trading up or down, it is wise to figure out first what price range makes sense for your budget.

Roughly speaking, you can afford to buy a house that's about three times your gross annual income. But more precisely, the price you can afford will depend on six key factors:

- Your income
- The amount of cash you have available for the down payment and closing costs
- Your outstanding debts
- Your credit history
- The type of mortgage you select
- Current interest rates

The easiest way to find out what size mortgage you qualify for is to meet with a local loan agent to be lender prequalified. Take information with you regarding your income, current debts, and assets. Be completely candid with your loan agent about the particulars of your financial situation, including the source of your cash down payment and the length of time at your current job.

Ask the loan agent to have your credit checked before you make an offer to buy a home. Should there be any credit problems that might interfere with your loan approval, you'll know up front. The best home loans (i.e., those with the best interest rates and terms) require impeccable credit. If you find a mistake in your credit report, ask your loan agent what you can do to correct it and take care of the problem before you get into

Multiply your annual gross income by three to determine your approximate price range.

1

a contract to buy a house. See Chapter 10 for more on financing for buyers whose credit is marginal. A credit report should cost about $50 per person.

Lenders look at two ratios when qualifying you for a home loan. One is the ratio of your monthly housing expense to your gross monthly income. The housing expense includes the principal and interest payment on your home loan, property taxes, and hazard insurance. These items are referred to jointly as PITI (Principal, Interest, Taxes, and Insurance). The other ratio is the ratio of your total monthly debt (PITI plus other debt obligations) to your gross monthly income.

Your housing expense-to-income ratio should fall in the 28 to 33 percent range, although some lenders will go as high as 40 percent if you can make a large down payment and have additional cash reserves in the bank. Generally, the higher the loan amount relative to the property value (in other words, the less cash down), the lower the qualifying ratio. Five to 10 percent cash down buyers may find that lenders will qualify them on a 28 percent housing expense-to-income ratio.

Your total debt-to-income ratio should be in the 34 to 38 percent range. If your lender tells you your ratios are 30/36, this means your housing expense-to-income ratio is 30 percent and your total debt-to-income ratio is 36 percent.

There is a certain satisfaction to be derived from calculating for yourself approximately what you can afford. A "Home Purchase Affordability Worksheet" is shown opposite for prospective buyers who are so inclined. Sellers, too, can benefit from familiarizing themselves with the worksheet. By examining the simple equations lenders use to qualify buyers for home loans, you should be able to avoid having your sale fall apart because the buyers couldn't arrange financing. Understanding the qualification process will enable you to determine at the time the buyers' offer is presented whether they will be able to qualify for the loan they need.

Skip the rest of this section if you have no interest in determining qualification yourself, but do get prequalified by a lender or mortgage broker. The home price you can afford using an adjustable rate mortgage (ARM) will be significantly more than the price you can afford if you get a fixed rate loan because the lower initial ARM interest rate makes qualifying easier. You'll find more general information about financing your home purchase in Chapter 10.

To calculate the loan amount you qualify for, divide your gross annual income (not net income) by 12 to arrive at your gross monthly income. If you'll be purchasing a home with another person, be sure to include the second income. For example, let's say your gross annual income is $50,000, which gives a gross monthly income of approximately $4,167. Multiply this figure by 36 percent to determine your affordable monthly debt, which in this example is approximately $1,500.

Have a loan agent or broker prequalify you before house hunting and pay to have your credit checked.

Home Purchase Affordability Worksheet

	Actual	Example
Gross Annual Income:	_____	$ 50,000
Divide by 12 to determine		
Gross Monthly Income:	_____	$ 4,167
Multiply by 36 percent (.36) to determine		
Affordable Monthly Debt:	_____	$ 1,500
Subtract		
Monthly Debts:	_____	$ 300
To determine the		
Affordable Monthly Housing Expense: **(PITI)**	_____	$ 1,200
Multiply by 85 percent (.85) to determine		
Affordable Mortgage Payment (PI): **(principal and interest only)**	_____	$ 1,020
Current Interest Rate:	_____	8%
Term of the Loan:	_____	30 year
See amortization schedule to determine		
Affordable Loan Amount:	_____	$ 138,000
Multiply by 4 percent (.04) to determine		
Closing Costs:	_____	$ 5,520
Total Cash Available:	_____	$ 41,000
Subtract		
Closing Costs:	_____	$ 5,520
To determine		
Down Payment Amount:	_____	$ 35,480
Add		
Affordable Loan Amount:	_____	$ 138,000
To determine your		
Approximate Affordable Purchase Price:	_____	$ 173,480

3

Next, subtract the total you pay each month on any long-term debts such as car payments, student loans, or installment loans. This number is your affordable monthly housing expense. In this case, let's say the buyers have a car payment of $300 a month which, when subtracted from $1,500, leaves $1,200 to apply toward the affordable monthly housing expense. If you have no long-term debt, simply multiply your gross monthly income by 30 percent to arrive at your affordable monthly housing expense.

The affordable monthly housing expense must cover your PITI. Monthly homeowner's association dues, if you are purchasing a condominium or townhouse, and private mortgage insurance (PMI), if it is required by the lender, will be added to the PITI in qualifying you for a loan. PMI is paid by the buyer to protect the lender in case the buyer defaults on the loan. It's usually required when a buyer puts less than 20 percent cash down. PMI costs vary with lenders but premiums usually run about one-half of a percent (0.50 percent) of the loan amount for the first year of the loan. (Divide this amount by 12 to figure the monthly PMI charge.)

The next step is to subtract an amount equal to your monthly property tax and hazard insurance liability (plus homeowner's dues and PMI, if applicable) from your affordable monthly housing expense. The resulting figure will represent your affordable mortgage payment (principal and interest only). Roughly 15 percent of the monthly PITI is usually applied toward taxes and insurance, so multiply your affordable monthly housing expense by 85 percent to arrive at your affordable mortgage payment.

Using our example, $1,200 multiplied by 85 percent (.85) results in an affordable mortgage payment of $1,020. The 85 percent figure is approximate and will vary with the purchase price and the loan amount. Simple formulas are provided below so you can check the amount deducted for taxes and insurance for accuracy after you have determined an affordable purchase price.

Your gross monthly income is one of two factors limiting the size of loan you qualify for. The other is current interest rates, which change over time and also vary from one type of loan to another. The interest rate charged on a loan amortized (paid off in full) over 15 or 20 years is usually lower than the interest rate on a similar loan amortized over thirty years. The initial interest rates on adjustable rate mortgages (ARMs) are lower than the interest rates charged on fixed-rate loans.

Affordability increases as interest rates decrease. It also increases if you use adjustable- rather than fixed-rate financing.

For information regarding current interest rates in your area, call several local lenders and ask for rate quotes on fixed- and adjustable-rate home loans. This is not the time to make a final decision about what kind of loan you want, but it's wise to start considering it. Looking at the monthly payments required to amortize a loan at different interest rates may help you to decide.

Turn to the amortization schedule at the back of the book. The tables are divided according to interest rates and the term of the loan (15 or 30 years). Remember, you have approximately $1,020 of your gross monthly income to apply toward your mortgage payment.

Suppose the interest rate on a fixed-rate loan amortized over 30 years is 8 percent. Find the 30-year column for that interest rate on the table. As you read down the list of monthly payments, look for the payment that most closely approximates $1,020. The table ends at $733.76, which is the monthly payment on a $100,000 loan. To find out how much more than $100,000 you can qualify for, subtract $733.76 from $1,020; the remainder is $286.24. Now read up the column. $286.24 falls about halfway between the monthly payments on a $30,000 and a $40,000 loan. Subtract $220.13 (the monthly payment required to amortize a $30,000 loan) from $286.24; the remainder is $66.11. Now read up the column again. The monthly payment closest to $66.11 is $58.70, which amortizes an $8,000 loan. Add $8,000, $30,000, and $100,000 for a total affordable loan amount of $138,000 for a 30-year, fixed-rate mortgage.

Compare this to the loan you qualify for if you select a 15-year fixed or an adjustable (amortized over thirty years). If the interest rate on a 15-year fixed loan is 7.5 percent, your affordable loan limit drops to approximately $110,000. On the other hand, selecting an adjustable 30-year loan with an initial interest rate of 6 percent will enable you to qualify for a loan amount of $170,000. Note that on some ARMs the lender will insist that you qualify at an interest rate that is 2 percent above the ARM start rate; others qualify you at the initial ARM interest rate. For more information about the pros and cons of fixed- and adjustable-rate home loans, see Chapter 10. An interest rate factor chart is included with the amortization schedule at the back of the book for home buyers who want more information on how to compute monthly payments and loan amounts.

5

To determine what home price you can afford, you now need to establish how much cash you have for a down payment and closing costs. Buyers who are selling one home to buy another will need to know the current market value of the home being sold, as well as an estimate of what the sale costs will be.

Buyers' closing costs (the fees associated with purchasing a home) include such expenses as loan origination fees; credit report and appraisal fees; escrow and title insurance fees (depending on where you buy); transfer taxes (again, this varies with location); document preparation and notary fees; proration of taxes; proration of homeowner's association dues; hazard insurance premium; inspection fees (termite, building, roof, etc.); and proration of interest owed on your new home loan. For more information about closing costs, see Chapter 11.

Returning to our worksheet, an approximate amount for closing costs is determined by multiplying your affordable loan amount by 4 percent. Subtract this amount from your total cash available to arrive at the down payment amount.

Then add the down payment to the loan amount; the total is your approximate affordable purchase price.

After you've established what price you can afford, check to make sure that the approximation used to arrive at your affordable mortgage payment is accurate. Remember, you multiplied the affordable monthly housing expense by 85 percent (.85) in order to reduce the PITI figure to principal and interest only. Annual property taxes in California are limited to 1 percent of the purchase price plus an additional amount to cover bonds for community improvements; a safe number is 1.25 percent, although this will vary from area to area. The cost of hazard insurance, almost always required by the lender, varies with location, deductible amount on the policy, and age of the home. A rough indicator of how much an annual policy will cost is found by multiplying the purchase price of the new home by .003 (0.3 percent). Add both figures together and divide by 12 to arrive at a monthly figure. Subtract this amount from your affordable monthly housing expense (PITI). The difference should be approximately the same as your affordable mortgage payment (principal and interest only).

The cash down payment required to purchase a home varies. Generally, the more cash down, the easier it is to qualify for a loan. But, there are loans available to qualified buyers who have as little as 5 percent cash down, or less. Buyers who are making a cash down payment equal to 10 percent of the purchase price, or less, will be required by most lenders to have extra cash reserves in the bank in order to qualify for a loan. Be sure to ask about additional cash reserve requirements when you get prequalified.

What you can qualify for may not be what you feel comfortable paying per month for your housing expense. Still, most buyers today apply for as much financing as they can afford, because the interest paid on a home loan is tax deductible, and other tax shelters have been severely curtailed by tax reform. But it's up to you to decide. It doesn't make sense to stretch far beyond your means, particularly if you're living on a fixed income or if future salary increases are uncertain.

Balancing Needs and Desires

Now that you know what you can afford, the next step is to decide what you want and need in a home.

Take a moment to indulge your fantasies—on paper that is. Buy a notebook and dedicate it to the search for your new home. On the first page, make a "wish list" of the features you desire in a home. Write down everything that comes to mind. For instance, maybe you're a hobby-oriented person who will be happier with a little extra space, even if it's a cubbyhole in a basement, to develop into a workspace or wine cellar.

Next, take a good hard look at the list, dividing it into two sections: your needs and your wants. Your needs can include such things as the number of bedrooms and baths, a kitchen large enough to accommodate your family, a formal dining room for entertaining, or a yard suitable for pets and children. Some home buyers have specialized needs, such as wheelchair access and one-level living to accommodate a disabled member of the family. If you and your spouse are both busy professionals, you may need a space for live-in help.

One variable that's often overlooked is the condition of the new home. If you're extremely busy, are short on cash, and have few mechanical skills, then "move-in condition" should be on your need list. On the other hand, if you can afford to hire professionals to remodel your new home, then "almost perfect condition" can be included on the want list. And if money is tight but you're skilled at house painting, plumbing, and carpentry, you may need to find a home that's not in move-in condition with the intention of working on it yourself. In this case, "fixer-upper" will be on the need list.

Home features that you want may include a swimming pool, a view, a family room with a fireplace, a gas stove, or a specific style of house (Mediterranean, English Tudor, or French Provincial). These are the features that distinguish a home that fits your dreams from one that merely suits your needs. They are items you can live without if necessary.

The final step in determining the kind of house you're looking for is to prioritize your wants and needs. The perfect house does not exist, not at any price. Knowing in advance which of your needs and wants are most important will help you to make a sensible decision.

7

What's in Store for You? The Psychological Aspects of Buying and Selling a Home

A striking, tall blond-haired woman nervously paced the room, puffing on a cigarette. "I stopped smoking, until recently," she sighed.

Another woman complained that she'd put on an extra 15 pounds over the past few months. "I was in great shape last year at this time. But I've been so depressed lately."

A tired looking 38-year-old man complained of sleepless nights and incessant worry.

What affliction do these unfortunate individuals have in common? They're all involved in buying or selling a home.

A lot has been written about the technical aspects of buying and selling a home. But what about the psychological aspects?

Few people are prepared for the emotional roller coaster that often accompanies a residential real estate transaction. The process requires a commitment of your time, energy, patience, and enthusiasm. At times you can expect to experience states of excitement and elation. And you can feel anxious, confused, cranky, even depressed.

Buying or selling a home is unlike any other business transaction you're likely to be involved in. There's a subjective and emotional component that rarely creeps into ordinary business deals. This is because it involves your home: your haven, your palace, your refuge from the problems of the outside world. Your identity is intimately intertwined with your home. Change your home and your identity is bound to be violated; this will be uncomfortable for most people.

Moving ranks high on the list of the most stressful events in life, like divorce, death, and loss of a job. Many of the critical elements involved in buying and selling a home are beyond your control. It's hard to tell, for instance, whether you'll find your next home in a few weeks or a few months. Your home may sell in a month or it may take six months. Once you're in escrow, you could have to change your plans completely and race to close early if interest rates start to rise. Or, a significant defect could surface during the house inspection, and you could find yourself back on the market again.

Having realistic expectations about the buying and selling process will help you cope with the experience. Understanding how the process works, which is what this book is about, will help you to feel more in control. Ask questions when you feel unsure, and don't hesitate to discuss your feelings.

Choose to work with an agent (or agents, if you're looking for a new home in several different areas) whom you relate to well. Select a Realtor® who is sensitive and understands your need to be updated continually on your purchase or sale. Work with someone who has good communication skills, someone who can demystify the process for you and explain the ins and outs of the business clearly.

Take time off during the purchase or sale, or have a little fun. Get out of town for a few days to take your mind off it all. When you're ready to give it all up because the pressure is too great, remember that thousands of people live through the process every year. To date, there's been no evidence to indicate that the experience is fatal. Like all things in life, this too will pass.

If buying and selling a home sounds like more trouble than it's worth, think again. Yes, it's time consuming. Yes, it can test the limits of your sanity. But, there's a huge reward at the end of the ordeal: a new home. And, as we all know, there's no place like home.

CHAPTER 2

TAXES *and* OTHER CONSIDERATIONS

Rarely is the *quest for tax relief the sole reason for buying a new home, but it's an important consideration. Buying or selling a residence has tax ramifications and it's wise to understand ahead of time how you'll be affected financially by your purchase or sale.*

The First-Time Buyer

Rent or Buy?

Affording the monthly payments is not the primary problem facing most first-time buyers. Statistics show that most renters pay approximately 29 percent of their income toward rent and receive none of the tax benefits of ownership. If you're currently paying in the neighborhood of $850 per month on rent and you earn $35,000 to $40,000 per year, you can probably qualify to buy a $120,000 home. Your monthly principal, interest, property tax, and insurance obligations (PITI; see Chapter 1) will be approximately $928 per month if you put 20 percent cash down and take out a $96,000 loan at a 9 percent interest rate (30-year term).

It will cost a mere $78 more per month to own your home, even before considering the tax savings. Most of the mortgage payment in the first year (approximately 99 percent on a loan amortized over 30 years) goes to paying interest, which, like property tax, is deductible from your income for tax purposes. In the first year of ownership, you would accumulate a write-off of over $10,000.

The after-tax monthly expense of your new home will vary depending on your tax bracket. Using the example above, your monthly mortgage interest and property tax expense for your first year of ownership will be approximately $890 per month. If you are in the 15 percent tax bracket, multiply $890 by .15 and subtract the result, $134, from your entire monthly housing expense (PITI) figure of $928. The balance, $794, is your monthly cost of ownership after considering your federal tax liability. If you're in the 5 percent state tax bracket, subtract an additional 5 percent from your mortgage interest and property tax expense. The higher your tax bracket, the larger the tax break, and the lower the after-tax cost of ownership.

The loan origination fees charged on a purchase mortgage (better known as "points," and customarily 1 to 2 percent of the loan amount) are treated as "prepaid" interest by the IRS and are tax deductible. (One point is equivalent to 1 percent of the loan amount.) If the lender charges two points to take out a $96,000 mortgage, it will cost you $1,920. In most cases this amount can be deducted from your income in the year of purchase, creating a considerable tax savings.

The above comparison of the expenses involved in renting versus buying doesn't discuss the hidden cost of home maintenance, which is normally not a renter's concern. A first-time buyer is wise to consider purchasing a relatively new home, condominium, or townhouse for which maintenance expenses are likely to be lower than for an older home. This example also doesn't take into account that a portion of the mortgage payment each month goes toward paying off the principal balance remaining on your home loan. This amounts to an enforced savings plan. If you were to continue to pay $850 in rent every month ($10,200 per year), you'd stand little chance of accumulating the equity necessary to allow you to trade up to a more desirable home in the future.

Home price appreciation is another important factor to take into consideration. It has averaged about 5 percent per year for the past 40 years, even though there have been periods when home prices rose faster than inflation as well as periods when prices were flat or declined.

Finally, there is a psychological benefit to owning a home which is often referred to as pride of ownership. It's hard to quantify this subjective factor. Among other things, it involves a sense of security that's derived from owning the roof over your head and from being your own landlord. An objective consideration is that, although home prices have fluctuated in recent years, rents have continued to rise and are expected to rise further in the future.

Accumulating the Cash for a Down Payment and Closing Costs

The biggest problem facing 70 percent of first-time buyers is accumulating the cash to cover a down payment and closing costs. This is understandable. With 29 percent of one's income going to rent and at least 20 percent going to income taxes, it's easy to see why many people find it difficult to save enough for a down payment even when they have the income to afford monthly mortgage payments.

Resourceful buyers have various options to consider if saving the customary 20 percent cash down payment seems impossible. The most obvious is to borrow the money from your parents. Approximately 30 percent of first-time buyers buy their first home with a loan or a money gift from their parents.

A credit from the seller for all or part of the buyer's nonrecurring closing costs reduces the amount of cash a buyer needs to close escrow.

Any taxpayer is permitted to give up to $10,000 per year to another person without having to pay a gift tax. If your parents have the financial ability and are so inclined, they can each give you and your partner up to $10,000 in one year (a total of $40,000). Lenders have restrictions on gifts from friends and relatives other than your parents. Also, if you are putting less than 20 percent down, most conventional lenders require that at least 5 percent of the purchase price be your own cash, not a gift. But if you have 20 percent or more cash to put down, the entire down payment can be a gift.

Be aware that lenders will require verification of the source of the funds needed to close escrow, unless the money has been in your bank account for at least five months. A gift letter from parents who are assisting their children is usually required by the lender. It specifies that the buyers are under no obligation to repay the "gift." Buyers are cautioned against claiming a loan from parents as a gift that doesn't need to be repaid. Lender fraud has severe consequences. If a lender were to discover that you falsified your loan application, the lender could demand immediate repayment of your loan in full.

It's wise to obtain the gift letter and cash from your parents before making an offer to purchase a piece of property, as it's not uncommon for relatives to change their minds about giving money. Don't find yourself in the awkward position of entering into a binding contract with a seller only to discover you're lacking a significant portion of your cash down payment.

The following is a list of additional ways to generate cash for a down payment and closing costs:

- Borrow against a 401(k) retirement plan or insurance policy.
- Liquidate, or borrow against, assets such as securities or a car.
- Borrow on an unsecured line of credit or charge card, if you can still qualify for a mortgage with the additional debt.
- Ask your employer to contribute part of the down payment.
- Get a loan from a friend or relative, if you can qualify with the additional debt.
- Ask the seller to pay your nonrecurring closing costs. (Lenders usually permit a credit of up to 3 to 6 percent of the purchase price.)
- Take a low-point or zero-point loan to reduce the amount of your closing costs.
- Ask the seller to carry financing.
- Explore the various city and county down payment assistance programs.
- Close escrow late in the month to reduce the proration of interest owed to the lender at closing.

11

Jill and John Smith had enough cash for a 10 percent down payment, but not enough to cover their closing costs. They made a $365,000 offer to purchase a home that had been on the market for some time. In the offer they asked the seller to credit them $10,000 in escrow for nonrecurring closing costs. Nonrecurring costs include such fees as title insurance, escrow fees, loan origination fee, and a city transfer tax. Since the house appraised for $365,000, the lender did not have a problem with this.

When buyers are short of the cash required to close escrow, it's often worth it to pay a slightly higher price for a home and take a credit from the seller to pay for nonrecurring closing costs. The house must appraise at the higher price, otherwise the lender will have a problem with this financing arrangement.

Financing for Buyers Short on Cash

Ninety and 95 percent financing is readily available from conventional lenders. Expect your closing costs to be higher for these loans than for 80 percent loans. An impound account (for the collection of property taxes and hazard insurance on a monthly basis) and property mortgage insurance (PMI) to protect the lender from foreclosure losses are required by most lenders when you put less than 20 percent cash down. In addition, most lenders will require that you have cash reserves in your bank account to cover several months of your housing expense.

Many portfolio lenders (lenders who make loans to hold in their own portfolios rather than to sell to investors) self-insure their 90 and 95 percent loans. They have more flexibility in approving their loans since they aren't sending them to an independent PMI company for approval. Self-insuring lenders usually don't charge a separate PMI fee. Instead, they increase the interest rate and/or loan fee (points) to cover the cost of self-insuring.

There are pros and cons to loans that self-insure for PMI. If you're paying a separate monthly PMI premium (which is not deductible for tax purposes) and you stay in the home long enough to build up a 20 percent equity, you can ask the lender to drop the PMI requirement and reduce your monthly payment. On a loan where the cost to self-insure for PMI is built into the cost of the loan, you can write this off for tax purposes since it's interest, but you're stuck with the increased fees for the term of the loan.

If you have 10 percent cash down and you know someone who is willing to loan you an additional 10 percent (a loan that will be secured by the property, not a gift), you can get an 80 percent loan from a conventional lender and avoid PMI and impound account payments. This is referred to as 80, 10, and 10 financing. The bank loans you 80 percent of the purchase price, you make a 10 percent cash down payment, and a third party makes you a 10 percent second loan. Sometimes a seller will be willing to carry the 10 percent second. Real estate agents and mortgage brokers are often in touch with individuals looking to make secure investments through second mortgages.

Fannie Mae (Federal National Mortgage Association) offers Community Home Buyer's Programs through participating lenders, including Countrywide Funding, GMAC, Home Savings of America, World Savings and Loan, First Interstate Bank, San Francisco Federal Savings and Loan, and American Savings Bank, to name a few. These loans require less cash down

> *Ten percent down buyers can avoid paying PMI if they can find an investor or seller to carry a second mortgage for 10 percent of the purchase price.*

and are easier to qualify for than are other conventional loans. A 5 percent down payment is required; however, up to 2 percent may be a gift or loan from a government or nonprofit agency. The borrower's income cannot exceed 115 percent of the area's median income, and the borrower must attend a seminar on home ownership and the home buying process. Large banks, such as Wells Fargo Bank and Bank of America, offer similar programs.

Fannie Mae also offers an employer-assisted home buying program, called MAGNET, which is similar to the program above except that employers make grants to borrowers for closing costs or for up to 2 percent of the required 5 percent down payment. For more information about Fannie Mae programs, call (202) 752-3421.

Veteran's Administration (VA) and Federal Housing Administration (FHA) financing are possibilities for eligible buyers who can't qualify for or afford 95 percent conventional financing. VA loans have no down payment requirement; FHA loans require about 3 percent down. These loan programs have strict limitations on loan amounts, the property must meet certain standards, the qualification process is lengthy, and the seller often pays costs not required when the buyer obtains conventional financing. VA and FHA financing are, therefore, not attractive options in areas where purchase prices are high or where the market strongly favors the seller. Cal-Vet (California Department of Veteran Affairs) offers attractive low-down loans to veterans who qualify.

CHFA (California Housing Finance Agency) has several home loan programs for buyers short of cash. The Home Mortgage Purchase Program is for first-time buyers with 5 percent down (10 percent for condominiums). Interest rates are usually below market rates, but income and purchase price limits apply. The CHFA Self-Help Housing Program provides loans to first-time buyers who use their own labor as a down payment. For more information, call (916) 322-3991 or (213) 736-2355.

Many cities and counties offer low-cost home loan programs for first-time buyers. For example, the Mortgage Credit Certificates Program allows eligible home buyers to take approximately 20 percent of their annual mortgage payments as an annual tax credit against federal income taxes. The tax credit is taken into consideration in qualifying the borrower for the loan; it increases the borrower's ability to qualify and reduces the effective interest rate on the loan by about 2 percentage points. Income, purchase price limits, and other restrictions apply on this and on other first-time buyer programs. Check with local housing agencies or the local Association/Board of Realtors® for more information.

Equity sharing is another possibility. Under this plan, a buyer purchases a home with an investor or a relative. The cash down payment, mortgage payments, tax benefits, and profits at time of sale are shared between the buyer and the investor. There are a few lenders, usually portfolio lenders, who offer equity share loans, and most lenders require that the buyers have at least 5 percent of their own cash for a down payment. Equity sharing is a less than ideal arrangement. Although the buyer has the exclusive right to occupy the property, ownership is shared. It's also difficult to find investors willing to invest in an equity share purchase unless home prices are appreciating at a healthy pace. Parents might be willing to participate in an equity share purchase to help their children get into their first home.

There are companies and brokers who specialize in bringing buyers and investors together for equity sharing ownership. Ask a real estate professional for a recommendation and exercise caution. Consult an attorney with experience in the area to assist you in drafting the necessary contracts and documents. Your agreement should include a provision that gives you the first right to buy out the investor and become the sole owner if you desire.

Another possibility is to purchase with a co-buyer. Under this arrangement, you share not only the financial aspects of ownership but also the living space with your partner. The benefit is that you and your partner can purchase a larger or more expensive home than might otherwise be possible. Again, consult an attorney with experience in drafting home ownership partnership agreements, and be sure you have a partnership arrangement agreed upon in writing before escrow closes.

In slower, "buyers'" markets, several other possibilities are available to buyers short on cash. Builders of new construction developments often offer attractive financing alternatives when they're having difficulty selling a project; these include low down payment financing for owner occupants or payment of a portion of the buyer's nonrecurring closing costs. Seller financing also becomes more prevalent when the real estate market slows down.

Finally, the lease option is a popular alternative to buyers and sellers in the real estate market when homes are difficult to sell. For a relatively small amount of cash (the option money, which is a negotiable amount), the buyer is able to lease a home for a specified period of time with an option to purchase the property for a specified price. The option money is applied to the purchase price if the buyer purchases the property, or is forfeited to the seller at the end of the option period if the buyer fails to complete the purchase. See Chapter 6 for more information about these options.

See Chapter 10 for more information about financing alternatives for marginally qualified buyers.

The Trade-up Buyer

The concerns of the trade-up buyer differ from those of the first-time buyer. Accumulating a cash down payment is usually not the major obstacle, since the repeat buyer usually has benefited from enforced savings through mortgage payments and home price appreciation.

Remodel or Move?

One dilemma for many homeowners is deciding whether to remodel their existing home or move to another. If you've been happy in your current home and neighborhood and you need more space or a different layout, remodeling is a possibility. Deciding to remodel, like deciding to move, requires careful consideration in order to avoid costly mistakes. The first step is to take a good close look at your wish list of needs and desires. Ask yourself if it's even possible to remodel your present home to suit your needs.

Sometimes it's not obvious whether remodeling will work, in which case you'll need the aid of an architect or contractor to help you make the decision. You're looking for an architect or contractor who'll listen to your needs and who'll design a plan that can be built within your price range (not double what you can afford). It's wise to have a consultation done in your home before engaging someone to draw a full set of plans. This will give you an opportunity to determine if the architect's ideas are in line with your own. The cost of a full set of plans is too much if they turn out to be of little use to you. Hire professionals to locate property boundary lines, easements, septic tanks, and wells to make sure your remodeling plans are feasible.

At some point in the decision-making process you need to consider whether you and your family can deal with the difficulties of remodeling. The process is very disruptive, particularly when it involves the kitchen and bathrooms.

Let's say you're still considering a major renovation and you have a set of plans. The next step is to have several licensed contractors bid on the job. While interviewing contractors you should also be determining the current market value of your home and looking into sources of remodel financing.

The easiest way to determine the current value of your home is to ask the real estate agent who sold you the home for a current market evaluation. You want to know the value of the home in its present, unremodeled condition. Also tell your agent what your remodeling plans are, and ask for an estimate of what your home's value will be after the improvements are completed. If you're adding a bedroom to a three-bedroom house, request comparable sales information on both three- and four-bedroom homes in your neighborhood. Your aim here is to determine whether you'll be overimproving your home for the neighborhood. The best house on the block is not generally thought to be the best investment.

Home improvements usually add value to a home, but you can't always recover the full cost when you sell. The value of the improvements will also depend on the amenities your home already has and how soon you sell after you remodel. Adding a second full bathroom and remodeling an outdated kitchen are improvements that usually return close to 100 percent of the investment. Other good investments (approximately 80 percent return) are a bathroom remodel, a master bedroom remodel, a family room addition, and adding a third bedroom, a deck, central air conditioning (in warm climates), or a fireplace (particularly if it's the only fireplace in the house). A swimming pool, on the other hand, will return only about 33 percent at the time of sale.

After you receive the contractors' bids, add the estimated cost of the improvements to the current market value of your home. Compare the total to the projected value of your home after the improvements are completed. If the total is considerably less than the projected value, you're probably making a secure investment.

15

You need to consider one last, but important, factor before making the decision to remodel or to move: tax consequences. You will, no doubt, have to take out a loan in either case. The points (loan fees, usually 1 to 2 percent of the loan amount) are treated differently by the IRS on refinance loans than they are on home purchase loans. With a home purchase, you can deduct the total amount of the points from your income in the year of purchase. On a refinance, however, the points must be deducted incrementally over the term of the loan (1/30 each year on a 30-year loan). You can claim any unclaimed points when you repay a refinance loan.

The 1986 Tax Reform Act preserved the deductibility of mortgage interest with specific limitations and qualifications which may be subject to revision. As of this writing, a taxpayer can deduct the interest paid per year on first mortgages secured by a first and second home up to $1 million of debt as long as this amount does not exceed the amounts paid on acquisition indebtedness and substantial improvements. In addition, a homeowner can deduct the interest paid per year on up to $100,000 of home equity debt (a second trust deed or secured line of credit).

If you have a large amount of equity in a home and a large income as well, it may make more sense to trade up than to remodel. For instance, a home that you paid $100,000 for 15 years ago, that's now worth $400,000, probably won't qualify for the maximum write-off due to IRS restrictions. If you sell this home, buy another for $500,000, and finance the purchase with an 80 percent loan, your new acquisition indebtedness will be $400,000. The interest on this loan is tax deductible each year, and the points paid to originate this loan are deductible in the year of purchase. Consult your tax advisor to determine the precise tax ramifications of moving or remodeling.

Buy or Sell First?

Often the biggest concern facing the trade-up buyer is whether to buy or sell first. The decision usually depends on the real estate market and your financial situation. Finding and purchasing your new home first lets you know precisely where you're going, and when, before you put your current home on the market. But if you need the equity out of your present home to close escrow on the new one, you may come up short if your current home doesn't sell for the anticipated price within the necessary time frame.

It's risky to make a non-contingent offer if you need the equity from your old home to buy a new one.

In a slow market, some sellers will agree to accept a purchase contract that is contingent upon the sale of the buyers' home. Sellers who accept a contingent sale offer often require the contract to contain an escape (or release) clause that allows them to continue offering their home to other buyers. The

16

time period specified in the escape clause is usually 72 hours, but this is negotiable. If the sellers receive another attractive offer, they can accept it in a secondary (or backup) position. They then give written notification to the buyers who are in first position that they have 72 hours to remove the contingency from the contract. If the first buyers remove the contingency within this time frame, they stay in contract. But their purchase is no longer contingent upon the sale of their current home. If the first buyers are unable to remove the sale contingency, the home goes to the second buyers and the first buyers start looking again.

A strategy that will work with some sellers is to make an offer contingent upon the sale of your home with a provision that the escape clause won't go into effect for a specified period of time, say two or three weeks. This will give you a chance to find a buyer for your current home without having to risk losing the new home to another buyer. The seller's concern will be that you might overprice your existing home, so don't be surprised if the sellers want their agent to approve your list price as a condition of the sale.

John and Linda Christopher were outgrowing their home, and they wanted a better school district. They couldn't afford to buy a new home without selling the old one. They started looking for a replacement home while they worked on getting their old home ready to market. They found a house that fit their wish list almost perfectly just before their old home went on the market. They offered the seller a little over the asking price, even though they weren't in competition with other buyers, in exchange for the privilege of having a contingent sale offer with a release clause that didn't go into effect for 21 days. On the twenty-first day, the Christophers sold their house and were able to complete the purchase.

17

In a fast-paced market, you're likely to have no trouble selling your home, but you probably won't find a seller willing to accept a contingent sale offer. The good homes sell fast in a seller's market, often with multiple offers. You'll find it impossible to compete with buyers who are able to purchase a new home without a contingency for the sale of another home.

Let's say you're a family of five. You need to liquidate the equity in your present home in order to move up, and the thought of selling first and moving to an interim rental is more than you can bear. What do you do in this case?

Start looking around for a new home first so you're sure that what you want is available, then list your home for sale with a condition that you may need a long close of escrow and/or a rent back.

A normal close of escrow is 30 to 60 days after an offer to purchase is accepted. A long close is 90 days or more. A seller rent-back provision allows the sellers to rent their home back from the buyers after the close of escrow, usually at a per diem (per day) cost equal to the buyers' principal, interest, taxes, and insurance (PITI). This may be more than what you're paying monthly to own your home currently, but after the escrow closes, you'll have your equity in cash, which will earn interest until you invest it in another home. Also, renting your own home back from the buyers enables you to avoid an interim move, which could be costly. Plus, you'll be in a good bargaining position when you find the home you want.

Although it's often difficult to find a seller who's willing to accept a contingent sale offer, it's easier to find sellers who will accept an offer contingent upon the close of escrow of another home that's already sold. In this case, you don't have to wait until your home closes escrow before purchasing your replacement home. But, it's wise to wait until your buyers have removed the inspection contingency from the purchase contract because sellers are often asked to pay to correct defects discovered during inspections. If you buy a new home before the inspection contingency is removed from your home sale and you end up having to re-roof your house in order to complete the sale, you could end up short of the cash needed to complete the purchase of your new home.

Occasionally, a house will be listed for sale before the seller has found a new home, contingent upon the seller finding a replacement home. This is not the way to sell a house for top dollar. As far as the buyer is concerned, the house is "maybe" for sale. Most buyers will be reluctant to start incurring expenses for such things as home inspections and loan application fees with no guarantee that the seller will complete the sale.

Buyers are often willing to allow you to rent back until you find a home as long as you agree to give them notification that you'll be vacating in sufficient time for them to give their landlord a 30-day notice. The buyers will at least know they have a house, even if they have to wait to move in. With the contingency for a seller to find a replacement home, however, the buyers have no guarantee that they'll ever be able to move in.

Buyers who agree to accept a contingency for the seller to find a replacement home usually require a price concession on the seller's part. The buyers will also customarily insist on an escape clause that allows them to continue to search for other homes. When they find one they like, they are free to withdraw from the contract and purchase the other home; this puts your house back on the market and leaves you searching for another buyer. If a home appears back on the market several times, it may acquire a stigma that will be difficult to overcome. Buyers often offer less for properties on which several deals have fallen apart, or they may shy away from making an offer at all if you develop a reputation for being a seller whose house is always on the market but not for sale.

Minimize risk by selling your home with a provision to rent it back from the buyers after closing escrow if necessary.

Another solution to the "buy first, sell first" dilemma is interim financing, also called "swing" or "bridge" financing. A swing loan is a short-term loan, normally for six months (sometimes with an option to renew for an additional six months), that allows a seller to convert some of the equity in the present home to cash before the house is sold. Interest rates and fees vary, as do qualifying parameters. The amount of cash you can borrow on an interim basis is usually equivalent to 70 or 75 percent of the current market value of the home minus existing debt secured against the property.

The borrower must have the financial ability to qualify to carry the mortgage payments on the old and new homes simultaneously. In addition to the expense involved, there's a risk that the old home might not sell within the six-month term of the interim loan.

> **Rita Jennings bought a townhouse she fell in love with using a swing loan secured by her large family home. She then listed her home for sale just as the market slowed down and prices dropped. Eight months later, her home hadn't sold so she had to put the townhouse on the market in order to avoid foreclosure. She sold the townhouse at a loss. The unfortunate experience cost her $65,000 and put her no closer to realizing her goal of moving to a more manageable home. To make matters worse, Rita's accountant confirmed that the IRS would not permit her to take a tax write-off to cover the amount of the loss.**

19

A final strategy to consider if you have the financial wherewithal—and the thought of owning two homes is something you can live with—is to buy the new home before you sell the old one and use a "teaser rate" adjustable-rate mortgage (ARM) for the new home loan. A teaser rate ARM is a loan with a discounted, or below market, initial interest rate. You must have the cash available to put down on the new home. And your income must be sufficient to carry the new home loan and the loan on your current home, if your current home hasn't sold and closed escrow by the time you close escrow on the new one. Using a teaser rate ARM loan to purchase the new home will keep the monthly payments to a minimum until the initial ARM interest rate adjusts—in several months to one year. After your old home has sold and closed, you can either refinance the loan on the new home or make a substantial principal pay-down on the ARM and keep that loan. Another benefit of using an ARM, if you plan to keep the loan, is that the payments on an ARM loan are reamortized periodically. If you make a large principal pay-down before the next reamortization of the loan, your monthly payments will be reduced accordingly. When you make a large principal pay-down on a fixed-rate mortgage, the monthly payments aren't adjusted; the pay-down shortens the term of the loan. Also, some fixed-rate mortgages have prepayment penalties; ARM loans usually do not.

The Rollover Residence Replacement Rule

A final word on the tax consequences of trading up. The 1986 Tax Reform Act abolished favorable tax treatment for capital gains reported on real estate sales, so the gain is now taxed as ordinary income (to a maximum rate of 28%). If, however, you sell your principal residence and purchase another principal residence within two years, you can defer your gain on the sale. This is the rollover residence replacement rule. To qualify to defer your entire capital gain liability, the price of your new home must be equal to, or exceed, the adjusted sales price of your old home. The adjusted sales price is defined by the IRS as the selling price less the selling costs and fix-up expenses incurred within 90 days before sale. If you buy a less expensive home, you will pay tax either on the gain realized on the sale or on the difference between the adjusted sale price and the purchase price of the new home, whichever is less. The cost of capital improvements you've made to the property (not routine maintenance expenses) can be used to offset capital gain. See Internal Revenue Service publications 521 and 523 for more information on calculating capital gain liability or talk to your accountant.

Trade-up buyers who are building a new home or who buy a less expensive home and reconstruct it are permitted to defer the gain on the sale of the previous residence if the acquisition, construction, and reconstruction costs of the new house exceed the adjusted sales price of the old home and the work is completed within two years before or after the sale of the old home.

Be aware, if you're considering buying your next home first and renting the old one for a time if it doesn't sell, that you must sell the old home within two years of buying the new one if you want to defer tax owed on your capital gain. There may be other tax consequences of renting a single-family residence so be sure to consult your tax advisor before making a move.

The Trade-Down Buyer

The trade-down buyer is typically the buyer who owns and lives in a home designed for raising a family, but whose children no longer live at home. Increased longevity is turning the older adult group into the fastest growing segment of our population. The over-fifty-five population has, on the average, two to four times the buying power of the trade-up buyer. Seventy-five percent of this group own their own homes, and 84 percent of those who do own them free and clear—the home mortgage has been paid off in full.

Deciding to move is rarely an easy decision for the older homeowner. The home may have become a nuisance and sometimes a major expense, but it's usually the source of many fond memories. The major predicament facing this buyer is deciding where to move. If health considerations don't enter into the decision-making process, a different but smaller house is an alternative. Another option is to move to an adult retirement community that offers services and security. And finally, if health care is a consideration, there are living facilities that offer full-scale medical services.

Again, the tax consequences of a move are best considered before even starting to look for a new home. The rollover residence replacement rule applies to all taxpayers, so if you purchased a retirement home within two years of selling your current home, the IRS will allow you to roll the gain from the sale of this home into the retirement home. But if you purchased your retirement home five years before selling your primary residence, you cannot roll the gain from the primary residence into the retirement property.

One-Time Break for Taxpayers Over 55

Since most trade-down buyers purchase less expensive homes, the sale of the current home is likely to result in a taxable gain. Remember, in order to have no taxable gain at the time of sale, the homeowner must purchase a replacement home that is at least equal in price to the adjusted sales price of the current home. Fortunately, the IRS allows taxpayers aged 55 and over to take a one-time exclusion of up to $125,000 on the gain from the sale of a principal residence. The exempted amount will not be taxed as a gain by the IRS.

To qualify for this exclusion, you or your spouse must be 55 or older on the day your current home closes escrow. If you are not yet 55 and your spouse, who would have been 55, is deceased, check with your tax advisor to see if you qualify for the exclusion. Also, there is a residency and ownership requirement that you must have owned and lived in the home you're selling for at least three of the last five years. The $125,000 exclusion is not automatic; you must choose to take it and notify the IRS by submitting a written, signed statement with your tax return. If you take less than the $125,000 maximum exemption allowed, you are *not* entitled to take the unused portion at a later date. Also, a divorced person whose spouse has used the exemption is not allowed to take further exemptions.

21

Apart from the one-time exclusion, an installment sale can be used to defer tax paid on a capital gain. With an installment sale the seller carries a loan for the buyer for part of the sale price. Tax on the gain is paid as the loan is repaid. Consult your tax advisor before entering into an installment sale agreement.

Property Tax Relief for Trade-Down Buyers Over 55

In the past, a deterrent to trading down for many older buyers was the inevitability of property tax reassessment. Let's say, for instance, you own a 2,500-square-foot home on one-third of an acre, worth $200,000. You paid $65,000 for the home in 1975, and your current property taxes are $850 per year. If you sold this home and purchased a 1,500-square-foot, low-maintenance townhouse for $195,000, your new property taxes would be approximately $2,200 per year.

California Assembly Bill 60, which went into effect in 1987, helps to make retirement more affordable for homeowners aged 55 and over by giving them the option on a one-time basis of transferring their existing property tax base to a replacement home of equal or lesser value. Rather than paying property taxes based on the market value (purchase price) of the replacement residence (as is ordinarily the case), homeowners who qualify pay property tax on the replacement home based on the assessed value of their current home.

Several restrictions apply. One owner must be 55 or older when the current residence is sold, and the replacement residence must be purchased within two years before or after the current residence is sold. Both residences must be located in the same county, and the purchase price of the replacement home cannot exceed 100 percent of the sale price of the current home if the replacement home is purchased prior to the sale of the current home. This limit increases to 105 percent if the replacement home is purchased within one year after the sale, and to 110 percent if purchased within two years. Proposition 90, passed overwhelmingly by California voters in 1988, authorizes the legislature to extend the benefits of A.B. 60 to seniors who purchase a replacement home located in a different county, but only if that county's board of supervisors elects to participate in the program and accepts transfers from other counties. Because your current property tax assessment will not automatically be transferred to your replacement residence, you must file a form with the county assessor's office in order to take advantage of these benefits.

Trade-down buyers who want to transfer the low tax assessment on their old home to a new one are wise to sell the old home first. The tax base transfer will be disallowed by the county tax assessor if you close escrow on your replacement home first and your old home subsequently sells for less than you paid for the replacement. If you close on the replacement home a day or so after the close of escrow on your old home, you are allowed to pay 5 percent more for the new home and still maintain the same tax base.

22

June and John Williams lived in a charming, architect-designed Berkeley home for over 40 years. Convinced that they would have no problem selling their prime property, they bought a condominium in a continuous-care facility for $335,000 before putting their home on the market. After waiting through a slow market, they finally sold their home for $313,500, which was not enough to enable them to transfer their property tax base to the new condominium.

Rather Than Move: Other Options

Many of today's senior citizens do not trade down, preferring to remain in the family home, which they usually own free of debt. One problem they face, however, is that they're living on a fixed retirement income which may not be sufficient to cover living expenses.

One way to tap equity that's tied up in the family home is a home equity line of credit. Once you qualify for a credit line, it is secured as a lien against the home, and you have the ability to write checks up to your approved loan amount limit. You are permitted to pay back the amount borrowed over a number of years.

Since the IRS allows you to deduct interest paid on up to $100,000 of home equity debt per year, the credit line is an attractive alternative for seniors who pay taxes. Most home equity credit lines have flexible interest rates, so be sure you fully understand how the loan works before it becomes a lien against your home.

An innovative mortgage geared to the over-62 group is the reverse mortgage. This loan is particularly suited to middle- and low-income seniors who have a large amount of equity in their home but who are short on cash. The home is used as collateral for the loan, and the lender makes payments (monthly or in one lump sum) to the homeowner. The monthly payment is tax-free, and these payments usually don't jeopardize Social Security or Medicare benefits. The loan is paid back to the lender when the homeowner dies, sells the home, or at the end of the term of the loan, whichever comes first.

Unfortunately, not many lenders are interested in reverse mortgages. Also, fees and terms vary with lenders, so shop around before making a commitment. Some lenders insist on sharing in some of the home's future appreciation. Maximum loan limits apply, and monthly payments are determined by the borrower's age and the market value of the home. Reverse mortgages provide a steady income, but they deplete the equity in your home. Be sure to obtain professional estate planning advice before proceeding with a reverse loan.

For more information about reverse mortgages, contact the National Center for Home Equity Conversion (NCHEC) (1210 E. College Drive, Suite 300, Marshall, MN 56258-2078); the American Association of Retired Persons' Home Equity Information Center (601 "E" Street NW, Washington, DC 20049); and the Federal Housing Authority (FHA) at (800) 245-2691.

Another possibility for the older homeowner who prefers to stay put is the sale-leaseback. With this arrangement, the homeowner sells the home to a relative or investor and then leases it back either for a fixed period or for the remainder of his or her life. The seller receives cash proceeds from the sale but continues to occupy the home. The investor may receive tax benefits from owning the property as a rental investment, in addition to equity build-up and price appreciation. Consult an attorney to assist you in drawing up a sale-leaseback agreement, and be sure to investigate the estate planning ramifications, particularly if you're entering into this sort of an agreement with a child or heir.

The Temporary Trade-Down Move

Older adults are not the only candidates for a trade-down move. Others include homeowners who are desiring relief from exorbitant mortgage payments, seeking a change in lifestyle, considering a career change, or divorcing.

If you're trading down in order to permanently reduce housing expense payments, don't forget that you'll have to pay tax on the portion of capital gain that will not be reinvested in a replacement home. Only homeowners over 55 qualify for the $125,000 exclusion, and capital gain (which previously received preferential tax treatment) is now taxed as ordinary income. Any taxpayer, however, can

23

defer tax paid on a capital gain by use of an installment sale. Consult with a knowledgeable tax advisor before making the final decision.

Homeowners seeking temporary relief from high mortgage payments or the expenses of home maintenance might be wise to sell the current home and rent awhile. This way you can buy a grace period and still defer capital gains as long as you purchase a replacement home within two years of selling the current home. Keep in mind that you'll need funds for the down payment when you do buy the replacement home. Also, factor in the costs of selling and purchasing a home, and consider that qualifying for a new home loan will be difficult if you're unemployed or new on a job. Refinancing, rather than moving, is another option if interest rates are low.

The Transferred Homeowner

No move is easy, but the family that is moving a long distance is faced with a particularly traumatic experience. Fortunately, steps can be taken to ease the anxiety. Relocation assistance is sometimes provided by large companies, but even without corporate help, you can assist yourself by asking your new employer to recommend several real estate agents.

Your move will be made easier if you work with a real estate agent who has experience assisting relocated buyers. This means selecting an agent who understands the transferee's special needs and the emotional turmoil the relocation process entails. Ask the agents for names and phone numbers of other buyers they helped to relocate. Find out whether or not these people would choose to work with the agent again.

Another way to find an agent in your new area is to call a local branch of a large national real estate firm and get recommendations from someone in the relocation department. This person can also provide you with a relocation package, which should contain maps of the local area; information on public transportation, hotels, and restaurants; data on schools and test scores; community activities and amenities; a sampling of current home prices; and calendars of current cultural and recreational activities.

Once in contact with an agent in the new location, ask to be kept informed of local events. Have your agent send you newspaper clippings about school and neighborhood events as well as information about new listings. Whenever possible, subscribe to the newspaper, or ask your agent to send the Sunday real estate section to you.

Transferees who have the benefit of corporate assistance are the most fortunate. Since executives typically make four moves during their professional careers, relocation companies have developed to help large corporations simplify the moving process. Their services include assistance in finding a home; reimbursement for all or part of the closing, moving, storage, and temporary housing costs; help with financing the new home; equity advance (interim financing);

grants for cost of living allowances; counseling; help in finding spousal employment in the new community; and guaranteed home purchase.

The guaranteed home purchase is probably the biggest plum most relocation packages have to offer. With guaranteed purchase programs, the transferring employer contracts with a third-party home purchase company to buy the transferee's old home if it hasn't sold by a designated time. The home purchase company sets a buy-out price that the homeowners have to accept after a certain period of time, usually 30 to 60 days. During this time, if the sellers receive a better offer than the buy-out price, they can usually accept that offer, and the home purchase company will handle the transaction to the close of escrow.

Sellers who have the option of a company buy-out should insert a clause in the listing agreement allowing them to assign the listing to a third-party home purchase company at any time and at their discretion. Most brokers will accept this condition as long as they have a reasonable period of time to attempt to sell the property. The buy-out provision enables a seller who runs out of time to turn the listing over to the corporate transfer company and take the buy-out offer, in which case no commission is owed to the initial listing broker.

The IRS allows transferred taxpayers to deduct the costs of moving, with certain restrictions. Briefly, deductions are allowed if the location of your new job is at least 50 miles farther away from your current home than was your old job.

Nonresident Seller Withholding Requirement

25

State law requires income tax withholding of 3.33 percent of the sales price on a nonresident's sale of a California property. The withholding requirement applies when the seller shows an out-of-state address or when the proceeds from the sale are to be disbursed to a financial intermediary of the seller. There is no withholding requirement if the sales price is $100,000 or less or if the seller had a California homeowner property tax exemption on the property in the year of sale. Other provisions apply, so check with a local title or escrow company if you have any questions about how California Internal Revenue Code Sections 18805 and 18815 might affect you.

California home sellers of foreign nationality must comply with a withholding requirement of 10 percent of their sale proceeds if the sale price is $300,000 or more, according to the Federal Investment in Real Property Tax Act. Ironically, it's the buyer's legal responsibility to make sure the seller complies with the withholding requirement. Your real estate agent and escrow officer can make sure the appropriate paperwork is filed at closing.

CHAPTER 3

WORKING *with* REAL *ESTATE* AGENTS

Agents, Brokers, Realtors: Defining the Terms

Generally speaking, a real estate agent is anyone who helps people buy and sell real estate. Technically, however, the individual who is helping you buy or sell a home is usually acting under the umbrella of a real estate broker who legally must supervise all sales transactions. Thus, it is the broker who is actually your agent.

Anyone who sells real estate in California is licensed by the state, either as a salesperson or as a broker. Real estate salespeople and brokers are often referred to as licensees. Salespeople must work under the supervision of a licensed broker and cannot sell real estate on their own. To obtain a broker's license generally requires sales experience, college-level course work, and the satisfactory completion of the broker's licensing exam.

Real estate brokers can work independently, or they can serve as the broker of record for other licensed salespeople. A broker may also choose to work for another broker. The words "Broker Associate" on an agent's business card indicate that the agent is a licensed real estate broker working as an associate of another licensed broker. A broker can be either an individual or a corporation, like Coldwell Banker or Century 21.

You'll often hear agents refer to the "listing agent" or "selling agent." The listing agent is the person who lists and markets the house. The selling agent is the person who writes the offer for the property buyer. These terms do not necessarily indicate the agency representation relationships that exist in the transaction. Agent representation is discussed further in the agency disclosure section below.

There is another important designation in the industry: the Realtor®. The title "Realtor®" next to an agent's name indicates that he or she is not only a licensed salesperson or broker but is also a member of the National Association of Realtors® (NAR), which is a trade organization. The significance of this designation for the prospective home buyer or seller is that members of NAR subscribe to a strict code of ethics. By agreeing to the NAR code of ethics, real estate licensees pledge that their real estate activities will conform to a high standard of ethical and professional conduct. Consumers can file a complaint with a local Board of Realtors® against a Realtor® who violates this code of ethics. Penalties can range from a letter of censure to expulsion from the association.

Don't assume that every real estate agent is a member of the NAR; in fact, only about two out of three real estate agents are Realtors®. If you don't see a Realtor trademark on the agent's business card, call your local Board of Realtors® to find out if he or she is a Realtor®. Membership in a local Board of Realtors® in the state of California automatically entitles an agent to membership to the California Association of Realtors (CAR) and the NAR.

The letters GRI (Graduate Real Estate Institute) or CRS (Certified Residential Specialist) next to an agent's name indicate that the agent has completed advanced training. The CRS designation is the more advanced of the two.

How to Shop for an Agent

One of the most important decisions you'll make when buying or selling a home is selecting a real estate agent to represent you. An honest, experienced, hard working, and capable agent can make the difference between a smooth real estate transaction and a nightmare. It's a good idea to interview several real estate agents before selecting one, unless you're a repeat buyer or seller who already has a good working relationship with a particular agent.

There are various ways to find good agents. The best sources of contacts are friends or associates who have bought or sold recently and can recommend agents. Be sure to ask your colleagues if they would use the agent again. If personal contacts don't generate enough leads, call the managers of reputable local real estate companies and ask for recommendations of agents who specialize in the neighborhood of your current home if you're selling, or in the area where you're considering moving if you're buying. If you're a first-time buyer, ask to speak to agents who are good at, and who enjoy, working with novices.

Visiting Sunday open houses is another way to become acquainted with real estate agents. This gives you an opportunity to see an agent in action, as well as to preview the inventory of homes for sale. Drive around your neighborhood and make note of the real estate signs you see most frequently. If you see one agent's name repeatedly, that agent may specialize in the area.

When you walk into a local real estate office and ask to talk to an agent, you'll most likely be turned over to the "floor agent," the person on duty to answer calls and inquiries from prospective customers. You don't need an appointment to interview the floor agent, and this visit will give you an opportunity to scrutinize the real estate office.

One innovative buyer called several escrow companies and asked escrow officers to recommend three good agents, then selected the one agent mentioned by all three. Why call an escrow company? Because once a house is bought or sold in California, an agent usually opens escrow at an escrow or title company. The escrow officer and real estate agent then work closely with one another throughout the transaction and, as a result, are familiar with one another's professional reputations.

Beware of the out-of-the-area broker. You'll get the best service working with an agent who's an expert in selling real estate in your community. An agent from

27

several counties away who's anxious to help you sell your home probably doesn't have enough local business to stay busy. Also, an out-of-the-area agent is less likely to be informed about local customs and practices. If the agent is a friend, ask to be referred to an agent who specializes in your area.

Regardless of how you connect with agents, it's essential that you carefully interview each agent and that you obtain names and phone numbers of several of their past clients. Talk to these references to find out if they'd work with the agent again. Be sure the clients have worked with the agent recently and that they aren't just good friends who bought or sold a home ten years ago.

What Qualities to Look for in an Agent

Real estate agents usually work on commissioned income, not on salary. They are usually paid only at the end of a home purchase or sale transaction, and the amount they earn depends on the price of the home. Consequently, there is a potential conflict of interest in the agent-client relationship. This is why it's imperative that you select your agent carefully.

In California, when you work with a real estate agent, you establish a fiduciary relationship, which is one of trust that requires the agent to provide you with "utmost care, integrity, and loyalty." The agent, by law, is required to put your needs before his or her own, even if in doing so that agent will not earn a commission. If this seems impossible to you, consider that the most successful agents rely on referral business from a satisfied clientele for their livelihood. A satisfied customer who was advised by an agent not to proceed with a risky transaction will certainly give this agent a glowing recommendation.

Aside from honesty, what other qualities should you look for in an agent? Find out if the agent works full time at real estate and how much experience the agent has. Selecting a part-time real estate agent can be a big mistake in today's complex marketplace. Generally, the more experience an agent has, the better, but a well-trained new agent can work out fine if he or she is supervised by a broker with experience.

Find out how knowledgeable the agent is in all aspects of the buying and selling process, including home construction, real estate practices, inventory and sales in the area, local ordinances, and financing. Ask a lot of questions. How well you understand the answers will give you a clue about the agent's expertise and communication abilities. Good agents have the strength of character to answer "I don't know" to questions they're unsure of. But they also have the perseverance to find the answer for you or to direct you to the proper source for an answer. Watch out for the agent who tries to entice you into doing business by making negative

Ask agents you interview for references of clients who used their services recently.

28

remarks about competitors. This is a violation of the Realtor® code of ethics. Overstating the value of a property for the purposes of acquiring a listing is also a violation of the code, and it's illegal. Beware of the agent who's desperate to make a sale. Top agents manage their personal finances so that, even though they work on commissioned income, their livelihood doesn't depend on the success of a single transaction. If you sense desperation on the part of an agent, find another one.

Real estate is a people business, so naturally you want someone working for you who's skilled at working with people. The agent you select will be your personal representative in dealings with other real estate agents, loan brokers, title officers, prospective buyers or sellers, insurance agents, and property inspectors. Promptness and personal appearance are also factors to take into consideration.

The in-person interview is critical. But before making a final selection, be sure to interview agents on the phone. Since most of the critical work in a real estate transaction occurs over the telephone, an agent who can't communicate well this way is at a disadvantage.

Make sure an agent belongs to the local Multiple Listing Service (MLS). Agents submit their current listings to the MLS, and this information is distributed to all fellow members. The MLS provides an invaluable marketing service for a seller because it increases the amount of exposure a property receives. By the same token, buyers working with agents who participate in the MLS have access to many more homes listed for sale than they would if they worked with a nonmember agent.

A factor often overlooked, but equally important as honesty, experience, and professionalism, is rapport. Buying or selling a home is unlike any other business transaction. A house is not only the biggest purchase most people make, it's home. As such, personal psyches get intertwined with economic factors to create an element of subjectivity that isn't usually found in other businesses. Completing a real estate transaction will take anywhere from several months to a year or more. A successful real estate transaction depends on teamwork between the agent and the buyer or seller, which requires a good working relationship based on mutual trust, respect, and compatibility. Your real estate agent needn't be your best friend, but you should be able to relate well to one another. If the personal chemistry isn't there, find another agent.

Find out if an agent you're considering is a Realtor®. Remember, Realtors subscribe to a strict code of ethics. A dissatisfied buyer or seller can make a complaint to the local Board of Realtors®, which has procedures for handling grievances against their members.

Selecting a Listing Agent: The Comparative Market Analysis

Sellers should expect each prospective listing agent to provide a comparative market analysis of the home. This is a written estimate of the current market value of the home, based on a comparison with similar homes that have sold in

29

the neighborhood within the last six months. The comparative sales information of these other homes should include the property address, the sale price, the list price, the date the sale closed escrow, a brief description of the property, and the number of days the home was on the market. The analysis should also include information on similar homes that are presently being offered for sale in the area, as well as a list of the homes that were for sale but never sold (expired listings).

To complete an accurate comparative market analysis, an agent must first preview your home, paying particular attention to details. Agents should inquire about the age of the roof, the year the exterior was last painted, remodeling you've done, and any defects you're aware of such as drainage problems, roof leaks, or structural problems. The answers to these questions affect the market value of your home. Also, the kinds of questions an agent asks about your home will give you insight into how detail oriented the agent is.

Your second meeting, to review the comparative market analysis, will allow you to observe the agent's thoroughness and dependability. An agent who takes the time to personalize the presentation is telling you something about the level of service you can expect during the transaction. The presentation should include a written proposal for marketing your home that details precisely how the agent intends to accomplish the sale.

Don't list with an agent who won't complete a comparative market analysis. Some agents will guess at a price for your home at your first meeting. One step above this is the agent who shows up for the first appointment accompanied by several other agents from the office. The group waltzes through your home together, then huddles for a moment before producing a collective estimate on the price of your home. Neither of these approaches is sufficient. Insist on an agent who's willing to do the required homework.

Some people feel awkward about interviewing more than one real estate agent. It's understandable that you don't want to waste someone's time and you don't want to be misleading about your intentions. Real estate agents are accustomed to working in competition with other agents, however, and there's no obligation to work with an agent you've interviewed. As a courteous gesture, inform each agent you talk to that you're interviewing others. Once you've made a final decision, call the agents you didn't select and let them know how much you appreciate their efforts on your behalf. Pay special attention to the losing agents' responses. An agent who takes the news graciously should be at the top of your list if you run into trouble with your first choice and need to change agents later on.

Selecting an Agent: Advice to Buyers

Like sellers, buyers should interview several agents before selecting one. Buyers should expect a prospective agent to discuss their needs and desires as well as their financial capabilities before showing them a single house. Looking at houses that are out of your price range or that don't suit your needs is a waste of time—yours and the agent's. An agent who has endless time probably isn't selling many houses.

30

Make sure an agent you're considering will expose you to the full inventory of homes for sale that suit your needs, not just those houses listed with his or her brokerage firm. Also make sure than an agent you're interviewing has time to work with you and isn't overextended with other clients.

Don't be surprised if an agent asks for your loyalty. Many good agents refuse to work with buyers who won't commit to working with them exclusively, at least within their market area.

Even after you've selected an agent to work with, you may want to visit Sunday open houses on your own. Ask your agent to provide you with a list of Sunday opens that might work for you. And let other agents you come into contact with know that you already have an agent. Some buyers like to peruse the classified ads of homes for sale until they find a home to buy. If your agent is a member of the Multiple Listing Service, he or she will be able to give you information about homes advertised by other companies.

Most homes for sale are shown by appointment only when they're not open. And buyers must be accompanied by their agent. A good agent will have made appointments with the sellers in advance to show you their homes and will provide you with a map of your house tour, including address, price, and number of bedrooms and baths. After previewing four or five houses with you, the agent should have a good idea of what you're looking for. It's wise to save brochures or flyers from each house you see to refer back to.

After you've previewed the homes listed that might work for you, the frequency with which you can expect to see new listings will depend on the general market activity. In a fast market, where homes sell quickly, you may need to drop what you're doing and race to see a new listing the day it comes on the market. In slower markets, you may be able to wait days or until a Sunday open house. Let your agent know that you expect to hear from him or her on a weekly basis even if just to tell you there's nothing new in your price range that suits your needs. At least you'll know your agent is out there looking for you.

31

Buyers looking for new homes may not have the luxury of picking their own agent because builders often employ a sales staff to sell their houses. See Chapter 6 for more information about buying new homes.

Keep in mind that real estate agents are qualified to give real estate advice, but if you have questions regarding legal or tax matters, you should consult the appropriate professionals. Real estate agents also cannot discriminate, so you shouldn't expect them to discuss the racial or ethnic makeup of a neighborhood.

Real Estate Commissions Are Negotiable

Real estate commissions are negotiable between individual brokers and sellers. It is, however, perfectly legal for a real estate broker to have a set commission policy, say 6 or 7 percent of the sale price.

Most buyers and sellers have no idea what happens to a commission after the escrow has closed. A common misconception is that this amount goes directly to the listing agent. In most cases, this is not so. Ordinarily, the listing broker shares the commission fifty-fifty with the selling broker. Agents have predetermined commission split arrangements with the real estate brokers they work for, and this varies from broker to broker and from agent to agent. In most cases, the commission is split four ways—between two brokerage companies and two agents.

Many sellers wonder how to negotiate a commission. The first step is to ask. Few brokers are going to offer to reduce their fees unless you ask them to, although there are discount brokers you can interview if cutting the commission is a high priority. Whether or not you'll be successful negotiating a commission will hinge on several factors, including market conditions and the price range of the home you're selling. Real estate companies and agents need to make a profit in order to continue doing business. When listings are selling quickly with minimal marketing effort, brokers will be more likely to reduce their fees than in a slow market when it takes a long time to sell. In a low inventory market when listings are scarce and much in demand, you'll have an easier time negotiating the commission. A full service company that provides sellers with an extensive marketing program, including a large commitment to advertising, will probably deviate from its set commission policy less than a minimal service company might. Similarly, a top producing agent with more than enough business who gives clients 110 percent service is less likely to discount the commission than is an agent who's desperate for work. Sellers will have greater success negotiating a reduced commission with a top company or agent in a seller's market, particularly in the upper-end price ranges.

An agreement that stipulates a higher commission to the broker if the property sells quickly (say, 6 percent) and a lower rate (5 percent) if the property is not sold within a given time period is actually the reverse of what's sensible. A property that isn't selling will cost the broker more in market expense, not less. Plus, if the market is slow and a lot of homes are sitting around unsold, the homes that are most likely to sell are those offering attractive prices and commissions. The real estate commission owed to the selling broker is included in the Multiple Listing Service information on each house. If agents have a pick of five or so similar houses, it stands to reason that they will first show the houses on which the most generous commissions are being offered. In a slow market, you could negotiate yourself out of a sale by insisting on a cut in the commission. Commission rates are market-sensitive, just as home prices are.

Real estate brokers generally offer discounted commissions for clients who send them a high volume of business, such as builders and relocation companies. You also might find that an agent will agree to a commission reduction, even if this is contrary to company policy, if the commission is not being split with another selling broker or if the agent is representing one client in both a sale and a purchase.

There is a form of commission negotiation that most buyers and sellers are unaware of. Sometimes a broker will refuse to negotiate the commission at the time a listing is taken, but will later cut the fee in order to keep a transaction from falling apart.

> **Bill and Polly Harris sold their home after nine months on the market. The sale negotiations took several weeks with both the buyers and sellers making concessions in order to put the deal together. Two weeks later, the buyers' inspections revealed that the chimney needed work in order to make it safe to use. Rather than have the sale canceled over a $450 repair bill, and since the house was listed with a 6 percent commission, the brokers agreed to share the cost, each paying $225.**

Don't be shy about discussing commissions.with prospective agents. If one agent volunteers to represent you for a commission lower than what others are offering, let the competition know that someone has agreed to work for you for less. Give yourself the benefit of finding out if another agent will agree to match that fee.

Finally, commissions shouldn't be the only factor you consider in choosing an agent. Rapport, dependability, professionalism, comprehensive marketing, and service are the critical ingredients to a successful real estate transaction.

Whom Does a Real Estate Agent Represent?

In 1987, agency disclosure became law in California. Real estate agents are now required to provide buyers and sellers with a copy of a form entitled "Disclosure Regarding Real Estate Agency Relationships" before they enter into a contract to list or purchase a home. This form explains the various forms of representation that can exist in a transaction, and it defines the agent's duties and obligations to the principals involved. When a purchase agreement is accepted, part of that agreement includes a declaration stating who the agent(s) will represent in the transaction.

There are several possible representation arrangements. An agent can represent the seller or the buyer exclusively (single agency) or represent both the seller and the buyer (dual agency). An agent who represents a seller or buyer exclusively has a fiduciary responsibility to that person. A fiduciary relationship is one of trust that demands the highest duties known under the law. A dual agent owes a fiduciary duty to both the buyer and the seller. Since there is a potential conflict of interest with dual agency, California law states that a dual agent shall not disclose to the buyer that the seller will accept less than the list price, or disclose to the seller that the buyer will pay more than the offer price, without express written permission.

The listing (seller's) agent can never represent the buyer exclusively in a transaction because the listing agreement creates an agency relationship between the sellers and their agent. An agent working with a buyer can represent a seller exclusively under an arrangement called subagency. With subagency,

33

the agent writing the offer for the buyer does not owe a primary allegiance to the buyer, but to the seller. Although subagency isn't common in California today, it used to be the norm, and it's still common in other states. A buyer using a sub-agent of the seller should be careful about what is discussed with the agent. For instance, a seller's subagent would be obliged to tell a seller you're willing to pay more than your offer price if you mentioned this to the agent.

Regardless of agency relationships, California law is very clear on an agent's obligations to both the buyers and sellers in a transaction. These responsibilities include diligent performance of an agent's duties; honesty, fairness, and good faith to both parties; and a "duty to disclose all facts known to the agent materially affecting the value or desirability of the property that are not known to, or within the diligent attention and observation of, the parties."

Selecting the types of agency relationships that will exist in a transaction is not done at the discretion of the buyers and sellers involved. Brokers have policies regarding how they'll represent buyers and sellers. The most common arrangement is for a broker to represent principals as follows: a seller exclusively if another broker either represents the buyer exclusively or acts as a sub-agent of the seller; a buyer exclusively if the seller is represented exclusively by another broker; both the buyer and seller if the buyer is purchasing a property listed by the same broker.

Dual agency exists not just when one person represents both the buyer and seller but also when the seller's and buyer's agents both work for the same broker. If you find yourself in a situation where dual agency is the only possible representation arrangement available and you feel uncomfortable with this, ask your agent to refer you to a good agent with another brokerage company who can represent you exclusively as a buyer's agent. The two agents can work out an arrangement to share the commission owed to the selling agent between them through a referral fee system.

The real estate commission is usually paid by the seller from the sale proceeds. In California, it's legal for an agent to represent the buyers exclusively in the transaction and be paid a commission by the sellers. The seller actually pays the commission to the listing broker who then divides the commission according to arrangements worked out between the brokers.

It's also possible to hire a buyer's broker who will not only represent the buyer legally, but who will also be paid by the buyer, not by the seller. A disadvantage of this is that the buyer will have to pay cash for the broker's services rather than have the fee built in to the purchase price (which means it can be partially financed) as is the case when the seller pays the commission.

Study any buyer broker contract carefully. Many contracts include a provision for the broker to be paid when you buy a home, regardless of which agent finds you a home. Don't get caught paying the commission twice if you're looking with several agents in different areas. And, make sure there's a provision for canceling the contract if you find the broker to be unsatisfactory.

DISCLOSURE REGARDING
REAL ESTATE AGENCY RELATIONSHIPS
(As required by the Civil Code)
CALIFORNIA ASSOCIATION OF REALTORS® (CAR) STANDARD FORM

When you enter into a discussion with a real estate agent regarding a real estate transaction, you should from the outset understand what type of agency relationship or representation you wish to have with the agent in the transaction.

SELLER'S AGENT
A Seller's agent under a listing agreement with Seller acts as the agent for the Seller only. A Seller's agent or a subagent of that agent has the following affirmative obligations:
To the Seller:
(a) A Fiduciary duty of utmost care, integrity, honesty, and loyalty in dealings with the Seller.
To the Buyer & the Seller:
(a) Diligent exercise of reasonable skill and care in performance of the agent's duties.
(b) A duty of honest and fair dealing and good faith.
(c) A duty to disclose all facts known to the agent materially affecting the value or desirability of property that are not known to, or within the diligent attention and observation of, the parties.

An agent is not obligated to reveal to either party any confidential information obtained from the other party which does not involve the affirmative duties set forth above.

BUYER'S AGENT
A selling agent can, with a Buyer's consent, agree to act as agent for the Buyer only. In these situations, the agent is not the Seller's agent, even if by agreement the agent may receive compensation for services rendered, either in full or in part from the Seller. An agent acting only for a Buyer has the following affirmative obligations.
To the Buyer:
(a) A fiduciary duty of utmost care, integrity, honesty, and loyalty in dealings with the Buyer.
To the Buyer & Seller:
(a) Diligent exercise of reasonable skill and care in performance of the agent's duties.
(b) A duty of honest and fair dealing and good faith.
(c) A duty to disclose all facts known to the agent materially affecting the value or desirability of the property that are not known to, or within the diligent attention and observation of, the parties.

An agent is not obligated to reveal to either party any confidential information obtained from the other party which does not involve the affirmative duties set forth above.

AGENT REPRESENTING BOTH SELLER & BUYER
A real estate agent, either acting directly or through one or more associate licensees, can legally be the agent of both the Seller and the Buyer in a transaction, but only with the knowledge and consent of both the Seller and the Buyer.

In a dual agency situation, the agent has the following affirmative obligations to both the Seller and the Buyer:
(a) A fiduciary duty of utmost care, integrity, honesty and loyalty in the dealings with either Seller or the Buyer.
(b) Other duties to the Seller and the Buyer as stated above in their respective sections.

In representing both Seller and Buyer, the agent may not, without the express permission of the respective party, disclose to the other party that the Seller will accept a price less than the listing price or that the Buyer will pay a price greater than the price offered.

The above duties of the agent in a real estate transaction do not relieve a Seller or a Buyer from the responsibility to protect their own interests. You should carefully read all agreements to assure that they adequately express your understanding of the transaction. A real estate agent is a person qualified to advise about real estate. If legal or tax advice is desired, consult a competent professional.

Throughout your real property transaction you may receive more than one disclosure form, depending upon the number of agents assisting in the transaction. The law requires each agent with whom you have more than a casual relationship to present you with this disclosure form. You should read its contents each time it is presented to you, considering the relationship between you and the real estate agent in your specific transaction.

This disclosure form includes the provisions of article 2.5 (commencing with Section 2373) of Chapter 2 of Title 9 of Part 4 of Division 3 of the Civil Code set forth on the reverse hereof. Read it carefully.

I/WE ACKNOWLEDGE RECEIPT OF A COPY OF THIS DISCLOSURE.

BUYER/SELLER_____ Date_____ TIME_____ AM/PM

BUYER/SELLER_____ Date_____ TIME_____ AM/PM

AGENT _____ By _____ Date_____
(Please Print)   (Associate Licensee or Broker-Signature)

A REAL ESTATE BROKER IS QUALIFIED TO ADVISE ON REAL ESTATE. IF YOU DESIRE LEGAL ADVICE, CONSULT YOUR ATTORNEY.

This form is available for use by the entire real estate industry. The use of this form is not intended to identify the user as a REALTOR®. REALTOR® is a registered collective membership mark which may be used only by real estate licensees who are members of the NATIONAL ASSOCIATION OF REALTORS® and who subscribe to its Code of Ethics.

Copyright© 1987, CALIFORNIA ASSOCIATION OF REALTORS®
525 South Virgil Avenue, Los Angeles, California 90020   FORM AD-11

OFFICE USE ONLY
Reviewed by Broker or Designee _____
Date _____

35

CHAPTER 2 OF TITLE 9 OF PART 4 OF DIVISION 3 OF THE CIVIL CODE

Article 2.5 Agency Relationships in Residential Real Property Transactions

2373   As used in this article, the following terms have the following meanings.

(a) "Agent" means a person acting under provisions of this title in a real property transaction, and includes a person who is licensed as a real estate broker under Chapter 3 (commencing with Section 10130) of Part 1 of Division 4 of the Business & Professions Code, and under whose license a listing is executed or under which a purchase is obtained.

(b) "Associate licensee" means a person who is licensed as a real estate broker or salesperson under Chapter 3 (commencing with Section 10130) of Part 1 of Division 4 of the Business & Professions Code and who is either licensed under a broker or has entered into a written contract with a broker to act as the broker's agent in connection with acts requiring a real estate license and to function under the broker's supervision in the capacity of an associate licensee.

The agent in the real property transaction bears responsibility for his or her associate licensees who perform as agents of the agent. When an associate licensee owes a duty to any principal, or to any buyer or seller who is not a principal, in a real property transaction, that duty is equivalent to the duty owed to that party by the broker for whom the associate licensee functions.

(c) "Buyer" means a transferee in a real property transaction, and includes a person who executes an offer to purchase real property from a seller through an agent, or who seeks the services of an agent in more than a casual, transitory, or preliminary manner, with the object of entering into a real property transaction. "Buyer" includes vendee or lessee.

(d) "Dual agent" means an agent acting, either directly or through an associate licensee, as agent for both the seller and the buyer in a real property transaction.

(e) "Listing agreement" means a contract between an owner of real property and an agent, by which the agent has been authorized to sell the real property or to find or obtain a buyer.

(f) "Listing agent" means a person who has obtained a listing of real property to act as an agent for compensation.

(g) "Listing price" is the amount expressed in dollars specified in the listing for which the seller is willing to sell the real property through the listing agent.

(h) "Offering price" is the amount expressed in dollars specified in an offer to purchase for which the buyer is willing to buy the real property.

(i) "Offer to purchase" means a written contract executed by a buyer acting through a selling agent which becomes the contract for the sale of the real property upon acceptance by the seller.

(j) "Real property" means any estate specified by subdivision (1) or (2) of Section 761 in property which constitutes or is improved with one to four dwelling units, any leasehold in this type of property exceeding one year's duration, and mobilehomes, when offered for sale or sold through an agent pursuant to the authority contained in Section 10131.6 of the Business & Professions Code.

(k) "Real property transaction" means a transaction for the sale of real property in which an agent is employed by one or more of the principals to act in that transaction, and includes a listing or an offer to purchase.

(l) "Sell," "sale," or "sold" refers to a transaction for the transfer of real property from the seller to the buyer, and includes exchanges of real property between the seller and buyer, transactions for the creation of a real property sales contract within the meaning of Section 2985, and transactions for the creation of a leasehold exceeding one year's duration.

(m) "Seller" means the transferor in a real property transaction, and includes an owner who lists real property with an agent, whether or not a transfer results, or who receives an offer to purchase real property of which he or she is the owner from an agent on behalf of another. "Seller" includes both a vendor and a lessor.

(n) "Selling agent" means a listing agent who acts alone, or an agent who acts in cooperation with a listing agent, and who sells or finds and obtains a buyer for the real property, or an agent who locates property for a buyer for the property for which no listing exists and presents an offer to purchase to the seller.

(o) "Subagent" means a person to whom an agent delegates agency powers as provided in Article 5 (commencing with Section 2349) of Chapter I. However, "subagent" does not include an associate licensee who is acting under the supervision of an agent in a real property transaction.

2374   Listing agents and selling agents shall provide the seller and buyer in a real property transaction with a copy of the disclosure form specified in Section 2375, and, except as provided in subdivision (c), shall obtain a signed acknowledgement of receipt from that seller or buyer, except as provided in this section of Section 2374.5, as follows:

(a) The listing agent, if any, shall provide the disclosure form to the seller prior to entering into the listing agreement.

(b) The selling agent shall provide the disclosure form to the seller as soon as practicable prior to presenting the seller with an offer to purchase, unless the selling agent previously provided the seller with a copy of the disclosure form pursuant to subdivision (a).

(c) Where the selling agent does not deal on a face-to-face basis with the seller, the disclosure form prepared by the selling agent may be furnished to the seller (and acknowledgement of receipt obtained for the selling agent from the seller) by the listing agent, or the selling agent may deliver the disclosure form by certified mail addressed to the seller at his or her last known address, in which case no signed acknowledgement of receipt is required.

(d) The selling agent shall provide the disclosure form to the buyer as soon as practicable prior to execution of the buyer's offer to purchase, except that if the offer to purchase is not prepared by the selling agent, the selling agent shall present the disclosure form to the buyer not later than the next business day after the selling agent receives the offer to purchase from the buyer.

2374.5 In any circumstance in which the seller or buyer refuses to sign an acknowledgement of receipt pursuant to Section 2374, the agent, or an associate licensee acting for an agent, shall set forth, sign and date a written declaration of the facts of the refusal.

2375.5 (a) As soon as practicable, the selling agent shall disclose to the buyer and seller whether the selling agent is acting in the real property transaction exclusively as the buyer's agent, exclusively as the seller's agent, or as a dual agent representing both the buyer and the seller and this relationship shall be confirmed in the contract to purchase and sell real property or in a separate writing executed by the seller, the buyer, and the selling agent prior to or coincident with execution of that contract by the buyer and the seller, respectively.

(b) As soon as practicable, the listing agent shall disclose to the seller whether the listing agent is acting in the real property transaction exclusively as the seller's agent, or as a dual agent representing both the buyer and seller and this relationship shall be confirmed in the contract to purchase and sell real property or in a separate writing executed or acknowledged by the seller and the listing agent prior to or coincident with the execution of that contract by the seller.

(c) The confirmation required by subdivisions (a) and (b) shall be in the following form:

_____ is the agent of (check one)   _____ is the agent of (check one)
(Name of Listing Agent)   (Name of Selling Agent if not the same as the Listing Agent)

[   ] the seller exclusively; or   [   ] the buyer exclusively; or
[   ] both the buyer and seller.   [   ] the seller exclusively; or
                                                                                               [   ] both the buyer and seller.

(d) The disclosures and confirmation required by this section shall be in addition to the disclosure required by Section 2374.

2376   No selling agent in a real property transaction may act as an agent for the buyer only, when the selling agent is also acting as the listing agent in the transaction.

2377   The payment of compensation or the obligation to pay compensation to an agent by the seller or buyer is not necessarily determinative of a particular agency relationship between an agent and the seller or buyer. A listing agent and a selling agent may agree to share any compensation or commission paid, or any right to any compensation or commission for which an obligation arises as the result of a real estate transaction, and the terms of any such agreement shall not necessarily be determinative of a particular relationship.

2378   Nothing in this article prevents an agent from selecting, as a condition of the agent's employment, a specific form of agency relationship not specifically prohibited by this article if the requirements of Section 2374 and Section 2375.5 are complied with.

2379   A dual agent shall not disclose to the buyer that the seller is willing to sell the property at a price less than the listing price, without the express written consent of the seller. A dual agent shall not disclose to the seller that the buyer is willing to pay a price greater than the offering price, without the express written consent of the buyer.

This section does not alter in any way the duty or responsibility of a dual agent to any principal with respect to confidential information other than price.

2380   Nothing in this article precludes a listing agent from also being a selling agent, and the combination of these functions in one agent does not, of itself, make that agent a dual agent.

2381   A contract between the principal and agent may be modified or altered to change the agency relationship at any time before the performance of the act which is the object of the agency with the written consent of the parties to the agency relationship.

2382   Nothing in this article shall be construed to either diminish the duty of disclosure owed buyers and sellers by agents and their [...] agents, subagents, and employees or to relieve agents and their associate licensees, subagents, and employees from liability for their conduct in connection with acts governed [...] by breach of a fiduciary duty or a duty of disclosure.

36

Many states do not yet have an agency disclosure law. If you're buying a home outside California, find out if your agent is acting as a subagent of the seller. It might not be possible to have an agent represent you exclusively if the seller is paying the commission. If you don't want to work with an agent who's a subagent of the seller, you may have no alternative but to hire, and pay for, a buyer broker to represent you.

The Pros and Cons of Working with More Than One Agent

There's no written rule that says a buyer must look for a new home with only one agent. Practically speaking, however, working with one agent exclusively is usually the best arrangement. Since most buyers are in a hurry, working with one agent helps avoid the time-consuming duplication of efforts that can occur with several agents. Most homes are listed on the Multiple Listing Service, so if you work with an agent who belongs to the local MLS and who is active in the business, you're likely to be exposed to the full inventory of listings as they become available. Many good agents will only work with buyers who agree to work with them exclusively in their area.

As a seller, you really haven't got much choice. Most listing agents will work only on an exclusive basis. This is an aspect of the real estate business that causes confusion: it's possible to list with one agent and obtain maximum exposure at the same time. This is done by signing an Exclusive Listing Agreement, with a clause in the agreement that instructs the agent to list your home on the Multiple Listing Service. Again, to accomplish this you must list with an agent who belongs to the local MLS.

37

Be courteous to real estate agents, but don't let yourself be intimidated by them. Always remember that you're the boss. To avoid confusion, and to insulate yourself from unwanted agent solicitations, it's wise to inform agents whom you come into contact with (for instance, at open houses, or when calling real estate offices to inquire about signs or ads), that you already have an agent to represent you. Commission disputes between agents can arise if an agent other than your own exposes you to a home you want to purchase. If your agent is a member of the MLS, he or she has access to all of those listings and can show you a home regardless of who the listing broker is.

Common Complaints About Real Estate Agents

The most common complaint, often completely justified, is that buyers and sellers feel they're being hustled by real estate agents. Real estate is a competitive business, and the good agents are continually looking for new customers. It's also a very personal business, so you must relate well with an agent who represents you in order to have an agreeable transaction. If an agent's approach is too "hard sell" for your liking, find another agent. The most successful agents are masters at the "soft sell" approach to doing business.

Another common complaint is that the agent consistently shows homes that are above the buyer's price range. Good agents will qualify their buyers first and won't show homes out of the predetermined price range.

Buyers who have looked for some time and have found nothing often complain that their agent hasn't been listening to them and is always showing them houses that aren't quite right. Sometimes this is a valid complaint, but in many cases either the buyers aren't clearly communicating their wants and needs to their agent or what they're looking for isn't presently available.

Agents can't be expected to be mind readers. From an agent's standpoint, the hardest buyers to please are the ones who say nothing about what they like and don't like, or the ones who think every home they see is wonderful (which usually means they don't know what they like). If you're clear with your agent about what you're looking for, he or she should be able to describe your dream home after showing you no more than three or four houses.

A legitimate complaint made by both buyers and sellers is that their agent doesn't work hard enough for them. Buyers who discover they're missing out on one good house after another should find another agent who will work actively on their behalf. An even bigger problem occurs when buyers or sellers discover, after the purchase contract is negotiated, that their agent won't return phone calls and fails to follow through with the critical details of the escrow and closing.

A final complaint pertains to agents' egos interfering with the transaction. Good agents understand that they're not the decision makers. It's an agent's job to advise buyers and sellers on issues pertaining to their home purchase or sale; the principals decide how to proceed based on their specific needs and desires.

What to Do If You're Dissatisfied with Your Agent

Firing real estate agents before they're hired is easy enough: tell them you already have another agent to represent you. If, after you're into the escrow period, you discover that your agent has left you to fend for yourself, you have several ways to protect yourself.

Let your agent know you're unhappy with the lack of attention to your transaction. Ask to be informed every few days about the escrow's progress. If this still doesn't result in improved service, continue to call every day or so to monitor the transaction yourself.

Never forget that you're entitled to high-quality representation. If, after repeated discussions with your agent, you continue to be dissatisfied, call the agent's manager or broker of record. Be candid about your concerns. If the manager is unable to solve the problem, then request that another agent be assigned to handle your transaction.

Problems that can't be resolved at the broker level can be pursued by filing a complaint with the local Board of Realtors, if the agent is a member, or the California Department of Real Estate (DRE). The DRE licenses real estate agents and brokers in the state and can suspend or revoke licenses under certain circumstances. For more information about filing a complaint with the DRE, call (213) 897-3399.

Buying or Selling a Home Without an Agent

Although the law does not require that you buy or sell a home through an agent, statistics indicate that approximately 80 percent of real estate transactions are conducted with the help of a real estate agent.

Selling a home by yourself will save you the real estate commission. There is a price to pay, however. You'll need to cover the expenses of advertising on your own. You'll also need to make your home available for showings, be able to financially qualify prospective buyers so you don't waste your time, comply with various disclosure requirements and effectively negotiate face-to-face with interested parties.

Sellers who sell on their own (called FSBOs—For Sale By Owner) often offer to cooperate with a broker who represents a buyer for a reduced commission (say 2.5 to 3.5 percent of the sale price). Don't be surprised if a co-op broker insists on a dual agency representation, even though the FSBO sellers offer to represent themselves. Undisclosed dual agency is against the law and is grounds for rescinding a sale. Since the co-op agent will be the only agent involved in the transaction, the fear is that the FSBO sellers might rely on him or her for advice which would inadvertently create an illegal undisclosed dual agency relationship. This provides grounds for canceling the sale.

39

Finding a home and representing yourself as a buyer is a little more difficult. If you restrict your search to only those homes being offered for sale by owner, you'll have access to only 20 percent or less of the homes on the market. If you include homes that are listed for sale in your search, be aware that the seller has probably agreed to pay a commission regardless of whether or not the buyer is represented by another broker. Since real estate commissions can only be paid to licensed brokers, unlicensed buyers won't save money by trying to represent themselves. Also, in an active market, such buyers may miss out on good listings that sell through the brokerage community even before they're advertised to the public.

Aside from desiring to save money, some buyers and sellers want to conduct their home purchase or sale without a broker because they've had a bad experience with a real estate agent. As in any profession, there are good and bad agents The Department of Real Estate and the California Association of Realtors have made concerted efforts to raise the standard of care in the industry by requiring course work and continuing education as a part of the licensing process. Just because you had an unfortunate experience at one time doesn't mean you can't find a trustworthy professional to serve your current needs.

CHAPTER 4

LISTING YOUR HOME for SALE

When Is the Best Time to Sell?

Sellers commonly wonder when is the best time to sell. Statistics are available that can help determine the answer, and the Multiple Listing Service is continually compiling information on local real estate market conditions. Ask your agent: the length of time it's taking to sell homes similar to yours; the average percentage of listing price obtained; the number of recent sales in your neighborhood; the number of recent sales in your price range; the most common type of financing used; and how many unsold homes similar to yours are on the market in your neighborhood.

In an active real estate market, homes usually sell within 30 to 60 days for something close to the list price, and buyers usually obtain new financing to complete their purchases. In a slow market, you'll find fewer sales taking a longer period of time (90 days or longer), lower sale prices, and more seller financing.

Generally, a seller is better off selling in a seller's market, characterized by low inventory relative to the demand. In this type of market, there are more buyers looking for homes than there are homes for sale. This market condition tends to put an upward pressure on prices. Multiple offers on listings and bidding competitions between buyers are not uncommon.

Other factors come into play, too. For instance, the real estate market usually picks up during periods of low interest rates when housing is more affordable and it's easier for buyers to qualify for home loans. However, periods of low interest rates don't always result in active real estate markets. In 1992, for instance, low interest rates provided little stimulus to a stagnant real estate market plagued by recessionary influences such as high unemployment.

Consumer confidence also has a tremendous influence on the residential real estate market. When consumer confidence is up, more homes are sold than when confidence is low. For example, during the Persian Gulf War of 1991, consumers' worst fears of higher gas prices and a crippled economy failed to materialize. Instead, gas prices dropped and the stock market soared. Consumer confidence shot up and so did real estate sales. When the war ended, and the effect of a lingering recession took hold again, the confidence index dropped; so did home sale activity.

40

Sellers who are selling one home in order to buy another will find it easy to sell in a seller's market, but it may be difficult to find a replacement home. Selling in a buyer's market (also called a soft or flat market) will put you at a disadvantage as a seller, but you'll gain an edge once you've sold your home if you then become a buyer in that market. This will work to your advantage particularly if you're selling a less expensive home in order to trade up to a more expensive one. Although you may have to discount the price of the home you're selling, if you receive an equivalent discount on a pricier home that you're purchasing, you'll come out ahead. If you're moving from one marketplace to another, check local market conditions. Some transferees have been disappointed to find that they were selling in a soft market and buying into a seller's market.

In addition to supply and demand, and other economic factors, the time of year you choose to sell can make a difference both in the amount of time it takes you to sell your home and in the ultimate selling price. Weather conditions are less of a consideration in California than in other parts of the country. Consequently, we tend to see the real estate market here pick up as early as February, with the strongest selling season usually lasting through May. With the onset of summer, the market slows. July is often the slowest month for real estate sales due to a strong spring market putting possible upward pressure on interest rates. Also, many prospective home buyers and their agents take vacations during midsummer. Following the summer slowdown, real estate sales activity tends to pick up for a second, although less vigorous, season which usually lasts into November when the market slows again as buyers and sellers turn their attention to the holidays.

Sellers often wonder whether or not they should take their homes off the market for the holidays. Generally speaking, you'll have the best results if your house is available to show to prospective buyers continuously until it sells. Also, sometimes the real estate market is active in December, so check the supply and demand balance between buyers and sellers in your area before making a decision. If there's little inventory for sale and buyer activity is strong, you'll be better off keeping your home on the market.

It would be ideal if home sellers could decide to sell purely on the perceived right timing. This, unfortunately, is unrealistic. Most sellers, approximately 50 percent according to a recent survey, have an urgent need to sell, usually due to death, divorce, transfer, or financial need. For this reason, it's important to price your home competitively, particularly if you're selling in a relatively slow market.

Preparing Your House for Sale: The Five-Step Plan

Follow this five-step, fix-up-for-sale plan to maximize your chances of a speedy and profitable home sale:

1. Unclutter; remove excess.
2. Fix what's broken and update what's outmoded.
3. Depersonalize.

4. Clean thoroughly.
5. Set the stage.

There are two basic goals to aim for in fixing up your home for sale. One is to show your house off to its best advantage so that it looks great in comparison to the competition. The other is to repair defects that will either be detrimental to selling or will lower the market value of your home.

The entry to Jerry Thomas's house consisted of an immense deck and stairway system with such bad dry rot that Jerry had placed pots upside down over holes in the deck to keep guests from tripping and falling. The roof and gutters had deteriorated to the point that water poured from the roof onto the head of anyone standing at the front door during a rainstorm. Jerry's Realtor® predicted that, with the deck and roof in their current condition, the house would sell for around $200,000 and that the buyer would probably ask Jerry to pay for the repair work. The Realtor® convinced Jerry to replace the deck and roof before marketing the home. In addition, Jerry replaced old rust carpet, changed a few light fixtures, and painted dark brown cabinets off-white to lighten the interior and enhance the emotional appeal of the house. It sold with multiple offers for $250,000. Jerry more than doubled the return on the money he invested in fixing up the property for sale.

Start by taking a critical look at your home. Try to put yourself in the frame of mind of a picky buyer, and have a note pad handy. Ask your agent, or a friend with a critical eye, to walk through your home with you and make fix-up-for-sale recommendations. Compile a list of everything that should be repaired, replaced, or removed before you market the home.

Real estate agents often say that curb appeal (the way the property looks from the street) sells the house, so begin by making a study of the exterior. If you think this exercise is a waste of time, imagine yourself as a buyer walking up to a house that has a shoddy facade, fence posts hanging from rusty old nails, exterior house paint blistered and peeling, and crab grass growing everywhere. You immediately wonder what horrors await behind the front door.

First impressions are lasting; your fix-up work should start at the curb in front of your house.

Dead or dying shrubs should be removed and replaced. If the lawn is shot, consider rolling in new sod, but a sickly lawn may just need fertilizing and more water, so try this first. Replace missing fence slats and repair lopsided gates or shutters. Fix a leaky sprinkler system, and add color to the yard with flats of flowering annuals to line walkways and planting beds. Colorful container plants at the front entry provide a cheerful welcome.

Pay special attention to the condition of the driveway, particularly if it's in front of the house. Remove grease stains with a chemical solvent, patch holes, and consider resurfacing if the driveway is beyond repair. The impression you want to convey is that the property is well-maintained.

The exterior paint should be in good condition. If it looks good, touch up where necessary; otherwise, consider a complete paint job. Keep in mind that if you don't paint a house that needs it, the buyer will have to overcome a negative first impression, which may cost you more than it would have had you painted the house in advance.

Exterior color preferences change. It doesn't make sense to repaint your home without first considering a change in color scheme. This is particularly the case if a new color will make your home more salable or bring a higher price. Blue, yellow, green, black, purple, and slate gray have been difficult colors to sell in the past. A beige, taupe, white, or light gray with a contrasting trim is usually a safe bet, depending on the house style. Ask your agent and several painters for color recommendations. Drive around your neighborhood and note the color combinations that are particularly attractive. If you're still in doubt, contact a color consultant. And, even if you don't paint the whole house, it's usually a good idea to paint the front door.

The roof, gutters, and down drains should be in good repair. Caulk areas where you've had leaks in the past: chimneys, vent pipes, and skylights are common culprits. Replace loose, cracked, and missing shakes and shingles.

43

A word of caution about your fix-up projects: Keep a record of the items you're correcting that should be disclosed to the new buyer. For instance, a skylight that has leaked in the past and needs routine caulking should be disclosed. Informing the buyer, in writing, of the general maintenance items that must be taken care of to ensure the continued good condition of the property is likely to relieve you of future liability.

Before calling the roofer to make repairs or clean your gutters, look for signs of moisture entry from inside your house. Water stains and cracked, blistered, or peeling paint on ceilings or walls are the indicators. Have the roofer repair where indicated, and ask for a water test to be sure that the problem is corrected before making cosmetic repairs to the interior.

Other things to look out for in your yard are weeds, debris, fallen leaves, excess ivy, or murky water in the pool. Trim hedges and paths, clean up the yard, haul away broken yard furniture and debris, and have the pool water treated

Paint yields the biggest return on your investment: stick to neutral colors.

until it sparkles. Don't overlook the subterranean drainage system around your house. Call a rooting company to unclog plugged drains.

Be sure to emphasize good outdoor living, if this is a selling feature of your home. An empty deck or patio can be dressed up with outdoor furniture and containers of flowering plants. Good-looking, inexpensive varieties of patio furniture are available.

Now, for the inside. The areas that buyers will see first are the most important. Keep this in mind if you're short on time or funds. Before opening the front door, test the door bell and entry porch light. Purchase a new welcome mat to replace an old one that's frayed and weathered.

Imagine yourself as a prospective buyer. Open the door and walk inside. Stand in your entry hall and concentrate on the first impression. If the immediate surroundings appear dark, dingy, crowded, garish, or cluttered, change them to create an interior that's light, spacious, airy, and fresh.

Remove furniture from crowded rooms and hallways. Use the extra pieces elsewhere, or tag them for storage or sale. If you don't have room in your garage for extra pieces, rent a storage container. Generally speaking, underfurnished is better than overfurnished, because it creates an illusion of spaciousness. If you're having difficulty rearranging your belongings, ask your agent for help, or seek the advice of an interior decorator who specializes in fix-up-for-sale.

Dingy walls should first be cleaned, with specific effort directed toward removing crayon or pencil marks and fingerprints, particularly around light switch plates. If walls don't brighten with cleaning or if the existing colors are overpowering, repaper or paint as needed. Stick to neutral shades that won't clash with a buyer's decor.

44

Pay attention to floor coverings. Carpet that looks outdated, tattered, and worn should be replaced, unless you have hardwood flooring underneath the carpet. If the floors are in good shape, you can leave them bare and save the cost of recarpeting; if they are a bit rough, get several bids to determine the cost of refinishing. Find out from your agent whether hardwood floors or wall-to-wall carpets are more popular with buyers before deciding whether to refinish the floor or replace the carpet.

A good real estate agent will be able to recommend tradespeople to assist you with fixing up your home for sale. Get several bids for each major item such as painting and carpeting, and be sure to check references. You don't need to install top-of-the-line goods—a medium quality from a wholesale outlet is fine. But, be leery of using a product or contractor that's priced way under the competition. You may find the results unacceptable.

Unclutter your home so that buyers can concentrate on the house and not on your personal possessions.

Another reminder about disclosure obligations: Sellers who discover burn marks or stains in wood floors when they replace wall-to-wall carpet should disclose this to prospective buyers. If you patch, paint, or paper walls that are uneven, cracked, or have holes in them, disclose this, too, to avoid being accused of concealing a defect. Keep a record of these items as you redecorate for sale to aid you in filling out the seller disclosure form (discussed later in this chapter). Also, keep receipts for all of the fix-up work since some expenses are tax deductible.

Kitchens and bathrooms are focal points for most buyers. Be sure that both are spotless and free of clutter. Keep toilet articles out of sight; replace tired-looking shower curtains, bath mats, and towels. Antiquated light fixtures can be updated relatively inexpensively. Always keep in mind: the more light the better. If you've had a termite report that calls for replacing the kitchen or bathroom floor, consider having the work done before you market your home.

It doesn't make economic sense to completely remodel a kitchen just for the purpose of sale. But, an outdated kitchen with a good basic design can be turned from a liability into an asset by simply refacing cabinets, changing the floor covering, and installing new countertops.

Little improvements can make a big difference. Designer light switch plates throughout the house cost very little and can be added with a screwdriver. Old cabinets look new when battered knobs and pulls are replaced. Be sure to fix leaky faucets, a toilet that runs continually, and clogged drains. Add to your fix-up list torn screens, squeaky or sticky doors and windows, broken windows, or a sliding door that pops off its track. Tighten hardware, particularly loose door-knobs, and replace burned-out light bulbs and missing tiles.

45

Clean out and organize closets, because storage space is another top priority for most home buyers. Throw away anything you don't need; moving useless possessions is a waste of time and money. Consider investing in closet organizers if your closets are small. And don't forget to clean and reorganize the garage, attic, and basement to emphasize their storage potential.

Make the most out of every square inch of your house. Turn the junk room, for instance, into a room with a purpose. A room that's too small to be used as a bedroom might be ideal as an office, hobby center, nursery, study, or computer corner.

Don't overlook the views from your windows. Overgrown trees and hedges should be trimmed. Add a sheer window covering or a blind to a window that has an unpleasant outlook.

Pet and smoke odors are offensive to most buyers. Clean thoroughly and air out the house. Pet stores have products that eliminate most pet odors from carpets; the scentless variety is preferable.

Staged homes usually sell more quickly and for a higher price.

Depersonalize your home so that buyers can concentrate on what your home has to offer. Put away collections of photographs, knicknacks, trophies—anything that will distract a buyer. Also, conceal toothpaste tubes, toothbrushes, the coffee grinder, and even a portable microwave if it takes up precious countertop space. Your home may look sterile to you when you're done. Just remember that the way you live in a home and the way you sell it aren't the same.

The look you're aiming for is squeaky clean. Floors should be scrubbed and waxed. If you're not replacing carpets, have them professionally cleaned (or rent professional equipment and do it yourself), and, while you're at it, clean upholstered furniture. Wash all windows, inside and out.

> *Fix-up-for-sale expenses are tax deductible if the work is completed within 90 days before you sell. Ask your accountant for details.*

The final step is to stage your home for sale. Staging is a relatively new concept in the residential resale industry and was borrowed from builders who decorate model homes to assist their sales effort. A vacant house is difficult to sell because most buyers lack the imagination necessary to visualize themselves living in an unfurnished house. If you're selling a vacant house, consider renting furniture to aid in marketing. Sellers marketing furnished homes can make use of the model home analogy, too. Rearrange furniture to enhance the home's best features. Old furniture can be replaced with rental furniture if necessary. You can even rent decorative art work. Don't forget fresh flowers; select long-lasting varieties and replace them before they wilt.

Not everyone has a decorator's eye. It's possible to hire a decorator who specializes in helping sellers prepare their homes for sale. The cost varies, as does the cost of rental furniture. Some fix-up-for-sale decorators work on a per-hour basis; others charge a flat fee for the complete job. Ask your agent to recommend fix-up-for-sale decorators and furniture rental sources (or look under the "furniture rental" section in the Yellow Pages).

By now you're probably exhausted just thinking about all that needs to be done to get a home ready to sell. Working people will be particularly overwhelmed. Finalize the fix-up list and get bids for having the work done in advance. Take a few days off, if you can, to supervise or assist with the preparation. Hiring a professional cleaning company to come in after all the projects are completed will save you time, and it's worth the expense if you're busy. At the end of it all, don't be surprised if you find yourself wondering why you didn't take care of all these chores earlier. If you feel this way, you're not alone. Most people's homes never look as good as when they go on the market.

Pricing Your Home for Sale

You may have noticed that some homes listed for sale in your neighborhood sell quickly and for close to the asking price. Others sit on the market unsold, sometimes for months and sometimes without even a nibble from an interested buyer.

46

It's critical to price your home right in relationship to the current real estate market and to the conditions prevailing in your local marketplace. Since the real estate market is continually changing, and market fluctuations have an effect on property values, it's imperative to select your list price based on the most recent comparable sales in your neighborhood.

The Comparative Market Analysis (CMA), discussed in Chapter 3, provides the background data on which to base your list price decision. Study the comparable sales material presented to you by the different agents you interviewed initially. If the CMAs are over two or three months old, have your agent update the report for you. If all agents agreed on a price range for your home, go with the consensus.

Market value is the price a ready, willing, and able buyer will pay for the home at any given time. Occasionally, agents' opinions of the market value of a home will vary. In this case, ask your agent to bring other agents from his or her office through your home for the purpose of establishing a probable selling price. Be leery, by the way, of an agent you interview whose opinion of value is considerably higher than the others. This agent could have made an honest mistake, but some agents use overpricing as a method of getting listings. Then they work on sellers to reduce their price until the home sells. This practice is unethical; it's also illegal.

Pricing too high for the market can cost you money. Let's say your home is worth $250,000 and you list it for $325,000. Your home will appear overpriced to $325,000 buyers, in comparison to well-priced $325,000 listings, and buyers in the $250,000 price range won't even look at your house. When you drop your price to a range that will attract the right buyers, you can expect even lower offers because your home will then have the stigma of having been on the market for awhile.

There are a couple of pitfalls to avoid when pricing your home. Following your neighbors' lead will be a mistake if they've priced their home unrealistically high. Establishing a price according to what you think you'll need to get out of your home in order to buy your next home can be, at the least, a waste of your time if that price is too high for the market. If you go ahead and purchase a replacement home based on an unrealistically high list price, you could put yourself at financial risk. The value of your home is not determined by the price you want or need from your home; it's determined by what the market will bear.

Well-priced properties sell within 5 percent of the list price in most marketplaces and price ranges. This applies even to buyer's markets. Expect a bit more deviation, say up to 10 percent, in the over-$750,000 dollar price range. To arrive at a priced-to-sell list price for your home, divide the expected selling price by .95. The result will be a price that's

A well-priced listing is one that's listed within 5 percent of the expected selling price.

47

within 5 percent of the expected selling price. This price leaves you some negotiating room, but still looks attractive to buyers and agents. For example, a home that's expected to sell for $250,000 should be listed no higher than $263,000 ($250,000 divided by .95).

How you position yourself in the market, in relation to your competition, is very important. Some sellers find it helpful to visit Sunday open houses in their area. If the open house agent tells you that offers are being written and the home is new on the market, the home is probably priced right. A home that has been on the market for months with no offers is probably overpriced, particularly if similar homes in the area have sold quickly.

Psychology is important in pricing, and sometimes a minor price adjustment can make a big difference. For example, a $299,000 list price is likely to generate more activity than a $301,000 price. $299,000 sounds like a much better deal, even though it's only $2,000 less. Also, buyers often look up to a certain price, and won't consider anything listed over that price. Buyers whose price limit is $300,000 could miss a $301,000 listing completely if their agent relies on a computerized Multiple Listing Service to search for listings by price, which is how most agents set up their buyer tours. A computer MLS search for properties listed up to $300,000 will not report information about a $301,000 listing.

While overpricing can be a detriment to selling, setting your list price at a firm number from which you will not negotiate can also be a mistake. Most buyers like to feel they're getting a deal. No matter how much you hate negotiating, leave a little room in your list price so that you can come down some in your negotiations with a buyer.

In a strong seller's market, sellers are often afraid to price competitively for fear they'll sell too low and leave money on the table. To overcome this potential problem, expose your home to the market before accepting any offers. You may even want to instruct your agent to tell prospective buyers and their agents that you won't listen to offers until after the public and brokers' open houses. You virtually can't sell your house too low if you expose it to the market and let market forces rule.

Be aware that homes with defects (steep driveways, common driveways, traffic or freeway noise, many steps to the front door, a location on a busy street, structural problems, or a lot of deferred maintenance) will be easier to sell in a seller's market than in a buyer's market. In a seller's market, buyers are more willing to overlook such defects because there are fewer homes for sale to choose from. In a buyer's market, however, buyers are less willing to make compromises as they have a large inventory of homes to select from. Pricing below your competition is usually the only way to sell a home with a defect in a soft market.

Build a little, not a lot, of negotiating room into your list price.

48

You can sell a house in any market, even in a buyer's market, if it's priced right. Keep in mind that most home buyers cite price as the major factor in deciding whether to buy a given house. Price it right and it's sold.

The Exclusive Authorization and Right to Sell

Although there are several types of listing agreements, the most popular one in the residential home sale industry is the Exclusive Authorization and Right to Sell listing. Under this agreement, only the listing broker has the right to sell the home and will receive a commission, if the property is sold on the seller's terms and conditions, no matter who finds the buyer. Most exclusive listing contracts also contain provisions for the seller's broker to submit the property to the Multiple Listing Service and for the commission to be split between the listing and selling brokers. This way, the seller receives not only broker representation but maximum marketing exposure as well. A home may or may not sell during the time period of the listing agreement, but if it does, the listing broker will at least be compensated for the effort. Marketing a home comprehensively costs money, and few good brokers are willing to incur those expenses without at least having a chance of being compensated.

The listing agreement is an employment contract between you and your broker. The California Association of Realtors (CAR) has developed standard forms that are available for use by the entire real estate industry. A copy of the CAR "Exclusive Authorization and Right to Sell" listing is included and will be reviewed in this section. Individual real estate companies may have their own forms that differ somewhat from the CAR forms; however, there is consistency regarding the basic elements included in most exclusive right to sell listing agreements.

The listing agreement begins with a grant clause giving a real estate broker the exclusive right to sell a property for a specified period of time. The length of the listing period is negotiable, but it's usually 90 to 180 days. In an active real estate market, a well-priced home should sell within 90 days. In a slower market, a home may take in excess of six months to sell. The length of a listing can be extended by mutual consent of the seller and the broker. Sellers listing with an agent they haven't worked with before ought to list for 90 days and extend later if necessary. If you're not pleased with the agent's performance, you'll be free to find a replacement at that time.

The listing agreement contains a provision, under the Terms of Sale section, for specifying how the purchase price is to be paid. "All cash to seller" is the most common preference if the sellers need all of their equity in cash in order to buy a new home. In a slow market, or if a seller is trading down and doesn't need all the equity at the

The ideal term of a listing agreement is 90 days.

49

EXCLUSIVE AUTHORIZATION AND RIGHT TO SELL
MULTIPLE LISTING AUTHORIZATION
THIS IS INTENDED TO BE A LEGALLY BINDING AGREEMENT — READ IT CAREFULLY.
CALIFORNIA ASSOCIATION OF REALTORS® (CAR) STANDARD FORM

1. **EXCLUSIVE RIGHT TO SELL:** I hereby employ and grant _____
hereinafter called "Broker," the exclusive and irrevocable right commencing on _____, 19_____, and expiring at
midnight on _____, 19_____, to sell or exchange the real property situated in the City of _____,
County of _____, California described as follows: _____
_____

2. **TERMS OF SALE:** The purchase price shall be _____
_____ ($_____), to be paid as follows _____
_____

The following items of personal property are included in the above stated price: _____
_____

3. **MULTIPLE LISTING SERVICE (MLS):** Broker is a Participant of _____
ASSOCIATION/BOARD OF REALTORS® Multiple Listing Service (MLS) and this listing information will be provided to the MLS to be published and disseminated to its Participants in accordance with its Rules and Regulations. Broker is authorized to cooperate with other real estate brokers, to appoint subagents and to report the sale, its price, terms and financing for the publication, dissemination, information and use by authorized Association/Board members, MLS Participants and Subscribers.

4. **TITLE INSURANCE:** Evidence of title shall be a California Land Title Association policy of title insurance in the amount of the selling price.

Notice: **The amount or rate of real estate commissions is not fixed by law. They are set by each Broker individually and may be negotiable between the Seller and Broker.**

5. **COMPENSATION TO BROKER:** I hereby agree to compensate Broker, irrespective of agency relationship(s), as follows:
   (a) _____ percent of the selling price, or $_____, if the property is sold, conveyed or otherwise transferred within _____ calendar days after the
   or through any other person, or by me on the terms herein set forth, or any other price and terms I may accept, or _____ percent of the price shown in 2,
   or $_____, if said property is withdrawn from sale, transferred, conveyed, leased, or rented without the consent of Broker, or made
   unmarketable by my voluntary act during the term hereof or any extension thereof.
   (b) The compensation provided for in subparagraph (a) above if property is sold, conveyed or otherwise transferred within _____ calendar days after the termination of this authority or any extension thereof to anyone with whom Broker has had negotiations prior to final termination, provided I have received notice in writing, including the names of the prospective purchasers, before or upon termination of this agreement or any extension hereof. However, I shall not be obligated to pay the compensation provided for in subparagraph (a) if a valid listing agreement is entered into during the term of said protection period with another licensed real estate broker and a sale, lease or exchange of the property is made during the term of said valid listing agreement.
   (c) I authorize Broker to cooperate with other brokers, to appoint subagents, and to divide with other brokers such compensation in any manner acceptable to brokers.
   (d) In the event of an exchange, permission is hereby given Broker to represent all parties and collect compensation or commissions from them, provided there is full disclosure to all principals of such agency. Broker is authorized to divide with other brokers such compensation or commissions in any manner acceptable to brokers.
   (e) Seller shall execute and deliver an escrow instruction irrevocably assigning Broker's compensation in an amount equal to the compensation provided in subparagraph (a) (above) from the Seller's proceeds.

6. **DEPOSIT:** Broker is authorized to accept and hold on Seller's behalf a deposit to be applied toward purchase price.

7. **HOME PROTECTION PLAN:** Seller is informed that home protection plans are available. Such plans may provide additional protection and benefit to a Seller and Buyer. Cost and coverage may vary.

*8. **KEYBOX:** I authorize Broker to install a KEYBOX: _____ **(Initial)** YES (____/____) NO (____/____)
   Refer to reverse side for important keybox information.

9. **SIGN:** Authorization to install a FOR SALE/SOLD sign on the property: **(Initial)** YES (____/____) NO (____/____)

10. **PEST CONTROL:** Seller shall furnish a current Structural Pest Control Report of the main building
   and all structures of the property, except _____. **(Initial)** YES (____/____) NO (____/____)

11. **DISCLOSURE:** Unless exempt, Seller shall provide a Real Estate Transfer Disclosure Statement concerning the condition of the property. I agree to save and hold Broker harmless from all claims, disputes, litigation, and/or judgments arising from any incorrect information supplied by me, or from any material fact known by me which I fail to disclose. **(Initial)** (____/____)

*12. **TAX WITHHOLDING:** Seller agrees to perform any act reasonably necessary to carry out the provisions of FIRPTA (Internal Revenue Code §1445) and California Revenue and Taxation Code §§18805 and 26131, and regulations promulgated thereunder. Refer to the reverse side for withholding provisions and exemptions.

13. **EQUAL HOUSING OPPORTUNITY:** This property is offered in compliance with federal, state, and local anti-discrimination laws.

*14. **ARBITRATION OF DISPUTES: Any dispute or claim in law or equity arising out of this contract or any resulting transaction shall be decided by neutral binding arbitration in accordance with the rules of the American Arbitration Association, and not by court action except as provided by California law for judicial review of arbitration proceedings. Judgment upon the award rendered by the arbitrator(s) may be entered in any court ...diction thereof. The parties shall ha... ...o discovery in accordance with Code ... ...cedure §1283.05. The f... ...atters ...bitration he... ...al foreclosure or oth...**

time of sale, the listing might indicate "seller is willing to carry financing for a qualified buyer."

Sellers who have an existing assumable home loan should make a copy of the note available to the listing agent for prospective buyers to review. If the note has disappeared, ask your lender for a copy, along with an explanation of the terms under which the loan is assumable. Sometimes an agent can obtain this information for a seller. While you're at it, find out if your note contains a prepayment penalty, since if it does, this could drain thousands of dollars from your proceeds at closing. Be sure to verify in advance whether your net from the sale will be affected by a prepayment penalty.

A seller will usually specify in the listing agreement the items of personal property included in the purchase price. Appliances that are not built in (washer,

(e) Seller shall ~~row instruction irrevoc~~ ~~sation in an amount~~ ~~pensation provide~~
subparagraph (a) ~~from the Seller's proceeds.~~

6. **DEPOSIT:** Broker is authorized to accept and hold on Seller's behalf a deposit ~~to be~~ applied toward purchase price.
7. **HOME PROTECTION PLAN:** Seller is informed that home protection plans are available. Such plans may provide additional protection and benefit to a Seller and Buyer. Cost and coverage may vary.
*8. **KEYBOX:** I authorize Broker to install a KEYBOX: (Initial) YES (____/____) NO (____/____)
Refer to reverse side for important keybox information.
9. **SIGN:** Authorization to install a FOR SALE/SOLD sign on the property: (Initial) YES (____/____) NO (____/____)
10. **PEST CONTROL:** Seller shall furnish a current Structural Pest Control Report of the main building and all structures of the property, except _____.   (Initial) YES (____/____) NO (____/____)
11. **DISCLOSURE:** Unless exempt, Seller shall provide a Real Estate Transfer Disclosure Statement concerning the condition of the property. I agree to save and hold Broker harmless from all claims, disputes, litigation, and/or judgments arising from any incorrect information supplied by me, or from any material fact known by me which I fail to disclose.   (Initial) (____/____)
*12. **TAX WITHHOLDING:** Seller agrees to perform any act reasonably necessary to carry out the provisions of FIRPTA (Internal Revenue Code §1445) and California Revenue and Taxation Code §§18805 and 26131, and regulations promulgated thereunder. Refer to the reverse side for withholding provisions and exemptions.
13. **EQUAL HOUSING OPPORTUNITY:** This property is offered in compliance with federal, state, and local anti-discrimination laws.
*14. **ARBITRATION OF DISPUTES:** Any dispute or claim in law or equity arising out of this contract or any resulting transaction shall be decided by neutral binding arbitration in accordance with the rules of the American Arbitration Association, and not by court action except as provided by California law for judicial review of arbitration proceedings. Judgment upon the award rendered by the arbitrator(s) may be entered in any court having jurisdiction thereof. The parties shall have the right to discovery in accordance with Code of Civil Procedure §1283.05. The following matters are excluded from arbitration hereunder: (a) a judicial or non-judicial foreclosure or other action or proceeding to enforce a deed of trust, mortgage, or real property sales contract as defined in Civil Code §2985, (b) an unlawful detainer action, (c) the filing or enforcement of a mechanic's lien, (d) any matter which is within the jurisdiction of a probate court, or (e) an action for bodily injury or wrongful death, or for latent or patent defects to which Code of Civil Procedure §337.1 or §337.15 applies. The filing of a judicial action to enable the recording of a notice of pending action, for order of attachment, receivership, injunction, or other provisional remedies, shall not constitute a waiver of the right to arbitrate under this provision.
"NOTICE: BY INITIALLING IN THE SPACE BELOW YOU ARE AGREEING TO HAVE ANY DISPUTE ARISING OUT OF THE MATTERS INCLUDED IN THE 'ARBITRATION OF DISPUTES' PROVISION DECIDED BY NEUTRAL ARBITRATION AS PROVIDED BY CALIFORNIA LAW AND YOU ARE GIVING UP ANY RIGHTS YOU MIGHT POSSESS TO HAVE THE DISPUTE LITIGATED IN A COURT OR JURY TRIAL. BY INITIALLING IN THE SPACE BELOW YOU ARE GIVING UP YOUR JUDICIAL RIGHTS TO DISCOVERY AND APPEAL, UNLESS THOSE RIGHTS ARE SPECIFICALLY INCLUDED IN THE 'ARBITRATION OF DISPUTES' PROVISION. IF YOU REFUSE TO SUBMIT TO ARBITRATION AFTER AGREEING TO THIS PROVISION, YOU MAY BE COMPELLED TO ARBITRATE UNDER THE AUTHORITY OF THE CALIFORNIA CODE OF CIVIL PROCEDURE. YOUR AGREEMENT TO THIS ARBITRATION PROVISION IS VOLUNTARY."
"WE HAVE READ AND UNDERSTAND THE FOREGOING AND AGREE TO SUBMIT DISPUTES ARISING OUT OF THE MATTERS INCLUDED IN THE 'ARBITRATION OF DISPUTES' PROVISION TO NEUTRAL ARBITRATION."
(Initial) BROKER (____) SELLER (____/____)
15. **ATTORNEY'S FEES:** In any action, proceeding or arbitration arising out of this agreement, the prevailing party shall be entitled to reasonable attorney's fees and costs.
16. **ADDITIONAL TERMS:** _____
17. **ENTIRE AGREEMENT:** I, the Seller, warrant that I am the owner of the property or have the authority to execute this agreement. The Seller and Broker further intend that this agreement constitutes the complete and exclusive statement of its terms and that no extrinsic evidence whatsoever may be introduced in any judicial or arbitration proceeding, if any, involving this agreement.
I acknowledge that I have read and understand this agreement, including the information on the reverse side, and have received a copy.

Date _____ , 19 ___ _____, California
Seller _____ Address _____
Seller _____ City _____ State ___ Zip ___
In consideration of the above, Broker agrees to use diligence in procuring a purchaser.   Phone _____
Real Estate Broker _____ By _____
Address _____ City _____ Date _____

THIS STANDARDIZED DOCUMENT FOR USE IN SIMPLE TRANSACTIONS HAS BEEN APPROVED BY THE CALIFORNIA ASSOCIATION OF REALTORS® IN FORM ONLY. NO REPRESENTATION IS MADE AS TO THE APPROVAL OF THE FORM OF ANY SUPPLEMENTS NOT CURRENTLY PUBLISHED BY THE CALIFORNIA ASSOCIATION OF REALTORS® OR THE LEGAL VALIDITY OR ADEQUACY OF ANY PROVISION IN ANY SPECIFIC TRANSACTION. IT SHOULD NOT BE USED IN COMPLEX TRANSACTIONS OR WITH EXTENSIVE RIDERS OR ADDITIONS.
A REAL ESTATE BROKER IS THE PERSON QUALIFIED TO ADVISE ON REAL ESTATE TRANSACTIONS. IF YOU DESIRE LEGAL OR TAX ADVICE, CONSULT AN APPROPRIATE PROFESSIONAL.
This form is available for use by the entire real estate industry. The use of this form is not intended to identify the user as a REALTOR®. REALTOR® is a registered collective membership mark which may be used only by real estate licensees who are members of the NATIONAL ASSOCIATION OF REALTORS® and who subscribe to its Code of Ethics.
* REFER TO REVERSE SIDE FOR ADDITIONAL INFORMATION.
The copyright laws of the United States (17 U.S. Code) forbid the unauthorized reproduction of this form by any means including facsimile or computerized formats.
Copyright© 1988, CALIFORNIA ASSOCIATION OF REALTORS®
525 South Virgil Avenue, Los Angeles, California 90020
REVIEWED 2/91

FORM A-14

BROKER'S COPY

OFFICE USE ONLY
Reviewed by Broker or Designee _____
Date _____

EQUAL HOUSING OPPORTUNITY
M-SC-JAN-92

51

dryer, refrigerator, portable dishwasher, portable microwave, freestanding stove) are all negotiable. Sellers who are undecided at the time of listing about which appliances will stay with the house can either leave this section blank or state that the appliances are negotiable. Built-in appliances, window coverings, tacked down carpets, and fixtures permanently attached to the property are assumed to be included. So if you want to take your bedroom drapes because they match the bedspread, or a dining room chandelier that has sentimental value, you should specifically exclude these items from the sale.

The multiple listing authorization clause authorizes the broker to submit the listing information on the property to the Multiple Listing Service (MLS). To obtain access to the MLS an agent must be an MLS member, so list with an agent who's a member for the broadest marketing exposure. A home located in an area

8. **KEYBOX:** A keybox designed as a repository of a key to the above premises, will permit access to the interior of the premises by Participants of the Multiple Listing Service (MLS), their authorized licensees and prospective buyers. If property is not seller occupied, seller shall be responsible for obtaining occupants' written permission for use of the keybox. Neither listing nor selling broker, MLS or Board of REALTORS" is an insurer against theft, loss, vandalism or damage attributed to the use of keybox. SELLER is advised to verify the existence of, or obtain appropriate insurance through their own insurance broker.

12. **TAX WITHHOLDING:** (a) Under the Foreign Investment in Real Property Tax Act (FIRPTA), IRC §1445, every Buyer of U.S. real property must, unless an exemption applies. deduct and withhold from Seller's proceeds 10% of the gross sales price. The primary FIRPTA exemptions are: No withholding is required if (i) Seller provides Buyer with an affidavit under penalty of perjury, that Seller is not a "foreign person," or (ii) Seller provides Buyer with a "qualifying statement" issued by the Internal Revenue Service, or (iii) Buyer purchases real property for use as a residence and the purchase price is $300,000 or less and Buyer or a member of Buyer's family has definite plans to reside at the property for at least 50% of the number of days it is in use during each of the first two 12-month periods after transfer. (b) In addition, under California Revenue and Taxation Code §§18805 and 26131, every Buyer must, unless an exemption applies, deduct and withhold from the Seller's proceeds 3½% of the gross sales price if the Seller has a last known street address outside of California, or if the Seller's proceeds will be paid to a financial intermediary of the Seller. The primary exemptions are: No withholding is required if (i) the Seller has a homeowner's exemption for the subject property, for local property taxes, for the year in which the title transfers, or (ii) the property is selling for $100,000 or less, or (iii) the Franchise Tax Board issues a certificate authorizing a lower amount or no withholding, or (iv) the Seller signs an affidavit stating that the Seller is a California resident or a corporation qualified to do business in California. (c) Seller and Buyer agree to execute and deliver as directed any instrument, affidavit, or statement reasonably necessary to carry out those statutes and regulations promulgated thereunder.

14. **ARBITRATION:** Arbitration is the referral of a dispute to one or more impartial persons for final and binding determination. It is private and informal, designed for quick, practical, and inexpensive settlements. Arbitration is an orderly proceeding, governed by rules of procedure and standards of conduct prescribed by law.

ENFORCEMENT OF ARBITRATION AGREEMENTS
UNDER CALIFORNIA CODE OF CIVIL PROCEDURE SECTIONS 1281, 1282.4, 1283.1, 1283.05, 1287.4 & 1287.6

§ 1281. A written agreement to submit to arbitration an existing controversy or a controversy thereafter arising is valid, enforceable and irreversible, save upon such grounds as exist for the revocation of any contract.

§ 1282.4. A party to the arbitration has the right to be represented by an attorney at any proceeding or hearing in arbitration under this title. A waiver of this right may be revoked; but if a party revokes such waiver, the other party is entitled to a reasonable continuance for the purpose of procuring an attorney.

§ 1283.1. (a) All of the provisions of Section 1283.05 shall be conclusively deemed to be incorporated into, made a part of, and shall be applicable to, every agreement to arbitrate any dispute, controversy, or issue arising out of or resulting from any injury to, or death of, a person caused by the wrongful act or neglect of another.
  (b) Only if the parties by their agreement so provide, may the provisions of Section 1283.05 be incorporated into, made a part of, or made applicable to, any other arbitration agreement.

§ 1283.05. To the extent provided in Section 1283.1 depositions may be taken and discovery obtained in arbitration proceedings as follows:
  (a) After the appointment of the arbitrator or arbitrators, the parties to the arbitration shall have the right to take depositions and to obtain discovery regarding the subject matter of the arbitration, and, to that end, to use and exercise all of the same rights, remedies, and procedures, and be subject to all of the same duties, liabilities, and obligations in the arbitration with respect to the subject matter thereof, as provided in Chapter 2 (commencing with Section 1985) of, and Article 3 (commencing with Section 2016) of Chapter 3 of, Title 3 of Part 4 of this code, as if the subject matter of the arbitration were pending in a civil action before a superior court of this state, subject to the limitations as to depositions set forth in subdivision (e) of this section.
  (b) The arbitrator or arbitrators themselves shall have power, in addition to the power of determining the merits of the arbitration, to enforce the rights, remedies, procedures, duties, liabilities, and obligations of discovery by the imposition of the same terms, conditions, consequences, liabilities, sanctions, and penalties as can be or may be imposed in like circumstances in a civil action by a superior court of this state under the provisions of this code, except the power to order the arrest or imprisonment of a person.
  (c) The arbitrator or arbitrators may consider, determine, and make such orders imposing such terms, conditions, consequences, liabilities, sanctions, and penalties, whenever necessary or appropriate at any time or stage in the course of the arbitration, and such orders shall be as conclusive, final, and enforceable as an arbitration award on the merits, if the making of any such order that is equivalent to an award or correction of an award is subject to the same conditions, if any, as are applicable to the making of an award or correction of an award.
  (d) For the purpose of enforcing the duty to make discovery, to produce evidence or information, including books and records, and to produce persons to testify at a deposition or at a hearing, and to impose terms, conditions, consequences, liabilities, sanctions, and penalties upon a party for violation of any such duty, such party shall be deemed to include every affiliate of such party as defined in this section. For such purpose:
  (1) The personnel of every such affiliate shall be deemed to be the officers, directors, managing agents, agents, and employees of such party to the same degree as ~~~~~ them, respectively, bears such status to such ~~~iate; and
  ~~~~~ ks, and records of even~~~~~ ~~~~~med to be in the possession~~~~ ~~~~~ble of prod~~~~ ~~
  ~~~~~ ~~~~~udes any n~~~

52

within the marketing sphere of two boards should be included on both Multiple Listing Services.

Many sellers shy away from multiple listing their home because they think it's synonymous with an invasion of privacy. This needn't be the case because the listing agent can set up any showing arrangement that's agreeable to the sellers. It's advisable to make a home as accessible as possible for showing. However, if you're selling a multimillion-dollar property and you want prospective buyers to be financially prequalified before the property is shown, include this as a provision of the listing agreement.

Some agents will try to convince sellers to sell their homes "in-house," without multiple listing exposure. An in-house sale is one in which the listing (seller's) and selling (buyer's) agents both work for the same real estate firm. The only one to come out ahead with this arrangement is the real estate broker,

ENFORCEMENT OF ARBITRATION AGREEMENTS
UNDER CALIFORNIA CODE OF CIVIL PROCEDURE SECTIONS 1281, 1282.4, 1283.1, 1283.05, 1287.4 & 1287.6

§ 1281. A written agreement to submit to arbitration an existing controversy or a controversy thereafter arising is valid, enforceable and irreversible, save upon such grounds as exist for the revocation of any contract.

§ 1282.4. A party to the arbitration has the right to be represented by an attorney at any proceeding or hearing in arbitration under this title. A waiver of this right may be revoked; but if a party revokes such waiver, the other party is entitled to a reasonable continuance for the purpose of procuring an attorney.

§ 1283.1. (a) All of the provisions of Section 1283.05 shall be conclusively deemed to be incorporated into, made a part of, and shall be applicable to, every agreement to arbitrate any dispute, controversy, or issue arising out of or resulting from any injury to, or death of, a person caused by the wrongful act or neglect of another.
(b) Only if the parties by their agreement so provide, may the provisions of Section 1283.05 be incorporated into, made a part of, or made applicable to, any other arbitration agreement.

§ 1283.05. To the extent provided in Section 1283.1 depositions may be taken and discovery obtained in arbitration proceedings as follows:
(a) After the appointment of the arbitrator or arbitrators, the parties to the arbitration shall have the right to take depositions and to obtain discovery regarding the subject matter of the arbitration, and, to that end, to use and exercise all of the same rights, remedies, and procedures, and be subject to all of the same duties, liabilities, and obligations in the arbitration with respect to the subject matter thereof, as provided in Chapter 2 (commencing with Section 1985) of, and Article 3 (commencing with Section 2016) of Chapter 3 of, Title 3 of Part 4 of this code, as if the subject matter of the arbitration were pending in a civil action before a superior court of this state, subject to the limitations as to depositions set forth in subdivision (e) of this section.
(b) The arbitrator or arbitrators themselves shall have power, in addition to the power of determining the merits of the arbitration, to enforce the rights, remedies, procedures, duties, liabilities, and obligations of discovery by the imposition of the same terms, conditions, consequences, liabilities, sanctions, and penalties as can be or may be imposed in like circumstances in a civil action by a superior court of this state under the provisions of this code, except the power to order the arrest or imprisonment of a person.
(c) The arbitrator or arbitrators may consider, determine, and make such orders imposing such terms, conditions, consequences, liabilities, sanctions, and penalties, whenever necessary or appropriate at any time or stage in the course of the arbitration, and such orders shall be as conclusive, final, and enforceable as an arbitration award on the merits, if the making of any such order that is equivalent to an award or correction of an award is subject to the same conditions, if any, as are applicable to the making of an award or correction of an award.
(d) For the purpose of enforcing the duty to make discovery, to produce evidence or information, including books and records, and to produce persons to testify at a deposition or at a hearing, and to impose terms, conditions, consequences, liabilities, sanctions, and penalties upon a party for violation of any such duty, such party shall be deemed to include every affiliate of such party as defined in subdivision (e) of this section. For such purpose:
(1) The personnel of every such affiliate shall be deemed to be the officers, directors, managing agents, agents, and employees of such party to the same degree as each of them, respectively, bears such status to such affiliate; and
(2) The files, books, and records of every such affiliate shall be deemed to be in the possession and control of, and capable of production by, such party. As used in this section, "affiliate" of the party to the arbitration means and includes any party or person for whose immediate benefit the action or proceeding is prosecuted or defended, or an officer, director, superintendent, member, agent, employee, or managing agent of such party or persons.
(e) Depositions for discovery shall not be taken unless leave to do so is first granted by the arbitrator or arbitrators.

§ 1287.4. If an award is confirmed, judgment shall be entered in conformity therewith. The judgment so entered has the same force and effect as, and is subject to all the provisions of law relating to, a judgment in a civil action; and it may be enforced like any other judgment of the court in which it is entered.

§ 1287.6. An award that has not been confirmed or vacated has the same force and effect as a contract in writing between the parties to the arbitration.

53

who keeps marketing expenses down by effecting a quick sale and by not having to split the commission with an outside broker. The way to sell for top dollar is to expose a property as extensively as possible to all prospective buyers. Don't sell yourself short by accepting an in-house offer before your home has been adequately marketed. Exposure in a seller's market can result in multiple offers, sometimes for over the list price.

The Compensation to Broker portion of the listing agreement will be filled in according to the commission you and your broker agree upon.

Home protection plans are available, which may provide additional benefits to the seller and buyer after the close of escrow. A home protection plan is a service contract covering the major systems of the house: plumbing, electrical, furnace, hot water heater, and some appliances. Some contracts have limited roof coverage, and most have additional options available to cover the refrigerator, washer, dryer, spa, air conditioning, or pool equipment for an extra fee. The policy usually goes into effect at close of escrow and runs for one year. When a malfunction occurs in one of the covered systems, the buyer calls the protection plan company and pays a service charge; the protection plan company pays the cost of the repair work or replacement.

Sellers can offer to pay for a home protection plan when they list their home, or this may become a negotiable item in the purchase contract. If a policy is purchased before or at the close of escrow, the warranty company doesn't usually require an independent inspection of the property, and payment is usually made at the close of escrow. Policies are available for the marketing and escrow periods at a per diem cost. Read the policies carefully; limitations on coverage do apply. Ask your agent which companies are known for providing good customer service, and try to select a company that has no limitation on furnace coverage and one that doesn't exclude pre-existing conditions.

A seller must decide at the time of listing whether to have a keybox (also called a lockbox) installed on the property. A keybox is a metal box containing the house key, which is hung on, or close to, the front door. The keybox is opened by special keys issued only to agents who are members of the Multiple Listing Service. These keys can't be duplicated.

Having a keybox on your home makes the property easily accessible to agents and their buyers. It is not, however, mandatory. If you don't use the keybox, you should make a key available to agents through your listing agent. Be sure to get written authorization to have a keybox placed on the home if it is occupied by someone other than yourself (a tenant, for instance).

The "For Sale" sign is one of the best forms of advertising. If you shudder at the thought of a sign in your front yard, consider that most buyers drive around the neighborhoods where they want to live, and many call a real estate office or agent asking about houses where they've seen signs. They're usually inquiring about the price and size of the home. Contrast this with buyers who call inquiring about ads: they have no idea what the house looks like or where it's located.

Many sellers initially object to posting a sign because they don't want their neighbors to know their home is for sale. This is usually an emotional reaction to the thought of moving away from old friends. But in fact, sellers should want their neighbors to know their home is for sale. Often neighbors have friends who have asked to be kept informed of any new listing that comes on the market.

When you authorize a sign, you're also granting permission for a "Sold" sign to be put up once your home is sold. Ask your agent when this sign will be displayed: when an offer is accepted? when all contingencies are removed from the contract? or just prior to the close of escrow?

A "Pending Sale" sign is preferred by some agents because it lets the public know the seller has accepted an offer but that there may still be contingencies to be removed from the contract. A "Pending Sale" sign might encourage interested prospects to continue calling, so your agent can keep a list of interested people should the pending transaction fall apart. You can ask your agent to have a "Do Not Disturb Occupant" sign attached to the "For Sale" sign.

A Structural Pest Control ("termite") Report (now called a Wood Destroying Pests and Organisms Inspection Report) is obtained during the course of most home sales in California. Custom varies from one area to the next as to whether the buyer or seller pays the cost of the inspection report, which is approximately $135 for a house under 3000 square feet in size. Since it's usually the seller who pays the cost of the corrective work (and this could amount to thousands of dollars), it makes sense for the seller to order a report at the time the home is listed for sale. This way the sellers will know the extent of their liability before weighing an offer to purchase the home. Sellers who elect to provide a presale wood destroying pest report will want to limit that report to the main building, excluding old tool sheds or a detached garage. For more information about "termite" inspections, see Chapter 8.

Seller disclosure is a critical part of selling a home today. Effective January 1, 1987, a seller of residential property in California must provide a buyer with a completed Real Estate Transfer Disclosure Statement. (For more information about the Real Estate Transfer Disclosure Statement, read the remainder of this chapter, and see Chapter 9.)

The tax withholding clause of the listing agreement secures the seller's agreement to comply with the provisions of the Foreign Investment in Real Property Tax Act (FIRPTA). Briefly, FIRPTA requires every buyer of real property in the United States to withhold from the seller's proceeds 10 percent of the gross sales price if the seller is of foreign nationality. There are several exemptions, one of which is property with a sale price of less than $300,000 being purchased as a primary residence.

An arbitration clause will appear in some listing agreements that offers binding arbitration as an option to Realtors® and principals as a method of resolving disputes. The Additional Terms section of the listing agreement is provided for any other pertinent conditions that apply to the listing. A seller who has a number of additional conditions should enter "See Addendum to Listing Agreement attached" in the space provided. Title the supplement "Addendum to Listing Agreement" and have it signed by both you and your agent.

Additional terms can include a long close of escrow or a provision for the sellers to rent back their home after the close of escrow. The seller might require a close of escrow after a specific date, or the sale could be contingent upon the simultaneous close of escrow with the buyer's new home. Specific items of personal property could be included or excluded from the sale, or the seller might retain the right to assign the listing to a relocation company.

Sellers who are marketing tenant-occupied properties need to make it clear to prospective buyers that the property is currently occupied by renters who have certain legal rights. These rights depend upon rental arrangements and local rent control ordinances.

55

REAL ESTATE TRANSFER DISCLOSURE STATEMENT

(CALIFORNIA CIVIL CODE 1102, ET SEQ.)

CALIFORNIA ASSOCIATION OF REALTORS® (CAR) STANDARD FORM

THIS DISCLOSURE STATEMENT CONCERNS THE REAL PROPERTY SITUATED IN THE CITY OF_____
_____, COUNTY OF_____, STATE OF CALIFORNIA,
DESCRIBED AS_____.
THIS STATEMENT IS A DISCLOSURE OF THE CONDITION OF THE ABOVE DESCRIBED PROPERTY IN COMPLIANCE
WITH SECTION 1102 OF THE CIVIL CODE AS OF _____, 19_____. IT IS NOT A WARRANTY
OF ANY KIND BY THE SELLER(S) OR ANY AGENT(S) REPRESENTING ANY PRINCIPAL(S) IN THIS TRANSACTION,
AND IS NOT A SUBSTITUTE FOR ANY INSPECTIONS OR WARRANTIES THE PRINCIPAL(S) MAY WISH TO OBTAIN.

I
COORDINATION WITH OTHER DISCLOSURE FORMS

This Real Estate Transfer Disclosure Statement is made pursuant to Section 1102 of the Civil Code. Other statutes require disclosures, depending upon the details of the particular real estate transaction (for example: special study zone and purchase-money liens on residential property).

Substituted Disclosures: The following disclosures have or will be in connection with this real estate transfer, and are intended to satisfy the disclosure obligations on this form, where the subject matter is the same:_____
_____
_____

(LIST ALL SUBSTITUTED DISCLOSURE FORMS TO BE USED IN CONNECTION WITH THIS TRANSACTION)

II
SELLER'S INFORMATION

The Seller discloses the following information with the knowledge that even though this is not a warranty, prospective Buyers may rely on this information in deciding whether and on what terms to purchase the subject property. Seller hereby authorizes any agent(s) representing any principal(s) in this transaction to provide a copy of this statement to any person or entity in connection with any actual or anticipated sale of the property.

THE FOLLOWING ARE REPRESENTATIONS MADE BY THE SELLER(S) AND ARE NOT THE REPRESENTATIONS OF THE AGENT(S), IF ANY. THIS INFORMATION IS A DISCLOSURE AND IS NOT INTENDED TO BE PART OF ANY CONTRACT BETWEEN THE BUYER AND SELLER.

Seller ☐ is ☐ is not occupying the property.

A. The subject property has the items checked below (read across):

☐ Range	☐ Oven	☐ Microwave
☐ Dishwasher	☐ Trash Compactor	☐ Garbage Disposal
☐ Washer/Dryer Hookups	☐ Window Screens	☐ Rain Gutters
☐ Burglar Alarms	☐ Smoke Detector(s)	☐ Fire Alarm
☐ T.V. Antenna	☐ Satellite Dish	☐ Intercom
☐ Central Heating	☐ Central Air Conditioning	☐ Evaporator Cooler(s)
☐ Wall/Window Air Conditioning	☐ Sprinklers	☐ Public Sewer System
☐ Septic Tank	☐ Sump Pump	☐ Water Softener
☐ Patio/Decking	☐ Built-in Barbeque	☐ Gazebo
☐ Sauna	☐ Pool	☐ Spa ☐ Hot Tub
☐ Security Gate(s)	☐ Automatic Garage Door Opener(s)*	☐ Number of Remote Controls____

56

Occasionally, a friend or acquaintance of a prospective seller will express an interest in buying the home. It's possible to exclude such a person from the listing agreement. If someone specifically excluded from a listing agreement contracts with the seller to purchase the home, a commission is not owed to the listing agent.

An exclusion is worth considering as long as you keep several facts in mind. Most people who claim they want to buy your home, if you ever sell, never do. In addition, attempting to market a home with an exclusion in the listing agreement is difficult because an exclusion puts every other buyer at a disadvantage. Qualified buyers are sometimes reluctant to spend the time and energy required to make an offer on a property that they know someone else has the opportunity to purchase for less. Many busy agents refuse to work on properties with exclusions.

The best way to deal with someone who wants to be excluded from your listing agreement is to put a finite time on the length of the exclusion, say one or two

Seller ☐ is ~~~~~~~~ property.

A. The subject property has the items checked below (re~~~ ~~oss):

☐ Range	☐ Oven	☐ Microwave
☐ Dishwasher	☐ Trash Compactor	☐ Garbage Disposal
☐ Washer/Dryer Hookups	☐ Window Screens	☐ Rain Gutters
☐ Burglar Alarms	☐ Smoke Detector(s)	☐ Fire Alarm
☐ T.V. Antenna	☐ Satellite Dish	☐ Intercom
☐ Central Heating	☐ Central Air Conditioning	☐ Evaporator Cooler(s)
☐ Wall/Window Air Conditioning	☐ Sprinklers	☐ Public Sewer System
☐ Septic Tank	☐ Sump Pump	☐ Water Softener
☐ Patio/Decking	☐ Built-in Barbeque	☐ Gazebo
☐ Sauna	☐ Pool	☐ Spa ☐ Hot Tub
☐ Security Gate(s)	☐ Automatic Garage Door Opener(s)*	☐ Number of Remote Controls_____
Garage: ☐ Attached	☐ Not Attached	☐ Carport
Pool/Spa Heater: ☐ Gas	☐ Solar	☐ Electric
Water Heater: ☐ Gas	☐ Solar	☐ Electric
Water Supply: ☐ City	☐ Well	☐ Private Utility ☐ Other_____
Gas Supply: ☐ Utility	☐ Bottled	

Exhaust Fan(s) in_____220 Volt Wiring in_____
Fireplace(s) in_____ ☐ Gas Starter
☐ Roof(s): Type:_____Age:_____(approx.)
☐ Other:_____
Are there, to the best of your (Seller's) knowledge, any of the above that are not in operating condition? ☐ Yes ☐ No If yes, then describe. (Attach additional sheets if necessary.):_____
_____
_____

B. Are you (Seller) aware of any significant defects/malfunctions in any of the following? ☐ Yes ☐ No If yes, check **appropriate space(s) below.**
☐ Interior Walls ☐ Ceilings ☐ Floors ☐ Exterior Walls ☐ Insulation ☐ Roof(s) ☐ Windows ☐ Doors ☐ Foundation ☐ Slab(s)
☐ Driveways ☐ Sidewalks ☐ Walls/Fences ☐ Electrical Systems ☐ Plumbing/Sewers/Septics ☐ Other Structural Components
(Describe:_____
_____)

If any of the above is checked, explain. (Attach additional sheets if necessary):_____
_____
_____
_____

*This garage door opener may not be in compliance with the safety standards relating to automatic reversing devices as set forth in Chapter 12.5 (commencing with Section 19890) of Part 3 of Division 13 of the Health and Safety Code.
Buyer and Seller acknowledge receipt of copy of this page, which constitutes Page 1 of 2 Pages.
Buyer's Initials (_____) (_____) Seller's Initials (_____) (_____)

REAL ESTATE TRANSFER DISCLOSURE STATEMENT (TDS-14 PAGE 1 OF 2)

57

weeks at most. This will force the prospective buyer to make a decision, and a serious buyer will. It's advisable, in this situation, to hold off submitting the listing to the Multiple Listing Service until the person excluded has either purchased your home or is no longer excluded from the listing agreement. This way you don't muddy your marketing efforts by having to disclose an exclusion to prospective buyers. Keep in mind that your home is most salable when it first hits the market, so don't let anyone sabotage your initial market impact only to let you down later.

The Real Estate Transfer Disclosure Statement

California Civil Code Section 1102 requires sellers of residential property (one to four units) to provide a buyer with a Real Estate Transfer Disclosure Statement. A seller must comply with this requirement, whether or not there is a real estate agent involved in the transaction. Some residential property transfers are

---

DISCLOSURE

Sellers of real property should be aware of their disclosure obligations under the California Court Cases, Statutes and Real Estate Law commentaries excerpted or paraphrased below:

SELLER DISCLOSURE OBLIGATIONS
UNDER CIVIL CODE SECTION 1102, ET SEQ.

Effective January 1, 1987, a transferor (seller) of real property including a residential stock cooperative containing 1 to 4 residential units (unless exempted under §1102.1) must supply a transferee (buyer) with a completed Real Estate Transfer Disclosure Statement in the form prescribed in Civid Code §1102.6.

EXEMPTED TRANSFERS: Summary of exempted transfers (Civil Code Section 1102.1) where Real Estate Transfer Disclosure Statement is **not** required:

  a. Transfers requiring "a public report pursuant to §11018.1 of the Business & Professions Code" and transfers pursuant to §11010.4 of Business & Professions Code where no public report is required;

  b. "Transfers pursuant to court order" (such as probate sales, sales by a bankruptcy trustee, etc.);

  c. Transfers by foreclosure (including a deed in lieu of foreclosure and a transfer by a beneficiary who has acquired the property by foreclosure or deed in lieu of foreclosure);

  d. "Transfers by a fiduciary in the course of the administration of a decedent's estate, guardianship, conservatorship, or trust."

  e. "Transfers from one co-owner to one or more co-owners."

  f. "Transfer made to a spouse" or to a direct blood relative;

  g. "Transfers between spouses" in connection with a dissolution of marriage or similar proceeding;

  h. Transfers by the State Controller pursuant to the Unclaimed Property Law;

  i. Transfers as a result of failure to pay property taxes;

  j. "Transfers or exchanges to or from any government entity."

TIMING OF DISCLOSURE AND RIGHT TO CANCEL (CIVIL CODE SECTION 1102.2):

  a. In the case of a sale, the disclosures to the buyer shall be made "as soon as practicable before transfer of title."

  b. "In the case of transfer by a Real Property Sales Contract, (Installment Land Sales Contract) . . .or, by a lease together with an option to purchase, or ground lease coupled with improvements, as soon as practical before. . .the making or acceptance of an offer."

  "If any disclosure, or any material amendment of any disclosure, required to be made by this article, is delivered after the execution of an offer to purchase, the transferee shall have three days after delivery in person or five days after delivery by deposit in the mail, to terminate his or her offer by delivery of a written notice of termination to the transferor or the transferor's agent."

SUBSTITUTED DISCLOSURES: (CIVIL CODE SECTION 1102.4)

  a. Neither the transferor nor any listing or selling agent shall be liable for any error, inaccuracy, or omission of any information delivered pursuant to this article if the error, inaccuracy, or omission was not within the personal knowledge of the transferor or that listing or selling agent, was based on information timely provided by public agencies or by other persons providing information as specified in subdivision (c) that is required to be disclosed pursuant to this article, and ordinary care was exercised in obtaining and transmitting it.

  b. The delivery of any information required to be disclosed by this article to a prospective transferee by a public agency or other person providing information required to be disclosed pursuant to this article shall be deemed to comply with the requirements of this article and shall relieve the transferor or any listing or selling agent of any further duty under this article with respect to that item of information.

  c. The delivery of a report or opinion prepared by a licensed engineer, land surveyor, geologist, structural pest control operator, contractor, or other expert, dealing with matters within the scope of the professional's license or expertise, shall be sufficient compliance for application of the exemption provided by subdivision (a) if information is provided to the prospective transferee pursuant to a request therefor, whether written or oral. In responding to such a request, an expert may indicate, in writing, an understanding that the information provided will be used in fulfilling the requirements of Section 1102.6 and, if so, shall indicate the required disclosures, or
        reof, to which the informatic   d is applicable. Where such   furnished, the   be
            any it   her than thos

58

exempted from the requirement, such as probate, trustee, guardianship, foreclosure, and bankruptcy sales. A complete list of exempt transfers, along with explanatory material including an explicit citation of disclosure requirements, can be found on the reverse side of the first page of the disclosure form.

Much has been said about the care a buyer should take in making a home purchase. Equal care should be taken in selling a home. Ask your agent to supply you with a form before your listing appointment. Fill out as much of the form as you can on your own, checking any items you question. Ask your agent for an explanation of them, and complete them later when you better understand what is called for.

A seller has a duty to disclose "facts materially affecting the value or desirability of the property which are known or accessible only to him" and which

"If any disc_____mendment of any di_____e by this article, is _____r the execution of an offer to purchase, the transferee shall have three days afte_____ in person or five days after delivery by deposit in the mail, to terminate his or her offer by delivery of a written notice of termination to the transferor or the transferor's agent."

SUBSTITUTED DISCLOSURES: (CIVIL CODE SECTION 1102.4)

a. Neither the transferor nor any listing or selling agent shall be liable for any error, inaccuracy, or omission of any information delivered pursuant to this article if the error, inaccuracy, or omission was not within the personal knowledge of the transferor or that listing or selling agent, was based on information timely provided by public agencies or by other persons providing information as specified in subdivision (c) that is required to be disclosed pursuant to this article, and ordinary care was exercised in obtaining and transmitting it.

b. The delivery of any information required to be disclosed by this article to a prospective transferee by a public agency or other person providing information required to be disclosed pursuant to this article shall be deemed to comply with the requirements of this article and shall relieve the transferor or any listing or selling agent of any further duty under this article with respect to that item of information.

c. The delivery of a report or opinion prepared by a licensed engineer, land surveyor, geologist, structural pest control operator, contractor, or other expert, dealing with matters within the scope of the professional's license or expertise, shall be sufficient compliance for application of the exemption provided by subdivision (a) if information is provided to the prospective transferee pursuant to a request therefor, whether written or oral. In responding to such a request, an expert may indicate, in writing, an understanding that the information provided will be used in fulfilling the requirements of Section 1102.6 and, if so, shall indicate the required disclosures, or parts thereof, to which the information being furnished is applicable. Where such a statement is furnished, the expert shall not be responsible for any items of information, or parts thereof, other than those expressly set forth in the statement.

OTHER DISCLOSURE REQUIREMENTS

I   "...Where the seller knows of facts materially affecting the value or desirability of the property which are known or accessible only to him and also knows that such facts are not known to, or within the reach of the diligent attention and observation of the buyer, the seller is under a duty to disclose them to the buyer." Lingsch v. Savage, 213 Cal. App. 2d 729.

II   "Concealment may constitute actionable fraud where seller knows of facts which materially affect desirability of property and seller knows such facts are unknown to buyer." Koch v. Williams, 193 Cal. App. 2d 537, 541.

III   "Deceit may arise from mere nondisclosure." Massei v. Lettunich, 248 Cal. App. 2d 68, 72.

IV   Failure of the seller to fulfill such duty of disclosure constitutes actual fraud. [Civil Code Section 1572(3)]

V   **California Civil Code: §1709. Deceit—Damages** One who willfully deceives another with intent to induce him to alter his position to his injury or risk is liable for any damages which he thereby suffers. **§1710. Elements of Actionable Fraud** A deceit, within the meaning of the last section, is either: (1) The suggestion, as a fact, of that which is not true, by one who does not believe it to be true; (2) The assertion, as a fact, of that which is not true, by one who has no reasonable ground for believing it to be true; (3) The suppression of a fact, by one who is bound to disclose it, or who give information of other facts which are likely to mislead for want of communication of that fact; or (4) A promise, made without any intention of performing it.

VI   "The maker of a fraudulent misrepresentation (seller) is subject to liability...to another (buyer) who acts in justifiable reliance upon it if the misrepresentation, although not made directly to the other (buyer), and that it will influence his conduct..." [parenthetical material added]. Restatement (2d) or Torts §533.

VII   "The Seller may have an affirmative duty to disclose certain significant facts regarding the condition of his property. It is not enough for the seller to say nothing because he is not asked." California Real Estate Sales Transactions, §12.2, p.463 (Cal. C.E.B. 1967).

VIII   "A buyer who has been defrauded by the seller has the choice of either: (A) Using the seller's fraud as a defense when and if the buyer refuses to follow through with his obligation under the contract, or (B) Using the seller's fraud as a basis for an action for affirmative relief in the form of an action for damages or for recission of the contract."

IX   Exculpatory Clauses: "It is better for the seller to disclose the specific condition than to attempt to exculpate himself against its nondisclosure. In general, the exculpatory (e.g., "as is") clause provides little, if any, protection." California Real Estate Sales Transactions p.483 (Cal. C.E.B. 1967).

[The Above is a general statement of the seller disclosure obligations. Other disclosure may be required].

59

"facts are not known to, or within the reach of the diligent attention and observation of the buyer...." Failure to disclose can constitute fraud. Furthermore, it's not sufficient to fail to disclose something simply because you're not specifically asked to. For instance, if you're selling a condominium and your condominium association is currently involved in litigation against the builder, you must disclose this to a buyer, whether or not the buyer asks you about it. Precisely what is considered a material fact will differ from one situation to the next.

The disclosure form isn't complicated, but in most cases it should be supplemented with additional information from the seller. Section I (see sample form) asks the seller to itemize "substituted disclosures," and several spaces are allotted for this. A substitute disclosure is any documentation you have, or will obtain, that is intended to satisfy the disclosure obligations, such as wood destroying

□

Subject Property Address: _____ _____ , 19 _____

C. Are you (Seller) aware of any of the following:

1. Substances, materials, or products which may be an environmental hazard such as, but not limited to, asbestos, formaldehyde, radon gas, lead-based paint, fuel or chemical storage tanks, and contaminated soil or water on the subject property. .... ☐ Yes ☐ No
2. Features of the property shared in common with adjoining landowners, such as walls, fences, and driveways, whose use or responsibility for maintenance may have an effect on the subject property. .... ☐ Yes ☐ No
3. Any encroachments, easements or similar matters that may affect your interest in the subject property. .... ☐ Yes ☐ No
4. Room additions, structural modifications, or other alterations or repairs made without necessary permits. .... ☐ Yes ☐ No
5. Room additions, structural modifications, or other alterations or repairs not in compliance with building codes. ... ☐ Yes ☐ No
6. Landfill (compacted or otherwise) on the property or any portion thereof. .... ☐ Yes ☐ No
7. Any settling from any cause, or slippage, sliding, or other soil problems. .... ☐ Yes ☐ No
8. Flooding, drainage or grading problems. .... ☐ Yes ☐ No
9. Major damage to the property or any of the structures from fire, earthquake, floods, or landslides. .... ☐ Yes ☐ No
10. Any zoning violations, nonconforming uses, violations of "setback" requirements. .... ☐ Yes ☐ No
11. Neighborhood noise problems or other nuisances. .... ☐ Yes ☐ No
12. CC&R's or other deed restrictions or obligations. .... ☐ Yes ☐ No
13. Homeowners' Association which has any authority over the subject property. .... ☐ Yes ☐ No
14. Any "common area" (facilities such as pools, tennis courts, walkways, or other areas co-owned in undivided interest with others). .... ☐ Yes ☐ No
15. Any notices of abatement or citations against the property. .... ☐ Yes ☐ No
16. Any lawsuits against the seller threatening to or affecting this real property. .... ☐ Yes ☐ No

If the answer to any of these is yes, explain. (Attach additional sheets if necessary.): _____
_____
_____
_____

Seller certifies that the information herein is true and correct to the best of the Seller's knowledge as of the date signed by the Seller.

Seller_____ Date_____

Seller_____ Date_____

III
AGENT'S INSPECTION DISCLOSURE
(To be completed only if the seller is represented by an agent in this transaction.)
THE UNDERSIGNED, BASED ON THE ABOVE INQUIRY OF THE SELLER(S) AS TO THE CONDITION OF THE PROPERTY AND BASED ON A REASONABLY COMPETENT AND DILIGENT VISUAL INSPECTION OF THE ACCESSIBLE AREAS OF THE PROPERTY IN CONJUNCTION WITH THAT INQUIRY, STATES THE FOLLOWING:

_____
_____
_____

Agent (Broker
Representing Seller)_____ By_____ Date_____
                    (PLEASE PRINT)   (ASSOCIATE LICENSEE OR BROKER-SIGNATURE)

IV
INSPECTION DISCLOSURE

only if ... offer is ...

60

pests ("termite"), roof, drainage, soils, septic tank, well, structural, and general house inspection reports. Current as well as past reports should be listed, and relevant copies of each report or estimate for repair work should be attached to the disclosure statement.

Section II of the disclosure form has three parts. Part A asks if the seller occupies the property and what appliances and specific items are part of the property. If the dishwasher or microwave is portable and not included in the sale, don't check the boxes next to these items. Part A also asks if any of the items included with the property are not in operating condition. Part B asks if the seller is aware of any significant defects, and Part C is a list of 16 questions about the property. Explain each defect completely, attaching additional sheets of paper to the form if necessary. Don't forget to include any fix-up-for-sale work that

AGENT'S INSPECTION DISCLOSURE
(To be completed only if the seller is represented by an agent in this transaction.)
THE UNDERSIGNED, BASED ON THE ABOVE INQUIRY OF THE SELLER(S) AS TO THE CONDITION OF THE
PROPERTY AND BASED ON A REASONABLY COMPETENT AND DILIGENT VISUAL INSPECTION OF THE
ACCESSIBLE AREAS OF THE PROPERTY IN CONJUNCTION WITH THAT INQUIRY, STATES THE FOLLOWING:

_____
_____
_____

Agent (Broker
Representing Seller)_____ By_____ Date_____
　　　　　　　　　　　(PLEASE PRINT)　　　　　　　(ASSOCIATE LICENSEE OR BROKER-SIGNATURE)

IV
AGENT'S INSPECTION DISCLOSURE
(To be completed only if the agent who has obtained the offer is other than the agent above.)
THE UNDERSIGNED, BASED ON A REASONABLY COMPETENT AND DILIGENT VISUAL INSPECTION OF THE
ACCESSIBLE AREAS OF THE PROPERTY, STATES THE FOLLOWING:

_____
_____
_____

Agent (Broker
obtaining the Offer)_____ By_____ Date_____
　　　　　　　　　　　(PLEASE PRINT)　　　　　　　(ASSOCIATE LICENSEE OR BROKER-SIGNATURE)

V
BUYER(S) AND SELLER(S) MAY WISH TO OBTAIN PROFESSIONAL ADVICE AND/OR INSPECTIONS OF THE
PROPERTY AND TO PROVIDE FOR APPROPRIATE PROVISIONS IN A CONTRACT BETWEEN BUYER AND SELLER(S)
WITH RESPECT TO ANY ADVICE/INSPECTIONS/DEFECTS.

I/WE ACKNOWLEDGE RECEIPT OF A COPY OF THIS STATEMENT.

Seller_____ Date_____　　Buyer_____ Date_____

Seller_____ Date_____　　Buyer_____ Date_____

Agent (Broker
Representing Seller)_____ By_____ Date_____
　　　　　　　　　　　(PLEASE PRINT)　　　　　　　(ASSOCIATE LICENSEE OR BROKER-SIGNATURE)

Agent (Broker
obtaining the Offer)_____ By_____ Date_____
　　　　　　　　　　　(PLEASE PRINT)　　　　　　　(ASSOCIATE LICENSEE OR BROKER-SIGNATURE)

A REAL ESTATE BROKER IS QUALIFIED TO ADVISE ON REAL ESTATE. IF YOU DESIRE LEGAL ADVICE, CONSULT YOUR ATTORNEY.

This form is available for use by the entire real estate industry. The use of
this form is not intended to identify the user as a REALTOR®. REALTOR®
is a registered collective membership mark which may be used only by real
estate licensees who are members of the NATIONAL ASSOCIATION OF
REALTORS® and who subscribe to its Code of Ethics.

Copyright© 1990, CALIFORNIA ASSOCIATION OF REALTORS®
525 South Virgil Avenue, Los Angeles, California 90020

QUADRUPLICATE

Page 2 of _____ Pages.

OFFICE USE ONLY
Reviewed by Broker or Designee _____ _____
Date _____

EQUAL HOUSING
OPPORTUNITY
M-PM-8/92

61

REAL ESTATE TRANSFER DISCLOSURE STATEMENT (TDS-14 PAGE 2 OF 2)

conceals defects requiring disclosure (e.g., new carpet over stains on a wood
floor; wallpaper hiding cracks or voids in walls).

　　Be careful how you answer the questions in Part C. They ask if you're aware
of any of the conditions listed below. Don't guess when you answer the questions,
and don't make assumptions that you can't validate. Question 4, for instance, asks
the seller if you are aware of any additions, modifications, and repairs that were
made without necessary permits. Do you know, for example, if the family room
added by the previous owner was done with permits? If you have a copy of the
permits and the final inspection was signed off by the city, then you can validate
this work was done with permits. Otherwise, you may not know for sure. You can
write "unknown" next to a question even though the form only provides boxes for
"yes" and "no" responses.

Often sellers incorrectly assume that because they hired a contractor to remodel or repair, the work was done with permits. Sometimes contractors will do a job without obtaining the required permits in order to save time and costs, and to avoid problems with the bureaucracy. Be sure your contractor takes out the necessary permits, has the city do a final inspection, and gives you the originals. Attach copies of any permits you have to the disclosure form.

A word of caution about "in-law" or "granny" units, commonly a second living unit in a single-family home: These units are frequently rented out, often in violation of zoning laws. You must disclose the legal status of an in-law unit that's in your home. If you fail to disclose a zoning violation, and the buyer purchases the property foreseeing a steady stream of rental income only to have a neighbor report the infraction to the city after the close of escrow, chances are the buyer will have good cause for taking legal action against you. Don't take chances; complete and accurate disclosure will minimize your future liability.

Sellers who haven't recently occupied the house they're selling might want to include a statement on their disclosure form that indicates they have not occupied the property for a period of time; therefore, their knowledge of property defects may be limited.

The Real Estate Transfer Disclosure Statement was recently amended to add Question 1, which asks if you are aware of environmental hazards on the property. In addition to answering this question, make sure the buyers receive a copy of "Environmental Hazards: A Guide for Homeowners & Buyers." This booklet is available for $3.54 from the California Association of Realtors, 525 Virgil Avenue, Los Angeles, CA 90020; (213) 739-8227. The booklet includes a receipt for the buyers to sign to indicate they have received a copy. (For a more detailed discussion of environmental hazards, see Chapter 9.)

In addition to completing this two-page form, it's a good idea to attach a sheet to the form explaining repairs or replacements you have made to the property. You can entitle this "Addendum to Real Estate Transfer Disclosure Statement," and list it under the "Substituted Disclosures" clause of Section I. Briefly list what work was done, why, when, and by whom. Copies of paid receipts and workmen's guarantees or warranties can be attached to the disclosure form with your list.

By now you're probably wondering just how much you need to disclose. Should you mention, for instance, that the water pressure drops when two showers are running at the same time? Ask yourself if this is something you'd want to know before you purchase a home. Sometimes the answers to these questions aren't clear. But it's safe to say that if you're asking yourself whether something needs to be disclosed, it probably should be, so disclose it.

62

Sellers must complete the state-mandated disclosure statement whether or not an agent is involved in the sale.

Disclosing too much can't hurt; exposing too little can result in a lawsuit.

What you fail to disclose, your neighbor may disclose for you after the close of escrow. Friendly neighbor disclosures are more common than you'd think, and can result in costly settlements for the seller who was less than forthright. Also, be sure to give the buyers copies of past reports on the property. One of the biggest causes of claims is undisclosed reports.

Leslie Briggs stated in the Real Estate Transfer Disclosure Statement that there were no known problems with the roof of her home. During the general building inspection, the buyers' agent asked Leslie the age of the roof and was told that it was less than eight years old. Based on this information, and a phone call to a roofer who said the average life of a composition shingle roof is in excess of fifteen years, the buyers removed their inspection contingency without having a separate roof inspection. After the close of escrow, the buyers became chummy with a neighbor who told them Leslie was planning to replace the roof within a year if she stayed in the house. The buyers called in a roofer, who said the roof needed to be replaced before the next winter. The buyers sent a copy of the bid to reroof the house to Leslie along with a letter indicating they expected her to share in the expense. Leslie's attorney advised her to settle with the buyers to avoid a lawsuit.

63

Disclosure of a property defect does not constitute an agreement to fix it, nor does it absolve you of responsibility for fixing it. Most purchase contracts contain a warranty clause which states that all the house systems will be operative at close of escrow. If you have any questions about what you need to repair before closing, check your purchase contract and consult your agent or a real estate attorney.

Disclosure is not something for a seller to fear; failure to disclose has far more serious consequences. And the seller is not the only party who has obligations under the disclosure law. Agent responsibilities are discussed below, and the buyer in a residential real estate transaction has a duty under this law "to exercise reasonable care to protect himself or herself."

The Real Estate Transfer Disclosure Statement requires that both the seller's and buyer's agents complete "reasonably competent and diligent visual" inspections of the "accessible areas of the property." Their findings, which should include disclosure of defects, facts materially affecting the property value, and "red flags," are recorded in Sections III and IV of the disclosure form (with additional

If you're asking yourself if something needs to be disclosed, it's probably material to someone, so disclose it.

sheets attached when necessary). A red flag is a condition that may indicate an underlying problem, such as plaster cracks, sagging ceilings, cracks in retaining walls, warped doors, sloping floors, standing water, or cracked driveways.

Your agent will inform you of the results of the visual inspection and should ask if you have knowledge about any red flag items. This may jog your memory and help you to disclose something you had previously overlooked. Your agent may think a red flag that you mention might be the sign of a serious problem and recommend that you seek the advice of an appropriate professional before marketing your home.

Section V of the disclosure form admonishes the buyer and seller to seek professional advice or inspections and provides spaces for principals and agents to sign. Before you sign the bottom of this form, be sure that both agents have completed Sections III and IV. If an agent found nothing worth adding to what's already contained in the disclosure statement, he or she should indicate this in the space above the agent's signature with a statement like "No additional conditions were noted." A statement by the agent advising you to seek professional advice or inspections, without an accompanying statement indicating that the agent completed an inspection of the property, does not constitute an agent inspection. This is merely the agent's attempt to circumvent the duties mandated by state law. Be certain that this space is filled in correctly so you have proof that the agent complied with the requirements of the law.

64

It's important to complete the Real Estate Transfer Disclosure Statement as soon as possible after the property is listed. The Civil Code dictates that disclosures must be made to the buyer "as soon as practicable before transfer of title," and also contains a right of rescission period to protect the buyer. If the completed disclosure form or any amendment to this form is given to the buyer after the purchase contract is signed, the buyer has three days after personal receipt of the disclosure, or five days after the form is mailed, to terminate the contract by giving written notification of termination to the seller or his or her agent.

Remember that an offer which is made without the benefit of full disclosure may result in a terminated contract, so protect yourself by having your agent make copies of the disclosure form available to all prospective buyers before offers are written.

Earthquake Hazards Disclosure

Effective January 1, 1993, state law requires sellers of one- to four-unit buildings built before 1960 to give the buyer a copy of a booklet entitled *The Homeowner's Guide to Earthquake Safety*. The law also requires that home sellers, regardless of the age of the home, disclose any known earthquake hazards. So it's a good idea to make sure that buyers of homes built since 1960 also receive a copy of the booklet. The booklet includes a form called the "Residential Earthquake Hazards Report" for the seller to use to disclose any known earthquake weaknesses.

The law requires sellers to disclose knowledge of any of the following deficiencies: the absence of anchor bolts securing the sill plate to the foundation; unbraced perimeter cripple walls; unreinforced pier-and-post foundations; unbraced first-story walls; an unreinforced masonry perimeter foundation; unreinforced masonry dwelling walls; a house with walls, posts, or columns that are tall and unbraced; a living area above a garage; and a water heater that isn't anchored, strapped, or braced. Sellers also must describe work they have completed to correct any of these earthquake weaknesses.

The booklet tells you how to identify each of the weaknesses you're required to disclose, and it also tells you what you can do to strengthen them. The Residential Earthquake Hazards Report provided in the booklet can be completed without the aid of a contractor, but care should be taken filling out the form. Sellers should attach a sheet with additional explanations when necessary to avoid making inaccurate disclosures. Question 2, for instance, asks the homeowner: "Is the house anchored or bolted to the foundation?" There are four possible answers provided on the form: "yes," "no," "doesn't apply," and "don't know." If you've had anchor bolts installed you might be inclined to answer "yes" and leave it at that. But frequently the foundation of a house is not completely accessible for bolting, in which case it might have been only partially bolted. Rather than just answer "yes," it would be better to attach an explanation stating that the foundation was only bolted in the easily accessible areas and that some areas (behind finished walls, for example) remain unbolted.

The law requires disclosure; it does not require that a seller complete earthquake strengthening (also called retrofitting) before selling. The intent of the law is to raise homeowners' awareness of preventative measures that can be taken to improve a home's ability to withstand earthquakes. But, the booklet does state that "if you strengthen your house's earthquake weaknesses before you sell, you may get a better price for your house." Following the Loma Prieta quake of 1989, prospective home buyers became keenly aware of the benefits of earthquake retrofitting. It's a feature buyers look for, particularly in an older house. The cost to retrofit an unreinforced home is frequently taken into consideration by buyers, either at the time they make their offer to purchase a home or during the course of their inspections.

A word of caution about hiring contractors to complete earthquake strengthening. Contractors who don't specialize in earthquake retrofitting may cost less than professional specialists. But you may be paying for a false sense of security. Plywood panels that aren't the proper width or that aren't nailed or blocked correctly won't provide you with adequate strengthening. An improper retrofitting job can actually hurt a house by creating an unbalanced structure that could be thrown further out of balance by a strong quake.

Homeowners who are uncertain about whether their home may have earthquake weaknesses that need strengthening can obtain a copy of the new earthquake booklet for $2.25 from the California Seismic Safety Commission, 1900 K Street, Sacramento, California 94814-4186; (916) 322-4917. Your real estate agent can also provide you with a copy of the booklet and should take responsibility for giving a copy to the buyers. Make sure your agent has the buyers sign for receipt of the booklet and that you receive a copy of the signed receipt.

65

Additional Disclosure Requirements

Sellers are required to make disclosures in addition to those provided in the Real Estate Transfer Disclosure Statement and the earthquake safety booklet. For example, legislation requires the disclosure of a death on the property if it occurred within the last three years. Effective January 1, 1991, new garage door openers were required to have an automatic reversing device. A disclosure to indicate that an old garage door opener may not comply with current safety standards is included at the bottom of page 1 of the Real Estate Transfer Disclosure Statement. Sellers who are licensed to sell real estate in the state of California must disclose that fact to a buyer.

The Uniform Building Code requires that chimneys be fitted with spark arresters. In addition, smoke detectors are required in all dwelling units (not just single-family homes). A smoke detector is required in a central location outside each sleeping area. So if you have bedrooms located in two different wings of the house, you'll need two smoke detectors. If you're selling a new house or if you made additions, alterations, or repairs to an existing home that cost over $1,000 for which a permit is required, a smoke detector must be installed in each bedroom and also at a centrally located point outside the bedroom(s). Sellers must provide written confirmation that the property is in compliance with California's smoke detector law when they sell. For more information, contact the State Fire Marshal's office, (916) 262-1875.

66

Sellers also need to disclose to buyers if their property is located in a Flood Hazard, Seismic Hazard, or Special Study Zone. JCP Geologists, Inc., will complete a Geologic Disclosure Report to determine if a property is in, not in, or partially in a State Special Studies Zone, a Special Flood Zone, or a Seismic Hazard Zone for a nominal fee of approximately $55. To order a JCP report, call (415) 940-1514 or (408) 446-4426.

A home seller must make a good faith effort to obtain a notice of any "Mello Roos" assessments against the property and deliver a copy of the notice to the buyers. When a Mello Roos Community Facility District is established in an area, a special tax may be levied to support the sale of tax-exempt bonds for capital improvements and/or local schools. Information on Mello Roos assessments that may affect your property can be obtained from a preliminary title report, your property tax bill, or from the county tax assessor. Sellers must also disclose if their property is in a state fire responsibility area. For this information, call the local fire department.

In addition to state-mandated disclosure requirements, some local government entities impose point-of-sale ordinances that must be complied with when a property is sold. An energy retrofit ordinance is an example of a point-of-sale ordinance. Local governments also have restrictions and regulations on the use of private property, such as zoning restrictions and rent control laws. Check with your real estate agent, city planning department, or local title company for more information about local disclosure obligations.

CHAPTER 5

SHOW
and SELL

The primary objective, *once your home is listed for sale, is to sell for the highest possible price in the least amount of time. For some sellers, the notion of a relatively quick sale is unsettling. Keep in mind that there is usually an inverse relationship between the length of time a home is on the market and the percentage of list price that is realized when it sells. Generally, the longer the marketing period, the lower the ultimate sales price. Well-priced homes sell faster and for a higher amount (relative to the list price) than comparable properties that are priced too high. To protect yourself from selling too low in a strong seller's market, insist that your home be exposed to the market before entertaining an offer.*

67

Marketing Your Home to Real Estate Agents

One of the ways to ensure a profitable and timely sale is to market your home effectively to the local real estate community. To maximize your success with real estate agents, have accurate information about your home readily available, keep your home in top condition, and make it easy to show.

After filling out and signing the various forms associated with listing, you and your agent should sit down and verify the descriptive information to be used in marketing the home. Your agent should prepare a brochure or property information sheet describing the features and amenities of your home. This will help the real estate agents who show your home, since not every agent will know it as intimately as your listing agent does. Sometimes a house has features that aren't readily observable, such as an automatic sprinkler system or solar-assisted heating. The brochure or flyer should be something suitable for a buyer to take home as a reminder of what the home has to offer.

The accuracy of the information included in any marketing material, including newspaper advertisements, is very important. Pay particular attention to statements made about square footage and lot size, including acreage. The exact square footage in an older home may be difficult to verify; you should never rely on the previous owner's estimate. It's far better to refer to square footage and acreage in approximate terms. Using a room count (or the number of bedrooms and baths) is often preferable to referring to square footage at all.

Likewise, use caution when mentioning the age of the home, the character of the neighborhood (remember, housing discrimination is illegal), and subdivision feasibility. An illegal in-law unit should not be portrayed in such a way that implies guaranteed rental income. If you converted part of a basement into a "bedroom" without a permit, don't advertise this as an additional bedroom.

Your real estate agent will arrange for the other agents in the realty office to preview your home soon after it's listed. This is usually your first exposure to the real estate community. Have your home in glowing condition and be a gracious host if you're at home when the agents come through. Brace yourself for this event: many homeowners experience their first pangs of "seller's remorse" when they open their front door to a group of real estate professionals. It's perfectly normal to feel ambivalent about selling.

The next major event is usually an open house for the local real estate community. On the designated day, your home will be on a list with other homes in the area that have just come on the market. Agents from different real estate offices will caravan from one listing to another in order to preview the new inventory for prospective buyers. It's recommended that you leave the house during the brokers' open house, which will last for several hours. If you have a dog, particularly one that barks at visitors, take the dog with you.

The Perfect Showing

68

Making a home accessible for agents to show is an essential step toward selling it. For many sellers this is the hardest part of the marketing process, so don't be surprised if you feel resentful of the showing activity. Even though buying and selling homes is a business, it can also be a very emotional experience.

It's important that you and your agent establish an easy procedure for showing your home. The simplest plan, from the selling agent's perspective, is to have a lockbox on or near the front door. Lockbox use varies from area to area, so take guidance from your agent on this matter. If most homes for sale have lockboxes, so should yours.

The least desirable showing arrangement is one that requires the listing agent to accompany the prospective buyer and selling agent. This should be avoided, if possible, for two reasons. Buyers usually feel less inhibited if they can preview a new listing with their own agent. There's a lot of psychology involved in buying a new home, and it's important for a buyer to feel at ease, particularly when viewing a home for the first time.

Plan to leave the house during open houses and during showings to prospective buyers.

Also, coordinating schedules for a showing that requires two agents and a buyer might be difficult, particularly if you've listed with a successful agent who has a busy calendar. The harder it is to show a house, the less it will be shown.

It's critical to your marketing success to keep the house clean. Light is very important. Open drapes, even if you normally prefer a more private atmosphere. Leave lights on in dark rooms and hallways, and keep the house temperature at a comfortable level, especially if you're selling a vacant house in the middle of winter. Show off areas that might be missed by buyers or agents, such as large walk-in closets (leave a door ajar), attic storage, or a basement access. Tape a note to the door to direct agents to areas of the home they might otherwise miss.

Fresh flowers brighten the decor. A pleasant aroma is inviting, but don't go overboard. Turn television sets off and the radio down. If you're a smoker, empty ashtrays and air out the house before showings. While the house is on the market, try to smoke as little as possible inside or confine the activity to one room. Avoid cooking foods that leave strong lingering odors.

When an agent calls to make an appointment to show your home, be courteous and congenial. Don't get a reputation for being an uncooperative seller by refusing showings. Word travels fast through local real estate communities. If you're rude to agents and refuse to accommodate requests for showings, agents will shy away from showing your home at all.

Plan to leave the house when it's being shown. If that's out of the question, make yourself scarce. *Never* follow the real estate agent and a buyer around. This almost always guarantees a fruitless showing.

Mr. and Mrs. Simmons had owned their home for over 30 years when they decided to list it for sale and move to a retirement community. Mrs. Simmons was sure real estate agents would be unable to properly show her home unless she personally assisted, so the house was shown only by appointment with Mrs. Simmons; not even Mr. Simmons could be entrusted with the task. Mrs. Simmons hovered over each and every buyer pointing out the obvious, and refused to let agents conduct showings in a professional manner. The house never did sell and was withdrawn from the market at the end of the listing period.

69

Buyers are usually reluctant to say anything negative about a house in front of the seller. If they're not alone, they're less likely to look in closets and linger long enough to appreciate the house. It's natural to be curious about buyers' reactions to your home; the appropriate way to find out is to ask your agent.

Try to arrange showing appointments so that you don't have too many different groups of people coming at once. The last thing you want is for your spacious home to appear crowded. It's particularly important to stagger

Buyers usually need to express their objections to a home before they'll buy it, which they won't do if the seller is home during the showing.

appointments if you're selling a smaller home. Likewise, if you have a large family, plan to leave with the children during showings or send them outside to play. Try to present an environment that's free of distractions. While your home is on the market, make arrangements for your children to get together with friends at their homes, not yours.

Be sure to get a business card from each agent who shows your home. You should find an agent's card on a dining room or kitchen table if the house has been shown in your absence. If you find that agents are forgetting to leave their business cards, ask your agent to put a note next to your house brochures asking agents to please leave their cards. It's fine to answer agents' and buyers' questions, but avoid discussing the price, the terms of the sale, or the particulars of any offers. These questions should be referred to your agent.

Open Houses

Sunday open houses are an integral part of marketing residential real estate. Many sellers question their effectiveness, and some refuse to have their house held open to the public at all. From a marketing standpoint, however, a Sunday open house is a good idea, especially when a home is newly listed. It allows real estate agents who have previewed the home on the broker's caravan to bring or send their prospective buyers through.

A common seller complaint is that neighbors make up the biggest percentage of people who frequent Sunday open homes. While it's true that some people, who are not looking for a new home themselves, do frequent open houses, this is not necessarily a bad thing. Some neighbors, certainly, are simply curious to see what homes in the neighborhood are selling for. But others are keeping their eyes open for friends who'd like to move into the area.

Another misconception is that open houses are dangerous. The theory is that they provide potential burglars with an opportunity to examine the house before breaking into it. While there may be a small increased risk of theft when your home is listed for sale, statistically the odds are against it. It is a good idea, though, to put valuables away, particularly expensive breakable items that might be knocked over by a small child. If you're overly concerned, ask your agent if there have been any theft problems at open houses in the area recently.

Disgruntled sellers sometimes complain that an agent spent time during their open house selling another house to buyers who came through. Bear in mind that an open house will draw an assorted group of buyers with different housing needs and requirements. If the house is open to the public, it's open to anyone who wants to take a look.

How often to hold your home open to the public is something for you and your agent to decide. This is best done at the time of the listing so that there are no misunderstandings later. Don't have an open house too frequently, as this can give an impression of desperation and cause the house to become shopworn. Once every three weeks should be sufficient.

Try to remain flexible and avoid making dogmatic decisions about Sunday open houses. If houses are selling quickly and your house is priced right, you can probably sell it without opening it to the public. In slow markets, particularly if there are a lot of homes like yours on the market that aren't selling, you should have open houses periodically.

Selling a Tenant-Occupied Property

It's no wonder that sellers often have difficulties marketing tenant-occupied properties. Tenants who don't want to move might tell prospective buyers horror stories about the property (which may or may not be true) hoping that the house won't sell. Tenants can also make it difficult for a property to be shown by not permitting a lockbox, insisting on 24-hour notice before the property can be shown (which is usually within their rights), or refusing to allow agents to show the property at convenient times. Another problem is the tenant who lets the property get so run-down that there's no possibility of a good showing, even if an agent is successful in making an appointment.

Owners who have maintained a good relationship with their tenants will probably not experience such problems. To ensure cooperation from tenants, it's a good idea to offer them some kind of compensation for having to endure the marketing process. One possibility would be a rent reduction for each month that the home is on the market, payable to the tenant *after* the property is sold. If renters object to being disturbed during certain hours, set up an acceptable showing schedule and have your agent include this in the Multiple Listing Service information.

Sellers who encounter truly obstinate tenants should have occasional Sunday open houses so that agents can bring their prospective buyers through the property. If tenants have made the house difficult to show and you've finally made arrangements that are agreeable to them for a public open house, have your agent circulate a flyer throughout the real estate community to let agents know they can bring or send their clients through the house without encountering a confrontation by the tenants.

The Nitty-Gritty of Advertising

What's in an ad? Usually not a lot of information, just enough to make the phone ring at the real estate office. This is precisely the aim of a well-written real estate ad. It's intended to give readers enough information to pique their curiosity, but not so much that they can decide not to bother following up on it.

The marketing proposal you requested from the several agents you interviewed before listing your home for sale should contain detailed information about the company's advertising program, describing where the company places ads and how often you can expect to see your home advertised. A color photograph of the exterior of your home should be displayed in the window of your real estate broker's office. While it's not often that someone buys a house from a pic-

71

ture in the window, this has been known to happen. The general rule as far as marketing exposure is concerned is that no stone should be left unturned.

Coping with Having Your Home on the Market

Saying your home is on the market is a bit of a misnomer since, when your home is for sale, your whole life's on display. Dealing with the uncertainty of when your home will sell, the seemingly endless disruptions from showings or, even worse, no showings at all, is nerve-racking. There are steps you can take to make life easier.

Keeping the home in impeccable order is the biggest ordeal, particularly for a working family with children. Divide the labor and write up a schedule of when tasks are to be completed. Hire cleaning help every week or so, and buy extra cleaning supplies. You can close off rooms that aren't used much when the house isn't being shown. And pack away knicknacks: they gather dust, add clutter, and could be broken during the showing process.

Scheduling a vacation soon after you put your home on the market is not a bad idea because you'll need the rest after fixing the house up for sale. If this isn't possible, try taking a long weekend at some point during the marketing phase so that you can relax and get away from it all.

Many sellers get understandably upset when the showing process doesn't work just right. The first rule to remember is never to set yourself up to wait for agents and their buyers. If your home has a lockbox, you can leave whenever you like and agents can let themselves in. The problem usually arises when a seller with no lockbox needs to leave at precisely the time the agent and buyer are due to arrive, but they're late. To avoid this type of scenario, ask the agent to pick up your house key at the listing office. It's helpful to have a phone answering machine so that you don't miss calls from agents who want to show your home.

Occasionally, prospective buyers will be so excited about your home that they will ignore the "Do Not Disturb Occupant" sign and knock on your front door requesting to see the house. Keep a stack of your agent's business cards on hand for such occasions. You should never, no matter how desperate you are to sell your house, let anyone in unaccompanied by a real estate agent. Be polite, hand the buyers one of your agent's cards, and ask them to call your real estate office to make an appointment.

Monitoring the Marketing Activity

Sellers can assist with the sale of their homes; in return, they should expect to be kept up to date by their agents on the progress of the marketing efforts. Ask your agent to give you information after the real estate office tours your home. Do the agents have any recommendations regarding the condition of the property? What do they think of the list price? Some listing agents make it a practice to collect price estimates from each agent who previews a new listing. If this is common practice in your area, ask to see the sale price average and remember: The rule of thumb is to be listed within 5 percent of the expected selling price.

Ask your agent to request selling price estimates (also referred to as REVs, or Realtors' Estimates of Value) from the agents who attend the broker's open house. Your agent should provide you with the range of selling price estimates along with the average of all of the REVs collected.

Many people balk at the idea of a price reduction early in the marketing program. If a price modification is needed, make it as soon as possible, while your home is still fresh in the minds of the agents. A price reduction three months later, when the real estate community has forgotten your property, won't have quite the same effect, so make a correction early to ensure that your initial market impact is not lost.

> *Check your list price by having your agent collect Realtors' Estimates of Value (REVs) from the agents who attend the brokers' open house.*

In addition to following up on the individual showings and reporting comments from prospective buyers and their agents, your agent should keep you apprised of homes that have recently sold in your area (the most recent comparable sales), new listings in your neighborhood (your competition), as well as relevant changes in current market conditions (interest rate fluctuations or changes in supply and demand). Generally, the more buyers and the lower the availability of housing, the quicker the sale and the higher the sales price.

What to Do If Your Home Isn't Selling

If your home is sitting stale on the market, you'll need to adjust the list price. Coordinate a price modification with a second brokers' open house, and be sure your agent advertises the event to the real estate community. It's not easy to entice agents back to look at a house for a second time, but an agent who advertises a deli lunch, along with a new "priced to sell" list price, is likely to have a good turnout.

Usually a price reduction equal to 5 to 10 percent of the list price is necessary to stimulate renewed interest in your home. But, sometimes a relatively small reduction can have a big impact.

Bill and Jane Johnson had their home listed for sale for months during a time when prices were declining. Although the agents felt it was priced right, no one offered to buy it. One couple fell in love with the house and returned repeatedly to preview it without making an offer. Finally, the Johnson's agent suggested that the price be reduced a mere $10,000 to $339,000. The price reduction was the catalyst that got the buyers who loved the house to make an offer. They bought the house for $336,000.

73

In a buyer's market, particularly when prices are falling, buyers are so afraid of overpaying that they often shy away from making offers on homes that are priced too high, even ones that are priced just a little too high. If you're priced too high in a market where prices are declining, be a crusader and drop your price before your competition does. You're better off leading rather than following the market when it's moving down. In a declining market, the longer you wait to reduce your price, the lower the selling price will be.

Make your home easier to show. If showings have been difficult to arrange, change procedures. If agents have plenty of houses to show and sales activity is slow, it stands to reason that the homes that will be shown the most are the ones that have easiest access.

Consider making courtesy keys available at various reliable real estate offices if your home is not on lockbox and it's not located close to your listing office. A courtesy key, which your listing agent makes available to cooperating brokers, facilitates showing your home.

Ask your agent if there are any improvements you can make to the physical condition of your property. If agents have complained repeatedly that the colors in your living room and dining room are too overwhelming, consider repainting in a neutral color. Any major changes of this sort should be completed prior to your second brokers' caravan. Consider having a Sunday open house if you haven't had one. Ask your agent to circulate a flyer announcing the event.

74

Sellers often wonder if providing a sales incentive (a higher commission or free trip) to the selling agent will speed up the marketing process. Although it sounds like a good idea, it's rare that the result is a home sale, unless your home is one of many just like it for sale in your marketplace. If this is the case, the sales gimmick could result in more showings. Otherwise, you're better off dropping the price than providing a prize to the agent who sells your home. Buyers don't select one home over another so that their agent will make more money; they buy the most competitively priced home that best suits their needs.

After months on the market, it's natural to wonder if it's a good strategy to take your home off the market for awhile and put it back on later. Usually this isn't worth the effort, and you may miss a prime opportunity to sell your home if a transferee who's perfect for your home comes into town during your time off the market.

Sometimes sellers find themselves in the awkward position of having to move before their home is sold. Is it better to leave the house vacant or rent it out? If you can afford to furnish the home and leave it unoccupied, this is the best solution. But, not everyone can afford to do this. There are tax consequences of renting your single-family residence, so check with your accountant first. You'll probably be told that your home will need to stay on the market while it's rented in order to preserve your single-family residence tax status. If so, select your tenant carefully. Offer an incentive for the tenant to cooperate in showing the house. A rent reduction in the form of a rebate at the end of the marketing period is usually the best incentive.

Occasionally, a house that should be selling doesn't because the agent is not doing an effective job of marketing. Any change in your marketing program should be announced to the entire real estate community, either by way of the Multiple Listing Service or with a separate flyer to local real estate agents. Relevant information includes a reduced list price, new showing arrangements, cosmetic modifications to the property, or an open house announcement.

Sellers who are not satisfied with the quality of service they're receiving at the end of the listing period, particularly if their feelings of dissatisfaction have been previously communicated directly to the agent, should find a reliable replacement agent at that time.

CHAPTER 6

FINDING YOUR
DREAM HOME

Looking for a *new home can be the most enjoyable part of your real estate experience. Take a pad and pen with you on house hunting trips so you can make notes, and refer back to your list of needs and wants from time to time to help stay on track.*

Whenever possible, leave small children with a sitter or friend. Buyers can find it distracting to look at a house, especially for the first time, accompanied by youngsters. Minimize exhaustion and confusion by previewing no more than four or five houses at one time. If you're purchasing a home with someone else, set up an initial house tour with your agent at a time when both of you can attend. It won't take long for a good agent to understand your likes and dislikes. After this, one of you can do the house screening if it's inconvenient for both to go.

When Is the Best Time to Buy?

The principle of supply and demand applies to real estate as it does to the economy in general. When there are more buyers in the marketplace than there are sellers, a high demand for houses is created, which usually puts upward pressure on prices. Such a market is referred to as a seller's market. A buyer's market, on the other hand, is one in which there are more sellers than buyers, inventory is plentiful, and home prices are usually soft.

There are advantages and disadvantages to buying in a buyer's market. The advantages include plenty of inventory to choose from, low prices, and less competition from other buyers. Also, property taxes and many of the fees associated with buying (loan origination fees, title insurance and escrow fees, transfer taxes and real estate commissions) are calculated based on the purchase price. When prices are low, these costs will be less than in a stronger seller's market when prices are rising.

The main disadvantage of buying when the market is slow is that the market value of your new home may actually drop before it rises again. For this reason, it's unwise to buy in a buyer's market unless you plan to stay in your new home for four or five years. For example, San Francisco Bay Area home buyers who bought during the recession of 1981 and who sold a couple of years later barely broke even due to flat home prices. However, Bay Area residents who bought in 1981 and held on to their homes until 1989 saw the price of them more than double.

It's often said that the best time to buy is when there's a lot for sale. If this is so, then why don't more people buy in a buyer's market? Negative press during slow economic times tends to put a damper on consumer confidence which influences spending patterns. And don't discount the effect of the "herd syndrome." That's the principle of psychology that says most people will feel more comfortable buying when everyone else is. There's safety in numbers.

That secure feeling that comes with buying along with everyone else carries a premium. The more buyers there are in the market, the higher the demand for homes. The seller is at an advantage, therefore, and you may have to pay more for a home than if you purchased it during a buyer's market. In a hot seller's market, buyers may find themselves in stiff competition with other buyers for houses that end up selling over the asking price. But it's easy to rationalize paying a few thousand dollars extra when you're sure to make the money back after a few months of price appreciation.

Be wary of following the herd and buying when the market is booming. If the market has experienced high levels of appreciation for several years, it may not be a good time to buy because the market may be due for a downward correction. In contrast, when the market has risen at a rate less than the inflation rate for several years, it may be ready for a rebound. It could be a good time to buy.

The principle of supply and demand also applies to interest rates, and there's an intimate relationship between interest rates and a home buyer's ability to buy. When interest rates are low, more buyers can qualify for financing. But, an increase in demand for financing tends to put upward pressure on interest rates.

Don't rule out the possibility of buying when rates are high. These are usually the periods when buyers can find relatively good deals on home prices. Most buyers believe that it's impossible to buy when rates are high so they drop out of the market, leaving less competition for the enterprising few. There are always people who will need to sell no matter what the market is doing. Difficulties in financing during periods of high interest rates can be overcome by assuming a seller's low-interest adjustable mortgage, seller financing, or a combination of the two.

Interest rates are cyclical, and there seems to be no way to determine conclusively at any given time whether rates are rising or falling. But anyone can follow the financial markets by regularly reviewing the business section of a major metropolitan newspaper to track several indicators that have been relatively reliable in the past. Interest rates are influenced by activity in the national and international money markets; recently, the most accurate indicator of home loan rates has been the bond market. When bond prices soar, interest rates on home loans drop, and vice versa. The Federal Reserve Board discount rate is another figure to watch. This is the rate charged to banks when they borrow money. A drop in the discount rate is usually followed by a drop in the prime rate, and this is finally reflected in lower mortgage rates. Conversely, a rise in the discount rate

77

signals that mortgage rates will probably move higher. Don't be surprised if home loan rates rise or drop in anticipation of an increase or decrease in the Federal Reserve Board discount rate.

The amount of foreign currency invested in government securities affects mortgage interest rates as well. The more foreign investment, the less the government needs to borrow to support itself. A lower demand for money means a lower interest rate on your home loan. On the other hand, when foreign investors go elsewhere the government must borrow more; this creates a higher demand for money and higher interest rates usually follow.

Other indicators to watch are the rates charged on Treasury securities and the money supply figures. Higher Treasury bill (T-bill) rates usually predicate higher interest rates, as can money supply figures if they exceed government expectations.

Regardless of when you choose to buy, don't get yourself into the trap of waiting until the interest rate cycle bottoms out. It's risky to wait if you can qualify to buy and rates are already relatively low. Financial markets can change quickly, and often it's not apparent that interest rates have bottomed out until they're on their way back up again. The same applies to home prices. It's hard to know whether prices have hit their low or high point for the cycle until they're headed in the other direction.

It's important to carefully investigate the local marketplace when considering whether or not it's a good time to buy. The California real estate market has not cycled in perfect synchronization with the national real estate market. California has been strong when the rest of the country has lagged behind, and vice versa. Also, within California there is tremendous variability. For instance, the inland and coastal markets don't necessarily move in tandem, and the Northern and Southern California markets have differed considerably in the past. You'll even find variability within an area.

Deciding on the right time to buy is not only dependent on external economic factors. It's also a decision that is contingent on your personal needs, financial situation, and job security. The best time to buy is when you can afford to and you find a home that suits your needs.

The Canons of Real Estate

Most residential real estate professionals agree that the most important factor affecting the value of a property is its location. Your aim should be to find a home that suits your needs and is located in the best neighborhood you can afford. Homes located in the most desirable neighborhoods hold their value better and appreciate more than homes located in undesirable areas. If you can't afford to buy in the best communities, find a home that's adjacent to one of these areas. The peripheral neighborhoods often experience good appreciation when the general economy of the area is on the upswing.

The other location variable to keep in mind is where, within a given neighborhood, a home is situated. A home on a busy street corner may be difficult to sell when you decide to move again, as may a home that's subject to freeway noise, in the path of noxious odors from a nearby chemical plant, or located too close to commercial establishments. If you fail in love with a house that suffers from a location defect, be sure you get it for a good price relative to the value of other homes in the neighborhood. Also bear in mind that when you sell, you'll probably need to make a price accommodation for the next buyer, and it may take a bit longer for you to sell.

The second general guideline to consider in making a home purchase is that the most expensive home on the block is not the best investment. Conversely, the least expensive home is usually a better investment, with certain qualifications. The cheapest home may also be one that requires a lot of work, and if the house is very small, with no potential for expansion, your opportunities to improve its value are limited. A safe bet is a moderately sized and priced home surrounded by more expensive homes. The pricier homes in the neighborhood tend to pull the surrounding property values up.

A corollary to the second guideline is: don't overimprove for the neighborhood. If you're considering a home that will need extensive remodeling in order to make it suitable for your family, determine improvement costs and investigate property values in the neighborhood carefully before you buy. Turning the beast on the block into the beauty may not make sense if there's no chance of recovering your investment on resale. The top price a buyer will pay for a home is usually determined by the prices that similar homes in the area have recently sold for.

Finally, it usually makes sense to buy the most expensive house you can afford, although in uncertain economic times it's wise to be conservative. It's prudent to stretch a little and buy a more expensive home if it will suit your long-term needs and eliminate the necessity of an interim move. In most cases, the tax laws favor buying a home at the top of your affordability range and mortgaging it to the hilt in order to maximize your tax write-off. This sort of tax planning, however, does not make sense for everyone.

Buyers obtaining adjustable-rate financing are smart to set aside cash reserves to cover unanticipated increases in mortgage interest rates. This is particularly important for those living on a fixed income.

Be cautious in your expectations for the future. Buyers who make the decision to buy the most expensive home they can based on the promise of future salary increases, or with the hope that home prices will appreciate, may suffer serious disappointment if there's an economic downturn.

Lender Prequalification

Before you actually start looking for a new home, make certain you have determined your affordable price range correctly. Ask your agent to refer you to a good lender or mortgage broker for the purpose of getting "lender prequalified." It's important to take care of this detail at the beginning of your search. Have the lender explain the various financing options open to you. Find out the benefits and drawbacks of 15-year versus 30-year financing and become familiar with the

79

differences between fixed, adjustable, and hybrid (loans that combine fixed- and adjustable-rate features) mortgages. (See Chapter 10 for more information about financing.) All too often, buyers don't explore the options available to them until their offer to buy has been accepted. Those who have researched the financing alternatives in advance will be that much ahead of the game.

Buyers who have been prequalified are at an advantage, particularly in a multiple offer situation. Ask your lender or mortgage broker for a prequalification letter indicating that you are qualified for the loan amount specified in your offer (not the maximum you can qualify for). In a multiple offer presentation involving several full-price offers, a seller is going to be the most impressed with an offer from buyers who include written verification that they are prequalified for a loan.

Preapproval is even better than prequalification. To get preapproval you'll need to complete a loan application, including employment and down payment verification, and your credit will have to be checked. You are then approved for a loan subject to the lender's receipt of a satisfactory appraisal and preliminary title report on the property you want to buy. If you have a low cash down payment, and you find you're losing out in multiple offer competition to buyers with larger down payments, get preapproved by a lender to alleviate a seller's concern about your ability to qualify.

Evaluating Neighborhoods

80

You're buying more than a roof over your head when you purchase a new home; you're buying into a neighborhood whose character will have a direct impact on your day-to-day life. Your goal is to select a neighborhood that offers qualities compatible with your family's lifestyle. Although selecting a community is some-what subjective, there are certain quantifiable features to evaluate in making your decision.

Affordability will naturally narrow the choices. Once you've determined which areas you can afford, the most important considerations are proximity to your place of work, the quality of local schools, and the prospects for long-term appeal or value of the neighborhood.

Commute time is a common concern, so if you'll be driving, take test drives to work during rush hour from the various neighborhoods you're considering. Ask friends at work who live in these areas how they cope with commuting. Investigate car pooling and public transportation. Communities in close proximity to public transportation tend to have more appreciation potential than do outlying communities with none.

Make the commute to work during rush hour from any house you're seriously considering buying before you make an offer to buy it.

Home buyers with school-age children must find out where the closest schools are. Will the children be able to walk to school? If not, is local transportation available, or will you have to drive them? Visit the local school, meet with a counselor or the principal, and visit a class. Ask to see state test scores, inquire about extracurricular activities and special programs, and be sure to verify school district street boundaries. When researching a senior high school, determine what percentage of the students go on to college and which colleges they attend. Even if you don't have school-age children, the quality of the local schools is still an important consideration. Communities with good public schools tend to appreciate faster during good economic times and they hold their value better during economic downturns.

Evaluating the long-range appeal of a neighborhood does not require a degree in economics or a crystal ball. There are several factors that tend to indicate if a community is likely to hold, or increase, its value over time. A community with a diverse economic base with good possibilities for expansion and increased employment opportunities in the future is an excellent choice. Talk to local merchants and bankers, read local newspapers, and check with the Chamber of Commerce to find out if the community's employment is rising or falling. Look for signs of home improvement projects in the neighborhoods you're considering. This is an indication that homeowners are staying put rather than moving out. Ask your agent to find out if the gap between the list price and selling price of homes for sale in the neighborhood is widening or narrowing. A gap that is narrowing indicates a neighborhood on the upswing; a widening may indicate a market that's taking a downturn.

Most home buyers are concerned about how safe and stable a neighborhood is. Do some investigation on your own. After you've seen a home you like, drive by it during several different times of the day and night to get a sense of the neighborhood. Any agent with an ounce of sense will drive you to a house using the most scenic route. Find the least scenic route and see if you still like the looks of the neighborhood. If the houses on the block of the house you admire are perfectly groomed but the yards look shabby several blocks away, do some further investigating.

Too many "For Sale" signs in an area may indicate that a neighborhood is deteriorating. There is, however, an odd phenomenon that occurs periodically in the real estate business. Not a single house will be listed in an area for months; then all of a sudden, for no special reason, several homes on one block are put up for sale at the same time. If a lot of homes are for sale in a neighborhood you're considering, ask your agent to find out if this is simply a quirk or a trend to be concerned about.

Call the local police department and inquire about the incidence of crime. Some police departments provide statistics by street on crimes over the past year. Others have census tract information compiled by the category of the crime: burglary, assault, etc.

Verify school district boundaries by calling the local school district.

81

The more subjective qualities of a neighborhood may be important to you. For instance, if a sense of community is vital to your decision of where to buy, visit the neighborhood. Find out who your new neighbors would be by going to meet some of the locals in person. Do neighbors know one another? Is there a neighborhood association of homeowners? Are there annual neighborhood events? Don't be surprised if your agent is hesitant to make generalizations about the makeup of the neighborhood, however, as discussion of the racial, religious, or ethnic composition of an area is illegal.

Outdoor and sports-minded individuals will be interested in the proximity to parks, lakes, beaches, and recreational facilities. Cultural buffs will need to investigate the availability and location of libraries, art museums, and theaters. The weather may be important to you, or if you're short of time, one-stop shopping may be high on your priority list. Is there one place where you can go on a Saturday morning to take care of the weekly chores? Families with an older relative living in may need to be near a major health care facility.

Additional considerations that may be relevant are: What percentage of the local residences are rented? (This information can be obtained from the county tax rolls.) Are the streets busy or quiet? Are there hazardous traffic patterns? Are there local leash laws for pets? Are religious centers located nearby? What is the availability of day-care centers? Are the local utilities public? Is there adequate street lighting? Are there unreasonable homeowners' association restrictions?

82

What and Where to Buy: The First-Time Buyer

Although home prices dropped in California in recent years, prices still remain relatively high. The median price of a single-family detached residence in California in 1992 was approximately $201,000. This presents a problem for the first-time, entry-level buyer. What options are available for the first-time buyer who may be having difficulty finding affordable housing?

- Buy when interest rates are low. Housing affordability increases as interest rates drop. As interest rates decrease, the loan amount you qualify for increases.
- Inland areas of the state tend to be cheaper than coastal areas. The outskirts of town tend to be less expensive than neighborhoods closer to a major metropolitan area.
- Buy in affordable neighborhoods that are peripheral to expensive neighborhoods. Marginal neighborhoods often experience healthy appreciation during periods of economic prosperity.
- Buy with a friend or relative. Be sure to have a written partnership agreement before you close escrow.
- Buy with an equity-share investor. It's easier to find an investor when home prices are appreciating than in a down market.
- Buy into a Tenant-In-Common (called TIC). This is a form of ownership often found in cities with rent control and restrictions on condo conversions. A TIC is a multiunit dwelling that is owned in partnership. Be sure to

consult a knowledgeable real estate attorney who has experience with TICs to review all relevant agreements and paperwork before you buy.

- Buy a fixer-upper, ideally a cosmetic fixer. See more about buying fixer-uppers and probate sales later in this chapter.

- Buy a small house in an expensive neighborhood and add on to it later.

- Buy a condominium or townhouse. The median price for a condominium in California in 1992 was $156,500.

- Buy a foreclosure. See more about foreclosure sales later in this chapter.

- Buy a multiunit residential building. Occupy one unit and rent out the others to help offset your ownership costs. Beware of depending on an illegal "in-law" unit for income to cover part of your housing expense. The city could put a stop to your nonconforming use of the property.

- Lease a home with an option to buy. See more about lease options in this chapter.

- Buy a live-work space (usually a converted warehouse in a commercial urban area).

Don't expect to buy your dream home the first time around. The goal is to become a homeowner. Your first home will be just that: the first, not the ultimate, home you'll own.

83

The Anatomy of a Dream Home

Houses have character, and it's usually this subjective quality that draws a buyer to one home over another. Feeling comfortable in a home is an important prerequisite to buying it. A home is, after all, your personal haven from the outside world. Savor the moment you walk into a new listing, after weeks or months of looking, and say to yourself, "This is it!" Indulge yourself in the joy of the moment; then step back and face reality. Pull out your notebook and scrutinize the list of features you're looking for and make sure that the home meets at least the majority of your needs. If it fits the bill, there are a few more exercises you should perform, before submitting an offer.

Take a realistic look at the decor. Are you paying extra for someone else's good taste or decorating expertise? Will your furniture substitute satisfactorily for the seller's? What will it cost you to hire a decorator to recreate the ambiance you've fallen in love with?

After you've taken an objective look at the house, conduct a prepurchase inspection with the help of your agent. A friend who is knowledgeable about housing would be a suitable assistant in this process. This is not a formal inspection, which requires hired professionals, but a step in determining whether you're willing to spend the time and money involved in making an offer.

The first item to consider is the general layout, also known as the floor plan. Ideally a home should have areas appropriate for gatherings as well as those conducive to private activities. Family and living rooms should be located at a distance from bedrooms, particularly if the bedrooms are to be used by infants or students who need quiet for studying. If members of the family are involved in hobbies or crafts, there should be spaces away from the main family living areas for these endeavors.

The "flow" of a floor plan is very important. A layout that gives access to the primary rooms from a central hall is the best arrangement. The living room, particularly, should not be a pass-through space to reach other rooms. A house that allows for easy circulation is important for buyers who have children.

Because the kitchen is the focal point of most households, be sure it's laid out well, with a sufficiently large eating area and, ideally, a separate access to the outside. The work space should be set up so that the appliances and counters are located near one another.

Room size and storage space requirements vary from one buyer to the next. Bear in mind that too little storage, with no possibility of improving the situation, always poses a problem. Be sure that rooms are large enough to accommodate your furniture by taking measurements of large pieces of furniture and checking for fit at the new house.

Also take a moment and consider the home from the standpoint of its resale qualities. Features that are most in demand are spacious rooms, kitchens with eating areas, direct access from the garage to the house (ideally to the kitchen), a family room on the main living level (ideally off the kitchen), a driveway that provides easy access to the street, adequate parking area, level entry to a private yard, sunny exposure, at least one bathroom on each level, convenient washer and dryer locations, a fireplace in the living room, a formal entry hall (with a coat closet), sufficient electrical outlets, and central air conditioning in warm climates.

Pay attention to maintenance considerations. If the house has a pool, determine whether you have the time to clean it and, if not, whether you can afford to pay someone else to do the job. Trees over a pool will make the upkeep even more difficult.

Remember that large yards require a lot of work. Sometimes a small but secluded yard, away from neighbors, can convey the feeling of a large yard with much less work. Find out if the house is insulated and ask the owner for copies of recent utility bills to determine how much these tend to run during average and high expense months.

Have your agent obtain a copy of the seller's Real Estate Transfer Disclosure Statement as well as copies of any existing reports. Ask your agent to find out the age of the appliances and major systems such as the plumbing, electrical, and heating. Basic home systems will break down in

Pay attention to resale value when considering a home to purchase.

time. Have the systems been replaced or upgraded recently, or is this an expense that you should factor into your purchase price? If the systems are old, is the seller providing a Home Protection Plan? After reviewing these documents, take one last tour around and through the premises, this time with an eye to determining the general condition of the property.

One of the primary causes of structural defects in houses is water. Watch for signs of excessive moisture. The first rule of home maintenance is to be certain that all water is directed away from the house. Porches and patios should drain away from the foundation, and rainwater should be collected in gutters that empty into downspouts connected to drainpipes which take the water away from the building. If this is not possible, the water should at least not collect in puddles next to the house as this can cause the soil underneath a portion of foundation to become saturated and, ultimately, to drop or settle. Some settling is routine and can be expected, particularly in older homes. Every effort should be made, however, to improve the drainage in and around a house to avoid future problems.

Evidence of standing water should be investigated by a qualified professional. Water that collects in a basement area may indicate a need for a drainage system (which can be expensive). If you're buying during the dry season, look for stains on the basement floor or on foundation walls, as these are signs that water may have been present in the past. Other conditions that may be indicative of a drainage problem are large cracks in the soil or basement floor, cracks in the foundation, or erosion channels in the dirt underneath the house. A house with a sump pump, usually located in the basement, most certainly has excessive water under it, at least periodically. Find out from a drainage expert whether the sump pump is an adequate solution to an excessive moisture condition.

Look for signs of moisture entry inside the house. Water stains on window sills and around doors suggest that they may not be watertight, and stains on ceilings and walls, or peeling paint and wallpaper, may be a sign that the roof needs repair.

Examine the exterior condition of the roof. Moss growing on a wood shake or shingle roof may indicate a problem. A house with three layers of roofing, and evidence of moss and deterioration below the surface layer, should be investigated by a qualified roofer. An old roof that is one layer thick can usually be repaired by simply roofing over the existing surface, whereas a leaky roof that is already several layers thick will be more complicated to repair. Check the gutter and downspout system for voids, rust, and deterioration. If trees overhang the roof, you'll need to have gutters and downspouts routinely cleaned and serviced.

Check the fireplace and chimney from inside and out. Cracks inside can mean that the firebox needs work; a

Review the seller's Real Estate Transfer Disclosure Statement before making an offer to purchase a home.

85

chimney that leans away from the house may also signal a problem.

Check the condition of fences and gates around the property. Is the landscaping well-maintained, or will you need to consider redoing it in the near future?

Test the water pressure. Turn on the shower and sink faucets, and flush the toilet at the same time. Be aware that the electrical system may need upgrading if there are too few outlets and extension cords running everywhere.

Look for signs of settling problems from the interior of the house. Do the windowpanes on a set of French doors line up properly? Or does one door hang much lower than the other? If so, this might indicate a foundation problem. Do floors slope? Open and close doors and windows to see if they stick. Are doors and windows warped? Scrutinize door frames from the opposite side of a room. Are the tops of the doors parallel with the floor? Are the sides of the door jambs parallel with adjacent vertical walls?

Doors, floors, and windows that are out of plumb can indicate structural problems or poor workmanship; they can also simply signify routine settling. Hardwood floors that squeak and buckle may not be nailed properly. Wallpaper patterns that don't line up at the seams are usually the result of shoddy craftsmanship, although a sagging floor (indicative of a possible structural problem) could also be the cause.

The purpose of your prepurchase inspection is to find out if there are glaring and significant defects that you're certain you can't live with. Examine the property carefully, but don't take too long to make up your mind if buyers are waiting in line to make offers. Your cursory inspection should *not* be done in lieu of hiring qualified professional inspectors. If you decide to make an offer, make it contingent upon obtaining all inspections you feel are necessary to protect yourself.

Only a licensed contractor, engineer, or roofer can tell you whether a flaw is normal, considering environmental conditions and the age of the house, or whether it is something to be concerned about. Inspections that are done in addition to those that the seller has already ordered are customarily at the buyer's expense. The cost is generally in the range of $250 to $500, but if soils reports are involved, you may be looking at an out-of-pocket expense of over $1,000. Extra inspections are worth every penny if they make you feel secure about the integrity of a home, or if they prove that the home is not a good investment.

Buying a Newly Constructed Home

There are definite advantages to buying a newly constructed home. New homes are energy efficient; lower utility costs may enable you to afford a more expensive home. And because new homes are built to modern code requirements, you shouldn't have to remedy code violations as you often do with older homes. New homes are usually easier to maintain than older homes and are generally equipped with modern amenities.

If you purchase in a planned community development, your new home may entitle you to use recreational facilities such as a swimming pool, golf course, or

86

tennis courts. Planned community developments are subject to restrictions on use which are described in the Covenants, Conditions, and Restrictions (CC&Rs). Make sure you read and approve the CC&Rs as a condition of your purchase agreement.

One drawback of new homes is that they often lack distinctiveness. Older homes are often located in neighborhoods that were developed over a period of time and offer a variety of architectural styles. Established neighborhoods have mature landscaping which is usually lacking in new developments. New homes are frequently smaller than older homes, and their locations are sometimes not the best. Beware of the hidden costs of buying a new home; window coverings and landscaping, for instance, are often not included. If this is the case, don't forget to add these costs to the purchase price.

When you're shopping for a new home, don't fall in love with a designer-decorated model and assume that this is what you'll get at the close of escrow. If you're buying in a tract development, ask to see a sample home that hasn't been decorated for sale and find out what's included in the purchase price. How many of the classy upgrades displayed in the model do you have to pay extra for? Is the carpet in the model the same grade that you'll get in your new home, or do you have to pay extra for a better quality carpet? Are the light fixtures included in the price or do you pay extra? Do you have any choice in the finishing details?

Some builders will allow a buyer to select certain finishing details, such as floor coverings, cabinets, paint and tile quality and color, finish hardware, and light fixtures. Be sure that all modifications or upgrades are put in writing and signed by both the buyer and builder. This agreement should specify how much additions will cost, when they'll be paid for, and what credits the buyer will receive for deletions. Keep in mind that if houses in a development are selling well, there may be no opportunity for a buyer to negotiate the purchase price, aside from settling on finishing details and upgrades.

87

One way to protect yourself if the builder is to complete some of the finishing details after the close of escrow is to pay half the cost ahead of time and the other half upon completion of the work. Another possibility is to agree that a portion of the builder's proceeds from the sale will be held in an escrow account to be released when the work is completed.

Hire a professional to inspect a new home. Just because a house is new doesn't mean it was built correctly. Even though a house was built with permits, and was inspected and signed off by a city building inspector, is no guarantee that all the work was done to code specifications. City inspectors sometimes miss, or intentionally overlook, code violations. Ask the builder for copies of any reports on the property, including the soils report. Have the inspector review these and any construction documents. It's wise to include a contingency in your purchase contract for the builder to provide you with any and all building plans, soils and engineering reports, surveys, city inspection reports, and permits for you to read and approve.

Before you buy a new home, investigate the reputation of the builder. A brand new roof can leak. Does the builder have a reputation for responding to calls from buyers when unsuspected defects appear? Is the problem then remedied quickly and without undue hassle? Contact a real estate attorney or the state contractor's licensing agency for the answers to questions about the builder's liability for defects. You may want to include a provision in your purchase contract for the contractor to correct any latent defects that might appear in the first year, at no cost to you. There are also home protection plans that builders can purchase that specifically cover new construction.

Ask to see other homes the builder has constructed to check out the quality of the workmanship. Be sure to talk to the homeowners, and investigate the builder's reputation with lenders and material suppliers. You will have difficulty getting a builder to remedy defects if the company files for bankruptcy or goes out of business after you purchase the home. Check at the county courthouse to see if any suits have been filed against the builder. The local Better Business Bureau and the Contractors' State License Board can tell you if they have received complaints about the builder. Talk to subcontractors who worked for the builder. Ask if the builder cut corners during construction and if he paid his bills on time.

Special care should be taken when buying a new home from an occasional builder (someone who builds less than a dozen homes a year). Some of these contractors build the best new homes on the market; others are unprofessional and may not be in the business a year or so after you purchase. Make sure the builder has a good reputation, will give you a warranty on latent defects (you may want to ask an attorney to draft a warranty agreement), lives locally, and will be available to come back if necessary to take care of problems. If you're buying a home in a tract development constructed by a builder who's new to the industry, ask the builder to purchase a new home warranty policy from an independent insurance company. This will provide you protection if defects surface and the builder is out of business.

Complete the final inspection of a new home at least a week before the close of escrow. Take a note pad with you and make a list, commonly called a "punch" list, of items the builder is to complete before the close of escrow or within a reasonable amount of time thereafter. Make the punch list a part of your purchase contract, and get the builder to sign it. Do not accept a cash settlement from the builder at the close of escrow in lieu of an agreement to complete the items on your list, and don't trust a builder who denies you reasonable access to the property to complete any inspections you deem necessary.

Investigate the builder's professional reputation before you buy a newly constructed home.

88

You finance a new home purchase the same way you finance the purchase of a used home. Sometimes a developer will have an arrangement worked out with one or several lenders who will provide competitive financing for prospective buyers. A builder cannot insist that you use a particular lender. However, it might work to your advantage to use a lender who is familiar with the project you're buying into. The loan processing and escrow will probably go more smoothly than if you use a lender who has had no experience doing loans for buyers of homes in the development.

In a strong seller's market, you may find that there's no opportunity to negotiate the price on a new home. In a buyer's market, builders are more willing to negotiate on price. If you can't get a developer to budge on his price, see if he'll provide upgrades at no additional cost. In a slow market, you might be able to negotiate with the builder to pay some or all of your nonrecurring closing costs or buy down the interest rate on a loan for you.

Builders of large projects will usually have their own staff of sales agents and a specific sales contract designed for use by these agents. If this is the case, you will not be allowed representation by your own outside agent, so you may want to pay an agent a consulting fee or hire a real estate attorney to review the sales contract to be sure you're adequately protected. The project sales agents may act as dual agents or they may represent the builder exclusively in the sale transaction. And you can expect a different sort of sales approach in new home developments than in the resale market. Project sales agents are only interested in selling you one product—a home in their subdivision. Anticipate a more focused, and perhaps harder sell. Take your list of wants and needs with you to help you stay focused on what you really want in a home. Don't let someone talk you into buying something you don't want.

Some new developments advertise that they cooperate with brokers. This usually means that a real estate agent will receive a commission if he or she introduces a buyer to a project who subsequently buys a home there. If you're working with an agent and you want him or her to be involved in your purchase in a broker co-op development, make sure that your agent is with you the first time you visit the project; otherwise the builder probably won't pay your agent a commission. Even if a developer encourages broker cooperation, your offer still might have to be written up by a member of the developer's sales staff and on the developer's standard contract. But, if your agent is receiving a share of the commission, you can receive consultation without having to pay an additional fee. Call a development in advance to find out if you'll have to pay a higher price if an outside agent is involved.

There are often unanticipated delays in building a new home. If you enter into an agreement to buy a new home before it's completed, and you're selling another home in order to purchase the new one, negotiate a provision in the sale of your old home to have the option to rent it back from the new owners if the completion date of your new home is delayed. Also, try to include a clause in the

89

new home contract that makes the builder responsible for paying the cost of your rent-back (or the cost of a hotel room) if construction is delayed due to the fault of the builder rather than unavoidable circumstances such as bad weather.

Make sure to investigate the cost of any Mello-Roos assessments that affect a new home you're considering buying. The Mello-Roos act allows local governments to establish special tax assessment districts to finance the cost of public works projects such as new roads, libraries, fire stations, and schools. Developers usually pay the cost of Mello-Roos assessments until the development is completed and sold. Then the individual home buyers take over the assessment burden. Fees can run anywhere from a few dollars to several thousand dollars per year. These fees may not be tax deductible; check with your tax advisor.

Be careful buying into a new project in a down market, particularly if the project is only partially built and you're one of the first buyers. If the project isn't selling well, the builder might not be able to complete future phases. Or the builder might find that he has to drastically discount the price on newer models to sell them. This will have a negative effect on the value of your home.

Buying an Older Home

One benefit of purchasing an existing home is that you're buying into an established neighborhood. The schools may be better than in newer areas, tree-lined streets are commonplace, and yards are usually landscaped. Older neighborhoods are often centrally located, offering good access to freeways, places of employment, theaters, entertainment, cultural activities, and shopping centers.

The major appeal of an older home is its architectural uniqueness. Established areas usually contain a mix of styles, and buyers who are influenced by "curb appeal" (what a house looks like from the street) are often attracted to older homes. These homes may be characterized by a high level of craftsmanship, spacious rooms, hardwood floors, high ceilings, built-in bookcases, leaded or stained glass windows, and distinctive moldings that cannot be found in newly constructed homes. Existing homes also usually come equipped with window coverings and light fixtures.

An older home *may* be less expensive than a new home, but this will depend on its general condition. Low energy efficiency is costly, as is the expense of insulating. Maintenance may be higher on an older home if major components such as the roof, kitchen appliances, furnace, and hot water heater have not been replaced recently, so be sure to have a home protection plan to cover the major systems in place at the close of escrow.

Older homes often were not built to modern building code requirements, and one consequence of this is that they may not be able to withstand the shock of a major earthquake as well as new houses. If this concerns you, contact a contractor who specializes in equipping older homes to better withstand earthquakes (referred to as earthquake retrofitting); read the seller's disclosure regarding residential earthquake hazards; and study "The Homeowner's Guide to Earthquake Safety." (See Chapter 4 for more information.)

There's also a greater likelihood that an older home might contain materials that are environmentally hazardous. California home sellers are required by state law to disclose environmental hazards on the property if they are aware of any. Often sellers of older homes aren't aware of such hazards around their house, but this doesn't mean that there aren't any. Your real estate agent should give you a copy of a booklet entitled: "Environmental Hazards, a Guide for Homeowners and Buyers." Read this carefully, and hire the appropriate specialist to do further investigations of the property before you buy it if you have any suspicions that there might be environmental hazards present. (See Chapter 9 for more information about environmental hazards.)

Older homes have withstood the test of time, which is not the case with a new home. When you buy an older home, you have the benefit of knowing any problems that have developed during the current owner's period of ownership. Some problems (soils instability, structural and foundation defects) only become apparent over a period of time so they're often easier to detect in an old home than in a new one.

Buying a Fixer-Upper

Plenty has been written about the great profits to be reaped from buying a dilapidated home, slapping on a fresh coat of paint, and reselling it mere months later for a handsome markup. Turning the ugliest house on the block into a jewel may sound like easy money; it's not. First, you must be able to distinguish a house with profit potential from a lousy investment. Cosmetic repairs can be relatively inexpensive and usually pay back double their cost. But the expense of correcting major structural defects might not add a penny to the market value of a home and could conceivably run a project into the red.

91

Evaluating the floor plan is critical. A good basic layout with a hideous decor is a great combination in a fixer-upper. A minimal investment may well turn such a property around. A house with a maze of rooms, on the other hand, may have a defective floor plan that no amount of paint and paper will remedy.

Check the major components of the house very carefully. Hire a professional inspector and, if you're anticipating a major renovation that will entail moving walls, consult with an architect before you buy to be sure that it's feasible.

Location is vitally important to the success of a fix-up project. You should buy in the best neighborhood you can afford, and make certain that you won't be overimproving for the area. Consult your real estate agent and check the comparable sales in the neighborhood carefully before committing to the project. Be wary of the agent who promises there are huge profits to be made by rehabilitating a fixer. Examine the comparable sales carefully, and be sure you're reading the market correctly.

A cosmetic fixer-upper, which is structurally sound, usually has the most profit potential.

Luke Friedman learned his first renovation lesson the hard way. He bought the smallest and least expensive house he could find in an affluent neighborhood, installed a new kitchen and bathroom, and gave the house a cosmetic face lift. When the refurbished house went back on the market, it was priced lower than any other house in the area. It was also still the smallest house on the block. The house sat on the market for nine months and finally sold only after numerous price reductions, leaving Luke with a sizable tax write-off and no profit. If Luke had done his homework first, he would have discovered that buyers for homes in this particular neighborhood were looking for large family homes, not compact homes on postage stamp lots.

Financing the renovation is a major consideration, and often the costs will have to be paid in cash. It will be easier to obtain a loan if you intend to occupy the home; however, it's unrealistic to expect you and your family to live in a home that will be a construction zone for a period of time.

Asking a seller to carry the financing is a possibility if the property is free of other liens and if the seller has been unable to sell for all cash. Sometimes a seller who won't carry a first loan will carry a small second, say for 10 percent of the purchase price. The buyer obtains the new first loan and pays the seller the major portion of the purchase price at the close of escrow (90 percent in this case). The balance is paid to the seller in a relatively short period of time when the buyer has finished the fix-up work and sells the home.

Financing the purchase of a fixer-upper with a new adjustable-rate mortgage that is assumable by a subsequent buyer makes good sense. The interest rate will be lower than on a fixed-rate loan and, if financing is difficult to obtain by the time the renovator is ready to sell, there will be a loan in place on the property that can be taken over by a qualified buyer.

An unsecured line of credit can also be used to pay for the fix-up work if the buyer qualifies. This indebtedness does not have to be paid back when the house is sold since it isn't secured as a lien against the house, and the interest on the loan may be tax deductible as a cost of doing business.

Successful renovators have used the lease option as another way to finance a fix-up project. The buyer gives the seller a relatively small amount of cash to apply toward a predetermined purchase price and then leases the property from the seller for a specified period of time. During the lease period, the buyer fixes up the property; then, when the project is done, the buyer exercises the option, completes the purchase, and immediately sells the house to another buyer for a profit.

There is some risk to the buyer here because title to the property remains in the seller's name during the lease period. The buyer is paying to fix up someone else's property, so it's imperative to check a preliminary title report very carefully before entering into this sort of agreement. Further protection is obtained by recording the lease so that it will have priority over future liens the seller may secure against the property. Also, the buyer cannot use a secured line of credit to finance the rehabilitation work since the property will still be in the seller's name during the fix-up period. Another problem with lease options is that few sellers are agreeable to selling for anything less than all cash in a strong seller's market. Also many sellers would object to the buyer turning the house into a construction zone before title transfers into the buyer's name.

Whether you take a lease option or purchase a fixer-upper outright, the cost of leasing or owning the property during the rehabilitation period must be considered in calculating the profit potential. This is particularly true if you won't be occupying the property. Experienced renovators will tell you that fix-up projects generally cost more and take longer than anticipated, so figure an extra amount into the budget to cover any cost overruns.

Novices should carefully consider whether they're temperamentally suited to be successful renovators. Fix-up projects have to be carefully supervised to keep them on time and close to budget. The renovator must have a critical eye, be attentive to details, have an ability to organize, and be able to deal effectively with total chaos and endless frustration.

In planning your renovation, keep in mind that kitchens, bathrooms, and storage spaces are important to today's home buyers. The kitchen-family room combination is particularly desirable and can often be created in an older home by knocking out the walls that separate the kitchen from a breakfast room or maid's room. A spacious master bedroom suite with a private bath and large walk-in closet is also attractive to most buyers.

A home with a large structural pest control ("termite") problem might provide a good fix-up opportunity, but it's important to evaluate ahead of time what sort of work is required. If the bathroom floor, walls, and shower are rotted and the "termite" report calls for replacing them, a buyer might be wise to negotiate a credit from the seller for the dollar amount required to complete these repairs. Since "termite" estimates are usually on the high side compared to a contractor's cost, the credit might pay for a whole new bathroom. Make certain that the lender will allow escrow to close without requiring a notice of completion from a structural pest control operator if new financing is a part of the transaction.

Curb appeal is important, so plan on improving the landscaping and front entry. Stick to neutral color schemes, and put a little extra into less expensive items such as light fixtures, hardware (doorknobs, light switch plates, cabinet pulls and knobs), and bathroom plumbing fixtures. Quality sells a home, and extra attention to detail will build you a good reputation, which is important if you intend to rehabilitate more properties in the area.

The best time to buy a fixer-upper, if your intention is to turn the house around for immediate profit, is when home prices are climbing. Be careful that you don't get caught up in the buying frenzy that can occur in a hot market and end up overpaying for the house. This will cut into your profit margin, which is exactly what happened to many speculators in 1989 who bought as the market peaked and then couldn't afford to renovate the house for a profit. There's less risk involved if you're buying a fixer home to live in for several years while you

93

fix it up. Also, look out for environmentally hazardous materials on the property. If you miss something that a future buyer insists you remedy when you sell (such as asbestos on furnace pipes or a buried heating oil tank), you could see your profit decline significantly.

Buying a Townhouse or Condominium

One way for first-timers to buy in a desirable location, where the prices of single-family homes are out of their reach, is to opt for a condominium or townhouse. Condos and townhouses are not only attractive to first-time buyers; they are an ideal compromise for anyone who desires the tax benefits of home ownership without the cost and trouble of home maintenance.

When you buy into a townhouse or condominium complex, you purchase a specific unit which you own individually. In addition, you share in the ownership of common areas, such as hallways, elevators, exterior grounds, pools, tennis courts, or clubhouse. You automatically become a member of a homeowners' association to which you pay monthly, or annual, dues to cover expenses such as common area maintenance.

Condominium ownership is not for everyone, since you must be agreeable to living in close proximity to your neighbors and, in some cases, to sacrificing privacy. The tradeoff is low maintenance and a secure lifestyle.

Location is critical in determining the value of the investment and the potential for appreciation. Some well-located and well-managed condo projects demonstrate a good history of appreciation; many more, however, have not appreciated much, if at all, in recent years. The detached residence is currently more in demand than condominiums or townhouses, but this will probably change in the years ahead as the population ages, creating a larger demand for low-maintenance living environments. From a resale standpoint, a one- or two-bedroom condo is a better investment than a studio, if you can afford it.

In evaluating a condo development, find out what percentage of the units are owner-occupied as opposed to tenant-occupied. The more owner occupants, the better. Owners usually demand a higher caliber of management and maintenance, since they have an investment in the condition of the project. Sometimes a high percentage of renters indicates that the original developer was unable to sell the project when it was new. Find out how many of the units are still owned by the original developer. Some lenders won't approve new mortgages for buyers purchasing into condo developments with a large percentage of renters.

Find out how much the monthly association fee is and what expenses it covers. It usually includes garbage collection, maintenance of exterior grounds, homeowner's insurance, and sometimes exterior maintenance of individual units. Pay particular attention to the insurance coverage that's provided for the association, as this usually does not include coverage for your personal possessions or for damage to the interior of your unit. It probably won't include a personal liability rider, either.

Other important questions regarding the maintenance fee are: How often has it been raised in the past? Are there any anticipated increases in the near future? How much of a reserve does the homeowners' association maintain to cover the cost of repairs to common areas such as pools and tennis courts? Is the homeowners' association involved in any litigation against the builder for structural defects? If the association loses and cannot recover the cost to repair defects, what is the potential amount that individual owners will pay to remedy the problems? Find out how many homeowners are delinquent in making their monthly maintenance dues payments. A high percentage of delinquencies might indicate dissatisfaction with the management of the association. Be aware, by the way, that homeowner's dues projections listed at new construction sites are sometimes unrealistically low. If so, anticipate that they will go up in the future and budget for this increase. Older projects will tend to have higher monthly dues than will newer projects. Also be aware that your association dues are not tax deductible.

Read the CC&Rs (Covenants, Conditions, and Restrictions) and bylaws of the homeowners' association carefully. One drawback of living in a planned community development is that you don't have unrestricted ownership privileges. The CC&Rs may prohibit pets and may also include remodeling, rental, and resale restrictions. A seller is required by law to provide buyers with copies of CC&Rs, articles of incorporation, bylaws, current rules and regulations, and current financial statements to read and approve before escrow closes. Your lender will probably want to see a copy of these documents as well. The seller must also disclose any pending litigation, claims, or special assessments.

The size of a condominium or townhouse project is a relevant consideration. A large project may seem impersonal to you, but large complexes usually have a homeowners' association board of directors, elected by the homeowners, who take care of the maintenance and financial details. In a smaller, more intimate, complex you may be required to be more active in the association's affairs. If you want to get away from home maintenance concerns altogether, you may be better off buying in a large, well-run complex.

Have a building inspector assess the general quality of construction and examine the common facilities for any major structural defects that could result in future assessments against the homeowners' association. A Wood Destroying Pests and Organisms ("termite") inspection of the individual unit is also recommended.

Investigate the parking and additional storage provisions thoroughly. Will you have an assigned parking place or is parking on a "first come, first serve" basis? Find out if the building is adequately soundproofed. Talk to several owners who currently live in the complex to find out what they like and don't like about it.

California law prohibits homeowners' associations from charging exorbitant transfer fees. The law limits fees to the actual cost of changing the association's records plus the cost of sending the required notices to prospective buyers. Double-check to be sure you're not being unlawfully overcharged.

95

Lenders will not fund loans for buyers of units in new condominium and townhouse developments until a certain percentage (usually 50 to 70 percent) of the total units in the development, or a phase of the development, are presold. Keep this in mind if you're one of the first buyers in a new project. Don't give your landlord 30-days' notice that you're moving out until you know that you and the development are approved for financing.

Buying Foreclosures

A foreclosure or distressed sale begins when the owner stops making the mortgage payments. After the delinquent owner has missed several payments, the lender will record a notice of default against the property. This initiates a three month and 21-day time period during which the owner can pay back mortgage payments and cure the default. If the owner doesn't cure the default, a trustee sale is held, and the property is sold to the highest bidder. A property that doesn't sell at the trustee sale reverts to the lender and is referred to as an REO, which is industry jargon for "Real Estate Owned." REOs are then usually offered for sale, often through a real estate broker.

You may get an incredibly good deal by buying a foreclosure property. Like buying a fixer-upper, buying foreclosures is often touted as a quick way to get rich. But extreme care should be used if you're considering buying a distressed sale property. Buying foreclosures requires a lot of hard work and expertise and it's not recommended for novice home buyers.

There are typically three opportunities to buy a foreclosure: after the borrower is delinquent on the mortgage payments but before the trustee sale; at the trustee sale; or from the foreclosing lender after the trustee sale.

Some newspapers carry a list of notices of default or you can research these at the County Recorder's Office. Then approach the delinquent owners and attempt to purchase the property directly from them.

At the end of the three-month and 21-day reinstatement period, the foreclosing lender will sell the property at a trustee sale if the loan is not cured by that time. Trustee sales are advertised in advance and they require an all cash bid. The lender who holds the first loan on the property will start the bidding at the amount of the loan being foreclosed.

Be careful when you're buying directly from a delinquent owner or at a trustee sale that you don't overpay for the property. If home prices have fallen since the delinquent loan was secured on the property, the remaining loan balance could exceed the current market value of the property. Also, a trustee sale is an "as is" arrangement, so be sure to have the property thoroughly inspected to your satisfaction before the sale.

Lending institutions often offer attractive prices, terms, and financing to prospective buyers in an attempt to sell excess REO properties. Whether or not such a deal makes sense for you depends on several factors. Be aware that evaluating an REO requires more care than is necessary in other potential purchase situations.

Make sure that the price is truly a bargain. If the current value of the house was actually in excess of the loan amount, the owners could have sold the property themselves, thereby recouping some or all of their equity investment and avoiding a damaged credit rating. However, some homeowners facing foreclosure don't act quickly enough, sometimes due to denial.

Check property values in the neighborhood carefully. Also, find out what similar homes in the area were selling for six months ago to be sure that you're not buying into a neighborhood where property values are declining.

REOs are usually sold in their "as is" condition, and you probably will not have the benefit of reviewing a Real Estate Transfer Disclosure Statement. Make sure you see the property yourself before purchasing, and hire professional inspectors because many distressed sale properties are also in poor physical condition.

Insist that the lender provide you with clear title to the property, and purchase title insurance to protect yourself. Owners who let mortgage payments slide might have had other debts they couldn't handle, so make certain that you'll have no liability to the previous owner's creditors.

On the bright side, if you do find an REO that meets your specifications, the lender may be willing to provide you with attractive financing, sometimes at lower interest rates. You may even receive assistance with some of your closing costs.

Lenders are often not aggressive in marketing their REO properties. If this sort of property intrigues you, call lenders directly and talk to the person in charge of REOs. Another source is the federal government. The Federal Housing Administration (FHA) and Veterans Administration (VA) periodically announce the availability of these properties, usually in newspaper ads. The Resolution Trust Corporation (RTC) was established to sell properties acquired from insolvent savings and loan associations. Further information about the RTC can be obtained from calling the general information number (800-431-0600) or the Irvine Sales Center (800-542-6135). Call your local Board of Realtors and ask for a recommendation of an agent who specializes in foreclosures.

97

Many repossessed properties are tenant-occupied, in which case it's wise to make your purchase conditioned on the lender delivering the property to you vacant. Otherwise you might be faced with having to evict a tenant who is unwilling to leave the premises.

Another word of caution: if you're purchasing a property from a seller who's in the midst of a bankruptcy proceeding, be sure to consult with an expert such as a real estate professional with experience working on bankruptcies and foreclosures or a knowledgeable real estate attorney.

Buying a Probate Property

Generally speaking, a probate sale refers to a property that's being sold because the owner is deceased and the sale is necessary to settle the estate. More specifically, a probate sale is one in which the sale of the property must be confirmed in a court of law, either by a judge or by a probate commissioner.

California state law requires that a probate property be advertised according to statute provisions. Any offer that's accepted must be for at least 90 percent of the property's court-appraised value. Following acceptance, a court date is set so that the sale can be confirmed. Any interested buyer can attend this court hearing, at which time the property is offered for open bidding before the sale is approved.

A buyer interested in bidding in court must make a minimal overbid, the formula for which is set by probate law. The overbid must be for at least 10 percent of the first $10,000 of the initial buyer's bid plus 5 percent of the remaining balance; otherwise it won't be considered by the court. For instance, if the first buyer's accepted offer was $250,000, the minimal acceptable overbid would be $263,000 (10 percent of $10,000 is $1,000; 5 percent of $240,000 is $12,000; the total is $13,000 which, when added to the initial bid of $250,000, equals $263,000). Subsequent overbid increments are set at the discretion of the court.

In soft real estate markets, you're not likely to be overbid in court if you're paying fair market value for the property. You're more likely to find yourself in an overbid situation in a low-inventory seller's market where there are multiple buyers for virtually every new listing that comes on the market. If you find yourself in this situation, be careful when you go to court that you don't let yourself get carried away by the overbidding process. Decide in advance the top price you can afford to pay for the property and be willing to let it go if other bidders take the price higher.

Will Banner, a speculator, had just completed a successful renovation project and was looking for another one. He decided to bid on a probate property that already had an accepted offer. When the offer went to court for confirmation, Will entered into a bidding match with the buyer who made the initial offer. Their duel sent the price up over $50,000 above the initial offer price. Will was delighted to be the successful bidder until he completed the rehab project and found that he couldn't sell the property for enough to cover his costs.

Probate properties are usually sold "as is," a condition provided by law to protect the heirs who may have no first-hand knowledge about the property. You probably won't have the benefit of a Real Estate Transfer Disclosure Statement, since probates are exempt from this requirement. Make sure you have the property thoroughly inspected before you go to court for confirmation. A probate property listed for a low price may be no bargain at all if there's a lot of deferred maintenance or structural defects.

Additionally, any offers made must be contingency-free. This means that financing, inspection, and any other contingencies must be satisfied before the court date. The law also requires the buyer of a probate property to make a deposit to the estate equal to 10 percent of the purchase price. The deposit will often have to be in the form of a cashier's check made payable to the estate of the deceased.

Some buyers often shy away from listings that require court confirmation because they don't like the idea of not knowing if they can have the home until they've gone to court. Those involved in a purchase requiring court confirmation may want to make the sale of their current house contingent upon that confirmation, or at least make arrangements to rent it back in case they get overbid in court.

Until 1985, all estate sales routinely required court confirmation. The process was simplified when state law changed to allow for the sale of estate properties without court confirmation under the Independent Administration of Estates Act. Consult with an attorney if you are selling an estate property to determine the most advantageous way to proceed. Buyers don't like the court confirmation process because it aggravates moving anxiety. It may be an unavoidable necessity, however, in cases when an estate is being divided among disputing heirs.

Leasing with an Option to Buy

Leasing a home with an option to buy is one way that buyers can become homeowners when they're short of the cash needed for a down payment and closing costs. A lease option works like this: The prospective buyer leases the home from the seller for a period of time (usually one to five years). The lease includes a provision that allows the lessee to purchase the property at the end of the lease period, or earlier, at a predetermined price. In exchange for the privilege of tying up the seller's home for the lease period, the optionee/buyer pays a sum (called option money) to the seller. The option money is applied to the purchase price if the buyers complete the purchase; if they don't, the option money is forfeited and retained by the seller.

Sometimes the monthly rent paid on a lease option is higher than market rent, but often a portion of this is applied to the purchase price if the optionee completes the purchase. The purchase price on a lease option might also be higher than market price to accommodate the seller for anticipated future appreciation.

Most sellers prefer to sell for all cash, therefore lease options are not as prevalent as all cash sales. You'll find more lease option offerings during slow markets when sellers are having difficulty selling their homes. Make sure that you're not overpaying for the privilege of a lease option agreement and make sure that you're not buying a house that has a serious flaw. Has the house not sold due to the market, or is there something inherently wrong with the house that will make it difficult for you to sell in the future?

Not all sellers can accept a lease option. If the sellers need all their equity out of their home in order to move to their new home, a lease option won't work. In addition to homes that are multiple listed, look through the "For Rent" ads. Some landlords can be talked into a lease option agreement, but you may have to suggest this to the owner if the rental isn't being offered as such.

A lease option benefits a buyer in areas where prices are escalating. It allows the buyer to move into the house with a comparatively small cash outlay. Over the term of the lease, the lessee will hopefully save the balance of the cash needed to exercise the option and complete the purchase. It also gives the optionee the opportunity to live in the house before actually purchasing it, which is not possible with a conventional home purchase.

But, make sure your decision to lease option a property is well thought out because if you decide not to exercise your option at the end of the lease term, you'll be out the option money. A recent study concluded that most lease option tenants do not exercise their option. Get prequalified by a lender to make sure you'll be able to qualify for a home loan when you do accumulate the necessary cash to complete the sale. Also, be aware that some lenders won't allow your rent credit to apply toward your down payment.

Have the property inspected before you enter into the lease to make sure that there aren't any defects that you can't live with. Pay to have a preliminary title report run on the property to make sure that it's not overencumbered. Make sure the seller continues to pay the mortgage payments and property taxes during the lease period so that the property doesn't fall into foreclosure. Also, have the lease option agreement recorded against the property so that the seller can't sell it to someone else. And, your lease option agreement should state specifically who is responsible for property maintenance.

Sellers should make sure that the lease option agreement contains a provision that requires the optionees to repair damage they cause to the property. It should also detail what improvements, if any, the tenants can make to the property during the term of the agreement.

The elements of the lease option agreement are negotiable: the length of the lease; the purchase price; the amount of the option money; the amount of rent; and the portion of rent, if any, that's credited to the purchase price. Be sure to have a lease option agreement reviewed by a knowledgeable real estate attorney, particularly if you don't have a real estate agent handle the transaction. The California Association of Realtors® has a four-page lease option agreement, a copy of which is included at the back of this book. If an agent is involved in the transaction, the commission is usually paid as follows: A lease commission is paid at the time the lease is consummated. This amount is subtracted from the sale commission at the time the option is exercised and the optionee completes the purchase. If the optionee fails to complete the purchase, no more commission is owed to the agent(s).

Buying a Retirement Home

The basic principles that apply to buying any home apply to buying a retirement home. The one caveat is that retirees usually need to do more research before buying, particularly if they're living on a fixed income and are purchasing in an area where they've never lived before.

Lower taxes is often the impetus to make a retirement move. Write to the local Chamber of Commerce for details on the area's property taxes. If you're thinking of moving to another state, find out from that state what income, sales, and inheritance taxes will affect you. Find out if your pension will continue to be taxed by California and if the state you'll be moving to will give you any credit for those taxes.

Visit the community you're planning to move to several different times of the year before making the move. Ask retirees who've already made the move what unanticipated expenses they've encountered. Find out the cost of utilities, health care, auto insurance, food, clothing, and recreation. Subscribe to the local Sunday newspaper, and consider renting in the new community for awhile before buying.

Becoming an Expert on Prices

Buyers often wonder how they'll know what to pay when they do find a home they want to buy. The key to learning market value is to look at a lot of property. Some of this leg work you can do on your own. Hit the Sunday open house circuit. Then let your agent know what houses you've seen. Ask to be kept informed when any house you've seen sells. You'll want to know the selling price, how long it took to sell, and how close the selling price was to the list price. It helps to keep a written record. After you've seen a number of homes come on the market and sell, you'll know a well-priced home when it comes along.

If you feel unfamiliar with local property values, have your agent prepare a comparative market analysis of a home you're interested in before you make an offer. This doesn't have to be as complete a market analysis as what an agent prepares for prospective sellers who are attempting to set the list price on their home. It can be as simple as a computer printout of multiple listing information on similar homes that have been sold recently. Also ask for information regarding other properties being offered for sale in the neighborhood. Compare the amenities and list prices of these properties with those of your home of choice. But keep in mind that selling prices, not listing prices, are the true indicators of current market value.

101

Find out how long the neighboring properties were on the market and how close the final sale price was to the initial list price. In addition, find out how long the subject property has been on the market. Have there been other offers? Why were they rejected? Is there any flexibility in the price? A listing agent cannot divulge that the seller will accept less than the asking price unless the seller has given express permission for the agent to do so. If the agent is unsure about what the seller will accept, it may be because the agent doesn't know or has been advised not to say.

Often a buyer will want to know what a seller paid for the property, how long ago, and what improvements have been completed during the current ownership. County property ownership records will indicate the length of ownership. And it's usually possible to figure out what the seller paid for a property, even if the seller won't divulge this information. In California, when a property transfers title from one owner to the next, the seller pays a documentary transfer tax, the amount of which is stamped on the face of the grant deed when it is recorded. These documents are part of the public record. The tax is equal to $1.10 per thousand dollars of transfer price. Divide the amount of the tax paid by 1.1 and multiply this figure by $1,000 to arrive at the approximate sale price at the time of transfer. For example, a documentary transfer tax of $110, divided by 1.1, equals $100. Multiply this figure by $1,000 for an indicated sale price of $100,000. This figure may not be accurate if the seller carried financing for the buyer, in which case the figure may reflect the sale price minus the amount of seller financing.

When sufficient comparable sales data is not available, a buyer will often look at the seller's original purchase price and add allowances for price appreciation during the seller's period of ownership (your realtor should be able to provide rough approximations) as well as increases in value attributable to the seller's improvements to the property. This method of determining property value is approximate at best since it doesn't take local market conditions into account.

In a seller's market, the comparable sales figures may be out of date, and analyzing average price appreciation to determine what the house "should" be worth may be irrelevant. Conversely, in a sour market, yesterday's comparable sales may indicate a value higher than what similar properties are worth today.

Many buyers wonder if they should hire a licensed appraiser to complete an evaluation of a property before an offer is made. Most good real estate agents can provide you with all the relevant data you need to make an intelligent decision, and it won't cost you a dime extra.

CHAPTER 7

NEGOTIATING
the PURCHASE
CONTRACT

What Price Should You Offer?

How much you offer to pay for a home should be based on the following factors:
- Current real estate market conditions: Is it a soft buyer's or hot seller's market?
- How well-priced the home is
- The price you can afford to pay
- The seller's motivation

Most houses don't sell for the full list price. Exceptions usually occur when the real estate market is hot, or the rare occasion when a house is listed below its market value. In these situations, houses can sell for the full asking price, or more. Ordinarily, however, houses sell for less than the list price after negotiations between the buyer and seller to arrive at a mutually acceptable price.

How much under the seller's asking price you should offer will depend on supply and demand in your local market and on how well-priced the home is. In a high inventory soft market, where there are a lot of homes for sale and relatively few buyers, you'll have more room to negotiate than in a low inventory market with high demand. In a hot market, a desirable house could attract offers from several buyers (called "multiple offers"), in which case you might want to offer the full asking price, or more, to have a chance at being the successful bidder. Ask your agent how long it's taking to sell homes similar to the one you're interested in buying, and how active the local market is.

After you determine the market conditions, the next step is to figure out how well-priced the home is. See the last section of Chapter 6 for information on how to become knowledgeable about home prices. A home that's well-priced for the market will sell more quickly, and for closer to the list price, than a home that's overpriced for the market.

Buyers purchasing in a new development may find that the builder won't negotiate the price at all if the project is selling well. Ask a sales agent to give you information about recent sales in the development. In a slow market, developers are more willing to negotiate the price.

How much you can afford to pay is determined by how large a loan you can qualify for and the amount of cash you have available for a down payment and closing costs. Remember, if you're stretching to buy a house you're in love with, you can afford to pay a higher price if you take an adjustable-rate, rather than a fixed-rate, home loan. If you're short on cash, you might be able to ask the seller or builder to credit an amount to cover some or all of your nonrecurring closing costs. You should expect to pay a higher price in exchange for such a credit and the house will have to appraise at the higher price or the lender won't allow the credit.

What you can afford will set an upper limit to what you will pay for a home; you shouldn't exceed this amount. And, property condition ought to be factored into the affordability equation. If you know, for instance, that the house needs a new roof, budget this into your purchase. Make sure you have enough money left after you close on the new house to pay for the roof.

Be careful, if you're buying in a hot seller's market, that you don't get caught up in the frenzy of a multiple offer competition. Buyers have been known to pay over what they could afford in such circumstances.

Find out all you can about the seller's motivation and needs. How long has the house been on the market? Have there been other offers? If so, why weren't they acceptable to the seller? Why is the seller selling? Has the seller already bought another home? Is there any flexibility in the seller's price? Has the seller been transferred?

There's more to an offer than the price. By finding out as much as possible about the seller's situation, you may be able to offer the seller a benefit, such as a quick close of escrow or an "as is" sale with respect to the "termite" work, in exchange for a price concession.

Except for the situation where you're making an offer in a heated market in competition against other buyers, you'll want to start your negotiations at a price that's lower than what you're ultimately willing to pay. However, making an unreasonably low initial offer could insult a seller to the extent that he or she might refuse to consider your offer at all. Or, a very low offer could elicit an extremely high counter price from the sellers. This doesn't mean that you won't ultimately reach a common meeting ground; it just might take longer. If you're making a low offer, one that's more than 10 percent below the asking price, keep it simple. The more complicated the offer (usually the more contingencies, the more complicated), the more difficult it'll be to negotiate the price. For instance, you can usually negotiate a better price if your offer is not contingent upon the sale of another property.

An effective strategy for buying a home at the best price is to offer slightly under what you think the market value is for the home. A realistic and motivated seller might accept an offer that's close to market value rather than risk losing a good buyer by making a counteroffer at a higher price.

104

Getting Ready to Negotiate

Ideally, your negotiations should start before you sit down to write up an offer to purchase. The preliminaries can start with a verbal dialogue between your agent and the listing agent. Ask your agent to convey your interest in the property to the other agent, and to find out if there are other interested buyers. If there are, you'll want to be kept informed if it looks like any other buyers are getting ready to make offers.

Call your loan agent and make arrangements to get a prequalification, or preapproval, letter. Proof of your financial means can tip the scales in your favor, particularly if you're making an offer in competition with other buyers. Buyers who are qualified to pay more than they're offering can ask their loan broker or lender to give them a prequalification letter for the loan amount specified in the offer. If the sellers counter back at a higher price, you can provide another prequalification letter for the higher loan amount at that time.

In slower markets, you can use a verbal prenegotiation strategy to your advantage. This also works to the sellers' advantage because it prepares them to be receptive to your written offer so that you can ultimately consummate a sale. Let's say you're interested in a property that has been on the market for some time, but you think it's overpriced. You don't want to make an insultingly low offer and offend the sellers, so you have your agent call the seller's agent to explain your situation: You like the house but you can't afford to pay the seller's price. Your agent should find out if the sellers will entertain selling at a lower price. If they say yes, proceed with a written offer. It may help, if the sellers are occupying the property, to visit the house on several occasions and let the seller's agent know you're trying to decide between several houses. This might give the sellers the impetus to acquiesce on their price rather than lose you to other sellers. If the sellers are stuck on their price, move on to a more motivated seller.

105

Sometimes hypothetical sale price figures are exchanged between agents and their principals during verbal prenegotiations. Verbal agreements to sell real estate are not binding. If you arrive verbally at a mutually agreeable sales price, get it in writing as soon as possible. This is particularly important if you're dealing directly with a seller. Until it's in writing, the seller can sell the property to another buyer for a higher price.

The Real Estate Purchase Contract and Receipt for Deposit

The terms "deposit receipt" and "purchase contract" are often used interchangeably. A purchase contract is also called a deposit receipt because prospective buyers agree to put some of their hard-earned dollars toward the purchase in the form of a deposit when they make an offer to buy a home. But, the deposit receipt is more than just a receipt for money, it's a legally binding contract. It should be read and completed carefully.

In California, a real estate purchase contract must be in writing in order to be enforceable. In some states a real estate purchase agreement is prepared by an attorney; in California, however, licensed real estate agents are permitted to complete standard form purchase agreements. The sample contract included in this book is a standardized California Association of Realtors® form. Individual real estate company forms will deviate from this standard form somewhat, although most purchase contracts used in the state contain many of the same basic elements. The CAR Real Estate Purchase Contract And Receipt For Deposit is comprehensive and much more detailed than most contracts designed by individual real estate companies. The CAR contract includes common contract contingencies as well as disclosure requirements. Many of the provisions don't apply unless they're relevant to your specific situation. Some brokers have addenda to their purchase contracts that encompass elements contained in the CAR purchase contract. If you find that your broker's contract lacks some key provisions contained in the CAR contract, these can be incorporated by attaching an addendum to the contract including the CAR verbiage. The CAR contract may include language that you don't want in your purchase agreement. Paragraphs can be deleted if necessary, by referencing deletions in an addendum.

Most buyers and sellers never read the deposit receipt, which is a mistake because it's a complicated legal document that contains all the terms and conditions of the home purchase agreement. Never assume that you don't have to read the contract thinking your agent has already done this for you. Many agents are also guilty of not reading contracts, particularly the fine print. The more familiar buyers and sellers are with the standard form purchase agreement, the easier it'll be for them to draft and review agreements with their agents. Ask your agent to provide you with copies of the forms you'll be using when you make an offer, if they aren't CAR forms, so that you can review them in advance. Offers are often written hastily, particularly if there are multiple prospective buyers interested in the property.

This section will take you step-by-step through the CAR purchase contract. If you have any questions about specific contract clauses, your legal responsibilities and rights, or the legal consequences of signing a contract, ask your real estate agent or a knowledgeable real estate attorney. Don't assume any question is frivolous; there are no stupid questions when it comes to buying and selling real estate.

Read and understand the entire purchase contract before you sign it.

The opening section of the contract includes spaces for the property address, the contract date, the buyer's name, the deposit amount, and the purchase price. It's important to fill in the date the contract is drafted, since any addenda or counteroffers to the contract will refer to the original contract date.

106

The Financing section (paragraph 1) of the contract specifies the manner in which the buyers plan to finance the purchase. It also states that the buyers' ability to obtain financing is a contingency of the purchase agreement. This means that if the buyers are unable to obtain the financing proposed in the contract (after using diligent and good faith efforts), they are not obligated to complete the purchase and their deposit will be refunded.

Item A in the Financing section deals with the manner in which the financing contingency will be removed. Check either box 1 or 2. If box 1 is checked, the contingency will be removed when the lender either funds the loan or approves an assumption. If box 2 is checked, the financing contingency will be removed by the buyer in writing within the time specified. Most sellers and agents will prefer the second option.

Item B states that the buyer's ability to obtain the deposit and down payment is *not* a contingency. If you don't currently have the funds needed to close, and there's any possibility that these funds might not be available in time to close, you should protect yourself with a contingency. For example, if part of your down payment is coming from the sale of another property, make your purchase agreement contingent upon the successful close of that escrow. The CAR contract includes a contingent sale provision (see paragraph 20). Or, if you're using equity from another property you own for part of the down payment, but you need to refinance that property in order to do so, make this a contingency of the contract. This contingency can be added under item M of the Financing section (Additional Financing Terms) and could be worded like this: "This offer is contingent upon buyer's ability to refinance his property located at 456 James St., Our Town, within 30 days of acceptance for a loan amount of no less than $150,000."

> *The basic elements of an offer include:*
> - *Deposit amount*
> - *Purchase price*
> - *Financing contingency*
> - *Close of escrow and possession*
> - *How closing costs are shared*
> - *Physical inspection contingency*
> - *Various disclosures*
> - *Pest Control inspection and repairs*
> - *Additional terms and conditions*

Item C refers to the buyer's deposit: where and when it will be deposited, and what form it will take. Item D is completed if the deposit will be increased before close of escrow. Buyers frequently make their deposit in two stages. An initial deposit accompanies the offer. The deposit amount is increased at a later date, usually at the time the buyers remove their inspection or financing contingency.

Regarding item E, the balance of down payment will need to be deposited with the escrow holder no later than the day before close of escrow. The escrow holder must have negotiable funds (wired funds or a cashier's check drawn on a California bank) in the escrow account the day before closing. The balance of

CALIFORNIA ASSOCIATION OF REALTORS

☐

REAL ESTATE PURCHASE CONTRACT AND RECEIPT FOR DEPOSIT
THIS IS MORE THAN A RECEIPT FOR MONEY. IT IS INTENDED TO BE A LEGALLY BINDING CONTRACT. READ IT CAREFULLY.
CALIFORNIA ASSOCIATION OF REALTORS® (CAR) STANDARD FORM

DATE: _____, 19____ AT _____, California,

RECEIVED FROM _____ ("Buyer")

THE SUM OF _____ Dollars $_____

as a deposit to be applied toward the

PURCHASE PRICE OF _____ Dollars $_____

FOR PURCHASE OF PROPERTY SITUATED IN _____, COUNTY OF _____, California,

DESCRIBED AS _____ ("Property").

1. **FINANCING:** THE OBTAINING OF THE LOAN(S) BELOW IS A CONTINGENCY OF THIS AGREEMENT. Buyer shall act diligently and in good faith to obtain all applicable financing.

   A. FINANCING CONTINGENCY shall remain in effect until (Check ONLY ONE of the following):

       1. ☐ (If checked). The designated loan(s) is/are funded and/or the assumption of existing financing is approved by Lender.

       OR 2. ☐ (If checked). _____ calendar days after acceptance of the offer. Buyer shall remove the financing contingency in writing within this time. If Buyer fails to do so, then Seller may cancel this agreement by giving written notice of cancellation to Buyer.

   B. OBTAINING OF DEPOSIT AND DOWN PAYMENT by the Buyer is NOT a contingency, unless otherwise agreed in writing.

   C. DEPOSIT to be deposited ☐ with Escrow Holder, ☐ into Broker's trust account, or ☐ _____ $ _____

       BY ☐ Personal check, ☐ Cashier's check, ☐ Cash, or ☐ _____,

       PAYABLE TO _____

       TO BE HELD UNCASHED UNTIL the next business day after acceptance of the offer, or ☐ _____.

   D. INCREASED DEPOSIT, within _____ calendar days after acceptance of the offer, to be deposited ☐ with Escrow Holder, ☐ into Broker's trust account, or ☐ _____ $ _____

   E. BALANCE OF DOWN PAYMENT to be deposited with Escrow Holder on demand of Escrow Holder . . . . $ _____

   F. FIRST LOAN IN THE AMOUNT OF . . . . $ _____

       ☐ NEW First Deed of Trust in favor of ☐ LENDER, ☐ SELLER; or

       ☐ ASSUMPTION of existing First Deed of Trust; or ☐ _____;

       encumbering the Property, securing a note payable at approximately $_____ per month (☐ or more), to include ☐ principal and interest, ☐ interest only, at maximum interest of _____% ☐ fixed rate, ☐ initial adjustable rate, with a maximum lifetime interest rate increase of _____% over the initial rate, balance due in _____ years. Buyer shall pay loan fees/points not to exceed _____.

   G. SECOND LOAN IN THE AMOUNT OF . . . . $ _____

       ☐ NEW Second Deed of Trust in favor of ☐ LENDER, ☐ SELLER; or

       ☐ ASSUMPTION of Existing Second Deed of Trust; or ☐ _____;

       encumbering the Property, securing a note payable at approximately $_____ per month (☐ or more), to include ☐ principal and interest, ☐ interest only, at maximum interest of _____% ☐ fixed rate, ☐ initial adjustable rate, with a maximum lifetime interest rate increase of _____% over the initial rate, balance due in _____ years. Buyer shall pay loan fees/points not to exceed _____.

   H. TOTAL PURCHASE PRICE, not including costs of obtaining loans and other closing costs . . . . $ _____

   I. LOAN APPLICATIONS: Buyer shall, within the time specified in paragraph 26B(1), submit to lender(s) (or to Seller for applicable Seller financing), a completed loan or assumption application(s), and provide to Seller written acknowledgment of Buyer's compliance. For Seller financing: (1) Buyer shall submit a completed loan application on FNMA Form 1003; (2) Buyer authorizes Seller and/or Broker(s) to obtain, at Buyer's expense, a copy of Buyer's credit report; and (3) Seller may cancel this purchase and sale agreement upon disapproval of either the application or the credit report, by providing to Buyer written notice within 7 (or ☐ _____) calendar days after receipt of those documents.

   J. EXISTING LOANS: For existing loans to be taken over by Buyer, Seller shall promptly request and upon receipt provide to Buyer copies of all applicable notes and deeds of trust, loan balances, and current interest rates. Buyer may give Seller written notice of disapproval within the time specified in paragraph 26B(5). Differences between estimated and actual loan balance(s) shall be adjusted at close of escrow by: _____ payment, or ☐ _____

the down payment should be equal to the total cash down minus the deposit amount(s), since deposits are ordinarily applied toward the total purchase price.

Items F and G specify the additional financing terms the buyers are proposing to complete the purchase; only the relevant clauses should be filled in. The "or more" box after the monthly payment amount is checked to indicate you won't accept a loan with a prepayment penalty.

Some buyers object to providing specific financing terms such as the interest rate and loan fee and would rather state simply: "terms acceptable to buyer." Most attorneys, however, feel this is not advisable since if a dispute were to arise between the buyers and sellers, a judge might rule the contract to be unenforceable due to the vagueness of its terms. Specifying an interest rate protects the buyers in case rates rise drastically during the financing contingency time period.

☐ NEW Se̶c̶ or ☐ LENDER, ☐
☐ ASSUMPTION of Existing Second Deed of Trust; or ☐ _____ ;
encumbering the Property, securing a note payable at approximately $_____ per month (☐ or more), to include
☐ principal and interest, ☐ interest only, at maximum interest of _____% ☐ fixed rate, ☐ initial adjustable rate, with a maximum
lifetime interest rate increase of _____% over the initial rate, balance due in _____ years. Buyer shall pay loan fees/points not to
exceed _____ .

H. TOTAL PURCHASE PRICE, not including costs of obtaining loans and other closing costs .... $ _____

I. LOAN APPLICATIONS: Buyer shall, within the time specified in paragraph 26B(1), submit to lender(s) (or to Seller for applicable Seller financing), a completed
loan or assumption application(s), and provide to Seller written acknowledgment of Buyer's compliance. For Seller financing: (1) Buyer shall submit a completed
loan application on FNMA Form 1003; (2) Buyer authorizes Seller and/or Broker(s) to obtain, at Buyer's expense, a copy of Buyer's credit report; and (3) Seller
may cancel this purchase and sale agreement upon disapproval of either the application or the credit report, by providing to Buyer written notice within
7 (or ☐ _____) calendar days after receipt of those documents.

J. EXISTING LOANS: For existing loans to be taken over by Buyer, Seller shall promptly request and upon receipt provide to Buyer copies of all applicable notes
and deeds of trust, loan balances, and current interest rates. Buyer may give Seller written notice of disapproval within the time specified in paragraph 26B(5).
Differences between estimated and actual loan balance(s) shall be adjusted at close of escrow by:
☐ Cash downpayment, or ☐ _____ .
Impound account(s), if any, shall be: ☐ Charged to Buyer and credited to Seller, or ☐ _____ .

K. LOAN FEATURES: LOANS/DOCUMENTS CONTAIN A NUMBER OF IMPORTANT FEATURES AFFECTING THE RIGHTS OF THE BORROWER AND LENDER.
READ ALL LOAN DOCUMENTS CAREFULLY.

L. ADDITIONAL SELLER FINANCING TERMS: The following terms apply ONLY to financing extended by Seller under this agreement. The rate specified as
the maximum interest rate in F or G above, as applicable, shall be the actual fixed interest rate for seller financing. Any promissory note and/or deed of trust
given by Buyer to Seller shall contain, but not be limited to, the following additional terms:

1. REQUEST FOR NOTICE OF DEFAULT on senior loans.
2. Buyer shall execute and pay for a REQUEST FOR NOTICE OF DELINQUENCY in escrow and at any future time if requested by Seller.
3. Acceleration clause making the loan due, when permitted by law, at Seller's option, upon the sale or transfer of the Property or any interest in it.
4. A late charge of 6.0% of the installment due, or $5.00, whichever is greater, if the installment is not received within 10 days of the date it is due.
5. Title insurance coverage in the form of a joint protection policy shall be provided insuring Seller's deed of trust interest in the Property.
6. Tax Service shall be obtained and paid for by Buyer to notify Seller if property taxes have not been paid.
7. Buyer shall provide fire and extended coverage insurance during the period of the seller financing, in an amount sufficient to replace all improvements
   on the Property, or the total encumbrances against the Property, whichever is less, with a loss payable endorsement in favor of Seller.
8. The addition, deletion, or substitution of any person or entity under this agreement, or to title prior to close of escrow, shall require Seller's written
   consent. Seller may grant or withhold consent in Seller's sole discretion. Any additional or substituted person or entity shall, if requested by Seller, submit
   to Seller the same documentation as required for the original named Buyer. Seller and/or Broker(s) may obtain a credit report on any such person or entity.
9. If the Property contains 1 to 4 dwelling units, Buyer and Seller shall execute a Seller Financing Disclosure Statement (CAR FORM SFD-14) (Civil Code
   §§2956-2967), if applicable, as provided by arranger of credit, as soon as practicable prior to execution of security documents.

M. ADDITIONAL FINANCING TERMS: _____
_____
_____

Buyer and Seller acknowledge receipt of copy of this page, which constitutes Page 1 of _____ Pages.
Buyer's Initials (_____) (_____) Seller's Initials (_____) (_____)

OFFICE USE ONLY
Reviewed by Broker or Designee _____
Date _____

M-PM-7/93

BUYER'S COPY
REAL ESTATE PURCHASE CONTRACT AND RECEIPT FOR DEPOSIT (DLF-14 PAGE 1 OF 6)

109

If interest rates rise higher than the rate agreed to in the contract, the buyers are
not obliged to complete the purchase. Or, they can proceed at their option, if they
can still qualify for a loan at the higher rate. Alternatively, they can try to renegotiate the price with the seller to offset some of their increased financing costs.

The amount of the purchase price is filled in at item H. The total of the
deposit amount(s), the balance of the down payment, and the loan amount(s)
should be equal to the purchase price.

Item I covers the loan application process. It states that the buyers are to
submit a completed loan application, either to the lender or to the seller directly
if the seller is carrying financing for the buyer, within the time specified in paragraph 26. If the seller is carrying financing, the seller's agent is authorized to
obtain a credit report on the buyer and the seller has the right to disapprove the

☐

Property Address: _____ _____ , 19____

2. ATTACHED SUPPLEMENTS: The following ATTACHED supplements are incorporated in this agreement:

☐ _____ ☐ _____

☐ _____ ☐ _____

3. ESCROW: Escrow instructions shall be signed by Buyer and Seller and delivered to _____, the designated Escrow Holder, within _____ calendar days after acceptance of the offer (or ☐ at least _____ calendar days before close of escrow). Buyer and Seller hereby jointly instruct Escrow Holder and Broker(s) that Buyer's deposit(s) placed into escrow or into Broker's trust account will be held as a good faith deposit toward the completion of this transaction. Release of Buyer's funds will require mutual, signed release instructions from both Buyer and Seller, judicial decision, or arbitration award. Escrow shall close ☐ on _____ , 19___ , or ☐ within _____ calendar days after acceptance of the offer. Escrow fee to be paid as follows: _____ .

4. OCCUPANCY: Buyer ☐ does, ☐ does not intend to occupy Property as Buyer's primary residence.

5. POSSESSION AND KEYS: Seller shall deliver possession and occupancy of the Property to Buyer ☐ on the date of recordation of the deed at _____ AM/PM, or ☐ no later than _____ calendar days after date of recordation at _____ AM/PM, or ☐ _____ . Property shall be vacant unless otherwise agreed in writing. If applicable, Seller and Buyer shall execute Interim Occupancy Agreement (CAR FORM IOA-14) or Residential Lease Agreement After Sale (CAR FORM RLAS-11). Seller shall provide keys and/or means to operate all Property locks, mailboxes, security systems, alarms, garage door openers, and Homeowners' Association facilities.

6. TITLE AND VESTING: Buyer shall be provided a current preliminary (title) report at _____ expense. Buyer shall, within the time specified in paragraph 26B(5), provide written notice to Seller of any items reasonably disapproved. (A preliminary report is only an offer by the title insurer to issue a policy of title insurance and may not contain every item affecting title.) At close of escrow: (a) Title shall be transferred by grant deed; (b) title shall be free of liens, except as provided in this agreement; (c) title shall be free of other encumbrances, easements, restrictions, rights, and conditions of record or known to Seller, except for: (1) all matters shown in the preliminary (title) report which are not disapproved in writing by Buyer as above, and (2) _____ ; (d) Buyer shall receive a California Land Title Association (CLTA) policy issued by _____ Company, at _____ expense. (An ALTA-R policy may provide greater protection for Buyer and may be available at the same or slightly higher cost than a CLTA policy. The designated title company can provide information, at Buyer's request, about availability and desirability of other types of title insurance.) For Seller financing, paragraph 1L(5) provides for a joint protection policy. Title shall vest as designated in Buyer's escrow instructions. **(THE MANNER OF TAKING TITLE MAY HAVE SIGNIFICANT LEGAL AND TAX CONSEQUENCES; THEREFORE, BUYER SHOULD GIVE THIS MATTER SERIOUS CONSIDERATION.)**

7. PRORATIONS:

A. Real property taxes and assessments, interest, rents, Homeowners' Association regular dues and regular assessments, premiums on insurance assumed by Buyer, payments on bonds and assessments assumed by Buyer, and _____ shall be paid current and prorated between Buyer and Seller, unless otherwise shown in paragraph 7B or 7C, as of: ☐ date of recordation of the deed, or ☐ _____ .

B. Mello-Roos and other Special Assessment District bonds and assessments which are now a lien shall be: ☐ paid current by Seller as of the date shown in paragraph 7A (payments that are not yet due shall be assumed by Buyer without credit toward the purchase price); or ☐ _____ .

C. Homeowners' Association special assessments, which are now a lien, shall be: ☐ paid current by Seller as of the date shown in paragraph 7A (payments that are not yet due shall be assumed by Buyer without credit toward the purchase price); or ☐ _____ .

D. County transfer tax or transfer fee shall be paid by _____ . City transfer tax or transfer fee shall be paid by _____ . Homeowners' Association transfer fee shall be paid by _____ .

E. THE PROPERTY WILL BE REASSESSED UPON CHANGE OF OWNERSHIP. THIS WILL AFFECT THE TAXES TO BE PAID. Any supplemental tax bills shall be paid as follows: (1) for periods after close of escrow, by Buyer (or by final acquiring party, if part of an exchange), and (2) for periods prior to close of escrow, by Seller. TAX BILLS ISSUED AFTER CLOSE OF ESCROW SHALL BE HANDLED DIRECTLY BETWEEN BUYER AND SELLER.

8. CONDOMINIUM/P.D.: If the Property is in a condominium/planned development: (a) the Property has _____ assigned parking space(s); (b) the current regular Homeowners' Association dues/assessments are $_____ ☐ monthly, or ☐ _____ ; (c) Seller shall promptly disclose in writing to Buyer any known pending special assessments, claims, or litigation; and (d) Seller shall promptly request, and, upon receipt, provide to Buyer copies of covenants, conditions, and restrictions; articles of incorporation; by-laws; other governing documents; most current financial statement distributed (Civil Code §1365); statement regarding limited enforceability of age restrictions, if applicable; current Homeowners' Association statement showing any unpaid assessments (Civil Code §1368); any other documents required by law; most recent six months Homeowners' Association minutes, if available; and _____ . Buyer shall, within the time specified in paragraph 26B(5), provide written notice to Seller of any items disapproved. READ PARAGRAPH 7 FOR PRORATIONS AND TRANSFER FEES.

9. INSPECTION OF PROPERTY: ... shall have the right to conduct ... tests ... in paragraph ...

110

buyers' loan application or credit report within seven calendar days after receiving those documents.

The Existing Loans clause gives buyers who are assuming the seller's existing loan(s) on the property the opportunity to disapprove notes and deeds of trust, loan balances, and interest rates. This item covers how differences between the estimated and actual loan balance(s) will be resolved, and how impound account(s) will be reconciled. Buyers making an offer contingent upon taking over an existing loan would be wise to determine the existing lender's policy regarding takeovers before they make an offer. Many existing loans, particularly fixed-rate loans, have enforceable "due on sale" clauses, and there may be a risk that the lender will call the loan due, and even start foreclosure proceedings, if the property transfers to a new buyer and the existing loan is not paid off at that time.

C. Homeowners ~~... assessments, which are now a~~ ~~...ent by Seller as of the da~~ ~~...paragraph 7A (paymen~~ that are not yet due shall be assumed by Buyer without credit toward the ~~...se~~ price); or ☐ _____

D. County transfer tax or transfer fee shall be paid by _____ . City transfer tax or transfer fee shall be paid by _____ . Homeowners' Association transfer fee shall be paid by _____

E. THE PROPERTY WILL BE REASSESSED UPON CHANGE OF OWNERSHIP. THIS WILL AFFECT THE TAXES TO BE PAID. Any supplemental tax bills shall be paid as follows: (1) for periods after close of escrow, by Buyer (or by final acquiring party, if part of an exchange), and (2) for periods prior to close of escrow, by Seller. TAX BILLS ISSUED AFTER CLOSE OF ESCROW SHALL BE HANDLED DIRECTLY BETWEEN BUYER AND SELLER.

8. **CONDOMINIUM/P.D.:** If the Property is in a condominium/planned development: (a) the Property has _____ assigned parking space(s); (b) the current regular Homeowners' Association dues/assessments are $_____ ☐ monthly, or ☐ _____ ; (c) Seller shall promptly disclose in writing to Buyer any known pending special assessments, claims, or litigation; and (d) Seller shall promptly request, and, upon receipt, provide to Buyer copies of covenants, conditions, and restrictions; articles of incorporation; by-laws; other governing documents; most current financial statement distributed (Civil Code §1365); statement regarding limited enforceability of age restrictions, if applicable; current Homeowners' Association statement showing any unpaid assessments (Civil Code §1368); any other documents required by law; most recent six months Homeowners' Association minutes, if available; and _____ . Buyer shall, within the time specified in paragraph 26B(5), provide written notice to Seller of any items disapproved. READ PARAGRAPH 7 FOR PRORATIONS AND TRANSFER FEES.

9. **BUYER'S INVESTIGATION OF PROPERTY CONDITION:** Buyer shall have the right to conduct inspections, investigations, tests, surveys, and other studies ("Inspections") at Buyer's expense. Buyer shall, within the times specified in paragraphs 26B(2) and (3), complete these Inspections and shall notify Seller in writing of any item(s) disapproved. Buyer is strongly advised to exercise this right and to make Buyer's own selection of professionals with appropriate qualifications to conduct Inspections of the entire Property. If Buyer does not exercise this right to conduct Inspections, Buyer is acting against the advice of Broker(s). In any event, Buyer is relying upon Inspections made or obtained by Buyer. **BUYER AND SELLER ARE AWARE THAT THE BROKER(S) DO(ES) NOT GUARANTEE, AND IN NO WAY ASSUME(S) RESPONSIBILITY FOR, THE CONDITION OF THE PROPERTY. BUYER IS ALSO AWARE OF BUYER'S AFFIRMATIVE DUTY TO EXERCISE REASONABLE CARE TO PROTECT HIMSELF OR HERSELF, INCLUDING THOSE FACTS WHICH ARE KNOWN TO OR WITHIN THE DILIGENT ATTENTION AND OBSERVATION OF THE BUYER (Civil Code §2079.5).**
Seller shall make the Property available for all Inspections. Buyer shall keep the Property free and clear of liens; shall indemnify and hold Seller harmless from all liability, claims, demands, damages, and costs; and shall repair all damages arising from the Inspections.
No Inspections may be made by any building or zoning inspector or government employee without the prior written consent of Seller. Buyer shall provide to Seller, at no cost, upon request of Seller, complete copies of all Inspection reports obtained by Buyer concerning the Property.
BUYER IS STRONGLY ADVISED TO INVESTIGATE THE CONDITION AND SUITABILITY OF ALL ASPECTS OF THE PROPERTY AND ALL MATTERS AFFECTING THE VALUE OR DESIRABILITY OF THE PROPERTY, INCLUDING, BUT NOT LIMITED TO, THE FOLLOWING:

A. Built-in appliances, structural, foundation, roof, plumbing, heating, air conditioning, electrical, mechanical, security, pool/spa systems and components, and any personal property included in the sale.

B. Square footage, room dimensions, lot size, and age of Property improvements. (Any numerical statements regarding these items are APPROXIMATIONS ONLY and should not be relied upon.)

C. Property lines and boundaries. (Fences, hedges, walls, and other natural or constructed barriers or markers do not necessarily identify true Property boundaries. Property lines may be verified by survey.)

D. Sewer, septic, and well systems and components. (Property may not be connected to sewer, and applicable fees may not have been paid. Septic tank may need to be pumped and leach field may need to be inspected.)

E. Limitations, restrictions, and requirements regarding Property use, future development, zoning, building, size, governmental permits, and inspections.

F. Water and utility availability and use restrictions.

G. Potential environmental hazards including asbestos, formaldehyde, radon gas, lead-based paint, other lead contamination, fuel or chemical storage tanks, contaminated soil or water, hazardous waste, electromagnetic fields, nuclear sources, and other substances, materials, products, or conditions.

H. Geologic/seismic conditions, soil and terrain stability, suitability, and drainage.

I. Neighborhood or Property conditions including schools, proximity and adequacy of law enforcement, proximity to commercial, industrial, or agricultural activities, crime statistics, fire protection, other governmental services, existing and proposed transportation, construction and development, airport noise, noise or odor from any source, other nuisances, hazards, or circumstances, and any conditions or influences of significance to certain cultures and/or religions.

J. Buyer is advised to make further inquiries and to consult government agencies, lenders, insurance agents, architects, and other appropriate persons and entities concerning the use of the Property under applicable building, zoning, fire, health, and safety codes, and for evaluation of potential hazards.

K. Other: _____

_____ .

Buyer and Seller acknowledge receipt of copy of this page, which constitutes Page 2 of _____ Pages.

Buyer's Initials (_____) (_____)   Seller's Initials (_____) (_____)

OFFICE USE ONLY
Reviewed by Broker or Designee _____
Date _____

M-PM-7/93

BUYER'S COPY

REAL ESTATE PURCHASE CONTRACT AND RECEIPT FOR DEPOSIT (DLF-14 PAGE 2 OF 6)

111

Some existing loans, particularly the newer adjustable-rate mortgages, can be assumed by a subsequent buyer, but only on certain terms and conditions. Usually, the buyers must be creditworthy and must make formal application to assume the loan. Also, fees are often involved, and terms of the original loan may change when it is assumed by the new buyer.

Item L applies if the buyer is asking the seller to carry all or a portion of the financing. Although these provisions are standard and reasonable, any one or more can be deleted (as can any other provisions included in this contract) by specifying this in an addendum. Be specific if you want to delete a contract clause. For instance, "Number 3 under item L of the purchase contract is deleted."

In California, a Seller Financing Disclosure Statement must be completed giving full disclosure of the financing terms to the buyers and sellers when an "arranger" of credit is part of a one- to four-unit property sale in which the seller carries financing. A real estate broker representing buyers or sellers in such a property transfer is considered an "arranger" of credit. Number 9 under item L specifies that this form, a copy of which is included in the "Seller Financing" section of Chapter 10, will be completed as soon as practicable.

Section M can be used to include additional financing terms that will apply. Buyers who are concerned that they may have overpaid for a property might want to include a provision stating that the offer is contingent upon the property appraising for the purchase price. If the appraisal comes in low, the buyers can withdraw from the contract. Or they could renegotiate with the sellers to either lower the price or to carry some of the financing. Buyers who need an interim (swing or bridge) loan to complete the purchase will want to include this as a contingency under item M. If additional space is needed, an addendum can be made to the contract by stipulating this under the Attached Supplements section (section 2 of the contract). Buyers making offers in competitive bidding situations, or who simply want to impress the sellers with their earnest intent, might include a provision under section M that states that the buyers will provide the sellers with a prequalification letter from a lender, or loan broker, within several days of acceptance. It's preferable, however, to have a prequalification letter at the time an offer is made.

The total number of contract pages should be filled in at the bottom of each page and the buyer should initial each page to acknowledge receipt. The property address is filled in at the top of each page.

The CAR contract is a standard form; it's also a legally binding contract. Although your agent can assist in completing the contract, he or she can't give legal or tax advice unless he or she is also an attorney or a tax advisor. If you have legal or tax questions, consult the appropriate professional.

The Attached Supplements section at the top of page 2 allows for the incorporation of additional relevant forms into the contract. An Interim Occupancy Agreement should be included if the buyer wants to occupy the property prior to the close of escrow; or a Residential Lease Agreement After Sale is incorporated when the seller is to retain possession of the property after the close of escrow. If the buyer is applying for VA or FHA financing, VA or FHA Amendments can be included which state that the buyer won't be obliged to complete the purchase if the property is not appraised at the purchase price.

The name of the escrow holder, usually an escrow or title company, is entered on the first line of the Escrow section. The escrow holder is often chosen by the buyer, but this can also be a negotiable item. Buyers who are selling a home, and who want to have escrow on the old and new homes close simultaneously, should use the same escrow holder for both transactions. If the two properties aren't located in the same county, it may be difficult to accomplish a simultaneous close; in this case, make sure that the escrow on the old home closes a day or so before the escrow on the new home. This is critical if the proceeds from the sale of the old home are to provide the down payment for the purchase of the new one. If a real estate broker involved in the transaction has a financial interest in the escrow or title company, this must be disclosed in writing in the purchase agreement.

Escrow procedures differ somewhat in Southern and Northern California. In Southern California, it's customary for the buyer and seller to deliver escrow instructions to the escrow holder soon after the seller's acceptance, say within five days. In Northern California, escrow instructions are usually not given to the escrow holder until sometime within the last few weeks before closing. Fill in the close of escrow either as a specific date or as a number of days after acceptance of the contract. Be aware that Monday is not a good day of the week to close escrow. This is because the buyer's lender must fund the loan the day before the escrow closes and will start charging the buyer interest from the funding date. A lender must fund a Monday closing on the previous Friday, which means the buyer pays interest for three days before actually owning the property. If you're proposing to close a set number of days after acceptance, you may want to include a provision that states that if escrow closing falls on a Monday, buyers and sellers agree to close escrow on the following day. You won't know what the precise close date will be until the contract negotiations are complete, which could take days or weeks. Buyers who are short on cash may want to close escrow toward the end of the month in order to reduce the amount of prorated interest owed to the lender at closing. This will reduce the amount of their closing costs. Who pays the escrow fee varies from county to county.

Check the appropriate box at paragraph 4 (Occupancy). Whether or not you'll personally occupy the property as your primary residence will make a difference to the lender. Most lenders offer their best rates and terms to borrowers who intend to occupy the property.

113

The Possession and Keys clause specifies when occupancy of the property is to be delivered to the buyer. Sellers often don't feel comfortable moving out until they're certain that escrow has closed. Sometimes the buyer will allow the seller a courtesy day or two to move free of charge. If the seller is going to remain in possession for a longer period of time after the close of escrow, it's customary for the seller to compensate the buyer by paying rent. This is usually equal to the total of the buyer's principal, interest, taxes, and insurance (PITI), prorated on a per diem basis.

When sellers have made it a condition of the listing that they be able to rent the property back for a period of time, this can be detailed in the "or" space of the possession clause. For instance, such a condition might read, "Sellers have option to rent back property for up to thirty days after close of escrow, at a cost equal to buyer's PITI, prorated on a per diem basis. Sellers to give buyer written notice thirty days prior to vacating." If more space is required, an addendum can be attached to the contract (referenced by "See Addendum attached and made a part hereof"). The buyer and seller should make an "Interim Occupancy Agreement" or "Residential Lease Agreement After Sale" a part of the contract.

The Title and Vesting section is intended to protect the buyer in the event the seller is unable to deliver clear title to the property. Who pays the cost of a preliminary title report and the title insurance policy is negotiable, but it's often the buyer in Northern California and the seller in Southern California. It's the buyer's responsibility to disapprove of any unacceptable title matter in writing within a specific time after receiving the preliminary title report. The time period for buyer disapproval should be indicated in paragraph 26. If a buyer disapproves of the preliminary title report, it's then the seller's responsibility to remedy the defect by close of escrow. If the seller is unable to do so, the buyer doesn't have to complete the purchase. (See Chapter 11 for more information about title insurance policies and how to hold title.)

Paragraph 7 covers the payment of recurrent liens and assessments against the property, as well as transfer taxes and fees, if there are any. Normally, prorations are as of the close of escrow. Assessments are usually paid current by the seller; future payments are assumed by the buyer. The county transfer tax is often paid by the seller, as is a Homeowners' Association transfer fee. A city tax, if there is one, is frequently shared equally by the buyer and seller. However, who pays these fees is negotiable and is usually governed by local custom. Item E under this section notifies the buyer that the property will be reassessed upon change of ownership which will affect future property tax bills. This section also indicates who is responsible for supplemental tax bills. For periods after the close of escrow, the buyer will be responsible. For periods before the close of escrow, the seller will be responsible, even if the supplemental bill arrives after the close of escrow. It takes awhile for the county to reassess a property and mail a supplemental tax bill to the property owner. A new home will probably be reassessed at the time it's completed, and again when it sells. The supplemental bill for the period from completion until sale will be the responsibility of the seller. Probate properties are often reassessed at the time of the owner's death. Even if the supplemental tax bill isn't available until after the close of escrow, it will be the responsibility of the estate. Although supplemental tax bills don't usually arrive promptly, they are retroactive to the date the property was reassessed.

The number of parking spaces and the amount of Homeowners' Association dues should be indicated in paragraph 8 (Condominium/P.D.) if the property is in a condominium or a planned development. This paragraph also includes a provision for the seller to supply pertinent disclosure documentation regarding the planned development to the buyers for their approval within the times specified in paragraph 26. This documentation should include copies of the CC&Rs (Covenants, Conditions, and Restrictions); the articles of incorporation, bylaws, rules, and regulations; financing statements; and any notices of delinquent or pending assessments, claims, or litigation.

Paragraph 9 (Buyer's Investigation of Property Condition) gives the buyer the right to have professionals inspect the property. Inspections are at the buyer's expense. If conditions unacceptable to the buyer are discovered, the buyer must notify the seller of this in writing within the time frame specified in paragraph 26.

114

According to paragraph 9, the buyers agree to give the sellers copies of all inspection reports obtained by the buyers if the seller requests copies. If the seller is unwilling or unable to correct defects claimed by the buyer, the buyer may cancel the agreement and have the deposit refunded. Implicit in this contingency is the seller's right to remedy defects that are unacceptable to the buyer. Buyers often think the inspection contingency gives them an automatic right to cancel the contract, which it does not. If the buyers want approval or disapproval of the inspection contingency to be at their sole discretion, this must be written in as an additional provision of the contract. Also, if you intend to purchase the property only if your inspections result in specific findings, such as the feasibility of a building or remodeling project, you're wise to include this as a separate contingency rather than assume that it's covered under the inspection contingency. Section 9 strongly advises the buyer to have the property inspected. Don't take this recommendation lightly. This clause also advises buyers that they have an affirmative duty to exercise reasonable care to protect themselves. Most properties should be carefully inspected by qualified professionals, even new homes, condominiums, and townhouses.

Under paragraph 10 (Condition of Property), either item A or B should be initialed, not both. Item A is a Seller Warranty provision, which is typically included in most home purchase agreements. It says that when the house is turned over to the buyer, the roof and showers will be free of leaks; built-in appliances and mechanical systems will be operative; the property will be free of all debris and personal property not included in the sale; cracked and broken glass will be replaced; and the property will be in substantially the same condition it was in on the date of acceptance.

115

Item B under paragraph 10 is an "as is" clause, which states that the buyer will purchase the property in its present condition and without warranty. This clause is typically initialed if the property is being sold to settle a probate or foreclosure. If the property is to be purchased "as is" with respect to structural pest control ("termite") repairs, this should be indicated under paragraph 19 below. Even with an "as is" sale, the seller is still obliged to disclose material defects and the buyer has the right to have the property inspected by professionals as defined in paragraph 9.

Paragraph 11 requires the seller, unless exempt, to provide the buyer with a Real Estate Transfer Disclosure Statement within the number of days specified. If the buyer hasn't already received and signed a completed disclosure statement before making the offer, the buyer has the right to give written notice of termination of the contract to the seller within three days of personal delivery of the form, or within five days after the form is mailed to the buyer. The Real Estate Transfer Disclosure Statement isn't complete until both the buyer's and seller's agents have done their diligent visual inspections of the property and noted their findings on the form. Disclosure of defects doesn't relieve sellers of the obligation

☐
Property Address: _____ _____, 19____

10. CONDITION OF PROPERTY: (Initial ONLY paragraph A or B; DO NOT initial both.)
Buyer's initials   Seller's initials

_____/   _____/   **A. SELLER WARRANTY: (If A is initialled, DO NOT initial B.)** Seller warrants that on the date possession is made available to Buyer: (1) Roof shall be free of KNOWN leaks; (2) built-in appliances (including free-standing oven and range, if included in sale), plumbing, heating, air conditioning, electrical, water, sewer/septic, and pool/spa systems, if any, shall be operative; (3) plumbing systems, shower pan(s), and shower enclosure(s) shall be free of leaks; (4) all broken or cracked glass shall be replaced; (5) Property, including pool/spa, landscaping, and grounds, shall be maintained in substantially the same condition as on the date of acceptance of the offer; (6) all debris and all personal property not included in the sale shall be removed; (7)_____

NOTE TO BUYER: This warranty is limited to items specified in this paragraph A. Items discovered in Buyer's Inspections which are not covered by this paragraph shall be governed by the procedure in paragraphs 9 and 26.
NOTE TO SELLER: Disclosures in the Real Estate Transfer Disclosure Statement (CAR FORM TDS-14), and items discovered in Buyer's Inspections, do NOT eliminate Seller's obligations under this warranty unless specifically agreed in writing.

OR
Buyer's initials   Seller's initials

_____/   _____/   **B. "AS-IS" CONDITION: (If B is initialled, DO NOT initial A.)** Property is sold "AS-IS," in its present condition, without warranty. Seller shall not be responsible for making corrections or repairs of any nature except: (1) Structural pest control repairs, if applicable under paragraph 19, and (2)_____
Buyer retains the right to disapprove the condition of the Property based upon items discovered in Buyer's Inspections under paragraph 9. **SELLER REMAINS OBLIGATED TO DISCLOSE ADVERSE MATERIAL FACTS WHICH ARE KNOWN TO SELLER AND TO MAKE OTHER DISCLOSURES REQUIRED BY LAW.**

11. TRANSFER DISCLOSURE STATEMENT: Unless exempt, a Real Estate Transfer Disclosure Statement ("TDS") (CAR FORM TDS-14) shall be completed by Seller and delivered to Buyer (Civil Code §§1102-1102.15). Buyer shall sign and return a copy of the TDS to Seller or Seller's agent: (a) ☐ Buyer has received a TDS prior to execution of the offer, **OR** (b) ☐ Buyer shall be provided a TDS within _____ calendar days after acceptance of the offer. If the TDS is delivered to Buyer after the offer is executed, Buyer shall have the right to terminate this agreement within three (3) days after delivery in person, or five (5) days after delivery by deposit in the mail by giving written notice of termination to Seller or Seller's agent. DISCLOSURES IN THE TDS DO NOT ELIMINATE SELLER'S OBLIGATIONS, IF ANY, UNDER PARAGRAPH 10.

12. PROPERTY DISCLOSURES: When applicable to the Property and required by law, Seller shall provide to Buyer, at Seller's expense, the following disclosures and information. Buyer shall then, within the time specified in paragraph 26B(5) and (6), investigate the disclosures and information and provide written notice to Seller of any item disapproved pursuant to A-C and E1(b) below.

   A. GEOLOGIC/SEISMIC HAZARD ZONES DISCLOSURE: If the Property is located in a Special Studies Zone (SSZ) (Public Resources Code §§2621-2625), Seismic Hazard Zone (SHZ) (Public Resources Code §§2690-2699.6), or in a locally designated geological, seismic, or other hazard zone(s) or area(s) where disclosure is required by law, Seller shall, within the time specified in paragraph 26B(7), disclose in writing to Buyer this fact(s) and any other information required by law. (GEOLOGIC, SEISMIC AND FLOOD HAZARD DISCLOSURE (CAR FORM GFD-14) SHALL SATISFY THIS REQUIREMENT.) Construction or development of any structure may be restricted. Disclosure of SSZs and SHZs is required only where the maps, or information contained in the maps, are "reasonably available" as defined in Public Resources Code §§2621.9(c)(1) and 2694(c)(1).

   B. SPECIAL FLOOD HAZARD AREAS: If the Property is located in a Special Flood Hazard Area designated by the Federal Emergency Management Agency (FEMA), Seller shall, within the time specified in paragraph 26B(7), disclose this fact in writing to Buyer. (GEOLOGIC, SEISMIC AND FLOOD HAZARD DISCLOSURE (CAR FORM GFD-14) SHALL SATISFY THIS REQUIREMENT.) Government regulations may impose building restrictions and requirements which may substantially impact and limit construction and remodeling of improvements. Flood insurance may be required by lender.

   C. STATE FIRE RESPONSIBILITY AREAS: If the Property is located in a State Fire Responsibility Area, Seller shall, within the time specified in paragraph 26B(7), disclose this fact in writing to Buyer (Public Resources Code §4136). Disclosure may be made in the Real Estate Transfer Disclosure Statement (CAR FORM TDS-14). Government regulations may impose building restrictions and requirements which may substantially impact and limit construction and remodeling of improvements. Disclosure of these areas is required only if the Seller has actual knowledge that the Property is located in such an area or if maps of such areas have been provided to the county assessor's office.

   D. MELLO-ROOS: Seller shall make a good faith effort to obtain a disclosure notice from any local agencies which levy on the Property a special tax pursuant to the Mello-Roos Community Facilities Act, and shall deliver to Buyer any such notice made available by those agencies.

   E. EARTHQUAKE SAFETY:

      1. PRE-1960 PROPERTIES: If the Property was built prior to 1960, and contains ONE-TO-FOUR DWELLING UNITS of conventional light frame construction, Seller shall, unless exempt, within the time specified in paragraph 26B(7), provide to Buyer: (a) a copy of "The Homeowner's Guide to Earthquake Safety," and (b) written disclosure of known seismic deficiencies (Government Code §§8897-8897.5).

      2. PRE-1975 PROPERTIES: If the Property was built prior to 1975, and contains RESIDENTIAL, COMMERCIAL, OR OTHER STRUCTURES constructed of masonry or precast concrete, with wood frame floors or roofs, Seller shall, unless exempt, within the time specified in paragraph 26B(7), provide to Buyer a copy of "The Commercial Property Owner's Guide to Earthquake Safety" (Government Code §§8893-8893.5).

      3. ALL PROPERTIES: If the booklets described in paragraphs E1 and E2 are not required, Buyer is advised that they are available and contain important information that may be useful for ALL TYPES OF PROPERTY (Civil Code §§2079.8 and 2079.9).

   F. SMOKE DETECTOR(S): State law requires that residences be equipped with operable smoke detector(s). Local ordinances may have additional requirements. Unless exempt, Seller shall, prior to close of escrow, provide to Buyer a written statement of compliance and any other documents required, in accordance with applicable state and local law. (SMOKE DETECTOR STATEMENT OF COMPLIANCE (CAR FORM SDC-11) SHALL SATISFY THE STATE PORTION OF THIS REQUIREMENT.) Additional smoke detector(s), if required, shall be installed by Seller at Seller's expense prior to close of escrow.

   G. ENVIRONMENTAL HAZARDS BOOKLET: The booklet, "Environmental Hazards: Guide for Homeowners and Buyers," is published by the California Department ___Estate, and contains information that may be ___ful for ALL TYPES OF PROPERTY (Civil C___ §§079.7).

116

to fix them. Unless the property is being purchased "as is," any defect that the seller doesn't intend to repair as a part of the sale should be specifically referenced in the purchase contract.

    Paragraph 12 (Property Disclosures) incorporates a number of disclosures into the contract. When applicable to the property, a seller must provide the buyer with the disclosure information as required by law within the time frame specified in paragraph 26. The buyer then has the period of time specified in paragraph 26 to investigate disclosures and disapprove any item. Items A through C apply if the property is located within a Geologic/Seismic Hazard Zone, a Special Flood Hazard Area, or a State Fire Responsibility Area. If a property is located in one of these areas, there may be restrictions on construction, development, and remodeling. A lender will probably require flood insurance if the property is in a flood hazard zone. For information about Special Flood Hazard

FORM ~~...~~ ...pose bu~~...~~ ...ch may su~~...~~ ...ent constru~~...~~
remodeling or ~~...~~ ...osure of these areas is requir~~...~~ ...actual knowledge that the Prope~~...~~ ...ty is located in such an area o~~...~~
if maps of such areas have been provided to the county assessor's o~~...~~

D. MELLO-ROOS: Seller shall make a good faith effort to obtain a disclosure notice from any local agencies which levy on the Property a special tax pursuant to the Mello-Roos Community Facilities Act, and shall deliver to Buyer any such notice made available by those agencies.

E. EARTHQUAKE SAFETY:
1. PRE-1960 PROPERTIES: If the Property was built prior to 1960, and contains ONE-TO-FOUR DWELLING UNITS of conventional light frame construction, Seller shall, unless exempt, within the time specified in paragraph 26B(7), provide to Buyer: (a) a copy of "The Homeowner's Guide to Earthquake Safety," and (b) written disclosure of known seismic deficiencies (Government Code §§8897-8897.5).
2. PRE-1975 PROPERTIES: If the Property was built prior to 1975, and contains RESIDENTIAL, COMMERCIAL, OR OTHER STRUCTURES constructed of masonry or precast concrete, with wood frame floors or roofs, Seller shall, unless exempt, within the time specified in paragraph 26B(7), provide to Buyer a copy of "The Commercial Property Owner's Guide to Earthquake Safety" (Government Code §§8893-8893.5).
3. ALL PROPERTIES: If the booklets described in paragraphs E1 and E2 are not required, Buyer is advised that they are available and contain important information that may be useful for ALL TYPES OF PROPERTY (Civil Code §§2079.8 and 2079.9).

F. SMOKE DETECTOR(S): State law requires that residences be equipped with operable smoke detector(s). Local ordinances may have additional requirements. Unless exempt, Seller shall, prior to close of escrow, provide to Buyer a written statement of compliance and any other documents required, in accordance with applicable state and local law. (SMOKE DETECTOR STATEMENT OF COMPLIANCE (CAR FORM SDC-11) SHALL SATISFY THE STATE PORTION OF THIS REQUIREMENT.) Additional smoke detector(s), if required, shall be installed by Seller at Seller's expense prior to close of escrow.

G. ENVIRONMENTAL HAZARDS BOOKLET: The booklet, "Environmental Hazards: Guide for Homeowners and Buyers," is published by the California Department of Real Estate, and contains information that may be useful for ALL TYPES OF PROPERTY (Civil Code §2079.7).

H. LEAD BASED PAINT: Buyers obtaining new FHA-insured financing on residential properties constructed prior to 1978 are required to sign a lead paint disclosure form. (NOTICE TO PURCHASERS OF HOUSING CONSTRUCTED BEFORE 1978 (CAR FORM LPD-14) SHALL SATISFY THIS REQUIREMENT.)

I. OTHER: _____

13. GOVERNMENTAL COMPLIANCE: Seller shall promptly disclose to Buyer any improvements, additions, alterations, or repairs ("Improvements") made by Seller or known to Seller to have been made without required governmental permits, final inspections, and approvals. In addition, Seller represents that Seller has no knowledge of any notice of violations of City, County, State, or Federal building, zoning, fire, or health laws, codes, statutes, ordinances, regulations, or rules filed or issued against the Property. If Seller receives notice of any of the above violations prior to close of escrow, Seller shall immediately notify Buyer in writing. Buyer shall, within the time specified in paragraph 26B(5), provide written notice to Seller of any items disapproved.

14. RETROFIT: Compliance with any minimum mandatory government retrofit standards, including but not limited to energy and utility efficiency requirements and proof of compliance, shall be paid for by ☐ Buyer, ☐ Seller.

15. FIXTURES: All existing fixtures and fittings that are attached to the Property or for which special openings have been made are INCLUDED IN THE PURCHASE PRICE (unless excluded below) and are to be transferred free of liens. These include, but are not limited to, electrical, lighting, plumbing and heating fixtures, fireplace inserts, solar systems, built-in appliances, screens, awnings, shutters, window coverings, attached floor coverings, television antennas/satellite dishes and related equipment, private integrated telephone systems, air coolers/conditioners, pool/spa equipment, water softeners (if owned by Seller), security systems/alarms (if owned by Seller), garage door openers/remote controls, attached fireplace equipment, mailbox, in-ground landscaping including trees/shrubs, and

ITEMS EXCLUDED: _____ .

16. PERSONAL PROPERTY: The following items of personal property, free of liens and without warranty of condition (unless provided in paragraph 10A) or fitness for use, are included: _____

_____

17. HOME WARRANTY PLANS: Buyer and Seller are informed that home warranty plans are available. These plans may provide additional protection and benefit to Buyer and Seller. Broker(s) do not endorse, approve, or recommend any particular company or program. Buyer and Seller elect (Check ONLY ONE):
☐ To purchase a home warranty plan with the following optional coverage _____, at a cost not to exceed $_____, to be paid by _____, and to be issued by _____ Company,
OR
☐ Buyer and Seller elect NOT to purchase a home warranty plan.

18. SEPTIC SYSTEM: (If initialled by all parties.)
Buyer's Initials   Seller's Initials
_____/_____   _____/_____

☐ Buyer, ☐ Seller shall pay to have septic system pumped and certified. Evidence of compliance shall be provided to the other party before close of escrow.
☐ Buyer, ☐ Seller to pay for sewer connection if required by local ordinance.

	OFFICE USE ONLY
Buyer and Seller acknowledge receipt of copy of this page, which constitutes Page 3 of _____ Pages.	Reviewed by Broker or Designee _____
Buyer's Initials (_____) (_____) Seller's Initials (_____) (_____)	Date _____

BUYER'S COPY

REAL ESTATE PURCHASE CONTRACT AND RECEIPT FOR DEPOSIT (DLF-14 PAGE 3 OF 6)

M-PM-7/93

117

Areas, contact the Federal Emergency Management Agency (FEMA), (800) 638-6620. For information about Geologic/Seismic Hazards Zones, contact the California Department of Conservation's Division of Mines and Geology, (213) 620-3560 or (916) 445-5716. To find out if a property is located within a State Fire Responsibility Area, call the local fire department or the county assessor's office. Items D through H are disclosures regarding Mello-Roos assessments, earthquake safety, smoke detectors, environmental hazards, and lead-based paint. Item I (Other) provides a space to include other disclosures/ordinances that may apply.

The Governmental Compliance section requires sellers to disclose any improvements to the property made without necessary permits, inspections, or final approval. Sellers are also required to give written notification to the buyers of any known code violations. The buyers have the right to disapprove any such notice from the seller within the time specified in paragraph 26.

☐

Property Address: _____ , 19____

19. PEST CONTROL: (If initialled by all parties.)
Buyer's Initials   Seller's Initials

_____/_____   _____/_____

A. Seller shall, within the time specified in paragraph 26B(8), provide to Buyer a current written Wood Destroying Pests and Organisms Inspection Report. Report shall be at the expense of ☐ Buyer, ☐ Seller, to be performed by _____ , a registered Structural Pest Control Company, covering the main building and **(If checked):**
    ☐ detached garage(s) or carport(s); ☐ the following other structures on the Property: _____ .

B. If requested by Buyer or Seller, the report shall separately identify each recommendation for corrective work as follows:
"Section 1": Infestation or infection which is evident.
"Section 2": Conditions that are present which are deemed likely to lead to infestation or infection.

C. If no infestation or infection by wood destroying pests or organisms is found, the report shall include a written Certification that on the inspection date no evidence of active infestation was found (Business and Professions Code §8519(a).)

D. Work recommended to correct conditions described in "Section 1" shall be at the expense of ☐ Buyer, ☐ Seller.

E. Work recommended to correct conditions described in "Section 2," **if requested by Buyer,** shall be at the expense of ☐ Buyer, ☐ Seller.

F. Work to be performed at Seller's expense may be performed by Seller or through others, provided that: (a) all required permits and final inspections are obtained, and (b) upon completion of repairs a written Certification is issued by a registered Structural Pest Control Company showing that the inspected property "is now free of evidence of active infestation or infection." (Business and Professions Code §8519(b).)

G. If inspection of inaccessible areas is recommended in the report, Buyer has the option to accept and approve the report, or request in writing within 5 (or ☐ _____) calendar days of receipt of the report that further inspection be made. BUYER'S FAILURE TO NOTIFY SELLER IN WRITING OF SUCH REQUEST SHALL CONCLUSIVELY BE CONSIDERED APPROVAL OF THE REPORT. If further inspection recommends "Section 1" and/or "Section 2" corrective work, such work, and the inspection, entry, and closing of the inaccessible areas, shall be at the expense of the respective party designated in paragraphs (A), (D) and/or (E). If no infestation or infection is found, the inspection, entry, and closing of the inaccessible areas shall be at the expense of Buyer.

H. Inspections, corrective work, and certification under this paragraph shall not include roof coverings. Read paragraph 9A concerning inspection of roof coverings.

I. Work shall be performed in a skillful manner with materials of comparable quality, and shall include repair of leaking shower stalls and pans and replacement of tiles and other materials removed for repair. It is understood that exact restoration of appearance or cosmetic items following all such work is not included.

J. Funds for work agreed in writing to be performed after close of escrow shall be held in escrow and disbursed upon receipt of a written Certification that the inspected property "is now free of evidence of active infestation or infection." (Business and Professions Code §8519(b).)

K. Other: _____ .

20. SALE OF BUYER'S PROPERTY: (If initialled by all parties.)
Buyer's Initials   Seller's Initials

_____/_____   _____/_____

This agreement is contingent upon the close of escrow of Buyer's property described as _____ situated in _____ . Buyer's property is: ☐ Listed with _____ Company, ☐ In escrow No. _____ with _____ Company, scheduled to close escrow on _____ , 19____ .

A. (Check ONE:) ☐ Seller shall have the right to continue to offer the Property for sale, ☐ Seller shall NOT have the right to continue to offer the Property for sale (other than for back-up offers), ☐ Seller shall NOT have the right to continue to offer the Property for sale (other than for back-up offers) until _____ calendar days after acceptance of the offer.

B. If Seller has the right to continue to offer the Property for sale (other than for back-up offers) and Seller accepts another offer, Seller shall give Buyer written notice to (1) remove this contingency in writing and (2) comply with the following additional requirements _____ .
_____ .
If Buyer fails to complete those actions within _____ hours or _____ calendar days after receipt of such Notice from Seller, then this agreement and any escrow shall terminate and the deposit (less costs incurred) shall be returned to Buyer.

C. If Seller does not give the Notice above and Buyer's property does not close escrow by the date specified in paragraph 3 for close of escrow of this Property, then either Seller or Buyer may cancel this agreement and any escrow by giving the other party written notice of cancellation, and the Buyer's deposit (less costs incurred) shall be returned to Buyer.

21. CANCELLATION OF PRIOR SALE/BACK-UP OFFER: (If initialled by all parties.)
Buyer's Initials   Seller's Initials

_____/_____   _____/_____

Buyer understands that Seller has entered into one or more contracts to sell the Property to a different buyer(s). The parties to any prior sale may mutually agree to modify or amend the terms of that sale(s). This agreement is contingent upon the written cancellation of the previous purchase and sale agreement(s) and any related escrow(s).
(Check ONLY ONE of the following.)
~~...ON OF PRIOR SALE: If writt~~ ~~previous agreement(s) is not rec~~
~~...ller may can~~ ~~...giving the other pa~~

118

Paragraph 14, Retrofit, applies if compliance with government retrofit standards is required. Check the appropriate box to indicate if buyer or seller will pay any associated costs.

Fixtures, paragraph 15, includes all items permanently attached to the property as opposed to personal property, which is movable. Fixtures excluded from the sale are listed after "Items Excluded." If the sellers are excluding the dining room chandelier, for example, include a provision for the sellers to replace the chandelier by close of escrow, or to credit you money in escrow so that you can buy a replacement.

Under Personal Property, list unattached items that are included in the sale, such as freestanding kitchen appliances, a fireplace screen, and swimming pool equipment. Refrigerators, freezers, washers, and dryers are sometimes included. Buyers usually ask for what they want; sellers can always say no, in the form of a until _____ _____ ~~the offer.~~

B. If Seller has the rig~~____~~ _____ue to offer the Property for sale (other ~~_____~~ ~~_rs)~~ and Seller accepts another offer, Seller shall give Buyer written notice to (1) remove this contingency in writing and (2) comply with the following additional requirements_____

_____ .

If Buyer fails to complete those actions within _____ hours or _____ calendar days after receipt of such Notice from Seller, then this agreement and any escrow shall terminate and the deposit (less costs incurred) shall be returned to Buyer.

C. If Seller does not give the Notice above and Buyer's property does not close escrow by the date specified in paragraph 3 for close of escrow of this Property, then either Seller or Buyer may cancel this agreement and any escrow by giving the other party written notice of cancellation, and the Buyer's deposit (less costs incurred) shall be returned to Buyer.

21. CANCELLATION OF PRIOR SALE/BACK-UP OFFER: (If initialled by all parties.)

Buyer's initials _____   Seller's initials _____
_____/_____   _____/_____

Buyer understands that Seller has entered into one or more contracts to sell the Property to a different buyer(s). The parties to any prior sale may mutually agree to modify or amend the terms of that sale(s). This agreement is contingent upon the written cancellation of the previous purchase and sale agreement(s) and any related escrow(s).
(Check ONLY ONE of the following.)

☐ CANCELLATION OF PRIOR SALE: If written cancellation of the previous agreement(s) is not received on or before _____, 19____, then either Buyer or Seller may cancel this agreement and any escrow by giving the other party written notice of cancellation. Buyer's deposit, less costs incurred, shall then be returned to Buyer.

☐ BACK-UP OFFER: This is a back-up offer in back-up position No. _____. BUYER'S DEPOSIT CHECK SHALL BE HELD UNCASHED until a copy of the written cancellation(s) signed by all parties to the prior sale(s) is provided to Buyer. Until Buyer receives a copy of such cancellation(s), Buyer may cancel this agreement by providing written notice to Seller. Buyer's deposit shall then be returned to Buyer. AS RELATES TO A BACK-UP OFFER, TIME PERIODS IN THIS AGREEMENT WHICH ARE STATED AS A NUMBER OF DAYS SHALL BEGIN ON THE DATE SELLER GIVES TO BUYER WRITTEN NOTICE THAT ANY PRIOR CONTRACT(S) HAS BEEN CANCELLED. IF CLOSE OF ESCROW OR ANY OTHER EVENT IS SHOWN AS A SPECIFIC DATE, THAT DATE SHALL NOT BE EXTENDED UNLESS BUYER AND SELLER SPECIFICALLY AGREE IN WRITING.

22. COURT CONFIRMATION: (If initialled by all parties.)

Buyer's initials _____   Seller's initials _____
_____/_____   _____/_____

This agreement is contingent upon court confirmation on or before _____, 19____. The court may allow open, competitive bidding, resulting in the Property being sold to the highest bidder. Buyer has been advised to be in court when the offer is considered for confirmation. Court confirmation may be required in a probate, conservatorship, guardianship, receivership, bankruptcy, or other proceeding. Buyer understands that the Property may continue to be marketed by Broker(s) and others, and that Broker(s) and others may represent other competitive bidders prior to and at the court confirmation. If court confirmation is not obtained by date shown above, Buyer may cancel this agreement by giving written notice of cancellation to Seller.

23. NOTICES: Notices given pursuant to this agreement shall, unless otherwise required by law, be deemed delivered to Buyer when personally received by Buyer or _____, who is authorized to receive it for Buyer, or to Seller when personally received by Seller or _____, who is authorized to receive it for Seller. Delivery may be in person, by mail, or facsimile.

24. TAX WITHHOLDING:

A. Under the Foreign Investment in Real Property Tax Act (FIRPTA), IRC §1445, every Buyer must, unless an exemption applies, deduct and withhold 10% of the gross sales price from Seller's proceeds and send it to the Internal Revenue Service, if the Seller is a "foreign person" under that statute.

B. In addition, under California Revenue and Taxation Code §§18805 and 26131, every Buyer must, unless an exemption applies, deduct and withhold 3-1/3% of the gross sales price from Seller's proceeds and send it to the Franchise Tax Board if the Seller has a last known address outside of California or if the Seller's proceeds will be paid to a financial intermediary of the Seller.

C. Penalties may be imposed on a responsible party for non-compliance with the requirements of these statutes and related regulations. Seller and Buyer agree to execute and deliver any instrument, affidavit, statement, or instruction reasonably necessary to carry out these requirements, and to withholding of tax under those statutes if required. (SELLER'S AFFIDAVIT OF NON-FOREIGN STATUS AND/OR CALIFORNIA RESIDENCY (CAR FORM AS-14), OR BUYER'S AFFIDAVIT (CAR FORM AB-11), IF APPLICABLE, SHALL SATISFY THESE REQUIREMENTS.)

25. RISK OF LOSS: Except as otherwise provided in this agreement, all risk of loss to the Property which occurs after the offer is accepted shall be borne by Seller until either the title has been transferred, or possession has been given to Buyer, whichever occurs first. Any damage totalling 1.0 (one) % or less of the purchase price shall be repaired by Seller in accordance with paragraph 10, if applicable. If the land or improvements to the Property are destroyed or materially damaged prior to transfer of title in an amount exceeding 1.0 (one) % of the purchase price, then Buyer shall have the option to either terminate this agreement and recover the full deposit or purchase the Property in its then present condition. Any expenses paid by Buyer or Seller for credit reports, appraisals, title examination, or inspections of any kind shall remain that party's responsibility. If Buyer elects to purchase the Property and the loss is covered by insurance, Seller shall assign to Buyer all insurance proceeds covering the loss. If transfer of title and possession do not occur at the same time, BUYER AND SELLER ARE ADVISED TO SEEK ADVICE OF THEIR INSURANCE ADVISORS as to the insurance consequences thereof.

Buyer and Seller acknowledge receipt of copy of this page, which constitutes Page 4 of _____ Pages.

Buyer's Initials (_____) (_____) Seller's Initials (_____) (_____)

OFFICE USE ONLY
Reviewed by Broker or Designee _____
Date _____

M-PM-7/93

BUYER'S COPY
REAL ESTATE PURCHASE CONTRACT AND RECEIPT FOR DEPOSIT (DLF-14 PAGE 4 OF 6)

119

counteroffer, if they need to take the items requested with them. Beware of the seller who wants to include old freestanding appliances in order to avoid having to move them. The buyer should specify, in writing, that the seller remove unwanted items from the property by close of escrow. Items of personal property are usually included without warranty.

The Home Warranty Plans clause informs the buyer and seller that home protection plans are available and that they may provide additional protection. Buyers and sellers should direct any questions they might have about coverage directly to the protection plan company. If a protection plan is to be a part of the agreement, fill in the spaces provided for: optional coverage, the cost of the plan, who is to pay for the plan, and the company name. If the company name is not known at contract time, enter "to follow" in that space. If a protection plan is not to be a part of the contract, the appropriate box should be checked.

The Septic System clause is included if it's separately initialed by both parties. This clause specifies who pays to have a septic system pumped and certified, and who pays for a sewer connection if this is required. Buyers purchasing a home on a septic system should find out if the local municipality has any rules or regulations that might restrict future use of the system.

The Pest Control clause, paragraph 19, is included in the contract if it's separately initialed by both the buyer and seller in the spaces provided. The clause requires the seller to provide a current Wood Destroying Pests and Organisms Inspection Report within the time specified in paragraph 26. It's almost always advisable to have a property you're purchasing inspected for wood destroying pests. Who will pay for the report, the name of the licensed structural pest control operator, additional structures to be inspected, and who will be responsible for the Section I and Section II work recommended should be indicated in the spaces and boxes provided. Paragraph 19 allows the sellers to have repair work completed by themselves or others so long as required permits and final inspections are obtained and upon completion of repairs, a written Certification (Standard Notice of Work Completed and Not Completed) is issued by a licensed structural pest control company stating the property is free of active infestation. The clause also details who will pay for further inspections and recommended repair work. The cost to complete further inspections, make recommended repairs, and close up inaccessible areas will be paid by whoever is designated to pay for Section I and Section II work in subsections D and E of paragraph 19. If no infestation is found, the inspection and closing of inaccessible areas shall be at the expense of the buyer.

Paragraph 19 does not specifically require that recommended structural pest control work be completed by close of escrow. Some lenders require a Notice of Work Completed and Not Completed from a licensed structural pest control operator indicating that the property is free of infestation before close of escrow. If your lender will require this, include a provision for the seller to provide you with a completion notice by filling in the "Other" space (subsection K of paragraph 19). Some lenders will allow structural pest control repairs to be completed after close of escrow, with funds held in the escrow account, to be released when the escrow holder receives a completion notice indicating the property is free of infestation. Often the lender will want the buyer or seller to leave surplus funds in the escrow account pending completion of the work. However, paragraph 19 doesn't specify how surplus funds held in the escrow account will be disbursed after the work is completed. This should be clarified in subsection K. Frequently lenders won't allow funds to be held for pest control work, even though there's insufficient time to complete the work by closing. In this case, the lender may allow a credit for the amount of the work, but the credit may have to be designated as a credit for the buyer's nonrecurring closing costs. Check with your lender before you write an offer to purchase to find out what kind of restrictions, if any, the lender has regarding structural pest control repair work.

The "Other" section of the pest control clause can be used to propose alternatives such as, "Buyer waives the right to have a Wood Destroying Pests and Organisms Inspection" or, "Buyer accepts seller's existing pest control report completed by [a specific termite company], on [a specific date]; seller to pay for work recommended in this report." The buyer might be willing to take the property in "as is" condition with respect to pest control work, subject to reviewing and approving a current pest control report. See Chapter 8 for more information about Wood Destroying Pest and Organisms ("termite") reports and repairs.

When separately initialed by the buyer and seller, the "Sale of Buyer's Property" clause makes the contract contingent upon the close of escrow of the buyer's property which should be described in the spaces provided. The listing and escrow information can be included when applicable. The appropriate box should be checked in item A to indicate whether or not the sellers have the right to continue to offer their property for sale. If they do have this right, item B under paragraph 20 allows the sellers to deliver notice to the buyers that the sellers have accepted another offer subject to the cancellation of this contract. The buyers then have the time period specified (usually 72 hours, or 3 days, but this is negotiable) within which to remove the sale contingency, and fulfill any additional requirements specified in subsection 2 of 20B. Additional requirements might include increasing the deposit amount and providing confirmation that the buyers' home is sold, or that the buyers have secured alternate financing. If the buyers fail to perform, the sellers can cancel the agreement and proceed with the other offer. The buyers' deposit would be returned in this case. Buyers who don't want item B to be a part of the agreement should indicate that paragraph 20B is deleted from the contract. This can be included in paragraph 34 (Other Terms and Conditions). Most sellers will want 20B to be a part of the contract.

121

Paragraph 21 (the name of this clause in the CAR contract has been changed to "Cancellation of Prior Sale/Backup Offer") is included in the contract if it's separately initialed by the buyer and seller. This paragraph should be included if the sellers have already accepted another offer(s) that will take precedence over this one. A space is provided to indicate the backup position (backup offer number 1, 2, and so on). A date by which written cancellation of the prior agreement must be received should be filled in at the appropriate space. If a cancellation notion is not received by that date, either the buyer or the seller may cancel this agreement. The buyers' deposit check is held uncashed, and the buyers are free to withdraw their offer until the sellers give written notice to the buyers that the backup offer is in primary position. The day that the buyers receive such notification is deemed the acceptance date, and time periods for performance in the contract commence as of that date.

The Court Confirmation clause is included if it's separately initialed by buyer and seller. This clause makes the agreement contingent upon court confirmation on or before the date included in the spaces provided. This clause also puts the buyers on notice that the property will continue to be marketed until the sale is

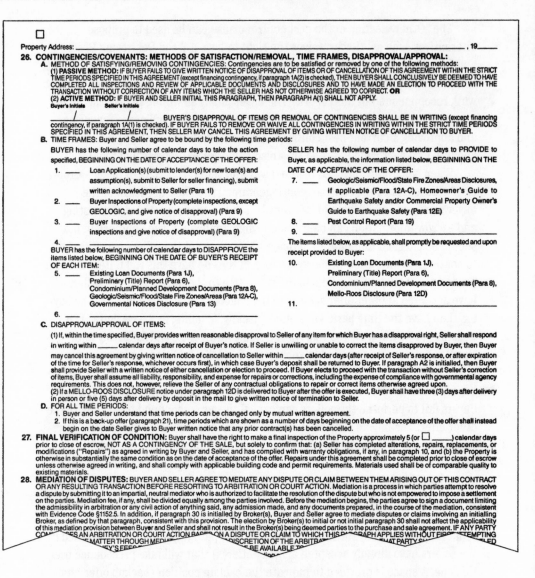

☐
Property Address: _____   _____ , 19____

26. CONTINGENCIES/COVENANTS: METHODS OF SATISFACTION/REMOVAL, TIME FRAMES, DISAPPROVAL/APPROVAL:

A. METHOD OF SATISFYING/REMOVING CONTINGENCIES: Contingencies are to be satisfied or removed by one of the following methods:
(1) **PASSIVE METHOD:** IF BUYER FAILS TO GIVE WRITTEN NOTICE OF DISAPPROVAL OF ITEMS OR OF CANCELLATION OF THIS AGREEMENT WITHIN THE STRICT TIME PERIODS SPECIFIED IN THIS AGREEMENT (except financing contingency, if paragraph 1A(2) is checked), THEN BUYER SHALL CONCLUSIVELY BE DEEMED TO HAVE COMPLETED ALL INSPECTIONS AND REVIEW OF APPLICABLE DOCUMENTS AND DISCLOSURES AND TO HAVE MADE AN ELECTION TO PROCEED WITH THE TRANSACTION WITHOUT CORRECTION OF ANY ITEMS WHICH THE SELLER HAS NOT OTHERWISE AGREED TO CORRECT. **OR**
(2) **ACTIVE METHOD:** IF BUYER AND SELLER INITIAL THIS PARAGRAPH, THEN PARAGRAPH A(1) SHALL NOT APPLY.

Buyer's Initials   Seller's Initials

_____/_____   _____/_____   BUYER'S DISAPPROVAL OF ITEMS OR REMOVAL OF CONTINGENCIES SHALL BE IN WRITING (except financing contingency, if paragraph 1A(1) is checked). IF BUYER FAILS TO REMOVE OR WAIVE ALL CONTINGENCIES IN WRITING WITHIN THE STRICT TIME PERIODS SPECIFIED IN THIS AGREEMENT, THEN SELLER MAY CANCEL THIS AGREEMENT BY GIVING WRITTEN NOTICE OF CANCELLATION TO BUYER.

B. TIME FRAMES: Buyer and Seller agree to be bound by the following time periods:

BUYER has the following number of calendar days to take the action specified, BEGINNING ON THE DATE OF ACCEPTANCE OF THE OFFER:

1. _____ Loan Application(s) (submit to lender(s) for new loan(s) and assumption(s), submit to Seller for seller financing), submit written acknowledgment to Seller (Para 1l)

2. _____ Buyer Inspections of Property (complete inspections, except GEOLOGIC, and give notice of disapproval) (Para 9)

3. _____ Buyer Inspections of Property (complete GEOLOGIC inspections and give notice of disapproval) (Para 9)

4. _____

BUYER has the following number of calendar days to DISAPPROVE the items listed below, BEGINNING ON THE DATE OF BUYER'S RECEIPT OF EACH ITEM:

5. _____ Existing Loan Documents (Para 1J),
Preliminary (Title) Report (Para 6),
Condominium/Planned Development Documents (Para 8),
Geologic/Seismic/Flood/State Fire Zones/Areas (Para 12A-C),
Governmental Notices Disclosure (Para 13)

6. _____

SELLER has the following number of calendar days to PROVIDE to Buyer, as applicable, the information listed below, BEGINNING ON THE DATE OF ACCEPTANCE OF THE OFFER:

7. _____ Geologic/Seismic/Flood/State Fire Zones/Areas Disclosures, if applicable (Para 12A-C), Homeowner's Guide to Earthquake Safety and/or Commercial Property Owner's Guide to Earthquake Safety (Para 12E)

8. _____ Pest Control Report (Para 19)

9. _____

The items listed below, as applicable, shall promptly be requested and upon receipt provided to Buyer:

10. _____ Existing Loan Documents (Para 1J),
Preliminary (Title) Report (Para 6),
Condominium/Planned Development Documents (Para 8),
Mello-Roos Disclosure (Para 12D)

11. _____

C. DISAPPROVAL/APPROVAL OF ITEMS:
(1) If, within the time specified, Buyer provides written reasonable disapproval to Seller of any item for which Buyer has a disapproval right, Seller shall respond in writing within _____ calendar days after receipt of Buyer's notice. If Seller is unwilling or unable to correct the items disapproved by Buyer, then Buyer may cancel this agreement by giving written notice of cancellation to Seller within _____ calendar days (after receipt of Seller's response, or after expiration of the time for Seller's response, whichever occurs first), in which case Buyer's deposit shall be returned to Buyer. If paragraph A2 is initialed, then Buyer shall provide Seller with a written notice of either cancellation or election to proceed. If Buyer elects to proceed with the transaction without Seller's correction of items, Buyer shall assume all liability, responsibility, and expense for repairs or corrections, including the expense of compliance with governmental agency requirements. This does not, however, relieve the Seller of any contractual obligations to repair or correct items otherwise agreed upon.
(2) If a MELLO-ROOS DISCLOSURE notice under paragraph 12D is delivered to Buyer after the offer is executed, Buyer shall have three (3) days after delivery in person or five (5) days after delivery by deposit in the mail to give written notice of termination to Seller.

D. FOR ALL TIME PERIODS:
1. Buyer and Seller understand that time periods can be changed only by mutual written agreement.
2. If this is a back-up offer (paragraph 21), time periods which are shown as a number of days beginning on the date of acceptance of the offer shall instead begin on the date Seller gives to Buyer written notice that any prior contract(s) has been cancelled.

27. FINAL VERIFICATION OF CONDITION: Buyer shall have the right to make a final inspection of the Property approximately 5 (or ☐ _____) calendar days prior to close of escrow, NOT AS A CONTINGENCY OF THE SALE, but solely to confirm that: (a) Seller has completed alterations, repairs, replacements, or modifications ("Repairs") as agreed in writing by Buyer and Seller, and has complied with warranty obligations, if any, in paragraph 10, and (b) the Property is otherwise in substantially the same condition as on the date of acceptance of the offer. Repairs under this agreement shall be completed prior to close of escrow unless otherwise agreed in writing, and shall comply with applicable building code and permit requirements. Materials used shall be of comparable quality to existing materials.

28. MEDIATION OF DISPUTES: BUYER AND SELLER AGREE TO MEDIATE ANY DISPUTE OR CLAIM BETWEEN THEM ARISING OUT OF THIS CONTRACT OR ANY RESULTING TRANSACTION BEFORE RESORTING TO ARBITRATION OR COURT ACTION. Mediation is a process in which parties attempt to resolve a dispute by submitting it to an impartial, neutral mediator who is authorized to facilitate the resolution of the dispute but who is not empowered to impose a settlement on the parties. Mediation fee, if any, shall be divided equally among the parties involved. Before the mediation begins, the parties agree to sign a document limiting the admissibility in arbitration or any civil action of anything said, any admission made, and any documents prepared, in the course of the mediation, consistent with Evidence Code §1152.5. In addition, if paragraph 30 is initialled by Broker(s), Buyer and Seller agree to mediate disputes or claims involving an initialling Broker, as defined by that paragraph, consistent with this provision. The election by Broker(s) to initial or not initial paragraph 30 shall not affect the applicability of this mediation provision between Buyer and Seller and shall not result in the Broker(s) being deemed parties to the purchase and sale agreement. IF ANY PARTY COM____CES AN ARBITRATION OR COURT ACTION BAS__ ON A DISPUTE OR CLAIM TO WHICH THIS P_____APH APPLIES WITHOUT FIR_____TTEMPTING _____E MATTER THROUGH MEDI_____, ____DISCRETION OF THE ARBITR_____AT PARTY S____ ____TLED _____EY'S FEE_____BE AVAILABLE T_____

court confirmed, and that the sale is subject to open, competitive bidding in court.

Paragraph 23 clarifies how and when notices pertaining to this agreement will be made. Space is provided to authorize the buyer's and seller's agents to receive notices on behalf of their respective clients.

Federal and state tax withholding requirements are explained in paragraph 24. See Chapter 2 for more information.

Paragraph 25 explains who's responsible if the property is materially damaged or destroyed. Briefly, the seller is responsible until title to the property transfers to the buyer. If the property is damaged before close of escrow in an amount that exceeds one percent of the purchase price, the buyer can terminate the purchase agreement.

requirement... Seller o... ...correct...
(2) If a MELLO... notice under paragraph 12b... ...offer is executed, Buyer s... ...three (3) days after delivery... in person or five (5) days after delivery by deposit in the mail to give w... or termination to Seller.

D. FOR ALL TIME PERIODS:
   1. Buyer and Seller understand that time periods can be changed only by mutual written agreement.
   2. If this is a back-up offer (paragraph 21), time periods which are shown as a number of days beginning on the date of acceptance of the offer shall instead begin on the date Seller gives to Buyer written notice that any prior contract(s) has been cancelled.

27. FINAL VERIFICATION OF CONDITION: Buyer shall have the right to make a final inspection of the Property approximately 5 (or ☐ _____) calendar days prior to close of escrow, NOT AS A CONTINGENCY OF THE SALE, but solely to confirm that: (a) Seller has completed alterations, repairs, replacements, or modifications ("Repairs") as agreed in writing by Buyer and Seller, and has complied with warranty obligations, if any, in paragraph 10, and (b) the Property is otherwise in substantially the same condition as on the date of acceptance of the offer. Repairs under this agreement shall be completed prior to close of escrow unless otherwise agreed in writing, and shall comply with applicable building code and permit requirements. Materials used shall be of comparable quality to existing materials.

28. MEDIATION OF DISPUTES: BUYER AND SELLER AGREE TO MEDIATE ANY DISPUTE OR CLAIM BETWEEN THEM ARISING OUT OF THIS CONTRACT OR ANY RESULTING TRANSACTION BEFORE RESORTING TO ARBITRATION OR COURT ACTION. Mediation is a process in which parties attempt to resolve a dispute by submitting it to an impartial, neutral mediator who is authorized to facilitate the resolution of the dispute but who is not empowered to impose a settlement on the parties. Mediation fee, if any, shall be divided equally among the parties involved. Before the mediation begins, the parties agree to sign a document limiting the admissibility in arbitration or any civil action of anything said, any admission made, and any documents prepared, in the course of the mediation, consistent with Evidence Code §1152.5. In addition, if paragraph 30 is initialled by Broker(s), Buyer and Seller agree to mediate disputes or claims involving an initialling Broker, as defined by that paragraph, consistent with this provision. The election by Broker(s) to initial or not initial paragraph 30 shall not affect the applicability of this mediation provision between Buyer and Seller and shall not result in the Broker(s) being deemed parties to the purchase and sale agreement. IF ANY PARTY COMMENCES AN ARBITRATION OR COURT ACTION BASED ON A DISPUTE OR CLAIM TO WHICH THIS PARGRAPH APPLIES WITHOUT FIRST ATTEMPTING TO RESOLVE THE MATTER THROUGH MEDIATION, THEN IN THE DISCRETION OF THE ARBITRATOR(S) OR JUDGE, THAT PARTY SHALL NOT BE ENTITLED TO RECOVER ATTORNEY'S FEES EVEN IF THEY WOULD OTHERWISE BE AVAILABLE TO THAT PARTY IN ANY SUCH ARBITRATION OR COURT ACTION. However, the filing of a judicial action to enable the recording of a notice of pending action, for order of attachment, receivership, injunction, or other provisional remedies, shall not in itself constitute a loss of the right to recover attorney's fees under this provision. The following matters are excluded from the requirement of mediation hereunder: (a) a judicial or non-judicial foreclosure or other action or proceeding to enforce a deed of trust, mortgage, or installment land sale contract as defined in Civil Code §2985, (b) an unlawful detainer action, (c) the filing or enforcement of a mechanic's lien, and (d) any matter which is within the jurisdiction of a probate court.

29. ARBITRATION OF DISPUTES: Any dispute or claim in law or equity between Buyer and Seller arising out of this contract or any resulting transaction which is not settled through mediation shall be decided by neutral, binding arbitration and not by court action, except as provided by California law for judicial review of arbitration proceedings. In addition, if paragraph 30 is initialled by Broker(s), Buyer and Seller agree to arbitrate disputes or claims involving an initialling Broker, as defined by that paragraph, consistent with this provision. The election by Broker(s) to initial or not initial paragraph 30 shall not affect the applicability of the arbitration provision between Buyer and Seller, and shall not result in the Broker(s) being deemed parties to the purchase and sale agreement.
   The arbitration shall be conducted in accordance with the rules of either the American Arbitration Association (AAA) or Judicial Arbitration and Mediation Services, Inc. (JAMS). The selection between AAA and JAMS rules shall be made by the claimant first filing for the arbitration. The parties to an arbitration may agree in writing to use different rules and/or arbitrator(s). In all other respects, the arbitration shall be conducted in accordance with Part III, Title 9 of the California Code of Civil Procedure. Judgment upon the award rendered by the arbitrator(s) may be entered in any court having jurisdiction thereof. The parties shall have the right to discovery in accordance with Code of Civil Procedure §1283.05. The following matters are excluded from arbitration hereunder: (a) a judicial or non-judicial foreclosure or other action or proceeding to enforce a deed of trust, mortgage, or installment land sale contract as defined in Civil Code §2985, (b) an unlawful detainer action, (c) the filing or enforcement of a mechanic's lien, (d) any matter which is within the jurisdiction of a probate or small claims court, and (e) an action for bodily injury or wrongful death, or for latent or patent defects, to which Code of Civil Procedure §337.1 or §337.15 applies. The filing of a judicial action to enable the recording of a notice of pending action, for order of attachment, receivership, injunction, or other provisional remedies, shall not constitute a waiver of the right to arbitrate under this provision.
   "NOTICE: BY INITIALLING IN THE SPACE BELOW YOU ARE AGREEING TO HAVE ANY DISPUTE ARISING OUT OF THE MATTERS INCLUDED IN THE 'ARBITRATION OF DISPUTES' PROVISION DECIDED BY NEUTRAL ARBITRATION AS PROVIDED BY CALIFORNIA LAW AND YOU ARE GIVING UP ANY RIGHTS YOU MIGHT POSSESS TO HAVE THE DISPUTE LITIGATED IN A COURT OR JURY TRIAL. BY INITIALLING IN THE SPACE BELOW YOU ARE GIVING UP YOUR JUDICIAL RIGHTS TO DISCOVERY AND APPEAL, UNLESS THOSE RIGHTS ARE SPECIFICALLY INCLUDED IN THE 'ARBITRATION OF DISPUTES' PROVISION. IF YOU REFUSE TO SUBMIT TO ARBITRATION AFTER AGREEING TO THIS PROVISION, YOU MAY BE COMPELLED TO ARBITRATE UNDER THE AUTHORITY OF THE CALIFORNIA CODE OF CIVIL PROCEDURE. YOUR AGREEMENT TO THIS ARBITRATION PROVISION IS VOLUNTARY."
   "WE HAVE READ AND UNDERSTAND THE FOREGOING AND AGREE TO SUBMIT DISPUTES ARISING OUT OF THE MATTERS INCLUDED IN THE 'ARBITRATION OF DISPUTES' PROVISION TO NEUTRAL ARBITRATION."

Buyer's Initials   Seller's Initials

_____/_____   _____/_____

123

Buyer and Seller acknowledge receipt of copy of this page, which constitutes Page 5 of _____ Pages.
   . Buyer's Initials (_____) (_____)   Seller's Initials (_____) (_____)

OFFICE USE ONLY
Reviewed by Broker or Designee _____
Date _____

M-PM-7/93

BUYER'S COPY
REAL ESTATE PURCHASE CONTRACT AND RECEIPT FOR DEPOSIT (DLF-14 PAGE 5 OF 6)

Paragraph 26 (Contingencies/Covenants: Methods of Satisfaction/Removal, Time Frames, Disapproval/Approval) is referenced frequently throughout the purchase contract.

Item A provides two methods for satisfying contingency removals. The Passive Method states that unless the buyers give written notice of disapproval or cancellation, it will be deemed that the buyers are proceeding with the transaction. This option will prevail unless the buyers and sellers initial the second option (the Active Method) which states that all buyer disapprovals and contingency removals will be in writing. The second option is usually preferable because it reduces uncertainty as to whether or not the buyers have removed their contract contingencies.

☐

Property Address: _____ _____ , 19____

30. BROKERS: (If initialled.) Any Broker who initials below agrees to (a) mediate any dispute or claim with Buyer, Seller, or other initialling Broker, arising out of this contract or any resulting transaction, consistent with paragraph 28, and (b) arbitrate any dispute or claim with Buyer, Seller, or other initialling Broker arising out of this contract or any resulting transaction, consistent with paragraph 29. However, if the dispute is solely between the Brokers, it shall instead be submitted for mediation and arbitration in accordance with the Board/Association of REALTORS® or MLS rules. If those entities decline to handle the matter, it shall be submitted pursuant to paragraphs 28 and 29. The initialling of this paragraph shall not result in any Broker being deemed a party to the purchase and sale agreement. As used in this paragraph, "Broker" means a brokerage firm and any licensed persons affiliated with that brokerage firm.

Selling Broker
By:

Listing Broker
By:

_____   _____
(Initials)   (Initials)

31. LIQUIDATED DAMAGES: (If initialled by all parties.)
Buyer's Initials   Seller's Initials

_____ / _____   Buyer and Seller agree that if Buyer fails to complete this purchase by reason of any default of Buyer:

A. Seller shall be released from obligation to sell the Property to Buyer.

B. Seller shall retain, as liquidated damages for breach of contract, the deposit actually paid. Buyer and Seller shall execute RECEIPT FOR INCREASED DEPOSIT/LIQUIDATED DAMAGES (CAR FORM RID-11) for any increased deposits. However, the amount retained shall be no more than 3% of the purchase price if Property is a dwelling with no more than four units, one of which Buyer intends to occupy as Buyer's residence. Any excess shall be promptly returned to Buyer.

C. Seller retains the right to proceed against Buyer for specific performance or any other claim or remedy Seller may have in law or equity, other than breach of contract damages.

D. In the event of a dispute, Funds deposited in trust accounts or escrow are not released automatically and require mutual, signed release Instructions from both Buyer and Seller, judicial decision, or arbitration award.

32. ATTORNEY'S FEES: In any action, proceeding, or arbitration between Buyer and Seller arising out of this agreement, the prevailing party shall be entitled to reasonable attorney's fees and costs, except as provided in paragraph 28.

33. MULTIPLE LISTING SERVICE: If Broker is a Participant of a multiple listing service (MLS), Broker is authorized to report the sale, price, terms, and financing for publication, dissemination, information, and use of the MLS, its parent entity, authorized members, participants, and subscribers.

34. OTHER TERMS AND CONDITIONS: _____
_____
_____
_____

35. TIME OF ESSENCE; ENTIRE CONTRACT; CHANGES: Time is of the essence. All prior agreements between the parties are incorporated in this agreement, which constitutes the entire contract. Its terms are intended by the parties as a final, complete and exclusive expression of their agreement with respect to its subject matter and may not be contradicted by evidence of any prior agreement or contemporaneous oral agreement. The captions in this agreement are for convenience of reference only and are not intended as part of this agreement. **This agreement may not be extended, amended, modified, altered, or changed in any respect whatsoever except by a further agreement in writing signed by Buyer and Seller.**

36. AGENCY CONFIRMATION: The following agency relationship(s) are hereby confirmed for this transaction:

Listing Agent: _____ is the agent of (check one):
(Print Firm Name)

☐ the Seller exclusively; or ☐ both the Buyer and Seller.

Selling Agent: _____ (if not same as Listing Agent) is the agent of (check one):
(Print Firm Name)

☐ the Buyer exclusively; or ☐ the Seller exclusively; or ☐ both the Buyer and Seller.

(IF THE PROPERTY CONTAINS 1-4 RESIDENTIAL DWELLING UNITS, BUYER AND SELLER MUST ALSO BE GIVEN ONE OR MORE DISCLOSURE REGARDING REAL ESTATE AGENCY RELATIONSHIPS FORMS (CAR FORM AD-11).)

37. OFFER: This is an offer to purchase the Property. **All paragraphs with spaces for initials by Buyer and Seller are incorporated in this agreement only if initialled by both parties.** If only one party initials, a Counter Offer is required until agreement is reached. Unless acceptance is signed by Seller and a signed copy delivered in person, by mail, or facsimile, and **personally received** by Buyer or by _____, who is authorized to receive it, by _____, 19___ at _____ AM/PM, the offer shall be deemed revoked and the deposit shall be returned. Buyer and Seller acknowledge that Broker(s) is/are not a party(ies) to the purchase and sale agreement. Buyer has read and acknowledges receipt of a copy of the offer and agrees to the above confirmation of agency relationships. This agreement and any supplement, addendum, or modification, including any photocopy or facsimile, may be executed in two or more counterparts, all of which shall constitute one and the same writing.

...osit is acknowledged: BUYER _____
                                  BUYER ___

124

Item B specifies the time periods that will be allowed for the buyer and seller to satisfy their respective contract contingencies. The standard contingencies referred to throughout the contract are listed with a space next to each one for the number of days that will apply. Spaces are provided to write in additional contingencies. If you need more room, write in "See addendum attached" in one of the blank spaces and include additional contingency time periods on the addendum.

Item C under paragraph 26 provides time frames for the seller to respond to the buyer's disapproval of any items listed under 26B. If the buyers disapprove of an item for which they have a disapproval right, the seller must respond within the time indicated. If the seller won't remedy the item, or doesn't respond, the buyer can either proceed with the transaction or give the seller notice of

Listing Agent: _____

(Print Firm Name)

☐ the Seller exclusively; or ☐ both the Buyer and Seller.

Selling Agent: _____ (if not same as Listing Agent) is the agent of (check one):

(Print Firm Name)

☐ the Buyer exclusively; or ☐ the Seller exclusively; or ☐ both the Buyer and Seller.

(IF THE PROPERTY CONTAINS 1-4 RESIDENTIAL DWELLING UNITS, BUYER AND SELLER MUST ALSO BE GIVEN ONE OR MORE DISCLOSURE REGARDING REAL ESTATE AGENCY RELATIONSHIPS FORMS (CAR FORM AD-11).)

37. OFFER: This is an offer to purchase the Property. All paragraphs with spaces for initials by Buyer and Seller are incorporated in this agreement only if initialled by both parties. If only one party initials, a Counter Offer is required until agreement is reached. Unless acceptance is signed by Seller and a signed copy delivered in person, by mail, or by facsimile, and **personally received** by Buyer or by _____, who is authorized to receive it, by _____, 19____ at _____ AM/PM, the offer shall be deemed revoked and the deposit shall be returned. Buyer and Seller acknowledge that Broker(s) is/are not a party(ies) to the purchase and sale agreement. Buyer has read and acknowledges receipt of a copy of the offer and agrees to the above confirmation of agency relationships. This agreement and any supplement, addendum, or modification, including any photocopy or facsimile, may be executed in two or more counterparts, all of which shall constitute one and the same writing.

Receipt for deposit is acknowledged:

BROKER _____

By _____

BUYER _____

BUYER _____

Address _____

Telephone _____ Fax _____

ACCEPTANCE

The undersigned Seller accepts the above and agrees to sell the Property on the above terms and conditions and agrees to the above confirmation of agency relationships (☐ subject to attached counter offer). Seller agrees to pay compensation for services as follows:

_____ to _____, Broker, and

_____ to _____, Broker,

payable: (a) on recordation of the deed or other evidence of title, or (b) if completion of sale is prevented by default of Seller, upon Seller's default, or (c) if completion of sale is prevented by default of Buyer, only if and when Seller collects damages from Buyer, by suit or otherwise, and then in an amount equal to one-half of the damages recovered, but not to exceed the above compensation, after first deducting title and escrow expenses and the expenses of collection, if any. Seller hereby irrevocably assigns to Broker(s) such compensation from Seller's proceeds in escrow. In any action, proceeding, or arbitration relating to the payment of such compensation, the prevailing party shall be entitled to reasonable attorney's fees and costs, except as provided in paragraph 28. The undersigned Seller has read, acknowledges receipt of a copy of this agreement, and authorizes Broker(s) to deliver a signed copy to Buyer.

Date _____ Telephone _____ Fax _____

Address _____

_____

SELLER _____

SELLER _____

Real Estate Broker(s) confirm(s) agency relationship(s) as above. (Real Estate Brokers are not parties to the purchase and sale agreement between Buyer and Seller.):

Real Estate Broker (Selling) _____ By _____ Date _____

Address _____ Telephone _____ Fax _____

Real Estate Broker (Listing) _____ By _____ Date _____

Address _____ Telephone _____ Fax _____

125

OFFICE USE ONLY

Reviewed by Broker or Designee _____

Date _____

M-PM-7/93

Page 6 of _____ Pages.

BUYER'S COPY
REAL ESTATE PURCHASE CONTRACT AND RECEIPT FOR DEPOSIT (DLF-14 PAGE 6 OF 6)

cancellation within the time indicated. Item C also states that a buyer who receives a Mello-Roos disclosure notice after the offer is accepted has three days after delivery in person or five days after the disclosure is mailed to give written notice of termination to the seller.

The Final Verification of Condition clause gives the buyer the right to perform a final "walk-through" inspection of the property approximately five days (or the number of days specified) before close of escrow. The final inspection is usually done within the week before closing. It's not a contingency, but gives the buyer the opportunity to confirm that the property has been maintained and that any repairs the sellers agreed to perform as part of the agreement are complete. Regarding repairs, including structural pest control repairs, this contract specifies that they be done in compliance with building code and permit requirements.

Agents should make sure the sellers understand this at the time the offer is presented. Often the fine print is glossed over during an offer presentation, which can be a mistake if the sellers then hire unlicensed quasi-professionals to complete substandard repair work that's unacceptable to the buyers.

Paragraph 28 (Mediation of Disputes) requires buyers, sellers, and their brokers to attempt to resolve disputes through mediation before pursuing arbitration or a court action. Mediation is a non-binding method of dispute resolution. Mediation fees will be shared between the parties involved. If any party doesn't attempt to mediate a dispute resolution before pursuing arbitration or other legal action, that party won't be entitled to recover attorney's fees, even if he or she is otherwise entitled to. Several matters are excluded from the mediation requirement, including matters within the jurisdiction of small claims court. This clause doesn't require the buyer's and seller's initials; it's automatically included as a provision of the purchase agreement.

Paragraph 29 (Arbitration of Disputes) is included as a provision in the contract if it's separately initialed by the buyers and sellers. If initialed, disputes arising out of the contract will be decided by neutral, binding arbitration, and not by court action. The arbitration process is usually a quicker and cheaper remedy to a dispute than a court action, but by agreeing to binding arbitration, you give up some legal rights. If you have any questions about whether or not you want binding arbitration to be a part of the agreement, talk to an attorney. As with the Liquidated Damages clause (paragraph 31 of the contract), only an attorney is qualified to advise you on this matter. Your real estate agent isn't qualified to counsel you on this, unless he or she is also an attorney. There are several matters that are excluded from the CAR Arbitration of Disputes clause, including matters within the jurisdiction of small claims court. In the case of a dispute involving monetary damages below the small claims limit of $5,000, the matter can be submitted to small claims court rather than to binding arbitration.

Paragraph 30 is initialed by the brokers involved if they agree to mediate and arbitrate disputes or claims arising from the contract or any resulting transaction.

The Liquidated Damages clause (paragraph 31) is included if it's separately initialed by the buyer and seller. This clause is a source of confusion for many buyers and sellers, and their agents. The clause, when initialed, states that the seller will retain the buyer's deposit(s) as liquidated damages if the buyer defaults. A default occurs when a buyer fails to go through with a purchase agreement for reasons not allowed for in the contract. For example, if the buyer is denied financing, after exercising due diligence to obtain a loan, a breach hasn't occurred and the buyer's deposit is returned. But, if the buyer fails to close escrow after all contingencies are removed from the contract, this would be a breach. Funds are not automatically released from an escrow account when a breach occurs; a release agreement must be signed by both buyer and seller. Also, in the absence of language to the contrary, the seller retains the right to proceed against a defaulting buyer for specific performance or any other legal remedy the seller may have, other than breach of contract damages.

In California, the law limits the amount of liquidated damages, in cases when the clause is initialed, to 3 percent of the purchase price, if the property is a one-to four-unit building and the buyers intend to occupy it as their residence. If the clause is initialed by the buyer and seller and there is to be an increased deposit, a separate form, called a Receipt for Increased Deposit, which restates the liqui-dated damages provision, must accompany the increased deposit and be signed by both buyer and seller in order for the liquidated damages clause to apply to the full amount of both the deposit and the increase. Many real estate agents over-look this critical detail.

Professional advice about the Liquidated Damages clause can only be obtained by consulting with an attorney. Real estate agents, who are not also attorneys, aren't qualified to advise you about the Liquidated Damages clause, although many will attempt to do so. If you can't decide what to do about this clause, consult a knowledgeable real estate attorney. The Liquidated Damages clause deals only with a buyer default, not a seller default.

Paragraph 32 (Attorney's Fees) states that the prevailing party in a legal action or arbitration arising from the contract shall be entitled to attorney's fees, except as provided in paragraph 28.

Paragraph 33 authorizes the broker to submit information about the prop-erty, and the sale, to the Multiple Listing Service.

Paragraph 34 (Other Terms and Conditions) is used to incorporate additional provisions into the contract. If the space provided is not sufficient, attach an addendum. If the buyer is a real estate agent licensed in the state of California, this fact should be disclosed here. Other terms might include a contingency for the offer to be approved by the buyer's attorney or tax advisor. If you're concerned about the cost of heating a large older home, include a contingency in this section for the seller to provide utility bills for the past year for your approval within several days to a week of receiving them. An agreement about repairs the seller is to make to the property, in addition to structural pest control repairs, can be included in this section. Buyers purchasing a new construction will want to include a contingency for the builder to provide copies of architectural plans, surveys, soils reports, engineering calculations, and related construction docu-mentation for the buyer's approval within a certain number of days of receiving them. Buyers of new homes might also want their attorney to approve the pur-chase contract if it's a form contract provided by the builder.

Buyers purchasing a tenant-occupied property will want to request that the property be vacant at the close of escrow, while those making an offer on a prop-erty where tenants will retain possession will want to request that any tenant deposits be turned over at the closing. Either provision can be included in para-graph 34. The Prorations clause (paragraph 7 of this purchase agreement)

127

provides for rents to be prorated. A buyer should also condition the offer upon the seller providing written verification from the appropriate local government authority regarding the legality of the rental units.

Local ordinances that must be complied with upon the transfer of title, or that may restrict the rights of property owners, should be included under Other Terms and Conditions (or in paragraph 12, item I above) with a provision stating who is to be responsible for compliance. A contingency requiring a buyer to qualify for swing financing should be here in wording similar to that used to describe the loan contingencies in paragraph 1 (Financing) of this purchase agreement, unless this is already included under paragraph 1M (Additional Financing Terms). Include the loan amount and term, interest rate, and fees involved, as well as a time period within which the buyer must qualify.

Paragraph 35 stipulates that time is of the essence; all prior agreements between the parties are incorporated in this contract; and that modifications to the contract must be in writing.

The Agency Confirmation section (paragraph 36) provides space for the listing and selling agents to identify themselves and to indicate whom they are representing in the transaction. The Agency Disclosure form should be reviewed and signed by the buyer and seller as soon as is practicable before entering into a real estate contract.

The Offer section is used to establish a date for expiration of the offer. If the seller doesn't respond to the buyer, or the buyer's agent, in writing (either in person, by mail, or facsimile) by the deadline specified in this paragraph, the offer is deemed revoked and the deposit is returned unless the buyer agrees to grant the seller an extension. While it's understandable that buyers want a response to their offer as soon as possible, it's unrealistic to expect an answer from the seller upon presentation; requesting this will offend some sellers. A day or two for response is reasonable in most cases.

The buyer signs below this section only after reading and understanding the entire contract, including all of the fine print. If a clause is unclear, and your real estate agent can't satisfactorily explain it to you, consult a real estate attorney before signing the contract. Also, be certain that the terms of the contract accurately reflect your intentions and capabilities. Once the purchase agreement is signed by all parties, it becomes a legally binding contract and penalties for noncompliance may be severe.

Consult your real estate agent, attorney, or tax advisor to be certain that you haven't overlooked any pertinent contingencies or conditions that should be made a part of the purchase agreement. Leaving terms of the contract open for future negotiation, such as closing and possession dates, can invite trouble.

After you've reviewed and signed the contract, have your agent complete a Buyer's Cost Sheet for you. This will give you an approximation of what costs you'll pay in addition to the down payment amount required to close the escrow. Be certain before you enter into a binding agreement that you'll be able to perform under the terms and conditions of the contract.

Finally, you should receive copies of each document you sign in the course of a real estate transaction: the agency disclosure form, copies of each page of the purchase agreement that you submit to the seller, and copies of property disclosure forms and reports. Dedicate a file to your real estate acquisition. The paperwork may seem cumbersome, but it's intended to protect you.

Presenting the Offer

The manner in which an offer is presented to a seller varies from area to area. Regardless of local custom, however, it's usually preferable to have the offer presented in person by the buyer's agent to the sellers and their agent. Buyers shouldn't attend the presentation as their presence might deter the sellers from asking questions and airing objections about the offer.

The presentation should be private, ideally in the conference room at the listing agent's office. The buyer's agent presents and reviews the offer thoroughly with the seller and the seller's agent. In addition, the buyer's agent should inform the seller of the buyer's financial capacity to perform under the terms of the contract. If the buyer has been prequalified by a lender, a letter confirming this should accompany the offer. Relevant financial information that the buyer's agent should have on hand at the presentation includes the buyer's occupation, the length of time the buyer has been employed in that occupation, the buyer's annual gross income, and the amount of any long-term outstanding debts. With this information, the seller and the seller's agent can determine if the buyer is qualified to obtain the financing terms proposed in the contract. Sellers, by the way, shouldn't let a buyer's agent talk them into hearing an offer without having their agent present.

129

Sellers will often want to know the offering price before the offer is presented, but there are several good reasons why it's better to wait to hear an offer presented in its entirety. In a dual agency situation, a potential conflict of interest is created if the listing agent has advance knowledge of another buyer's offer. Also, there is more to an offer than the price, and hearing a low initial bid can prejudice the seller against listening to the rest of the offer. A low offer from a qualified buyer that can be negotiated is far better than a full price offer from a buyer who can't qualify. So it's better to listen to all offers before categorically dismissing any.

Buyers should find out how their agent intends to present the offer before the presentation takes place. Agents' presentation styles differ. Some take an aggressive and combative stance in the hopes of coercing a seller into accepting a lower price. This rarely works and often angers sellers who usually

A spirit of cooperative negotiation yields the best results.

have an emotional attachment to their home. Make sure that your agent will approach the sellers with a spirit of cooperation, not confrontation. If you're making a low offer, your agent is usually better off blaming the price on external market conditions—an impersonal force over which no one has control—or on the buyer's affordability limitations, rather than insulting the sellers by insisting their high price is unrealistic. Your agent should compliment the sellers on their home, and build rapport. A good negotiator is a good listener. Your agent should find out the sellers' motivations so that you can work together to resolve issues and consummate a deal.

Buyers who aren't represented by an agent and who are presenting an offer directly to a seller should be aware of the value of remaining silent at key decision points during negotiations. After you've requested a concession from the seller, keep quiet and wait for a response, even if the wait seems interminable. Nervous chatter can compromise your efforts.

After the offer is presented and all questions answered to satisfaction, the buyer's agent should be excused so that the offer can be discussed by the selling party in private. At this point, the seller's agent should prepare a "Seller's Net Sheet" to indicate the amount of cash proceeds that will be realized if the offer is accepted.

Buying and selling long distance requires a slightly different procedure. If it's not feasible to coordinate an in-person presentation soon after the buyer's offer is written, a phone presentation should be arranged. The buyer's and seller's agents make a conference call to the seller and present the offer, as if the seller were present; the seller then wires acceptance or the terms of a counteroffer, or sends a facsimile. Related paperwork is express mailed to the seller for signature.

A seller's agent is legally required to present all offers, even the most ridiculously low, to the seller. You don't have to accept or even counter an offer if you don't want to, but your agent must present it to you.

Reviewing the Offer

Given the complexity of today's real estate purchase agreements, it's rare that an offer from a buyer is completely acceptable as written. Keep in mind that virtually everything in a purchase agreement is negotiable, including the form of the purchase contract itself. If the offer is written on an overly simplistic form that doesn't cover the items included in the CAR purchase agreement, your agent can rewrite it on the appropriate form. Even when the basic terms and conditions are satisfactory, the offer may be sloppily written, but with a little reworking it can be perfectly acceptable. Some offers are clearly written, but the terms might not be exactly what the sellers are looking for. The sellers and their agent need to weigh the pros and cons of an offer carefully. This is the time for the sellers to determine which terms they can live with and which require modification.

Starting at the top of the contract, make sure you know who is making an offer to purchase your home and that all buyers have signed the contract. Beware

130

of the phrase "and/or assignee" or "and/or nominee" next to a buyer's name. Insist that the nominee or assignee be named within a certain number of days following acceptance and that that party signs the original purchase agreement. Likewise, if a husband and wife are making an offer to purchase and only one of them has signed the contract, write into a counteroffer that the other party must sign within a day or two of acceptance. Ideally, all parties to the contract have seen the property by the time an offer is made. If the contract is subject to a buyer seeing and approving the property, make sure this contingency is removed within a brief period of time, say two or three days. Better yet, have the buyers remove this contingency by acceptance of the counteroffer, if possible.

A seller can request an increase in the deposit amount if the buyer's initial deposit is too low. There's no rule as to what amount is adequate. One percent of the purchase price is an average good faith deposit, but local custom will dictate how much is considered reasonable. A long close of escrow, particularly when at the buyer's request, should be accompanied by a substantial deposit. An increased deposit may be requested upon acceptance, several days after acceptance, upon removal of the inspection contingency, or upon removal of all contingencies. If the buyers and sellers agree to initial the Liquidated Damages clause, the sellers might want to request that the buyers' deposit be increased to three percent of the purchase price, the maximum allowed.

An offer accompanied with a deposit in the form of a promissory note rather than a personal or cashier's check should be countered with a provision that the note be replaced with a check within a day or two of acceptance. A promissory note is simply a promise to pay. A check, which is cashed by the escrow holder, is a more secure deposit.

131

The purchase price is probably the most frequently countered item in a purchase agreement. Many times the first offer is the best one a seller will receive, yet it may also be well below what the seller feels is reasonable. In evaluating an offer, there are a number of important factors to take into account in addition to the price. An offer from a qualified buyer with cash in the bank who can close escrow quickly may be worth more to a seller than a higher offer requiring a long close that's contingent upon the sale of another home. On the other hand, if your agent concurs that the offer is on the low side, try to get a sense from the buyer's agent during the presentation of whether there's any flexibility in the buyer's price. If you think the buyer or buyer's agent is unfamiliar with local property values, ask your agent to provide a list of comparable sales to support your price. If the offer is significantly under your asking price and your agent indicates that it's at, or close to, the fair market value for your property,

Counter any offer from a well-qualified buyer.

you need to do some serious soul searching. Your property will sell for the price a willing and able buyer will pay. If your house is only for sale if you can get a certain price, and that price is unrealistic for the current market, you need to consider the wisdom of having your house on the market at all. You're probably better off taking your home off the market and waiting for the market to improve. An overpriced listing becomes shop-worn and stale when it sits on the market too long. The longer it's on the market, the less you're likely to sell it for. Remember, if the market is declining and you do need to sell, you're better off selling sooner than later when the market will have dropped further, even if this means selling for less than you thought you would.

A buyer who makes a low initial offer price might be willing to come up to market value. You owe it to yourself to find out by presenting the buyer with a counterproposal. Don't be offended by a low offer, particularly if the market is slow. It's natural for buyers to want to test your price. In a soft market, you may want to counter the price a bit higher than your rock-bottom so that the buyer can counter again and have the last word, so to speak. In a fast market, where there's a sense of urgency and buyers want to tie up a property before other buyers put in bids, you can counter at your best price and let the buyer know that it's your final price.

Most offers will include a financing contingency. If the buyer's offer specifies that the financing contingency will be considered removed when the lender funds the loan, counter this with a specific number of days for the buyer to remove this contingency so that you don't wait until the last minute to find out that the buyer was denied a loan. Thirty days from acceptance is usually sufficient for loan approval. Approval of an assumption may take longer than this, and financing approval in general will take longer during fast markets, or when there's a lot of refinancing going on.

When considering the amount of the cash down payment, it's safe to say that the more cash down, the better. A loan for 90 percent of the purchase price will, in most cases, be more difficult for a buyer to obtain than a loan for 80 percent or less. A lender feels more secure about making a loan when a larger cash down payment is involved. This doesn't mean that a seller should refuse an offer from a buyer who needs to qualify for a 90-percent loan. There are plenty of well-qualified buyers with substantial incomes who are unable to accumulate large cash down payments, often because a good portion of their income goes to taxes. As a seller, you must keep in mind that the lender-qualifying procedure will be more rigorous than if the buyer were able to make a large cash down payment. Make certain in advance that the buyer can qualify for the proposed loan and that there are good comparable sales in the neighborhood to justify the purchase price to the lender's appraiser. Remember, if the house is appraised at less than the purchase price, a buyer applying for a 90-percent loan is unlikely to have the additional cash on hand to make up the difference.

If you have any question about the source of the buyer's funds, include a provision for the buyer to provide verification of the funds necessary to close

132

escrow within seven days, or so, of acceptance. It's particularly important to verify the source of funds if the buyer is making an all-cash offer without a financing contingency. If parents are providing all or part of the financing, ask them to verify their intent and ability to participate in writing, since it's not uncommon for buyers to think they can count on their parents for extra cash when in fact the parents have no desire to assist. Buyers who don't have a prequalification letter at the time they make an offer should be required to provide the sellers with a letter of lender prequalification, including satisfactory review of the buyer's credit, within three to five days of acceptance. The credit review is very important. Lenders have become sticklers about good credit. A prequalification letter without a credit review is worth very little.

Be certain that the interest rate and loan fee stated in the offer are readily available. If interest rates are heading upward or if the loan fee the buyer is proposing is on the low side (½ percent of the loan amount rather than 1 or 2 percent), include in a counteroffer a request that the buyer accept a loan with a higher interest rate or larger loan fee, if necessary. It's not advisable to counter that a buyer accept the "best prevailing interest rate," as a judge could interpret this phrase to be too vague to enforce should interest rates soar and the buyer fail to complete the purchase.

Normally, the buyer chooses the lender for the new first loan. Sometimes, however, a seller may want to have some say in that choice. During periods of unstable interest rates, for instance, a seller may be wise to counter that the buyer seek financing from a lender who will lock in an interest rate upon or soon after application. If rates rise, the buyer has the lender's promise to charge the lower rate, provided that the loan is approved and closes within a specified period of time.

Sellers who have a prepayment penalty on their loan should find out whether it may be waived if the buyer finances the home purchase through the same lender. This could result in a substantial savings to the sellers and, therefore, a lower purchase price for the buyers.

Ninety percent financing usually requires that the buyer and the property qualify for Private Mortgage Insurance (PMI) to protect the lender in case of default. PMI qualification can be a different process, although some lenders self-insure their 90-percent loans. Loan approval is usually easier to obtain from lenders that handle the entire process internally. If the buyer appears to be marginally qualified, you might counter that the buyer obtain financing through a portfolio lender who is less likely to be unreasonably rigorous in qualifying the buyer.

It's unwise for a seller to be overly restrictive about the buyer's choice of lender; after all, it's the buyer who has to live with the loan, not the seller. A seller should never insist that the buyer obtain a loan from a lender that the seller has a financial interest in.

Sometimes a buyer takes over an existing loan instead of obtaining a new one. In these situations, the seller will commonly prefer that the buyer formally assume the loan rather than take title "subject to" the existing loan. When the buyer formally assumes the loan, the lender looks primarily to the assuming borrower for repayment. With a "subject to" transfer, the seller may still be primarily responsible for payment. A "subject to" transfer may also involve an additional risk to the buyer, since most lenders will only permit an existing loan to be taken over through formal assumption and could start foreclosure proceedings following a "subject to" transfer if the note contains a valid "due on sale clause."

Sellers who carry back a note as part of the purchase price usually want to make a late charge part of the agreement. A late fee of 6 percent of the payment due is customarily charged if payment is not received within ten days of the due date. Likewise, a seller will want the buyer to provide a request for notice of default or sale and a request for notice of delinquency, both of which can be arranged through the title company. Sellers will also want title insurance and a tax service paid for by the buyer. A tax service notifies the lender (seller) if the borrowers are delinquent on their property tax payments.

The interest rate on an owner-carry loan is negotiable. Ask your agent to check with a mortgage broker to determine the current rate on institutional first (or second) loans. Seller financing is usually a little less expensive than conventional financing because loan fees (points) typically aren't charged. The interest rate on a seller-carry loan will also be influenced by current treasury bill and certificate of deposit rates. Sellers usually aren't willing to carry a loan for a lower return than they'd earn if their money was invested elsewhere.

134

Imputed interest rates are charged by the IRS if sellers carry back a note at too low an interest rate; in this case, sellers could be taxed on income they haven't received. Installment sale rules have changed several times in recent years, so have current information and understand the tax ramifications before entering into a legally binding contract.

The Escrow (paragraph 3) of the contract should specifically name the escrow holder to be used for the transaction. If the buyer's offer to purchase merely states "a reputable title/escrow company," include the name of a specific company in the counteroffer. Sellers who need to arrange a simultaneous close with another escrow, held by a different escrow holder, might request that the buyers change escrow holders to accommodate the sellers. The close of escrow date may require adjustment, depending on the buyer's situation and on how much the buyer and the buyer's agent knew about the seller's needs before drafting the offer. Who pays the escrow fee is negotiable and can be countered if necessary; local custom usually prevails.

The Possession and Keys section (paragraph 5) may need fine tuning, particularly if the buyer is selling a house and the seller is purchasing another home that's occupied. Occupancy dates will have to be staggered to allow each homeowner time to move out of the old home and into the new one. For instance, if you've agreed to give the seller of the home you're purchasing two days after close of escrow to move but you can't close that escrow until the one on your current home closes, then you'll need to ask the buyer to allow you to stay in possession of your current home for at least three days after it closes (and this will give you just one day to move). Sellers who stay in possession after the close need to keep their personal property and liability insurance in effect. The new buyer's insurance will cover the dwelling in case of fire, but it won't cover the seller's personal possessions. A "Residential Lease Agreement After Sale" should be made a part of the contract. Paragraph 5 says that the sellers will provide keys to all locks. If you can't supply keys to all locks, include this in a counteroffer.

Occasionally, a seller vacates a house before the close of escrow. This is quite common if the seller has been transferred. A buyer making an offer on a vacant home may request to take possession before the transfer of title, but there are potential problems with early possession, not the least of which is that the buyer may fall out of love with the home and move out before the closing. A seller who permits a buyer to take early occupancy should insist that the buyer carry insurance and that an Interim Occupancy Agreement be part of the contract.

It's never advisable for a seller to grant permission to a buyer to do cosmetic or structural work to a house prior to the closing. The buyer may think it's a good idea to do fix-up work while the house is empty, but if the escrow never closes for some unanticipated reason, the buyer will have paid to improve the seller's property. If the escrow doesn't close, the seller may be stuck with putting a half-painted house (or one that's painted atrociously) back on the market.

Who pays the cost of title insurance (paragraph 6: Title and Vesting) can be countered if necessary. Who pays this cost is negotiable, but local custom usually prevails.

135

Who pays the items included under the Prorations section is negotiable, but again custom often prevails.

Condominium, townhouse, and planned development owners should correct any inaccurate information included in paragraph 8 (Condominium/P.D.) in a counteroffer.

Physical inspections of the property (paragraph 9) are a necessary part of any real estate transaction. Sellers are advised to keep in mind that a property that has been well inspected during the course of the sale is less likely to be the source of a legal dispute afterwards. Encourage the buyer to complete all inspections deemed necessary, but request completion within a reasonable amount of time (within 10 to 14 days of acceptance).

The Condition of Property clause includes either a seller's warranty regarding the property or an "as is" provision. Sellers are cautioned against arbitrarily countering with an "as is" clause in an attempt to avoid disclosure requirements. Accurate, forthright, and thorough disclosure of a property's defects will help prevent after-escrow claims regarding undisclosed defects. Also, an "as is" provision, except where mandated by state law (such as in probate and foreclosure sales) can cause undue concern on the buyers' part and could result in the buyers withdrawing from the negotiations. Any known defects that won't be corrected by the close of escrow should be disclosed in writing, both in the purchase contract or counteroffer and in the Real Estate Transfer Disclosure Statement (RETDS).

It should be expressly stated that the seller doesn't warrant the condition of any such defective item. The Seller Warranty provision states that the seller will replace all cracked and broken glass, including shower enclosures, prior to close of escrow. If you don't intend to replace all cracked glass (for instance, a tiny crack in a stained glass pane), include this in writing in a counteroffer.

A reminder on the Real Estate Transfer Disclosure Statement (paragraph 11): The buyer has three days after personal delivery of this document to terminate the contract (five days if mailed). Complete the disclosure form and deliver it to the buyer's agent as soon as possible to avoid any last minute hang-ups in the transaction. Any serious defect that you don't intend to correct before the close of escrow should be listed separately in the purchase agreement or counteroffer. Disclosure of defects doesn't relieve the seller of the responsibility for fixing them. The buyer and seller must agree in writing that the property will be sold "as is" with respect to a given defect (such as a leaky roof or a broken stove burner). Also, the RETDS isn't complete until both agents have done their agent inspections. Even if the offer indicates that the buyers have received the RETDS, you may have to counter that you'll provide another one within a specific number of days if the disclosure is lacking agent inspections.

Agents, particularly if they're working outside of their regular area, may not be aware of local property disclosure requirements (paragraph 12). Include any oversights in a counteroffer. Sellers who are unsure if their property is located within a Geologic/Seismic or Flood Hazard Zone are wise to order a Geologic Disclosure Report from JCP Geologists, Inc. The cost is approximately $55. To order a JCP report, call (415) 940-1514 or (408) 446-4426. (See Chapter 4 for more information about seller disclosure requirements.)

Who pays the cost of compliance with mandatory retrofit requirements (paragraph 14) is usually negotiable.

Any fixtures (paragraph 15) that are excluded from the sale should be included in a counteroffer if they're not already itemized in the offer. Offers to purchase are often written hastily and without complete information. For instance, the buyer may not know which appliances are included in the sale and which fixtures are excluded.

Sellers who exclude light fixtures will often offer to provide the buyer with substitutes. Another alternative is to offer a credit in escrow, and let the buyer take responsibility for selecting and replacing the fixtures after closing.

Personal property (paragraph 16) that's included in the sale should be sold "as is" if it's old or no longer under a manufacturer's warranty. Any known defects should be disclosed in writing to the buyer.

Sellers can either agree or refuse to provide a Home Warranty Plan, or they

136

Don't be offended by a request you can't live with— counter it.

can propose that the cost of a plan be shared 50-50 by the buyers and sellers.

If paragraph 18 (Septic System) wasn't included, yet it should be, counter that buyer and seller agree to initial this clause and specify who is to pay which costs.

Regarding paragraph 19 (Pest Control), sellers who have obtained a presale Wood Destroying Pests and Organisms Report should ask the buyer to accept that report within several days. If the buyer insists on ordering a second report, the sellers should limit their liability for structural pest control corrective work to the amount stipulated in the first report. When the sellers don't have a current pest report at the time an offer to purchase is made, they should counter with a provision that the sellers will read and approve the new report within several days of receiving it. Alternatively, sellers can limit their liability for pest control work to a specific amount, with any amount over this limit subject to future negotiation. Who pays for a report and for pest control repairs is negotiable and can be countered. Sellers usually pay for Section I repairs, particularly in a soft market. If the buyers want detached structures inspected for wood destroying organisms, it's best to have this included in a separate report from the house report.

Contracts that include paragraph 20 (Sale of Buyer's Property) should be examined carefully to make sure the provisions included are acceptable. Sellers will usually want the right to continue to offer their property for sale, at least until the buyer's property is sold. The contingent sale contingency should run for a specific number of days, not until the close of escrow of the seller's property, so you'll need to include this in a counteroffer. If the number of days specified in paragraph 20, item B (seller's notice to buyer that another offer has been accepted and that the cancellation of sale clause is being invoked) is too long, this can be countered with a more reasonable time period (customarily 3 days, or 72 hours, but this is negotiable). When the buyers remove the contingency for the sale of their property, this should be accompanied by verification that they have the financial capability to perform under the contract. For more information about contingent sale offers, see the next section of this chapter.

137

Regarding paragraphs 21 and 22 (Backup Offer and Court Confirmation), if these clauses haven't been included, yet they should be, counter that buyer and seller agree to initial these clauses.

The offer will include time frames for the satisfaction and removal of contract contingencies (paragraph 26). The time frames can be countered to provide more or less time. For example, if the buyers have requested 30 days for an inspection contingency, this can be countered with a more reasonable time frame of 14 days or so. Or, if the buyers have asked the seller to provide a current Wood Destroying Pests and Organisms report within 5 days of acceptance, and the pest control company can't do the inspection for 7 days, this can be countered. Time frames for additional contingencies can be added as necessary. For instance, if the buyers included a contingency for their attorney to approve the contract, but they failed to specify a time frame for performance, this should be included in a counteroffer.

The time frames for approval and disapproval of items (paragraph 26C) can be modified in a counteroffer. And, if the purchase agreement doesn't include the provision for all contingencies to be removed in writing, add this to the counteroffer by asking the buyers to initial item 2 under section 26A, if it makes you feel more comfortable.

The Arbitration of Disputes and Liquidated Damages clauses (paragraphs 29 and 31) can be included or excluded in a counteroffer. Remember, only an attorney can advise you on these two clauses. Some real estate company purchase contracts have an arbitration clause that doesn't provide for a small claims court remedy to matters that are within the jurisdiction of that court. If you want arbitration, but only if the clause contains the small claims court provision, counter the offer to include this.

Just as the buyers have the right to include Other Terms and Conditions, so can the seller include additional provisions in a counteroffer. Examples: a contingency for the seller's attorney or tax advisor to approve the contract; a provision for a seller rent-back; or a contingency for the close of another escrow.

The Agency Confirmation clause can be countered, if necessary. The buyer's agent will usually call the sellers' agent before writing an offer to establish what agency relationships will apply. If this information wasn't available in advance and the agency relationships checked on the offer aren't accurate, the correct information can be included in a counteroffer.

138

Sometimes sellers are unable to respond to an offer within the time specified in the Offer section of the contract. If this is the case, and the buyers have indicated verbally that the sellers can have additional time, indicate in the counteroffer that the time period for acceptance has been extended to the date of the counteroffer.

The Acceptance section of the contract may have been filled in by the buyer's agent to indicate the compensation the seller will pay the broker(s). This may need to be countered if it's incorrect, or it may need to be filled in if the agent hasn't already done so. Check the box included in this section when acceptance of the contract is subject to an attached counteroffer.

Weighing the Risks of a Contingent Sale Offer

Let's say you've had your home on the market for months. You're desperate to sell; you've already bought and closed on another home. Finally, an offer comes in. The price is right. But, it's contingent on the sale of the buyer's property that's not yet on the market. What do you do under the circumstances?

You may be inclined to accept the offer. After all, isn't a contingent sale offer better than no offer? Not necessarily. Accepting a contingent sale could be a time-consuming and futile exercise, particularly if the buyers have difficulty selling their home.

One option would be to accept the buyers' offer with a provision for the sellers to have the right to continue to market their home (see paragraph 20 of the

CAR purchase contract). If the sellers receive another offer they want to accept, they deliver written notification of this fact to the buyers in primary position. The primary buyers then have the period of time agreed to in the contract (often 72 hours) within which to remove the contingency for the sale of their home. If they are unable to do so, the house goes to the second buyers. This cancellation provision is commonly referred to as a "release" or "escape" clause.

The problem with a contingent sale, even with a release clause, is that it can slow down the marketing effort. Particularly in a high-inventory market, where there are a lot of other properties to sell, agents often won't waste their time showing houses that have accepted offers with release clauses.

There are times when a contingent sale offer is worth the risk. For instance, suppose you have a mid-price range home, and the mid-range is soft. The buyers have a starter home in a desirable neighborhood where buyer activity is strong. The starter home is probably more salable than your mid-price range home. Just make sure that your agent previews the buyers' home, and include a contingency in a counteroffer for your agent to approve their list price. Even the most salable property won't move if it's overpriced.

If the buyers' home is located out of town, ask your agent to do some research for you before you get tied up with a deal that stands no chance of closing. Have your agent find out how salable the buyers' home is by calling agents in the area of the buyers' house. Get a reading on the local market conditions. If the buyers' house is already on the market, how much activity has there been? Does the house appear to be reasonably priced? No offer at all can be better than an offer that's contingent on the sale of a property that will never sell.

139

One strategy that can work effectively is to accept the buyers' contingent sale offer and include a provision stating that the sellers will stop offering their property for sale for two or three weeks. This gives the buyers an incentive to price their home to sell. If they can effectively market their home and find a buyer in two to three weeks, they don't have to risk losing the house to another buyer and the seller has a firm deal. This creates a true win-win situation.

No matter how fast you think the buyers' house will sell, markets have been known to change quickly. So be sure a contingent sale clause is structured in two phases. There should always be two time frames for performance. One time period, say 30 to 45 days, is for the buyers to find a buyer for their home. The other time period is for the escrow to close. The CAR purchase contract doesn't provide for two time frames, so you'll need to include this in a counteroffer.

Don't fall into the trap of accepting an offer that's written with one time period for the sale of the buyers' home and for closing the escrow. Such a contingency might read like this: "This offer is contingent upon the buyers' home selling and closing escrow within 90 days." This ties you up for a full 90 days. If the buyers don't have an offer by day 60, there's little likelihood they'll be able to close in 90 days. It's better to have a contingent sale provision that reads like this: "This offer is contingent upon the buyers' home selling within 30 (or 45) days. Escrow to close within 90 days, or sooner by mutual agreement." With a two-phase contingency, the sellers have the option of voiding the contract at the end of 30 or 45 days if the sellers find that the buyers' house isn't selling and the contingent sale is hindering the sellers' marketing effort. The sellers also have the option of extending the time period for the buyers to sell their house. But at least the sellers have some control over their destiny.

> *The basic counteroffer*
> *ingredients include:*
> • *Deposit amount • Purchase price*
> • *Close of escrow and possession*
> • *Who pays which fees and costs*
> • *Defects the sellers will and won't fix*
> • *Addition or modification of*
> *contingency time periods*
> • *Correction of oversights or*
> *inaccuracies in the offer*
> • *Additional terms and conditions*

Counteroffers

Whenever possible, respond to the buyer's offer as soon as possible. An offer to purchase can be withdrawn at any time prior to the moment that the seller's signed acceptance is delivered back to the buyer. Keep in mind that buyers are most enthusiastic about a house at the time they make an offer, so if you keep a buyer waiting the initial eagerness may wear off. Use the buyer's excitement to your own advantage, but be sure you consider your response carefully before making a formal counteroffer. Once the contract is signed by all parties, it's difficult if not impossible to change the terms.

140

Any counteroffer should be made in writing, on a separate form, such as the one included in this chapter. This is preferable to modifying and initialing items on the original contract. Oral offers and counteroffers aren't binding, since a real estate contract must be in writing to be enforceable. The sellers' agent will check the "subject to counteroffer" box at the bottom of the original purchase agreement, above the sellers' acceptance signature. When the sellers sign the purchase agreement, they are accepting the buyer's terms and conditions except those that are modified in the counteroffer.

The date of the original offer, the property address, and the names of the buyers and sellers should appear at the top of the counteroffer. The individual items to be modified are listed in the body of the counteroffer, with each change numbered and made in reference to a specific item on the original offer.

> *Until a counteroffer is signed by*
> *a buyer and delivered to the seller,*
> *it can be withdrawn and the seller*
> *can accept another offer.*

Any change requested to the terms proposed in the original offer creates a new offer that requires acceptance by the other party. The counteroffer is not legally binding and can be withdrawn by the party making it at any time up until it's signed by the other party and the signed acceptance is delivered back to the party making the counteroffer. A specific time period for acceptance should be stipulated in the counteroffer, after which the counter will become null and void if it's not accepted. Twenty-four hours is usually sufficient, unless the other party is out of town or somehow unable to respond within that time. If a response is made after the time period expires, it's wise to include a provision that indicates the time period for acceptance is extended to include the response date.

A counteroffer can be revoked by the maker at any time before it's signed by the other party and delivered back to the maker or agent. Such a revocation should be made in writing and delivered to the other party in order to avoid confusion, particularly if multiple offers are involved.

The delivery aspect is very important. To avoid any confusion, it's best to make specific arrangements to have the delivery made in person. It's also a good idea to have the seller sign for receipt of the ratified counteroffer so that there's no misunderstanding about whose offer takes priority should another offer be presented during the time that a counteroffer is outstanding.

There's no limit to how many times buyers and sellers can counter back and forth. If there's more than one counteroffer, number each one and note at the bottom, above the acceptance section, that counteroffer number two (three, four, etc.) is attached and made a part of the contract.

141

Negotiation Strategies

Consummating a real estate transaction depends on maintaining open communication between the buyer, the seller, and their respective agents. Contrary to the old school of thought which advocated adversarial negotiations based on attempts by each party to extract major concessions from the other, the current consensus is that a spirit of honest and enthusiastic cooperation usually yields the best results.

This doesn't mean that a buyer shouldn't try to obtain a property for the lowest price possible. And, sellers will certainly want to sell for the highest price obtainable. Although it may seem that buyers and sellers have conflicting interests, at least as far as the purchase price is concerned, both parties are definitely working toward the common goal of completing a house sale.

Some buyers and sellers have an aversion to bargaining and use a "take it or leave it" approach. Principals who are so inclined should have their agents talk with the other agent to determine if this straightforward approach will receive a positive reception. Some buyers and sellers feel a need to test the other party to see if there's any flexibility in price. If the sellers' agent feels his or her clients will counter any offer that's less than the list price, the buyers are better off offering less than their best price initially so that they have some room for upward movement when the sellers counter back with a higher price. That is unless there are several competing offers, in which case sincere buyers should make their very best offer at the outset.

The most important part of the negotiation process is to keep the momentum going. Lethargy or game-playing on the part of either party can result in a stalled transaction. If, after several rounds of counteroffers, it looks as if the buyers and sellers are stuck at prices that aren't too far apart, one approach that often works is to "split the difference" between the last two prices proposed. Settling on a compromise price can make both parties feel they're coming out ahead.

Don't expect the agents to know what price the other party will accept. Buyers and sellers frequently don't know themselves what price they'll be willing to accept until they're well into the negotiation process. There's much more to selling a house than agreeing on price, and often the other components of the purchase contract will be so desirable that a party will accept a price higher or lower than even they anticipated. For example, suppose the buyers and sellers haven't reached agreement on price and the sellers let it be known that they might make a price concession if the buyers agree to close escrow quickly. If the buyers are able to meet this condition, a deal can be made at a price that might be quite a bit lower than the sellers' list price.

Although it's wise to keep the momentum of the negotiations going in a forward direction, there are times when it's best to take a break. This means allowing the time period for response to a counteroffer to lapse. Let the sellers know, through your agent, that you're still interested but that you won't be responding at this time. If after a week or so, the sellers haven't received another offer and you're still interested in buying the house, rekindle the negotiations.

142

Janie Addison found a house she wanted to buy but it was overpriced. Janie's agent called the listing agent to see if the sellers would accept a reasonable price for the house. The sellers' agent thought they would since they'd already bought another home. Janie went ahead and made an offer which the sellers countered unrealistically high. Janie made it clear that she could only afford to pay so much for the house. At no time was there any discussion about the house being overpriced. The negotiations were abandoned temporarily on several occasions, which gave the sellers an opportunity to have numerous open houses and many more showings. No other offers were written and finally, one month later, the sellers accepted Janie's offer.

Buyers can usually afford the luxury of letting the negotiations lapse for a bit if it's impossible to move any closer and the market is slow. The worst thing that will happen is that someone else will come along and offer more for the house. But this shouldn't pose a problem for you because you should always be prepared to walk away from a house rather than overpay for it. Sellers, on the other hand, usually aren't afforded the same luxury. Sellers who call off a negotiation in midstream may not find a receptive buyer waiting for them when they decide they'd like to try another round. Or, if the buyers are still interested, the price they're willing to pay may be less if they sense the sellers are desperate.

All options should be explored before calling negotiations to a permanent halt. If the seller can't come down to your price, can you afford to pay more if the seller is willing to carry some financing for you? If the buyer can't come up to

Here are a few ways to break a negotiation impasse:
* *Split the difference in price.* • *Lower the purchase price, but make it "as is." * • *Seller can credit for some or all of the buyer's nonrecurring closing costs.* • *Seller can carry financing.* • *Buyer can use adjustable-rate, rather than fixed-rate, financing to keep costs down.* • *Offer the other party an "either/or" proposition (e.g., either a higher price with the seller carrying financing, or a lower price with all cash to seller).* • *Give up something you want (e.g., price, a long close of escrow, appliances) in exchange for something the other party wants.*

your price, can you sell for less if the buyer closes quickly? If you pay some of the buyers' nonrecurring closing costs, can they afford to pay more for your home? See the next section for more on ways to make your home more affordable.

During your negotiations, remember that buying and selling homes, unlike other business transactions, can be a very emotional process. If you have the opportunity to meet the other party in person before an agreement is finalized, be polite and diplomatic. Never insult the seller or engage in verbal fisticuffs.

143

Making Your Home More Affordable

A low offer may indicate that the buyers can't afford to pay more, no matter how much they love the house. There are several ways that willing buyers and sellers can work together for a successful transaction in this situation.

A buyer with mechanical skills, for instance, might be willing to purchase the property in "as is" condition with respect to "termite" work (after reading and approving a Wood Destroying Pest report, that is), thereby inducing the sellers, who would normally be paying for this work, to reduce the purchase price by the amount it would have cost them.

A seller can offer to pay all or a portion of the buyer's nonrecurring closing costs if the buyer is short on cash but otherwise qualified financially. These costs include such items as loan origination fees, title insurance and escrow fees (in areas where the buyer customarily pays for these), and transfer taxes. The lender will need to agree, since cash credits from the seller to the buyer are sometimes not permitted, particularly if the buyer is to receive cash at the close of escrow. Be sure to check with the lender in advance to avoid any last minute surprises. Also be aware that even if the lender does permit the seller to pay for the buyer's nonrecurring closing costs, the lender's appraiser might deem this to be a price concession on the part of the seller and adjust the appraised value accordingly. This could affect the size of a loan a lender will be willing to give the buyer.

Some lenders offer buy-down programs which permit a seller to pay a fee to the lender in return for a reduction in the buyer's interest rate on the new home loan for a certain number of years. This makes it easier for the buyer to qualify for the loan, since the initial monthly payments are discounted.

Seller financing is another way to make a home more affordable. Sellers who do not need all the cash proceeds from the sale of their home might offer to carry a first or second loan for the buyer. It's important that seller-assisted financing not inflate the value of the property if the buyer is obtaining a new first loan as a part of the purchase. For instance, if the fair market value of the home is $250,000 and you agree to sell for $260,000 including a seller carry-back second of $30,000, you may run into trouble when the lender of the new first loan is unable to appraise the property for the sale price or if the buyer defaults and you have to foreclose. If the purchase price is justifiable, you should have no problem.

Sellers who are in a position to carry a second mortgage equal to 10 percent of the purchase price for a buyer who only has enough cash to make a 10 percent down payment can make the buyer's purchase more affordable by enabling the buyer to obtain a loan for 80 percent of the purchase price. Eighty percent financing is preferable to 90 percent financing because the interest rate is usually lower and PMI (Property Mortgage Insurance) and an impound account are not required. It may be risky to carry a second mortgage for a buyer who's getting an ARM first loan that allows negative amortization. (See Chapter 10 for more information about financing.)

Sometimes the agents involved in a contract negotiation will be agreeable to reducing their commission in order to help make the transaction work. Granted this won't be a viable option where the buyer and seller are light-years apart. And, if you already negotiated a cut-rate commission with your broker at the time you listed the house, don't expect more commission cutting at the contract negotiation stage. But, if the brokers are willing to reduce their commission, this enables the seller to reduce the selling price to the buyer and thereby makes the house more affordable.

Multiple Offers

Sellers who list their homes during strong real estate markets may experience the good fortune of receiving multiple offers. Custom varies from area to area as to how multiple offers are presented to the sellers, but they should be handled in such a way as to ensure fairness to all parties and to protect the sellers from inadvertently selling the property to more than one buyer.

The preferred custom is to notify the sellers and each buyer's agent that there are multiple offers. The sellers' agent should refrain from reviewing the

144

terms of each offer before the presentation to ensure confidentiality and fair dealing. If the sellers' listing agent has written an offer for a prospective buyer, the agent's broker should step in to represent the sellers so that the listing agent is not privy to other buyers' offers.

Offers should be presented to the sellers and their agent in private by each buyer's agent. After hearing all offers, the sellers and their agent can confer privately to determine the appropriate course of action. Since there is only one house to sell and several willing buyers, it's advisable to counter only one offer in writing. Sellers who insist on countering more than one offer should rank them in order of priority and notify each buyer in writing that multiple written counters are being made. For instance, "This is counteroffer B, which is made subject to the collapse of counteroffer A."

Sellers listing a home in an active market, particularly if prices are increasing rapidly, should ensure that they get good market exposure before accepting any offer to purchase. It may be advisable to let agents know, when the property goes on the market, that offers will not be heard for several days (a specific date should be set). This will give agents an opportunity to show the home to their buyers and will maximize the sellers' chances of receiving multiple offers. Multiple offers don't always materialize at the same time, and the first buyer to make an offer is not necessarily the one who will end up with an acceptance.

Joyce Wong saw a house she loved on a Saturday morning and made an offer through her agent for less than the asking price. Since the house was new on the market and Joyce was the first buyer to see it, the sellers countered at full price. Joyce countered the sellers' counter at a compromise price and gave the sellers until Sunday night to decide. A second buyer walked through the open house Sunday afternoon, fell in love with the home, and wrote a full-price offer on the spot. The sellers accepted the second offer and notified Joyce that they rejected her counteroffer. Joyce was furious because she felt the sellers should have given her another opportunity to reconsider before even entertaining another offer. The sellers were under no obligation to do so, since Joyce had rejected their counter. Had Joyce signed the sellers' counter, the house would have been hers.

145

Backup Offers

A backup offer is an offer that's accepted subject to the collapse of the offer in primary position. It may be one of a number of multiple offers, or it may be an offer that's presented after the seller has already accepted another offer. Remember, all offers must be presented to the seller. A backup offer is negotiated just as if it were a primary offer, but the purchase agreement must contain a clause specifying that it is a backup offer and subject to the collapse of the primary offer (paragraph 21 of the CAR purchase agreement). There is no limit to how many backup offers you can have, but they must be numbered in order of priority so that there's no confusion or dispute on the part of the buyers as to whose offer has priority.

The benefit of being in backup position is that if something goes wrong with the first offer and that deal is canceled, your offer automatically moves into primary position, if you're in backup position number one, without the house being formally marketed to the public again.

A negative aspect of being in backup position is that it's difficult to continue to seriously look for another house when you have your heart set on getting the house on which you have made a backup offer. But you should continue to look, as hard as this might be.

A signed backup offer tends to solidify the first buyer's resolve to continue with the contract if unanticipated problems arise during the escrow period, such as property defects discovered during inspections.

In fairness to the buyers, a backup offer usually contains a provision allowing withdrawal from backup position at any time prior to written notification of elevation to first position. The buyer's notification of withdrawal should be in writing.

Backup buyers should read the backup-position clause carefully to make sure they understand what conditions apply. Some clauses permit the sellers to negotiate freely with the buyers in first position before canceling the contract. Backup buyers are often miffed to find out the sellers renegotiated their contract with the primary buyers in order to reach a satisfactory compromise without giving the backup buyers a chance to buy the house.

146

When Is a House Sold?

After the seller has accepted an offer to purchase, the escrow period begins. During this period, which can vary anywhere from a week to several months or more (45 to 60 days is customary), the property is said to have a pending sale. It's not technically sold until title transfers to the new buyer at the close of escrow.

It's advisable for a seller to continue to show the property to prospective buyers in the hopes of generating a backup offer, at least until inspection and buyer's loan prequalification contingencies have been satisfied. When another buyer's agent calls about the home, the seller should inform the agent that an offer has been accepted but that there are contingencies and the property is available for showing. A seller who has accepted an offer contingent upon the sale of another property should encourage showings until the other property has sold and the buyers have removed that contingency.

Many sellers make the mistake of telling prospective buyers or their

> *Sellers should continue to show their home to other prospective buyers after they have accepted an offer until their buyer's contingencies are removed from the purchase contract.*

agents that their home is sold when in fact they are still in the midst of negotiating a purchase contract. A sale is not pending until the purchase agreement and all counteroffers have been fully signed and accepted by all parties involved. Rumors spread fast within the real estate community, and the last thing sellers want is to have local agents think their home is sold when it's not.

Contract Contingencies

A clause stating that "time is of the essence" is a part of most residential real estate purchase agreements. If it doesn't exist in the preprinted contract it can be added in an addendum or counteroffer (see paragraph 35 of the purchase contract). This phrase means that the parties agree that timely performance is an important part of the agreement.

Confusion often arises concerning precisely what date a contingency is to be removed from the contract. To arrive at the correct date, count the acceptance date as day one. If the final day falls on a Sunday or government holiday, the contingency removal is due the following day. It's preferable to use calendar days, rather than business or working days, for contingency time periods, but some contracts specify business days, so check this carefully. Ask your agent to prepare a summary of the contract contingency dates and forward a copy to the other agent to ensure that everyone involved in the transaction is operating on the same time schedule.

Ideally, all contingencies (and waivers of contingencies) should be removed from the contract in writing. If this condition is not a part of your contract and you have any question regarding the status of a contingency, ask your agent to address your concern in a letter or inquiry to the other party or agent. If written approval or disapproval of contingencies is a part of your contract and a contingency is due but has not yet been removed, have your agent notify the other party in writing that either the contingency should be removed or a reasonable extension requested within 24 hours.

147

Coping with Buyer's and Seller's Remorse

Buyers and sellers may experience a peculiar reaction during the course of a real estate transaction. It's called remorse, and it usually sets in just after you've entered into a purchase agreement. The best thing to do if you start feeling you've made the wrong decision is to realize that this sort of emotional reaction is natural and will pass. Don't make the mistake of attaching more significance to these feelings than is warranted. Some people will be inclined to think that if their decision to buy was a good one, they wouldn't be feeling anxious. To the contrary, people who are prone to suffer from buyer's remorse will probably feel uncomfortable about making any major commitment.

Some sellers suffer a psychological jolt the first time they see a "For Sale" sign in front of their home. Or they feel resentful when they find a stack of Realtors' cards on the coffee table. This is understandable, since your home is both your haven and an extension of your identity. The selling process can seem like an intrusion on sacred territory.

Buyer's remorse can set in as early as the first time buyers see a house they really want to buy. Don't be surprised if you hear yourself saying, "I'm really not interested in this house," even though you've looked for months and have finally found the home of your dreams. An approach/avoidance response is quite common; change is difficult for most of us, even position change.

Buyer's remorse seems to be triggered by the uncertainty that results from relinquishing control. Even though your present house may no longer suit your needs, it's still home; it's comfortable and it feels secure. When you decide to buy a new home, you're forced to step outside your current comfort zone into the unknown. Your mind may try to compensate psychologically for feelings of uncertainty by mentally undoing the event. In other words, you may try to talk yourself out of buying the home you've fallen in love with. Couple feelings of uncertainty with the fear of making a long-term commitment and it's easy to understand why home buyers can suffer bouts of anxiety.

Some people won't experience remorse at all. Others will worry incessantly. Most buyers and sellers will fall somewhere in between the two extremes. A lot depends on the individual. For instance, if you have a high tolerance for uncertainty, you'll suffer less than someone who has a need to feel in control.

148

One way to minimize remorse is to do your homework before you buy or sell. Become knowledgeable about home prices in the area. Find out about different kinds of mortgages. Study the sample contracts you'll be using. Have the house you're buying thoroughly inspected to make sure you aren't buying unwanted problems. Budget your finances to make sure you aren't getting in over your head. Read this book from cover to cover before you enter into a buy or sell contract; refer back to it from time to time during the transaction when questions arise.

Revisit the house you're buying if you suffer from doubt; this will help you put your decision in proper prospective. Some buyers validate their purchase decisions by continuing to look at other houses until they have inspected the house they're buying and have financing lined up. Ask your agent to keep you informed about other sales in the area. Make sure your agent keeps you well informed during the transaction. This will help you to minimize any anxiety you have about this unfamiliar situation. A skillful and experienced agent will recognize early signs of remorse and be able to help you through a period of indecision without making you feel pressured.

CHAPTER 8

'TERMITE' *INSPECTIONS,* REPORTS, *and* REPAIRS

Let's Talk Termite

There's a common misconception that a "termite report" is concerned only with determining whether a property is infested with termites. In fact, a "termite report" is really a Wood Destroying Pests and Organisms Inspection Report (formerly called a Structural Pest Control Inspection Report). It documents the presence or absence of infestation or infection by wood destroying organisms, including dry rot, fungus, beetles, and other wood pests, not just termites. A Wood Destroying Pests and Organisms Inspection Report is prepared by a licensed structural pest control operator.

California state law does not require that a Wood Destroying Pests and Organisms report be completed when a home is sold, but many lenders require a pest report before they will approve a new loan. And some lenders insist that corrective work specified in the report be completed before the close of escrow, particularly if the buyer is putting down less than 20 percent cash or if the lender's appraiser recommends that wood destroying pest damage be repaired. "Termite reports" have, therefore, become an integral part of a home sale in California, and it's generally thought to be good protection for the buyer to require that the property be inspected by a licensed structural pest control operator as a condition of the purchase agreement.

Deciding when to order the report is a subject of debate. A seller listing an older home is advised to have the property inspected before listing or as soon after as possible. A caution regarding the presale inspection: It can become outdated if the home doesn't sell within a reasonable period of time. The inspector should put in writing how long the report and price estimates are good for and what the cost of a reinspection report would be.

In most parts of the state, it's customary for a buyer to ask the seller to pay for or complete structural pest control corrective work as part of the property sale agreement. Sellers who order a presale inspection report can ask the buyers to accept this report. If the buyers elect to obtain their own pest report on the property, the sellers will at least have a report that can be referred to in the contract, and they can limit their liability to the amount stated in this report.

Sellers who do not order a presale pest report are advised to make their acceptance of an offer to purchase their home contingent upon approving a current

149

report within several days of receiving one. Buyers will also want to approve the report. Sellers who agree to complete repairs for a buyer without having a concrete dollar amount for the required work are signing the equivalent of a blank check. Sellers should verify and approve the amount required for structural pest control work before they agree to pay for the work.

Structural pest control inspectors and companies are licensed by the state of California, which means that their activities are subject to specific rules and regulations. A structural pest control company is accountable to both the buyer and seller in a transaction, regardless of who pays for the inspection. In addition, state law requires the seller or the seller's agent to provide the buyer with a copy of the Wood Destroying Pests and Organisms inspection report of the property "as soon as practicable" before close of escrow. Legislation regarding the structural pest control inspection industry is constantly being amended to reflect current consumer needs, and the Structural Pest Control Board is available to hear consumer complaints.

> *Sellers must disclose all Wood Destroying Pests and Organisms inspection reports completed within two years.*

Selecting a 'Termite' Company and Ordering the Inspection

150

Selecting the right structural pest control company is a bit like choosing the right real estate agent. If you were pleased with the company that inspected your home when you purchased it, call them to complete a presale inspection report. Be wary of using an out-of-the-area company that might not be familiar with local conditions. Choose a local company with a good reputation for your presale inspection so that the buyers will feel comfortable accepting the report. Ask your agent for recommendations. Once you've settled on a company, call the Structural Pest Control Board in Sacramento, which free of charge will check any complaint history against the company for the past two years .

Sellers ordering an inspection report will want the report segregated into Section I and Section II findings. Section I findings are items of active infestation and/or damage resulting from infestation. Section II findings include conditions where no active infestation is present, but which will lead to future problems if left unchecked. If the lender requires that pest control work be completed as a condition of giving the buyer a new loan, it's usually only the Section I work that needs to be done. Often, who pays to correct the Section II work is subject to negotiation between the buyer and seller. In most cases, sellers will want to exclude detached structures, such as a garage

> *Sellers should ask the structural pest control company to divide the inspection report into Section I and Section II findings.*

or tool shed, from the inspection. A lender will usually not require that these be inspected.

If the structural pest control company is in the business of performing structural pest control repair work, ask for an itemized repair estimate. This will be important should you decide to have other contractors complete the recommended repair work. In this case, you may need to have the company who issued the report return to reinspect the property after the corrective work has been completed. If the company that inspected the property provided cost estimates as part of the original inspection report or thereafter, this company is required by law to complete a reinspection of the property—even if they do not perform the corrective work—as long as the reinspection is ordered within four months of the original inspection. The company can charge no more for the reinspection than was charged for the original inspection.

How to Read a 'Termite' Report

There are four basic parts to a Wood Destroying Pests and Organisms Inspection Report. The first is a grid itemizing structural pest control problems and the locations on the structure where the problems might be found. The pest control problems are listed across the top of the grid. The thirteen categories included are: Inaccessible Areas; Not Inspected; Further Inspection; Subterranean Termites; Drywood Termites; Fungus or Dry Rot; Other Wood Pests; Dampwood Termites; Earth-Wood Contacts; Faulty Grade Levels; Cellulose Debris; Excessive Moisture; and Shower Leaks. Eleven areas of the structure are listed along the side of the grid. The areas included are: Substructure Area; Stall Shower; Foundations; Porches-Steps; Ventilation; Abutments; Attic Spaces; Garages; Decks-Patios; Other-Interior; and Other-Exterior. The grid field is checked by the inspector to indicate pest control problems and where they are found.

151

The grid form will also specify where the inspector posted the inspection tag and if any other inspection tags were found. A licensed structural pest control operator is required by law to post an inspection tag (and a completion tag, if the company does the repair work) on the property. The tags are usually posted either at the entrance to the attic or subarea or in the garage and will include the name of the inspection company, the date of the inspection, and a statement that the tag is not to be removed.

The second part of the inspection report includes a diagram of the structure. A numeric/alpha numbering system is used to locate each structural pest control finding on the diagram. For example, the first area of the structure on the grid is the Substructure. The first structural pest control finding in the Substructure is designated as item number 1A on the diagram. The second finding in the Substructure is 1B, and so on. The second area of the structure on the grid is Stall Shower. The first Stall Shower finding is designated as 2A, the second is 2B, and so on.

The third part of the inspection report consists of a narrative description of the findings itemized on the diagram and recommendations for correcting each problem. The findings are listed 1 to 11 to correspond with each area of the structure included on the grid. If a number is omitted, this means that the inspector did not find a pest problem in this area of the structure. Below each item there will be an indication whether the finding is a Section I or Section II finding. Each section of findings should have a heading that will correspond with the area of the structure where the problem was found (Substructure, Stall Shower, Foundations, etc.). Structural pest control inspectors will customarily not inspect inaccessible areas (for instance, areas behind finished walls) that do not show any outward signs of infestation or infection. Also, they will not be responsible for damage subsequently found in inaccessible areas they did not inspect.

Finally, if the inspection company is in the business of correcting structural pest control defects, an itemized cost estimate of recommended repairs should be included as a part of the report. If an itemized cost estimate is not automatically included, request it. Each numbered item from the narrative description and diagram will have a corresponding price quote for correcting the problem.

Call the inspector who examined the property for a complete explanation if you have any questions. Watch out for statements like "if additional damage is found during the course of completing corrective work, a supplemental bill will be issued." An itemization of the costs of repair work should be complete and not open-ended. Occasionally, a structural pest control inspector will be unable to determine the extent of a problem without defacing the property, which you might not want done until your house is sold. In this case, have the inspector bid a worst case price so that at least you can negotiate with the buyer. If the work is then completed after escrow closes, at the seller's expense, specify in the purchase contract that any unused funds be returned to the seller. Insist that the termite company quote you a firm price before you authorize any work.

Sometimes a structural pest control company will find defects but suggest that another type of tradesperson (such as a plumber or tiler) do the work. The report may suggest that the homeowner consult the appropriate tradespeople for bids. Until you have obtained a bid for this work, you will not know the full extent of your structural pest control liability.

Who Pays for What?

The person obtaining the pest report usually pays the cost of the initial inspection, although one party can agree to reimburse the other if this is negotiated as part of the purchase agreement. Structural pest control companies often require payment for the inspection before issuing a written report. The cost of an inspection and report varies, but is usually around $150 for a structure of 3,000 square feet or less.

The seller usually pays to correct both the conditions that led to and the damage caused by active infestation and infection (the Section I work). The buyer usually takes responsibility for any work recommended to correct conditions that are deemed likely to lead to infestation or infection in the future (the Section II

152

work). The rationale behind this sharing of responsibility is that sellers should be liable for correcting problems that developed during their period of ownership and buyers should take care of problems that may develop after purchase.

Before agreeing to take responsibility for Section II findings, read them carefully and make sure you're not taking on a bigger project than you imagine. For instance, a large front stair and porch system that is at the end of its useful life, but that shows no signs of active infestation, could be noted as a Section II finding. If the porch will need replacing in another year or so and it will cost over $5,000 to fix, you may want to ask the seller to credit a few thousand dollars toward the future repair.

Who pays for structural pest control work, and how much, is negotiable. Some buyers prefer to buy a property in its "as is" condition with respect to these repairs, in which case they usually deduct the amount of the corrective work from the purchase price. In a strong buyer's market, sellers are more likely to be asked to pay for pest repairs than they are in a strong seller's market.

Inaccessible Areas and Further Inspections

The first thing you should do when reviewing a pest report is to see if the inspector checked any of the grid boxes under: Inaccessible Areas, Not Inspected, or Further Inspection. Although a seller may choose not to inspect a deteriorated detached garage or deck, a buyer should investigate the condition of all structures on the property. It's usually preferable to have detached structures inspected separately and not include the findings in the main dwelling report. If they are included in the main report, the lender may require all recommended repair work to be completed by close of escrow, which may be impractical. If detached structures are inspected separately, the buyers and sellers can negotiate a monetary compromise for needed repairs, either in the form of a credit for the buyer's nonrecurring closing costs or a price reduction. Or the buyers can buy the property "as is" with respect to detached structures, in which case the lender doesn't have to be involved.

A recommendation for further inspection signifies that the pest report is not complete. It's advisable, in most cases, to obtain a complete inspection. If a further inspection is not ordered when it's recommended, the structural pest control company won't take responsibility for subsequent damage or infestation that might be discovered in the uninspected area.

The CAR Purchase Contract and Receipt for Deposit makes a specific suggestion on how the payment for further inspections should be handled if they are recommended in the inspection report (see section 19 of the CAR Purchase

153

Buyers should order a further inspection if it's recommended in the pest report.

Contract included in Chapter 7). If the buyer requests that the further inspection be made, it's done at the buyer's expense. If infestation, infection, or damage is discovered, the cost to correct the condition plus the cost of entering and closing the inaccessible areas is paid by the respective party designated in paragraphs A, D, and/or E of section 19. If no infestation, infection, or damage is found, the buyer pays the cost of entering and closing the areas.

A seller should require that a buyer deposit funds with the structural pest control company to cover the opening and closing of inaccessible areas before the additional inspections are ordered. Or the buyers could give the escrow holder instructions to release part of their deposit to the pest control company to cover this expense, if this is acceptable to the sellers. If the transaction is terminated, the seller could otherwise have difficulty collecting this money directly from the buyer. Also, it should be a condition of the purchase agreement that both buyers and sellers read and approve all pest reports that were not available at the time the purchase contract was negotiated, including supplemental reports issued following inspections of inaccessible areas.

A word of caution about the recommendation for further inspections. A structural pest control inspector will not automatically complete a further inspection, as it will usually involve defacing a homeowner's property to some extent. The inspector will want the homeowner's permission first, which is understandable. However, if the owner is at home during the initial inspection, the inspector should inform the owner that further inspections are indicated and explain what will be involved. If the owner authorizes the work on the spot and the inspector does not need specialized equipment to complete the further inspection, it should be done at that time. A further inspection which requires the inspector to return to the property on a separate occasion will usually involve an additional fee. A seller who is home during the initial inspection and is not informed that further inspections are necessary should discuss this with the structural pest control company if the subsequent inspection report includes recommendations for further inspections which will only be completed by request and at additional expense.

The Pros and Cons of Getting a Second Report

There are several reasons why a buyer or seller might want to obtain a second, or even third, pest report. A buyer could have had a previous bad experience with the pest control company that issued the current report on the seller's home. Or the buyer may have been advised to get a second opinion, regardless of who completed the inspection report for the seller. Also, a seller could question the accuracy of the first report, in which case they might ask a second company to inspect the home.

When ordering an additional report, keep in mind that all Wood Destroying Pests and Organisms reports obtained during the past two years must be delivered

154

to the buyer, even any that you dispute. Full disclosure is required by law, and it's good practice for sellers to make all reports, no matter how old, available to buyers.

Also, be aware that the inspection process is somewhat subjective. One inspector may believe that a damaged piece of wood is still serviceable, while another might call for its complete replacement. Nonetheless, two pest reports on the same house should reflect similar findings regarding the presence of structural pest control damage, infestation, and infection. Large discrepancies need to be brought to the attention of the companies that completed the reports.

When sellers have an existing report and the buyers obtain a second opinion that reveals additional damage that was not itemized in the first report, the sellers should meet with their initial inspector at the property. Similarly, sellers who purchased their home within the last year, and who had all the recommended work completed by the structural pest control company at that time, should have a serious discussion with that company if a new inspection report reveals a large amount of pest control damage that could not possibly have occurred within one year. If a licensed structural pest control operator did not complete the job properly, the cost of remedying the problem should not be the homeowner's responsibility. Call the Pest Control Board or a knowledgeable real estate attorney if you are concerned about damage that might have been overlooked and you get no satisfaction from talking directly with a representative from the pest control company. Be aware that a structural pest control operator is permitted to modify a pest report to include additional damage and infestation if the revision is made before the company is paid for pest control repair work.

155

> **Gini Young listed her house for sale and had it inspected. She hired the same pest control company that completed the repair work on the house when she originally bought it. The inspector issued a report calling for about $1500 of repair work. When the buyer had the house inspected by a general house inspector, that inspector found something that had been overlooked by the structural pest control inspector. The pest control inspector returned to the property, admitted he had missed a major item, and amended his report to call for an additional $5,000 of necessary repair work. After serious negotiations between the inspector, the seller, and the real estate agents, the inspector agreed to do the work at his cost, but he refused to complete the work at no additional cost. The purchase contract then had to be renegotiated between the buyer and seller because the seller had limited her pest liability to the amount of the original report: $1,500.**

Although consumers are entitled to expect some consistency between the findings of two or more current reports on the same home, the recommendations on how to correct the defects will often vary from one company to the next, as will cost estimates for repairs.

Wood Destroying Pests and Organisms Inspection Reports become a part of the public record, and anyone can obtain copies of these reports and notices of completion that were filed on a property within the past two years by making a written request to the Structural Pest Control Board and paying a nominal fee.

How to Interpret Primary and Secondary Recommendations

Often a pest report will contain both a primary and a secondary recommendation for how to remedy a specific problem. The primary recommendation is the preferred method of repair; however, the secondary recommendation will be adequate for the purpose of issuing a notice of completion stating that the property is free and clear of active infestation.

Consult with an independent licensed contractor to determine if the primary recommendation is realistic or if it's an overassessment of what's necessary. A secondary recommendation may be satisfactory in terms of treating active infestation but might not be a long-term solution to a structural pest control problem.

Normally, the primary recommendation is more expensive; however, buyers should be aware that a secondary recommendation may require additional repairs in the future (at the buyer's expense), whereas a primary recommendation will often be a permanent solution to the problem. For instance, a wood retaining wall with earth-wood contact might exhibit some fungus damage but still be serviceable if chemical treatment is administered. In this case, chemical treatment would be a secondary recommendation.

The primary recommendation would be to tear out the existing wall and install an engineered concrete retaining wall in its place. This solution would effectively remove the earth-wood contact as well as take care of the existing infestation problem. The cost differential between these two procedures is significant. Whether primary or secondary recommendations are accepted can become a negotiable issue between buyers and sellers.

Sam and Teresa Watkins accepted a secondary recommendation to treat a fungus-damaged deck chemically when they purchased their home. Two years later, Sam was transferred out of state and the home had to be sold. Buyers made an offer conditioned upon Sam and Teresa providing a current pest report and repairing any damage. The new report called for total replacement of the deck, as it was now damaged beyond repair; no secondary recommendation was made. Sam complained to the inspector but to no avail. The chemical treatment had arrested the fungus deterioration but scattered pockets of dry rot were now evident throughout the deck, including the

156

support posts. The only way for Sam and Teresa to repair the damage was to have the deck torn down and rebuilt at considerable expense.

Scheduling Structural Pest Control Work

Scheduling structural pest control repair work requires that the seller (and buyer, if there is a pending sale on the property) sign a Work Authorization form. Normally, the structural pest control company will bill the escrow company if there is a pending sale and will receive payment from the seller's proceeds at or after the close of escrow. If the job is sizable (in excess of $5,000 or so), however, the company may require partial payment in advance.

It's important in active markets to schedule structural pest control inspections and repairs well in advance so the work can be completed by close of escrow. This is particularly important if a lender requires the work to be done before issuing a loan to the buyer. Some lenders will permit escrow to close without the repair work being completed. Such a lender will usually make it a condition of closing that the repair work be completed within 90 days following the close date. In addition, the lender may require that excess funds be left in an escrow account until the work is finished (usually one and a half or two times the cost of the repair work). The rationale behind this requirement is that if extra money is held, the work will be completed in a timely fashion. Most lenders cannot sell their loans to investors until the wood destroying pest repair work is done, so they are anxious to have the work done as soon as possible. It's usually the seller who is required to leave the extra money in escrow pending completion of structural pest control work on the property, although this is also negotiable.

157

One advantage to having structural pest control work completed after the close of escrow is that, while there is some inconvenience in having work done on a home after taking possession, at least then the buyer is in a position to supervise the work. After all, the buyer has to live with the structural pest control company's work in the future, not the seller.

Fran Goldberg and her sister Carol bought an older house that needed a lot of work. They negotiated to have the seller pay for the structural pest control work, which was considerable, and since the seller had already vacated the property, they scheduled the work to be done before the close of escrow. Imagine how devastated Fran and Carol were when their Realtor took them by the house to measure for drapes and they discovered the structural pest control contractors had demolished the wrong bathroom: the only decent room in the house. The pest control company did take responsibility for their mistake and retiled the bathroom, but there was no way to salvage the irreplaceable vintage tile.

A word of advice: If you take a credit for nonrecurring closing costs, or a price reduction, in lieu of having the seller complete pest repairs, be sure you have the work done after close of escrow. Many buyers fail to complete the work, often because they think it's not necessary. They are then unpleasantly surprised when they sell and find that the problems are much more expensive to fix.

Having 'Termite' Work Completed by Other Contractors

Buyers and sellers have expressed dissatisfaction with the Wood Destroying Pests and Organisms inspection process in California because frequently the company that inspects a property and issues the report is the same company that performs the required corrective work. It's possible to have other licensed contractors perform many of the recommended structural pest control repairs. This will sometimes result in a savings to the homeowner.

There are other reasons why you might use a contractor who isn't a licensed structural pest control operator to complete wood destroying pest repairs. Sometimes the company that issues the inspection report is not in the business of repairing structural pest defects. In active markets, the structural pest control company that performs the initial inspection on the property may be too busy to complete the repair work prior to close of escrow. Or sometimes a company known for performing competent inspections does not have a good reputation for the quality of their repair work.

158

Contractors should provide the homeowner with firm written bids for the work to be performed and obtain city building permits when necessary. All permits taken out to correct structural pest control defects should be signed off by the city building inspector before the contractors are paid in full. The homeowner will want to keep copies of all permits on file. After the work is completed, the homeowner needs to have the property reinspected by a licensed structural pest control operator in order for a notice of completion to be issued.

Occasionally, sellers will complete items on a pest report that do not require special expertise. One repair that's frequently performed by homeowners is removal of cellulose debris, which is nothing more than scraps or pieces of wood found in the substructure of the building. Cellulose debris is of concern to structural pest control inspectors because it can provide a nesting site for termites. Homeowners will often hire a handyman to complete other recommended repairs that do not require the skill of a licensed contractor or building permits.

One benefit of hiring a structural pest control company or licensed contractor to complete structural pest control repair work is that both are licensed by the state. If there's a problem with the corrective work after the close of escrow, the buyer will have recourse against the contractor. Make sure, as a seller, that you are not responsible for correcting future structural pest defects that arise as a result of shoddy work completed by unlicensed contractors. Remember also that even if a homeowner hires licensed contractors to complete termite repairs, only a structural pest control company can apply chemicals for treatment of infestation or infection.

Take special care in selecting a company to complete fumigation of a property. Since tenting a structure can result in damage to the roof, a structural pest company will usually require that the homeowner sign a hold-harmless clause which states that the company will not be held liable for inadvertent damage to the structure or landscaping.

The Notice of Completion

There is another misconception about the "termite" business. Buyers, sellers, agents, and lenders often refer to the notice that is issued by a structural pest control company after the recommended work has been completed as a "termite clearance." There is, however, no such thing as a "termite clearance." If a structural pest control inspector inspects a property and finds no infestation by wood destroying pests, an inspection report stating that the property is free and clear of active infestation will be issued. If pest control damage is found and is repaired, the termite company will then issue a completion notice.

Formally known as the "Standard Notice of Work Completed and Not Completed," this form refers to the original inspection report by number, date, and registration stamp number. It lists the repair recommendations completed by the company (as numbered in the original inspection report) as well as those not completed. The total cost of the repairs will also appear on the notice of completion.

When some of the items are handled by other contractors, the notice of completion should indicate the items, by number, that were "completed by others" in the section entitled "Recommendations not completed by this firm." If all the work recommended in the original inspection report has been completed, this should be indicated in a statement that the property is now free of evidence of active infestation or infection.

Sellers who complete all the recommended structural pest control work themselves will not receive a notice of completion from a structural pest control company. If, however, the company that originally inspected the property included repair cost estimates, the seller can order a reinspection report from the same company anytime within four months of the original report.

In order to issue a notice of completion, a structural pest control company must first have issued an inspection report on the property. Keep this in mind if you ask a second structural pest control company for a bid to complete the work recommended in another company's report. If you want the second company to do the work, be sure that company issues its own inspection report on the property first. Otherwise, the company will not be able to issue a notice of completion when the work is done.

Some structural pest control companies will guarantee their repair work, usually for a period of one year. They will not, however, guarantee work done by

159

others. This is why it's important for a seller to use a licensed contractor with a good reputation for customer service if some or all of the repair work is to be completed by someone other than the structural pest control company.

After the notice of completion is signed by the buyer and seller, the escrow company releases payment to the company that completed the repairs. Once in a while, there are excess funds left after the company is paid. These funds are normally released to the party who pays for the structural pest control repairs; confirmation of this should be made in writing and signed by both the buyers and sellers.

Handling Grievances

Occasionally, two pest reports will differ considerably in their findings. Alternatively, a homeowner might take issue with a specific finding contained in an inspection report, dispute a recommendation for correcting a defect, or be dissatisfied with the manner in which corrective work was completed. The homeowner's primary recourse is to discuss the matter with the inspector or the owner of the structural pest control company. In California, the Structural Pest Control Board regulates all licensed pest control operators. Serious disputes that cannot be settled directly should be brought to the attention of this board. If the board is unable to mediate a complaint, contact the Better Business Bureau or consult a real estate attorney. A two-year statute of limitations applies to all inspection reports and notices of completion. This means that a complaint must be filed with the board within two years of the inspection or notice of completion date. Wood destroying pest problems that develop after the date of inspection are not the responsibility of the structural pest control company.

160

Protect Your Investment

Prudent homeowners will have their property reinspected by a reliable structural pest control operator every two or three years so that there are no big surprises in store when it comes time to sell. Pest control problems often cost less to repair if they're detected and remedied in the early stages. The cost of an inspection report is minimal compared to the potential expense of ignoring a major defect.

Many buyers feel it's a waste of money to have a newly constructed home inspected for structural pest infestation. Again, the cost is minimal compared to possible consequences. Be aware that requirements of the Structural Pest Control Act differ from some modern building code requirements.

Periodic inspections by a structural pest control operator should be part of your home maintenance regime.

Even if there is no active infestation, the buyer of a newly constructed home should be made aware of conditions that may lead to infestation problems. Cellulose debris, for instance, is commonly found under new homes. It's also possible that the building materials could have been infested before construction, particularly by dry wood termites. A new construction site could require chemical treatment for the control of subterranean termites that are frequent inhabitants of the soils of Northern California.

Don't ignore Section II items. Some real estate agents downplay the importance of Section II findings, calling them merely maintenance notations. Ignoring a Section II finding can be costly in the long run. For instance, caulking a shower to prevent leakage is easy to take care of for minimal expense. Replacing a leaky shower, which will result if the caulking is overlooked, can run into thousands of dollars.

Once you've taken care of active infestation, establish a routine program of preventative maintenance to keep future pest control problems to a minimum. The biggest culprit in terms of wood pest damage is water. Keep gutters and downspouts clean and make sure water is directed away from the foundation. Seal exterior cracks before each rainy season and check windows for excessive moisture. Keep bathtubs, sinks, and toilets caulked and sealed, and check regularly for plumbing leaks. Have the roof and gutters checked every few years by a licensed professional. Old roofs and gutters can cause water to leak into exterior walls which can result in extensive damage.

161

CHAPTER 9

PHYSICAL *INSPECTIONS*

The Physical Inspection

A physical inspection is always necessary, regardless of how much you think you know about the structural integrity of a house. Ideally, the inspection contingency in the purchase contract should be written in a broad enough fashion to allow any and all inspections that are deemed necessary. It's often difficult to know in advance which inspections will be needed. For instance, you may not think you need a specific inspection of the drainage system, but your general house inspector could recommend this after taking a good look underneath the house. Don't trust yourself to do your own inspection. Even building contractors buying homes for themselves may suffer from myopia when it comes to detecting defects.

162

> Take the case of Randy Capp, a licensed contractor with years of experience building new homes, who purchased an older home to renovate for profit without obtaining an independent inspection. When Randy sold the home, the buyer's inspector recommended that the local utility company check the gas furnace since it appeared to be old and emitted a peculiar odor. The utility company shut the furnace down because it was cracked and leaking hazardous fumes. Randy never personally occupied the home and was unaware of this defective condition but, since he contracted to sell a house equipped with an operative furnace, he was obliged to install at his expense a new one before close of escrow.

Anyone who wants to buy badly enough can develop blinders to virtually any potential house problem. Don't make the mistake of waiving your rights to inspect a property just for the sake of relieving the anxiety of not knowing where you'll be moving to next. You won't be doing the seller a favor, either, if your folly results in a lawsuit regarding defects that might have been discovered ahead of time.

Many buyers think they're protected if a current Wood Destroying Pests and Organisms Inspection (commonly referred to as a "termite" report) has been completed on the property. Keep in mind that a pest report is limited to inspection for wood destroying organisms only, and may give little information regarding the condition of the roof, drainage system, and foundation, not to mention the mechanical systems of the home. A general physical inspection is a professional evaluation of the house and its major systems. Defects in any of the major components of a house can be expensive to repair.

Sometimes a pest report will mention conditions that are outside of its specific jurisdiction. For instance, if the structural pest control inspector sees cracks in a foundation, a roof that shows weathering, or a potential drainage problem, a disclaimer may be contained in the report suggesting that the buyer seek the advice of the appropriate professional. Such items should be reviewed by the buyers. Don't, however, count on a structural pest control inspection report to pinpoint problems that aren't the direct responsibility of the structural pest control inspector.

Even if you're purchasing a newly constructed home, or a condominium or townhouse, have it inspected by a general building inspector. One of the difficulties inherent in new homes is that they haven't weathered the years, so it's difficult to predict if problems will arise in the future. One advantage of buying an older home is that it's been put through the test of time.

When inspecting a new home, make the plans, soils report, engineering calculations, city inspector reports, and any other relevant documentation available to the building inspector. The inspector's review of these documents should reveal if the home has been properly constructed and if the removal of the inspection contingency needs to be conditioned upon the builder's completing or remedying unacceptable conditions. In addition, have the general building inspector help to complete a punch list of items that the builder must attend to before the close of escrow.

There are rare instances when a buyer won't be able to include a physical inspection contingency in the offer to purchase. Estate (probate) and foreclosure sales are usually "as is" sales and are exempted from the Transfer Disclosure requirement. When purchasing an estate or foreclosure property, it's imperative to have the property thoroughly inspected by both a structural pest control inspector and a general building inspector. In a normal home sale, the physical inspection is usually ordered by the buyer after the purchase offer has been signed by both buyer and seller. If the offer to purchase an estate or foreclosure property must be "as is," without any contingencies, have the property inspected in advance of presenting the purchase contract.

The Buyer's Investigation of Property Condition clause of the CAR purchase contract (paragraph 9) states that inspections are to be done at the buyer's expense, and that the buyer agrees to deliver copies of inspection reports to the seller if the seller so requests. Paragraph 24-E of the CAR contract allows the buyer to disapprove of any item discovered during the inspections. The seller then has the right to correct the item. If the seller is unwilling or unable to correct it, the buyer may cancel the contract. Implicit in this agreement is the notion that the buyer will not unreasonably withhold the approval of this contingency, but

163

will give the seller the opportunity to remedy defects. What this means is that the buyer will not use the inspection contingency as a way to back out of the contract for reasons other than the existence of defects that the seller is unwilling or unable to remedy.

How to Select a General Building Inspector

Home inspectors are not licensed in California, and recently, the home inspection business has been flooded with people who have marginal qualifications. Ideally, the general inspector you select should be either an engineer, an architect, or a contractor. When possible, hire an inspector who belongs to one of the home inspection trade organizations. The California Real Estate Inspection Association (CREIA) sets standards for member firms and, on a national level, the American Society of Home Inspectors (ASHI) has developed formal inspection guidelines and a professional code of ethics for its members. Membership to ASHI is not automatic; proven field experience and technical knowledge about structures and their various systems and appliances are a prerequisite.

General home inspections cost between $200 and $400, depending on the inspector and on whether the inspection includes an oral or a written report. It's generally preferable to have a written inspection report, as this may be helpful when you decide to sell the house at a later date. Also, if defects are discovered, a written report will provide documentation of the problem for the seller. An oral representation of a defect may not carry the same weight as a written disclosure, so if you select an inspector who only offers oral reports or whose written reports are extremely expensive, ask that significant defects be put in writing.

Definitely find an inspector who is knowledgeable about local properties and soil conditions. Don't use an inspector from out of the area, and don't hire an inspector who has a vested interest in the property. Find out if an inspector you're considering will take responsibility for defects missed during an inspection, and inquire if the inspector carries errors and omissions insurance. If you're buying the house with a contractor, have an independent, impartial contractor complete the inspection. The inspector should not be someone you intend to hire to repair any defects that are found or to complete work on the property at some later date.

The Scope of the General Inspection

Before the inspection begins, establish precisely what is to be included in the inspection. A general building inspection should cover the general site; the surrounding topography; sidewalks and streets adjacent to the property; the house exterior; the roof, downspouts, and gutter system; drainage in and around the house; the foundation, including basements and crawl spaces; the interior walls, floors, windows, and doors; the electrical, plumbing, and heating/cooling systems; the appliances; the attic; visible insulation; patios and decks; the fireplace; the garage; health hazards and code violations.

The buyer should accompany the building inspector if possible. This is perhaps the most important aspect of the home buying process, particularly for first-time buyers. Ask questions freely and request an oral summary of the findings at the end of the inspection. Bring along the seller's Transfer Disclosure statement, a current Wood Destroying Pests and Organisms Inspection Report, and any other reports you have, and ask the inspector to review them with you. Have the inspector pay particular attention to any red flag items noted by the listing or selling agent in the agent inspection portion of the Transfer Disclosure statement. For instance, if an agent mentions that there is a crack in the fireplace, find out if the inspector thinks this is a significant defect and if it warrants further inspection by a specialist. If you're buying a newly constructed home and have not ordered a Wood Destroying Pests and Organisms inspection report, ask the building inspector if there are indications that a report should be ordered.

Take a note pad to the inspection. One of the major benefits of a thorough inspection is learning precisely what routine maintenance the home will require. Make notes as you follow the inspector around the property.

Buyers purchasing a home long-distance should arrange for a relative or good friend who lives in the area of the home to attend the inspection. If this is not possible, ask your agent to tape-record the inspection and send the tape to you along with the written inspection report.

The ideal inspection is one that's conducted in the seller's absence. Sellers who must be present should not intrude. They can also have their agent follow up on the inspection and report back with a summary of the findings.

Buyers should understand, before they embark on a home inspection, that there will be some defects uncovered in almost any home. Have the inspector distinguish between insignificant flaws and major deficiencies. It's important to put the results of the inspection in perspective. A little bit of settling in an older home may be considered routine. Settling in a newly constructed home can indicate a bad foundation pour, which may be relatively insignificant, or improperly compacted fill (soil brought into the site in order to alter the ground level), which could be a major problem.

You will usually need the written report as soon as possible, since inspection contingencies are normally removed within the first two weeks after acceptance of a purchase contract. When you receive the report, don't be alarmed to find that it contains many disclaimers. Inspectors are well aware of their potential liability, and they usually build qualifications into written reports in order to protect themselves. If there's anything you don't understand in the report, call the inspector immediately and ask for clarification. Bring to the

Buyers should attend the general inspection of the home they're buying.

inspector's attention any qualifications in the report that seem unreasonable. Make notes of any such conversations you have with your inspector and, whenever possible, have the inspector respond to your questions in writing.

When to Order Additional Inspections

Any additional inspection recommended in the general report should be ordered and completed before the inspection contingency is removed from the purchase contract. For example, the report may suggest that the buyer seek the counsel of a licensed roofer, swimming pool inspector, drainage specialist, or soils expert in order to obtain a professional evaluation. Regardless of whether the recommendation is due to a suspected problem or merely a statement that certain systems have not been inspected conclusively, take the advice and follow through with the recommended reports.

Building code violations mentioned in a written inspection report need to be evaluated carefully. Most older homes do not conform to the current building code since code requirements have changed over the years. Sellers are usually not required to bring an older home up to modern code requirements before they sell, however.

If remodeling work has been done on a property, be aware that it may not have been covered by the required building permits. Owners and contractors often elect to bypass the building code process to avoid dealing with the bureaucracy, to save the cost of the permit, or to avoid a property tax reassessment. Lenders have started requesting verification that remodels were completed with permits in place before they will approve a loan. Ask the sellers to provide you with copies of any building permits on the property. If they don't have any and they're unsure whether structural improvements to the property were made with permits, check with the city building department.

Most city building departments will allow a homeowner to take out a permit for work that has already been completed. Keep in mind that to obtain final approval from the city on the finished renovation, you may have to open walls to verify that plumbing and electrical work was done according to code requirements.

Some code violations present health or safety hazards and should be corrected. Buyers who plan to remodel a home should be aware that they may be required to correct previous code violations.

When ordering additional inspections on the property, make certain in advance that you'll receive a report on the condition of the item in question and not merely a bid to replace it. Roofers, for instance, will often provide an estimate to replace an old roof with a new one with no evaluation at all of the existing roof. Roofs, septic systems, private wells, and swimming pools should always be examined by the appropriate qualified professional. There will usually be an additional charge if the location of the septic tank or well is unknown and needs to be determined as part of the inspection process.

Although obtaining additional inspections when they are recommended is critical, it's equally important to the successful completion of purchase negotia-

166

tions to approve or disapprove of all contract contingencies in a timely fashion. If the general inspector recommends a further inspection that cannot be completed before the contingency deadline, it's advisable that you remove the general inspection contingency (provided you're satisfied with the overall condition of the property) with the qualification that the contingency is being removed subject to the buyer's receiving a satisfactory report on that part of the property requiring further inspection.

A qualified contingency removal might be worded as follows: "Buyer removes inspection contingency, per paragraph 26 of the purchase agreement, pending acceptable documentation from the local gas company or a licensed heating contractor that the furnace is operable and in safe working order within ten calendar days."

An additional inspection by a soils or structural engineer will be expensive, often in excess of $1,000. If you're interested in purchasing the home so long as it's in safe condition, but your budget can't absorb the extra $1,000 and your inspector is concerned about the soil stability of the site, you might ask the seller to share the expense of further inspection. Most sellers would prefer to help with the cost rather than have a buyer terminate a contract.

Don't make the mistake of not ordering a further inspection on the assumption that the expense of repairing a system that breaks down following the close of escrow will automatically be covered by a home protection plan that you and the seller have agreed to purchase. If the seller is aware of pre-existing conditions in any of the systems or appliances to be covered by a home protection plan, these need to be disclosed to the home protection company at the time of application and will not be covered by the protection plan. The sellers are also required to disclose these defects to the buyers, and they may be required to repair them by close of escrow unless the buyers specifically agree in the purchase agreement to accept the defective items in their "as is" condition.

167

Environmental Hazards

Recently, concern has been raised about environmental hazards found in or on residential properties. Several years ago, the Real Estate Transfer Disclosure Statement was amended to specifically ask sellers if they are aware of any environmental hazards on their property. Environmental hazards that might exist on a residential property include asbestos, formaldehyde, radon gas, lead-based paint, fuel or chemical storage tanks, and contaminated water or soil, to name a few. A common problem is that many sellers are unaware of any such hazards on their property, but this doesn't mean they don't exist.

In 1989, the California legislature mandated the development of a consumer booklet on environmental hazards affecting residential properties. This booklet is to help homeowners and home buyers make informed decisions about environmental hazards. If this booklet is made available to a prospective home buyer, the sellers and real estate licensees are not required to provide any additional information on these hazards. However, sellers and real estate licensees must disclose the existence of any environmental hazards on the property that are known to them. A copy of *Environmental Hazards: A Guide For Homeowners and Buyers* can be obtained from the California Association of Realtors, 525 Virgil Avenue, Los Angeles, CA 90020 (213) 739-8227, at a cost of $3.54.

Asbestos has been used as both an insulating and a stiffening component in many home building products: ceiling tiles and sprayed ceilings; furnace, hot water pipe, boiler and stove insulation; roofing shingles and exterior siding; patching and sheetrock taping compounds; textured paints; vinyl floor tiles and sheet flooring; and appliances. Contact an asbestos-certified contractor for more information and a bid for proper asbestos removal or treatment if this is a concern to you. Do not attempt to remove asbestos yourself. Without proper handling, tiny asbestos particles can become airborne, creating a serious health hazard. If asbestos fibers are inhaled, the risk of contracting several types of cancer increases. It's doubtful that exposure to undisturbed asbestos is a health threat.

Determining if asbestos is present in a product may require chemical analysis, so don't let someone talk you into an expensive removal job without first determining conclusively whether the material in question contains a potentially hazardous amount of asbestos. Currently, there is no requirement for a seller to provide a buyer with an asbestos-free environment, although there has been a move in this direction in the California legislature.

Risk of exposure to radon gas is a concern to homeowners throughout the country because long-term exposure to high levels of radon may increase a person's risk of lung cancer. Radon appears to be less of a problem in California than elsewhere, although high levels have been found in Santa Barbara and Ventura counties, the north end of the San Fernando Valley, and in the Sierra Nevada Mountains. Radon is an invisible, odorless, and potentially deadly gas that is emitted from decaying underground uranium. Radon testing has not been standardized, and there is some concern that radon testing scams will become prevalent. Ask your real estate agent and general building inspector whether radon is a problem in your area. If it is, hire only an Environmental Protection Agency-approved tester. Call the California Department of Health Services Radon Program Hotline at (800) 745-7236 for a recommendation.

Excessive exposure to lead is a concern because it may cause damage to the kidneys, brain, and nervous system. Lead accumulates in the body, so even low levels of exposure may be harmful, particularly in children under the age of seven who are considered more vulnerable to the toxic effects of lead.

There's a good chance that homes built before 1978 will contain some lead-based paint, although the lead content in household paint was greatly reduced in 1950. The risk of lead poisoning from paint can be reduced by covering or replacing the painted surfaces. Don't attempt to remove lead-based paint yourself by sanding or torching. Contact your local health department to find qualified abatement contractors. Effective October 1, 1992, all applicants for FHA-insured mortgages who are buying homes built before 1978 must be provided with a Lead-Based Paint Notice.

Lead can also be found in drinking water, and it usually comes from lead solder or pipes. Lead pipes are usually found in older homes built before 1930, but the use of lead solder wasn't banned until 1988. If you suspect lead contamination of drinking water, have samples analyzed by a certified laboratory. Call your local health department for recommendations. Water testing kits are also available. For more information about paint and water testing kits, call the Lead Institute in San Francisco (415) 252-5530 or (800) 532-3837.

Formaldehyde, which has been used in the manufacturing of many home building products, is a colorless, pungent gas that is classified by the Environmental Protection Agency as a possible carcinogen. Air samples can be analyzed to determine levels of formaldehyde. Also, manufacturers will be able to tell you if a product contains formaldehyde.

Homes built before the 1930s that used heating oil for a period of time could still have a buried storage tank on the property. It's estimated that there are approximately 165,000 underground tanks in California. They can pose a problem if they leak and contaminate the surrounding soil and groundwater. Fuel oil tanks were usually capped off and abandoned when homeowners stopped using them in the 1940s. Often they were abandoned with oil still left in them, and in most cases, the current homeowners have no idea that there's an abandoned tank on the property.

The tanks eventually corrode and leak, if they were left partially filled. The cost to remove a residential tank is usually in the $5,000 to $15,000 range if there has been no contamination. Cleaning up a contaminated site can cost as much as $50,000 to $150,000, or more. Cities and counties vary in their regulations regarding the removal of abandoned underground storage tanks. The City of San Francisco, for example, requires the removal of a discovered tank at the homeowner's expense. Check with the hazardous materials division of your local city or county health department for more information about local regulations.

There are three indicators to look for in an older home to help determine if an abandoned tank might be present: a vent pipe, a fill pipe and cap, and capped-off pipes in the basement or crawl space of the house. If you're sure there's an abandoned tank on a property, but you can't find it, you may have to hire an environmental assessor to locate it.

There's an Underground Storage Cleanup Fund to help California homeowners with costly site cleanup. The fund is not available for tank removal, only for cleaning up a contaminated site. The homeowner pays the first $10,000; the fund covers the balance up to $1,000,000.

Homeowners and prospective buyers who are concerned about the proximity of a property to contaminated sites can order an environmental hazards report from either JCP Geologists in Cupertino, California, or Environmental Risk

169

Information and Imaging Services (ERIIS) in Alexandria, Virginia. Both reporting services rely on information from federal and state databases of known and suspected hazardous sites. Neither service provides an on-site analysis. You'll need to hire a local environmental consultant for an on-site investigation. The JCP report costs $85 and is ordered by calling (800) 748-5233. The ERIIS report (called the ERIIScan environmental property report) is available for $75 and is ordered by calling (800) 989-0403.

Recent studies have indicated that exposure to electromagnetic fields (EMF) produced by household appliances, electrical wiring, and high-tension power wires may cause cancer. As of this writing, these studies are inconclusive.

Abating an environmental hazard can be costly, and the laws covering environmental hazards are continually changing. If you suspect the presence of an environmental hazard on a property, be sure to consult the appropriate specialists so that you understand the full extent of the problem before proceeding with a purchase or sale.

Earthquake Retrofitting

Your general house inspector should examine the home to determine how well it's likely to withstand shaking from earthquakes. If your inspector doesn't have expertise in this area, hire an engineer or contractor who does to take a look at the house. Bring the seller's disclosure regarding earthquake hazards with you to the inspection. See Chapter 4 for more information about the seller's disclosure requirements on this subject.

Most houses that haven't been retrofitted for earthquakes can be strengthened to reduce the risk of earthquake damage. Although you're not required to strengthen your home to resist earthquakes, it's advisable to do so. The cost of retrofitting ranges from several hundred to thousands of dollars, depending on the age and condition of the house. The expense may be well worth it when you consider that earthquake insurance has a high deductible, usually 5 to 10 percent. Retrofitting can minimize the amount of damage, and therefore the amount you're likely to pay in future repairs.

To encourage earthquake retrofitting, the state provides a property tax exemption for such projects. That means that when you take out a permit to complete earthquake strengthening, your property taxes will not increase as they would with other remodeling projects. The tax exemption applies to projects completed on or after January 1, 1991 and completed on or before July 1, 2000. To ensure that you receive the exemption, you should file the appropriate form with the county tax assessor.

It's important to hire qualified engineers or contractors to create a set of retrofit specifications for your home. Then obtain competitive bids from several licensed contractors who have experience doing earthquake retrofit work. Many homeowners make the mistake of using unlicensed contractors who do inadequate retrofit work that has to be redone at additional expense by qualified professionals.

Reading and Approving the Transfer Disclosure Statement

Normally, the first order of business after entering into a purchase agreement is for the buyers to read and approve the seller's Transfer Disclosure Statement regarding material facts relating to the property. The Real Estate Transfer Disclosure Statement must be read and approved by the buyers within three days of receipt if the form is hand delivered, or within five days if it's mailed. Make certain that both the listing and selling agents have completed their written agent inspections.

Any inquiries you have about the disclosure statement should be directed to your agent. Buyers and sellers often wonder why real estate agents are so insistent that any questions that come up during the course of the transaction be handled through the agents. Real estate agents are apprehensive about buyers and sellers talking directly to one another about substantive matters because if a question arises involving a condition that may require a material disclosure, the details of the disclosure should be made in writing. Oral disclosures can lead to problems as they are hard to substantiate.

> **Judy and Joel Fink met with the seller of the home they were purchasing several days before the close of escrow to learn how to use the security alarm. During the training session, the seller mentioned that he used a hand-held pump to pump water out of the basement during heavy rains. Judy and Joel said nothing about this disclosure to their agent, who wasn't present for the meeting. Months later, the basement flooded during a heavy rainstorm. Joel and Judy reviewed the seller's Transfer Disclosure Statement, but it mentioned nothing about the property having a drainage or flooding problem. A lawsuit followed, which could have been avoided if the agents had been made aware of the issue before the escrow closed.**

171

It's far less time consuming, and usually less expensive, to resolve property defects before close of escrow than afterwards when attorney fees can mount up. If the agents had been aware of the flooding problem in the above example, they could have arranged to get specialists in before the close of escrow to give bids to remedy the problem. A compromise could have been worked out between the buyers and the seller thereby alleviating the need for a lawsuit.

Old Reports and Maintenance Records

Ask the sellers to provide you with all reports, regardless of age, concerning the property. Obtain copies of work contracts, proposals and invoices, or paid receipts for any major work. If major systems such as the furnace, hot water heater, or roof have been recently replaced, ask for copies of warranties and guarantees, and check with the contractor who performed the work to make sure that warranties are transferable to a new owner. Request that original building plans be left for the buyer at the close of escrow if they exist. They provide important additional documentation about the house and will prove useful if you remodel in the future.

If you have specific questions about the property that aren't answered by the documentation furnished by the sellers, ask your agent to put these additional questions in writing and ask for the sellers to provide a written response. It's a good idea to request copies of the seller's utility bills for several representative months of the year.

Amendments to the Transfer Disclosure Statement

Any material facts about a home that are discovered in the course of the transaction that might affect a buyer's decision to purchase, or influence the price a buyer would be willing to pay for the property, must be disclosed in writing. For instance, if a drainage problem that the sellers were unaware of when they listed the property is discovered during the property inspection process, it must be disclosed to the buyer in the form of an addendum to the Real Estate Transfer Disclosure Statement. Any addendum to the transfer disclosure institutes a new right of rescission period (three days from receipt if the addendum is hand delivered, or five days from the date of mailing) during which time the buyer has the right to terminate the contract.

It's important to amend the Real Estate Transfer Disclosure Statement as soon as possible if a previously undisclosed material defect becomes apparent to the sellers or their real estate agent. If the buyer is unwilling or unable to accept the property with the newly disclosed defective condition, it's better for the sellers to have this knowledge sooner rather than later so that they can begin to negotiate a sale with another buyer. It's far worse to have a buyer rescind the contract at the last minute, not to mention the fact that failure by the sellers or their agent to disclose a known material fact could have serious legal repercussions.

Dealing with Defects: Renegotiate or Terminate?

Reading the inspection report on the home you're purchasing or selling can be disheartening. Defects discovered during the inspection process can be dealt with in several ways. The buyers can accept the property with the disclosed faults or can ask the sellers to correct the conditions. Sometimes sellers will feel that the buyer's request to correct a problem is frivolous or is simply not within their budget. If this is the case, the buyers and sellers should attempt to negotiate an agreement to share the costs.

Renegotiations are bound to be stressful. The sellers may feel they compromised as much as they could during the initial negotiations. The buyers, on the other hand, may have already stretched their dollar as far as possible. Willing parties to a transaction can usually find a way to work out an equitable resolution if a serious defect is uncovered. Sometimes obtaining a second professional opinion or at least several cost estimates for the recommended repair work is all that's necessary.

Lenders will often not permit sellers to credit money to buyers to correct defects discovered during inspections. In this instance, the work may have to be completed by the sellers before the escrow closes. Sometimes, though, a lender will allow the sellers to credit money in escrow to the buyers to be applied toward the buyer's nonrecurring closing costs. If the sellers are not already crediting for nonrecurring costs, this might be a way to avoid having to complete the work by close of escrow. But, sellers should make sure that the contract clearly states that the credit for nonrecurring costs is in lieu of completing specific repairs requested by the buyers and that the buyers are to take full responsibility for making these repairs after the close of escrow. Lenders have restrictions on the amount they'll allow a seller to credit a buyer for nonrecurring costs, so make sure you get the lender's approval.

Sellers should keep in mind that it takes time to put a house back on the market, and it's often difficult to rekindle interest in a property that previous buyers have backed out of purchasing. Sellers who have a backup buyer waiting in the wings are in an enviable position. However, existing inspection reports must be disclosed to future prospective buyers, so if a serious problem exists, it's likely the new buyers will want to have it fixed. Buyers need to weigh the time and energy that will be involved in finding a suitable replacement home if they choose not to go through with an offer to purchase.

A home protection plan purchased by either buyer or seller at any time before the close of escrow will not require an inspection by protection plan company representatives. If the buyer's general building inspector indicates that the major support systems of the home are old, it might be a good idea to sign up for a protection plan if this is not already a part of the purchase contract. Be sure to request a copy of the protection plan policy before escrow closes to make certain that you are covered where you need to be. You may have to pay extra for covering a pool, spa, washer, dryer, or refrigerator.

Why Not Sell 'As Is'?

Many sellers hope to avoid their disclosure responsibilities by listing a home for sale "as is." Yet selling this way provides little protection to the sellers when the phrase is used generally as a catch-all clause. In addition, marketing a home for sale "as is" can have a negative impact on prospective buyers who fear that the sellers may have something to hide.

It is acceptable, however, to sell a home with the stipulation that a certain component of the property or an appliance that's included in the sale is being included in "as is" condition. If you know the roof is leaking, for instance, and you disclose this to a buyer, or if you're including the stove but the oven doesn't work and you've informed the buyer in writing of this defect, then selling the property "as is" with respect to these specific defects is fine as long as both parties agree to this in writing.

The primary reason for not selling with a general "as is" clause is that the provision will probably only apply to defects readily observable by the buyer. A defect that's not visibly apparent is not likely to be covered by an "as is" clause. Also, selling this way doesn't relieve the seller of legal responsibility for disclosing known material defects; withholding such information could be considered fraudulent in a court of law. It's far better to be straightforward regarding known defects rather than to assume an "as is" clause will provide any protection against a buyer's future claim.

This admonition applies to ordinary residential property transfers. Estate (probate) and foreclosure sales are exempt from the Real Estate Transfer Disclosure requirement, and the California statute dictates that these sales are to be "as is" sales. In both cases, the law protects the seller (usually an heir or a financial institution) who has recently acquired the property through adverse circumstances and may have little or no direct information about it.

Discovering Defects After the Close of Escrow

Homes need continual maintenance to function properly. An older home is bound to have some problems, and even new homes built to modern code requirements are not free of flaws. No matter how thorough the inspection process might be, there's always the possibility that an unanticipated breakdown will occur after the close of escrow.

How long, you may be asking yourself, after a house sells does the seller's responsibility end? Unfortunately, there's no clear-cut answer to this question. In California, there's an implied seller's warranty that the house being sold is habitable. Presumably, a habitable home has exterior walls, doors and windows that work, a functioning furnace and hot water heater, a potable water supply, a sanitary waste system, and a roof that doesn't leak, not to mention a sound foundation. Talk to a real estate attorney if you have any questions regarding what sellers are legally responsible for providing to buyers at the close of escrow.

The buyer's first course of action if a major system fails soon after the close (and the home protection company refuses to repair it) is to seek an amiable mediation with the sellers. The sooner the buyers make their complaint known to the sellers, the better; statutes of limitation on pursuing such claims do apply. If an inquiry doesn't remedy the problem, the buyers should consider sending a formal written claim to the sellers in care of their real estate agent. When all else fails, consult a real estate attorney.

CHAPTER 10

ALL *ABOUT* FINANCING

Finding your dream *home, negotiating the purchase contract, and having the home inspected by qualified professionals are all important parts of the home buying process. Equally important is financing your home purchase. Most home buyers use a loan to buy a home, and they make their offer to purchase that home contingent upon obtaining a loan commitment from a lender. Until the financing is secured, the sale is pending. Escrow can't close until the lender issues a check for the loan amount to the escrow holder.*

This chapter will help you get the loan you need to complete your purchase. It will explain the home loan qualification process, and it will help you decide which loan is best for you. Selecting the right loan is important because you may live with it for a long time, making monthly payments until you sell, refinance, or pay it off completely. Your choices are enormous, but don't let the variety of home loans in the marketplace intimidate you. It's not as complicated as it seems. What follows will decode and demystify the world of home financing so that you can make a sensible home loan selection.

In California, a deed of trust, rather than a mortgage, is the legal document used for the purposes of pledging real property as a guarantee for repayment of a home loan. The terms "mortgage" and "deed of trust" will be used interchangeably here, even though a mortgage is technically different.

Shopping for a Lender

The financing contingency in your purchase contract should specify the interest rate, origination fees, term (usually 15- or 30-year), and type of loan (fixed or adjustable rate) you'll need to complete your purchase. It should also specify a time period for you to obtain your loan commitment from the lender. A customary financing contingency time period is 30 days following acceptance of the purchase contract. This is usually sufficient time to receive formal approval from the lender, but in active real estate markets, a longer time period may be required. Your ability to remove the financing contingency and close the escrow on time will depend on your efforts during the first few days after you enter into a purchase contract. A completed loan application submitted later than five days after acceptance of the purchase contract stands little chance of being approved within a 30-day time period.

The most frequent sources of home purchase financing in California are mortgage brokers, commercial banks, mortgage banks, savings and loan companies, and credit unions. Ask friends and associates who bought a home or refinanced recently to recommend their lender or mortgage broker if they were satisfied with the service they received. Your real estate agent can provide you with rate sheets from various lenders and can make recommendations. Some real estate firms can help you shop for a home loan by using a computerized service, and major metropolitan newspapers usually print a summary of current home loan rates.

Don't overlook business connections when searching for a lender. Talk with a representative from the bank or savings and loan that handles your personal accounts. Associates of businesses with large commercial accounts can often arrange for better-than-market financing, since the bank considers you a valued customer. Employees of banks are usually offered a preferential interest rate or a discount on the loan origination fees. Credit unions, too, sometimes offer their members exceptional programs. Contact the lender that holds the loan on your current home: you may be able to get a break in the interest rate or loan fees by financing the new home through the same lender. If there's a prepayment penalty on your existing home loan, ask your lender to waive the penalty if you finance your new home through them.

176

Your ability to negotiate a break on loan fees will depend on current credit conditions. If money is tight, and there's more demand for money than money available to lend, you'll have little chance. When there's plenty of money available to lend and lenders are competing for your business, you can often find a lender who'll give you a break on the fees.

Lender Comparison Checklist

The following questions will help you find the lenders that can best serve your needs.

1. What types of home loan programs are offered? Some lenders offer only adjustable-rate mortgages (ARMs), while others have both fixed- and adjustable-rate loans. Some lenders that offer fixed loans provide either a 15- or 30-year variety but not both. Additional loan products are available through some lenders and not others. Examples include fixed loans with early call dates, convertible adjustables, biweekly payment plan loans, and Graduated Payment Mortgages (all explained later in this chapter). Since you may be undecided about the type of loan you want, it's important to keep track of which lenders are offering which loan programs.

2. What is the current interest rate? Although this will vary from one loan to another, ARMs usually have the lowest rates initially. The interest rate on a 15-year loan is usually lower than the rate on a 30-year loan. Conforming loans have lower interest rates than jumbo loans. A conforming loan is one that's packaged for sale to investors on the secondary money market (also called Fannie Mae or Freddie Mac loans). The loan amount limit for conforming loans is changed each year. In 1993, the conforming loan limit was set at $203,150. Loans over the conforming limits are referred to as jumbo loans.

3. What are the loan origination fees? These will also vary according to the loan and the individual lender but ARMs usually have lower startup fees than fixed-rate loans. Most lenders quote these fees as points, with one point equaling 1 percent of the loan amount. Be sure to ask about additional charges for credit reports, property appraisal, document preparation, or loan processing, which are often quoted in addition to the points. A credit report should cost about $50; the cost of an appraisal will vary depending on the price of the home, but expect about $300 for a $250,000 home. The fees for document preparation and underwriter review will vary, but can be as high as $700.

The interest rates and points charged by lenders will vary depending on the demand for money. When there is plenty of money to lend and the demand for financing drops, lenders usually offer lower interest rates and loan origination fees than during periods of high demand. There is also an inverse relationship between the points you pay and the interest rate on the loan: the higher the points, the lower the interest rate, and vice versa.

When comparing loans with different rates and points, keep in mind that 1 point is approximately equal to 0.125 percent on the interest rate on a 30-year loan (if you were to keep paying on the loan for the full 30 years, which most people don't). The longer you plan to keep the loan, the better off you are paying higher points and a lower interest rate. Calculate the interest rate savings each year on a lower versus a higher rate. Compare this to the difference in points and then consider how long you're likely to be paying on the loan. If you think you'll pay the lower rate long enough (before selling the home or refinancing) to more than offset the higher points, you're better off with the lower interest rate.

4. When are the loan origination fees paid? In most cases, you will pay for the credit report and appraisal in advance, at the time you submit your loan application. You will pay the points and document preparation and/or review fee at the close of escrow. But, this can vary from one lender to the next. Find out if any of the fees paid in advance will be refunded if your loan is not approved. Usually they won't be, but it's always best to ask.

5. What is the Annual Percentage Rate (APR)? The APR is the actual yearly interest rate paid by the borrower, figuring in the points charged to initiate the loan. When prospective borrowers call lenders for their current interest rates, the lenders will customarily quote only the interest rate on the note, not the APR. By law, the APR must be disclosed to a borrower but not necessarily at the time of the initial inquiry. The APR discloses the real cost of borrowing by adding on the points and by factoring in the assumption that the points will be paid off incrementally over the term of the loan (usually 15 or 30 years). The APR is usually about 0.5 percent higher than the note rate. There may be tax advantages to some borrowers in paying the points in one lump sum at the time the loan is originated.

6. What are your qualifying ratios? The qualifying ratio represents the relationship between the borrowers' projected PITI payments (principal, interest,

177

taxes, and insurance) and their gross monthly income. Conservatively, lenders like to see the PITI not exceed 30 to 33 percent of the borrowers' gross monthly income. Lenders also look at the ratio between the borrower's total debt, including the PITI, to income. This ratio usually needs to be in the 34 to 38 percent range. If a lender tells you they require a 30/36 ratio, this means the borrowers' PITI figure must not exceed 30 percent of their gross monthly income (housing expense-to-income ratio) and their PITI plus other long-term outstanding debts must not exceed 36 percent of their gross monthly income (debt-to-income ratio).

Some lenders are more lenient in their qualifying ratios, and generally, the larger the cash down payment, the easier it will be to qualify. A lender should be able to tell you over the phone if you'll qualify for a certain loan amount if you specify the amount of your cash down, the size of the loan you're looking for, your gross income, and the amount of any long-term outstanding debts. But, don't expect a lender or mortgage broker to fully prequalify you for a loan over the phone. This will usually require an in-person appointment.

7. Will the loan require Private Mortgage Insurance (PMI)? PMI insures the lender against a default on the part of the borrower; it's usually required when the borrower is making a cash down payment of less than 20 percent of the purchase price. PMI costs vary from one mortgage insurance firm to another, but premiums usually run about 0.50 percent of the loan amount for the first year of the loan. Most PMI premiums are a bit lower for subsequent years. The first year's mortgage insurance premium is usually paid in advance at the close of escrow, and there is usually a separate PMI approval process. In most cases, PMI can be dropped after you have built up 20 percent equity in your home, if your payment record has been good. Find out from your lender what procedure to follow to have PMI removed when your equity reaches 20 percent.

Some lenders (usually portfolio lenders, discussed later in this chapter) self-insure their loans with down payments of less than 20 percent. They usually don't charge an extra fee for PMI, but charge a higher interest rate instead, which can be written off for tax purposes by the borrower. A disadvantage is that you're stuck with the higher interest rate for the term of the loan.

8. Will the loan require an impound account? Most loans that require PMI also require an impound account, which is an account held by the lender for the payment of the borrower's property taxes and fire insurance. The borrower makes monthly payments to this account in addition to the mortgage payments, and the lender then pays the tax and insurance bills as they come due. Find out how much the lender will want at closing to fund your impound account. They will usually want enough to cover your hazard insurance, property tax, and second-year PMI payments for several months. Also, be sure to find out what additional cash reserves the lender will require you to have in your bank account (or in a 401(k) pension plan or IRA account) at closing. Most lenders want to know that you have enough extra cash to cover several months of your housing expense.

9. Is it possible to lock in an interest rate? During times of rising interest rates, this is a critical variable to consider in evaluating a loan program. When lenders lock in rates for a prospective borrower, they reserve money at a specified interest rate for a given period of time (usually 30 to 60 days). If rates increase during this period, the borrower's rate is protected as long as the loan is closed in time. Some lenders will lock in a rate (also called a rate lock) when the buyer submits a loan application, others when the loan is approved, and some only at the time that the loan documents are drawn. Get the lock-in commitment in writing, and find out whether the lender will honor the commitment if the loan doesn't close on time due to an error by the lender.

On fixed-rate loans, lenders charge for a lock-in by either increasing the interest rate on the loan or by charging a higher loan origination fee. You can expect to pay an extra 0.125 to 0.50 percent in interest rate, or an extra 0.25 to 0.625 percent of the loan amount in loan origination fees, for a rate-lock. The shorter the lock-in period, the lower the cost to lock in. It may cost nothing extra to lock in an initial interest rate on an ARM. If rates aren't rising, it's better not to lock in a rate on a fixed-rate loan because it costs extra and you usually won't get the benefit of a lower rate if rates drop during the rate-lock period. An ARM lender may pass the lower rate along to you if rates drop during your rate-lock period. If you do decide to lock in a rate, make sure your loan application and all supporting documentation get to the lender as soon as possible. This way you won't lose your interest rate should the lock-in time run out before your escrow is closed.

10. How long will it take to approve the loan? The approval process usually takes from two to four weeks after a completed loan application is submitted. Approval can take longer during active real estate markets or when interest rates are low and a lot of homeowners are refinancing.

11. Does loan approval and processing occur locally? Unanticipated delays are more likely to occur if formal approval and documentation must come from a corporate office located outside of the area.

12. Will the lender give a written loan commitment? Many lenders are more than happy to provide oral confirmation of approval but are reluctant to follow up with written confirmation. Insist on it. The commitment should include the interest rate, a summary of the terms of the loan, an itemization of the origination fees, and a date by which the escrow must be closed. The commitment letter will also include any conditions that must be met in order for the lender to fund the loan (issue the check for the loan amount). Don't remove your financing contingency from your purchase contract until all conditions beyond your control are removed. For example, if one condition of your loan approval calls for paying down a charge card and you have the ability, and are willing, to do this, go ahead and remove the contingency. But, if the loan condition is an acceptable underwriter's review of the appraisal, make sure this is done to the lender's satisfaction before you unconditionally remove your contingency.

13. Is the institution a portfolio lender? Portfolio lenders retain most of the loans they make for their own investment purposes. Other lenders make home loans with no intention of keeping them after the escrow closes. These loans

179

are usually sold on the secondary money market to Fannie Mae (Federal National Mortgage Association) or Freddie Mac (Federal Home Mortgage Corporation), two organizations that purchase home loans at a discount to resell to investors. Loans that are targeted for sale to Freddie Mac or Fannie Mae have rigid qualifying criteria and must be packaged for sale according to strict guidelines. The portfolio lender has greater flexibility in qualifying and more latitude in approving buyers.

14. Do the loans have prepayment penalties? A prepayment penalty is a fine charged by the lender for paying the loan off early. There are plenty of loans available that do not have prepayment penalties, so a loan that has one should be extra special. You should feel confident you won't be moving before the prepayment clause expires (usually five years following the note date) before accepting such a loan. Many zero-point loans have prepayment penalties.

15. Is the loan assumable? Fixed-rate loans usually are not, but adjustables often are. If the loan is assumable, will the subsequent buyer need to go through formal loan qualification? Will the loan be assumable on the same terms, or will they change to reflect current market conditions?

16. Will "termite" work need to be completed by the close of escrow? In a busy real estate market, this may be the determining factor between one loan program and another. If the structural pest control companies are backlogged with work and you have a short close of escrow, it may be impossible for the work to be completed before the close date. Loans that are packaged for sale to Fannie Mae or Freddie Mac will often require that the structural pest control work be completed before the loan can be sold to an investor. This is why conforming loans usually won't allow structural pest control work to be done after the escrow closes. Structural pest control work will need to be done before close of escrow if the buyer asks for the seller to do the work as a part of the purchase contract or if the appraiser recommends that structural pest control work be done before the lender funds the loan. Portfolio lenders have more flexibility because they set their own guidelines for loan approval. When lenders do permit structural pest control work to be completed after close of escrow, they will often want more than enough money than is needed to do the work to be put in an escrow account until the work is finished (usually one and a half to two times the required amount). This ensures that the work is done quickly. Who puts the extra money in escrow is negotiable between the buyer and seller; unused funds are usually returned after the work is completed to whomever put up the extra money.

18. Will the lender permit the seller to credit money to the buyer at close of escrow? When the lender won't allow a holdback for structural pest control or other repairs that the sellers have agreed to pay for, this can often be resolved with a credit from the seller to the buyer to cover the amount of the work. The work is then completed by the buyer after close of escrow. Many lenders, however, won't allow credits for repair work, but most will allow a credit toward the buyer's nonrecurring closing costs. Nonrecurring closing costs are paid on a one-time-only basis at closing. They include such fees as title insurance and escrow fees (in areas where the buyers pay these), the loan origination fee (points) and document preparation fee, and transfer taxes (if there are any). Lender's policies vary on how large a credit for nonrecurring costs they'll allow. They usually won't allow a credit that reduces the amount of the buyer's down payment, or that exceeds the total of the buyer's nonrecurring costs. Lenders often limit the amount the seller can credit for nonrecurring costs to 3 to 6 percent of the purchase price. Again, a portfolio lender may have more flexibility.

19. How long has the lender been in business? Beware of the new lender in town, with the deal of a lifetime, who runs out of money just prior to funding the loan.

20. Will the lender provide names and phone numbers of recent customers? Follow up by calling several borrowers who have recently obtained a loan from a lender you're seriously considering. Ask if they were satisfied with the service and if the lender delivered the loan as promised. Check with your agent and escrow officer to find out if either has worked previously with the lender. Were they satisfied? A poorly managed loan company that is understaffed during the peak home buying season may not be able to approve and fund your loan efficiently and close escrow on time.

The Pros and Cons of Working with a Mortgage Broker

181

Mortgage brokers are intermediaries between borrowers and lenders. They take your loan application, assemble your loan package, shop for a loan for you, and then place your loan package with a specific lender. Mortgage brokers usually have access to a multitude of loan products, and can frequently arrange financing that would not otherwise be available to a home buyer. Many lenders that work with mortgage brokers will not accept loans directly from an individual borrower. You'll want to work with a mortgage broker who's experienced, whose rates are competitive, and who provides excellent service.

Working with a good mortgage broker can save you time. Brokers are often available to meet with you evenings and weekends; some even make house calls. They can switch you from one loan program to another with relative ease. Let's say you apply for a fixed-rate loan, but rates climb so high you no longer qualify for the loan. A broker can pull your loan package from the fixed-rate lender and submit it to a lender with a lower-interest-rate adjustable loan program within a matter of hours.

Unfortunately, mortgage brokers don't have control over the lenders they work with. Also, some brokers will attempt to sell borrowers loans they don't want because it's easier to get some types of loans approved than others. If you're set on a 15-year fixed loan and you know you can qualify for it, don't let a mortgage broker talk you into a 30-year fixed or adjustable loan.

Mortgage brokers work on commission, just like real estate agents. The lender usually shares a portion of the points with the broker who originates the loan, or the lender gives the broker a rebate if the loan has no points. Some of the larger lending institutions that accept loan applications directly from prospective borrowers won't pay an outside mortgage broker for bringing in a loan. If the lender won't compensate the broker, the broker will charge the borrower an extra fee. Let your mortgage broker know up front that you don't want to pay extra for a loan that's readily available to you for less. But, if you've been turned down by several lenders and the broker has no alternative but to try a large institutional lender, then the extra fee may be fair compensation for the mortgage broker's efforts.

Take the experience of Linda Cornell, who selected a mortgage broker based on his promise to obtain a loan requiring minimum documentation and 20 percent down. One week before closing, the mortgage broker informed Linda that the loan program he promised her was no longer available, but he could secure a loan commitment for her from a large savings and loan if she was willing to put 25 percent down and pay a two-point loan origination fee. Linda was especially annoyed by the bait and switch routine, since she'd originally considered applying to the same savings and loan herself but didn't want to put 25 percent down if she didn't have to. If she'd gone directly to the lender, her loan fee would have been one and a half points, not two.

182

30-Year Versus 15-Year Loans

The 15-year home loan has been touted as the premium way to finance the purchase of a home for those who have a large enough income to support higher monthly payments (approximately $200 per month more than a 30-year fixed-rate loan for each $100,000 financed at a 10 percent interest rate). The amount of interest paid during the term of the loan is much less on a 15-year than on a 30-year; the longer the term of the loan, the larger the total finance charge paid by the borrower. In addition, 15-year home loans are offered at a lower interest rate than are 30-year loans: customarily 0.5 to 0.75 percent less. For example, the interest paid on a $150,000 15-year fixed-rate loan at 7.25 percent would be $96,473. On a 30-year fixed-rate loan at 8 percent, the interest paid will amount to $251,138.

It makes sense to finance your home purchase with a 15-year loan if you're planning to retire within the next 10 to 20 years and intend to stay in your present home. Or, if you're starting out with a low cash down but earn a large income and anticipate trading up to a more expensive home in the future, you might prefer a 15-year loan because it ensures enforced savings. The equity buildup on a 15-year loan increases at a much faster pace than on a 30-year loan: it takes 24½ years to pay down one half of a fixed loan that's amortized over 30 years. If you do select a 15-year loan in order to obtain maximum equity buildup in the shortest period of time, make certain that the lender will not charge a prepayment penalty, as this could diminish a good portion of your enforced savings.

To summarize the pros and cons of 15- and 30-year loan programs, consider the following: The 15-year loan has a lower interest rate, is paid off in a shorter period of time, costs much less in total financing charges during the term of the loan, and provides the borrower with quick equity buildup. On the other side of the coin, the 15-year loan is harder to qualify for, the monthly payments are higher, the borrower has less flexibility to adjust financing parameters, and it could provide less of a tax shelter.

A 30-year home loan leaves borrowers more in control of how much interest they ultimately pay, how much interest write-off and tax shelter they receive, and how much their monthly payments will be. Keep in mind that, barring explicit restriction, a 30-year fixed-rate loan can be paid off in half the time if the borrower makes double payments each month. The attractive feature of this loan is that it gives the borrower the flexibility to make additional payments, an option that can be critical for some home buyers, particularly those who are self-employed and are unsure about their future income.

Accelerated Loan Payoffs and Biweekly Mortgages

Although 15- and 30-year loans are the most popular home loans on the market, recently 20-year and even 10-year loans have increased in popularity. The appeal of both of these programs is that the loan is paid off earlier than a 30-year loan and the interest savings can be enormous. But, the drawbacks are the same as with a 15-year loan: higher monthly payments, less financial flexibility, and harder qualification.

A 30-year mortgage with a biweekly payment plan offers another compromise between the 15- and 30-year loans. The biweekly payment plan requires the buyer to make a payment once every two weeks rather than once a month. Each payment is equal to one half of the monthly payment on an ordinary 30-year loan. The interest rate or fee may be slightly higher on a biweekly loan to cover the increase in processing fees. The benefit to the borrower is that a 30-year loan on a biweekly schedule will be paid off in approximately 20 years, resulting in a large savings in total interest paid. For example, the total interest paid on a $100,000, 30-year fixed-rate loan at 10 percent is $215,314. On a biweekly payment plan, the interest paid over 20 1/2 years is only $137,679, a savings of $77,635.

If you have a 30-year fixed rate loan that is not set up for biweekly payments, don't send one half of your monthly payment to the lender on the fifteenth of the month expecting it to be credited toward reducing the remaining principal balance; it probably won't be. The lender will either send

A 30-year loan with a biweekly payment plan will be paid in full in approximately 20 years.

183

your check back to you or hold it until the other half of the monthly payment is received. In other words, the borrower usually can't arbitrarily convert to the biweekly plan; rather, the loan must be set up on this payment schedule initially.

Beware of middlemen who offer to turn your 30-year loan into a biweekly for you, for a sizable fee. These intermediaries arrange to have half your monthly payment withdrawn from your bank account every two weeks. Usually the middleman earns interest on your money while it sits in an escrow account until it's used to make your monthly payment, although this varies with the plan. The biweekly withdrawal creates an extra monthly payment each year. Making 13 monthly payments a year, rather than 12, reduces the term of your loan by about one third. With a little discipline, you can make the extra monthly payment on your own.

> By increasing your monthly payments by 5 percent on a 30-year loan you can reduce the length of your loan by about seven years.

You can shave thousands off the interest owed on a 30-year loan by increasing your principal payments by a mere $50 or $100 per month. The earlier you start making accelerated payments, the greater the savings since the principal on which you're paying interest is larger at the beginning of a loan than toward the end of its life. An advantage of making accelerated payments on your own, rather than taking a biweekly payment plan, is that you have flexibility to make additional payments when you can afford to.

Borrowers who plan to make periodic supplemental loan payments should check with their lender to make sure that there are no penalties for prepayment and that the payments will be properly recorded. Make a notation on the additional payment check to indicate that the money is to be applied to principal reduction; many lenders provide a space on the payment coupon to enter any extra principal payments. Check your year-end statement from the lender to confirm your extra payments were credited properly.

The benefit of making an early payoff on a 30-year fixed loan will depend on how low the interest rate on the note is. The lower the interest rate, the less advantageous an early loan payoff will be. Also, the lower the remaining loan balance, the less benefit of making an early prepayment. One factor to consider is how much the money you pay down on the loan could earn for you if it were in-vested elsewhere. Also, keep in mind that making extra principal payments on a 30-year loan doesn't relieve you of the responsibility of making regular monthly payments. You owe 12 monthly payments per year no matter how much extra you pay in any one month.

> You can pay off your 30-year loan in approximately 20 years by making one extra monthly payment per year.

184

Fixed- Versus Adjustable-Rate Mortgages

A fixed-rate home mortgage has a constant interest rate and equal monthly payments during the term of the loan; the interest rate and monthly payments of an adjustable-rate loan fluctuate. Lenders prefer adjustables because they shift the risk of future increases in interest rates to the borrower. However, it's a mistake to think that there is no risk involved in selecting a fixed-rate loan. Although such a loan is good protection against rising interest rates, the borrower is stuck with the initial rate if interest rates drop. Statistics show that home buyers who have chosen ARMs since 1981 have saved thousands of dollars. The percentage of home buyers applying for ARMs has risen substantially over the years, and adjustables currently account for about half of new home loans. As rates in general drop, home buyers tend to revert to the fixed loans; when rates rise, the preferred choice is the adjustable loan.

ARMs are favored by many home buyers, particularly when interest rates rise, because the lower initial interest rates makes it easier to qualify for a loan. Be aware, however, that with an ARM that has a discounted starting interest rate (also called a "teaser" rate), most lenders will use 2 percentage points above the teaser rate or 7 percent, whichever is higher, as the interest rate on which you'll be qualified for the loan.

There is usually a 2.0 to 2.5 percent difference in interest rates between an ARM and a 30-year fixed-rate loan. If you're planning on moving again within three or four years, an ARM makes sense even if rates do nothing but rise during that period of time. Calculate the difference between the initial cost of both loans (including the loan origination fees, which are almost always higher on a fixed-rate loan). Figure out what the savings will be during the first year or so of ownership if you select an ARM. The bottom line figure should speak for itself.

185

The index is the cost of funds that an ARM is tied to.

Always look at the worst case scenario. Compute what you'll pay in two or three years if you take an adjustable and interest rates go up and stay there. Can you live with the monthly payments if they increase to the maximum amount the lender is permitted to charge under the terms of the note? In the long run, a fixed-rate loan may be cheaper if you plan on staying in your home a long time.

Individuals on fixed incomes may want to consider a fixed-rate loan. The security of knowing that the monthly payments and interest rate will never change will often more than offset a possible disappointment if rates decline. Should rates drop and stay down for an extended period of time, there's always the option of refinancing. Be sure to find a lender who doesn't charge a penalty for early prepayment.

One benefit of ARMs that shouldn't be overlooked is that they're usually assumable. This is a particularly attractive feature if you don't plan to stay in your new home for an extended period of time. Having an assumable loan on your home may enable you to sell when others can't because of high interest rates or a shortage of mortgage money.

Understanding Adjustable-Rate Mortgages

The initial interest rate is important, but it shouldn't be the only factor in deciding which ARM is right for you. The starting interest rate on your ARM loan will be in effect for a finite period of time: usually one to twelve months. You'll have to live with the other features of the ARM until you pay the loan off, so you should examine the entire ARM program, not just the initial interest rate, before making a selection. This brief discussion will explain in general how ARMs work. The list of questions at the end of this section will help you to evaluate various ARM programs.

On a teaser rate ARM, the lender will usually qualify you based on an interest rate 2 percent above the initial discounted rate.

ARMs are tied to an index which is a measure of the lender's cost of borrowing money. The index is used as a basis for calculating the interest rate on an ARM loan. As the index rises, so will the interest rate on the adjustable loan. When the interest rate change becomes effective, and how it affects the monthly payment, will depend on the specific ARM program.

The most common indexes used in California are the Eleventh District Cost of Funds (an average of the cost of funds to the Eleventh Federal Home Loan Bank District institutions), Treasury Securities (T-Bills), Certificates of Deposit (CDs), and Libor (London inter-bank offering rate).

Historically, the Eleventh District Cost of Funds index has been more stable than Treasury Security indexes. This means that in periods of rising interest rates, ARMs tied to the Eleventh District index move up more slowly than do adjustables indexed to T-bills. In periods of falling interest rates, however, an ARM with an Eleventh District index drops more slowly. Although the Eleventh District Cost of Funds index has been the more stable index in the past, this should not be construed as a guarantee of how the index will behave in the future. When comparing one T-bill or CD index with another, keep in mind that the longer the term of the index, the more the borrower is protected from short-term erratic interest rate fluctuations. For

Generally, the longer the term of the index, the more stable the index will be.

186

example, an ARM with a six-month T-Bill, or six-month CD, index will be more volatile than one with a one-year Treasury Security average index. The Libor is a very volatile index.

Most metropolitan newspapers publish current ARM index rates, or you can call one of the following telephone services for an update. For the current Eleventh District Cost of Funds, call (415) 616-2600. For current T-Bill and CD rates, call (201) 838-8197 and (415) 974-2859.

> *An initial interest rate that starts below the fully indexed rate is called a "teaser" rate.*

The fully indexed interest rate on an ARM loan is calculated by adding a margin of a few percentage points to the index rate. The margin will vary from one loan program to the next but typically remains constant during the life of the loan. Avoid a loan that has a fluctuating margin or allows the lender to make modifications arbitrarily. To compare two ARMs tied to the same index, ask the loan officer for the current index rate and for the amount of the margin; then compare the resulting fully indexed rates. For instance, say you're considering two loans that are both tied to the six-month T-bill rate, which is currently at 3.5 percent. One loan has a 2 percent margin; the other 3 percent. In the first case the fully indexed interest rate would be 5.5 percent, as opposed to 6.5 percent in the second case. Often higher loan origination fees (points) are charged for the privilege of obtaining a loan with a lower margin, so be sure to compare the up-front fees charged before making a final determination.

187

Lenders will often offer an initial interest rate that is lower than the fully indexed rate. This is called a discounted, or "teaser," rate. For instance, rather than having a starting interest rate of 6.5 percent (the fully indexed rate), a loan might be offered at 5.5 percent initially. Again, check the amount of the loan origination fees charged; these could offset any savings to be gained by virtue of the lower initial rate. Also, find out how long the discounted rate will be in effect. Some loans have adjustment periods as frequently as every six months. If the index rate on the loan were to rise 2 percent during the first six months, your payment could rise very sharply within a short period of time. This rapid jump in payments is referred to as payment shock. The method of computing the initial increase in interest rate varies from lender to lender, so be sure to find out what happens to the interest rate at the first and subsequent adjustments. Also consider that a lower margin is usually better than a lower starting interest rate since the margin remains

> *The margin is the lender's profit.*

constant during the term of the loan whereas the initial discounted rate is temporary.

Conservative ARMs are available that protect the borrower in the unlikely eventuality of perpetually escalating interest rates. These ARMs have interest rate caps written into the note that set limits on how high the lender can raise the interest rate per adjustment period (periodic cap) and over the life of the loan (lifetime cap). These caps often set a lower limit on interest rate adjustments also, but this varies with the lender.

> Add the margin to the index to find the "fully indexed" interest rate.

Adjustment periods differ. They usually range from once every six months to once a year, although there are ARMs fixed for longer periods. There are also ARMs that adjust monthly. On an ARM that adjusts every six months, the cap per adjustment is usually 0.5 to 1.0 percent. ARMs that adjust once a year typically have an annual interest rate cap of 1 to 2 percent, lifetime caps in the 3.5 to 6 percent range. Often, the lower the initial interest rate, the higher the lifetime cap.

A lower periodic cap offers more protection for borrowers during periods of escalating interest rates; however, if rates drop significantly within a short period, it will take time for this drop to be reflected in the borrower's monthly mortgage payment if there is a periodic cap on how low the interest rate can go on each downward adjustment. Be aware that the periodic adjustment cap may not apply to the first adjustment if the initial rate on the loan is a teaser rate.

Some ARMs have actual payment caps which limit the amount that the monthly payment can increase at the time of each periodic adjustment. A payment cap usually limits an increase to 7.5 percent of the previous payment amount. This protects the borrower from a large jump in a monthly payment. However, if the payment increase is not sufficient to cover the increased interest owed, the unpaid interest is added to the remaining loan balance. In this case, the loan balance increases rather than decreases; this is called negative amortization.

> Periodic and lifetime caps limit how high or low the interest rate can adjust.

In periods of high appreciation, negative amortization is less risky than it is when prices are stable or dropping, particularly for the borrower who made a small cash down payment to begin with. The combination of negative amortization and depreciation in home prices can result in a loan balance that is higher than the market value of the home.

ARMs with payment caps and negative amortization are usually reamortized at some point so that the remaining loan balance can be fully paid off during the term of the loan. This could necessitate a substantial increase in the monthly payment. Most ARMs have a limit on the amount of negative amortization allowed, usually 110 to 125 percent of the original loan amount. If the loan balance exceeds this amount, the borrower has to start paying off the excess.

Negative amortization can be avoided by paying the additional interest owed monthly. ARMs that don't have payment caps usually don't have negative amortization.

A feature to beware of when shopping for an ARM is warehousing or shelving. This refers to the ability of the lender to save, hold over, or shelve any interest that couldn't be charged to the borrower at the time of an adjustment due to the periodic cap on the interest rate. If the loan permits the lender to warehouse uncharged interest, the borrowers could be stuck with a higher interest rate on their loan when interest rates in general have dropped. For

> *Negative amortization occurs when the monthly payment is insufficient to pay the total interest owed for the period.*

instance, if an ARM has a 2 percent annual interest rate cap and the index rate goes up 3 percent in a year, the lender can only increase the ARM interest rate by 2 percent at the next adjustment. But if rates drop 2 percent the following year, a lender who is permitted to shelve uncharged interest rate increases can charge the borrower the uncollected 1 percent the following year.

189

One of the benefits of the adjustable-rate mortgage is its assumability. Make sure that the loan is assumable by another qualified buyer at the same rates and terms available to you; some ARMs have provisions that entitle the lender to raise the index rate or margin at the time the loan is assumed. Also, make certain that the loan has no penalty for early prepayment.

ARMs are attractive to borrowers who want to make large principal paydowns from time to time. Doing this before an ARM loan adjusts for the period results in lower monthly payments based on the lower principal balance. This doesn't happen when a large principal pay-down is made on a fixed-rate loan; rather, it shortens the term of the loan and the monthly payments stay the same.

Questions to Ask About Adjustable-Rate Mortgages

1. What is the initial interest rate? Is this a discounted rate?
2. What is the fully indexed interest rate?
3. What interest rate is used to qualify the borrower?
4. What is the index?
5. What is the current index rate?
6. Will the lender provide a history of index rate changes?

7. What is the margin?
8. Is the margin constant throughout the term of the loan?
9. How often are interest rate adjustments made?
10. How much can the interest rate increase on the first adjustment?
11. What is the interest rate cap per adjustment (periodic cap)?
12. What is the lifetime interest rate cap?
13. Do the caps set upper limits on the interest rate or upper and lower limits?
14. Are the caps based on the fully indexed interest rate or on a teaser rate?
15. Is there a monthly mortgage payment cap?
16. Is there a possibility of negative amortization?
17. Is there a limit on the amount of negative amortization allowed? What is the limit? How will the limit affect future payments?
18. When is the loan reamortized?
19. Is the lender permitted to warehouse (or shelve) uncharged interest?
20. Is the loan assumable? On what terms and conditions?
21. Is there a prepayment penalty?
22. Is the loan convertible to a fixed-rate loan? On what terms and conditions?
23. Will the lender provide a full loan disclosure brochure?

These questions are to supplement the general list of questions provided in the section entitled "Lender Comparison Checklist." You will want to compare the points and other loan origination fees, lock-in policies, qualifying criteria, Property Mortgage Insurance, and impound account requirements, where applicable.

Convertibles and Hybrids

Some ARMs offer the borrower the option to convert to a fixed-rate loan at some time during the term of the loan. The interest rate on convertible adjustable loans will be about 0.5 percent higher than on ARMs without the conversion feature, and there's a fee charged to convert. The conversion fee is usually less than it would cost to refinance, but the fixed rate offered to you will probably not be the lowest fixed rate available in the marketplace at the time you convert. Convertibles usually aren't a great deal because they're expensive. But, they're worth considering if you plan to stay in your new home for a long time and the interest rate on fixed loans is high at the time you purchase. You can convert to a fixed rate when interest rates drop. Convertibles also make sense for some borrowers who can only qualify for an ARM when they buy, but who would ultimately like to have a fixed-rate loan.

ARMs with payment caps can result in negative amortization.

Shop carefully for a convertible adjustable. You may never convert the loan, so make sure you can live with the existing rate and terms; don't overpay for the conversion privilege. Also, compare the formulas used to compute the fixed rate at the time of conversion; if converting doesn't result in a fixed rate that's close to the then-current market rate, the convertible loan may not be worth it. Examine the restrictions on when you can convert. Ideally you'd like to be able to convert at anytime after an initial waiting period of a few years. Some convertibles only allow you to convert during specified time periods.

> *The adjustment period is the interval after which the interest rate can change.*

There are other hybrid mortgage products that combine features of some of the loans discussed above. For instance, there are loans that have a fixed interest rate for a period, then they convert to an ARM. There are fixed-rate loans with monthly payments based on a 30-year amortization that have an early call. A loan with an early call, or due date, must be paid off in full at that time—usually in five or seven years. You'll see these loans referred to as 30/5 or 30/7 (payments amortized over 30 years, all due in five or seven years). The trade off for the early call is an interest rate that's about 1 percent below a fixed-rate 30-year loan that's due in 30 years. It's possible to find a 30/5 or 30/7 with a guarantee refinance option to protect you in case rates are high when the loan comes due, but you'll pay extra for this feature. Early call loans are popular with buyers who know they'll be selling within five or seven years. Finally, there are fixed loans that have a one-time change in their interest rate during the term of the loan. You'll see these loans referred to, for example, as 5/25 or 7/23 (fixed at the initial rate for five or seven years and fixed at another rate for the remainder of the loan term).

191

Financing for the Marginally Qualified Buyer

Alternatives are available for prospective buyers who don't meet the conventional qualifying guidelines. But, restrictions apply to many of these programs. Don't waste time researching alternatives that you clearly won't qualify for. For example, if you're not a veteran, forget about looking into a VA or CalVet loan. Or, if you need a $225,000 loan amount, an FHA loan won't work due to restrictions on loan amounts. Instead, try a portfolio lender.

1. Portfolio lender. Enterprising buyers who can substantiate a job history and a good record of repayment of consumer debt should apply with a portfolio lender if they're told by a conventional lender that they don't meet their approval

> *Portfolio lenders have greater flexibility in qualifying borrowers.*

guidelines. Portfolio lenders package loans for their own investment portfolio rather than for sale on the secondary money market (to Freddie Mac or Fannie Mae). Therefore, they have more flexibility in loan approval and are more willing to stretch their qualifying limits for borrowers they feel are a good risk. But keep in mind that a portfolio lender may not offer the best interest rate.

2. Graduated Payment Mortgage (GPM). GPMs are a possibility for buyers who anticipate an increase in income in the future. These loans commence at an interest rate lower than the note rate, which makes them easier to qualify for. The rate will increase at predetermined intervals. There are fixed- and adjustable-rate GPMs. Negative amortization is usually a feature of GPMs because of the discounted initial interest rate. It's possible to avoid negative amortization by making a payment to cover the negative amount at the beginning of the loan. Perhaps you can negotiate with the seller to help make this payment.

3. Buy-downs. With an interest rate buy-down program, the seller agrees to pay toward either reducing a portion of the loan origination fees (points) or the interest rate (for a stipulated period of time), or both, for the buyer. If a seller buys down an interest rate, he prepays interest into an escrow account. This money is used to make up the difference between the interest rate on the note and the reduced rate the buyer will pay during the buy-down period. This not only saves the buyer on the monthly mortgage payment, it also makes qualifying easier because the buyer is qualified on the lower, buy-down interest rate. Frequently, builders who are having difficulty selling a new housing project due to slow sales activity will offer to buy down an interest rate for a buyer as a sales incentive. A 2/1 interest rate buy-down is a common program offered by builders. With a 2/1 buy-down, the first year's interest rate is 2 percent below the note rate; the second year's rate is 1 percent below the note rate. As with a teaser rate, the buyer should be aware that after the buy-down ceases, the preferential rate will stop and the buyer will begin paying the actual cost of the mortgage.

4. Quick qualifiers. Once touted as the easiest way to finance a home purchase, quick qualifier loans are scrutinized more carefully as a result of the savings and loan crisis. Formerly, a quick qualifier did not require the borrower to actually qualify for the loan and the source of the down payment money was usually not verified. A 20 to 25 percent cash down payment and good credit was all that was required. Today a quick qualifier loan requires a 20 to 25 percent down payment, good credit, verification of the source of the funds needed to close escrow, *and* the loan must make sense to the lender. The lender will want to see your financial statement, and the income and debt you report must fall within the debt-to-income ratios acceptable to the lender. The difference between a conventional loan and a quick qualifier is that a quick qualifier requires less documentation. The lender will take your word for a lot of the financial information you report on your application. Make sure that the information on your loan application is accurate. Another outgrowth of the savings and loan crisis is that some loan files are audited after close of escrow to check for accuracy. If the lender finds that you committed fraud on your loan application in order to get the loan, your loan could be called, which means you'd have to pay it off immediately. ARM quick qualifiers are easier to qualify for than fixed-rate quick qualifiers.

5. Veterans Administration (VA). The U.S. Department of Veteran Affairs offers a variety of loan programs to eligible veterans with no down payment, at below-market interest rates. The VA does not loan the money, but insures a portion of the loan. The current maximum loan amount is $184,000. There is no restriction on the purchase price as long as the buyers have the cash to make up the difference between the loan amount and the purchase price.

VA loans have been unpopular in the past because sellers were required to pay the buyer's points (loan origination fee). This put VA buyers at a disadvantage in fast-paced markets when there was a lot of competition from buyers using conventional financing. Recent changes in the VA program permit a buyer or a seller to pay the points, or the points can be shared by the buyer and seller. VA loan processing can take longer than with conventional financing. For this reason, VA financing may be an unpopular loan option when homes are selling quickly. It tends to increase in popularity in slower markets when sellers find it harder to sell and are willing to accept a longer financing contingency time period.

Some home builders advertise that they offer a "$1 down VA loan" program. This is a program that allows the seller to pay the closing costs (recurring and nonrecurring) and the loan initiation fee is financed (charged as a higher interest rate on the loan rather than as an up-front fee). For more information about VA financing, call (800) 827-1000.

193

6. Federal Housing Administration (FHA). The U.S. Department of Housing and Urban Development (HUD) offers a variety of loan insurance programs through FHA that require approximately 4 to 5 percent cash down. The down payment must be the buyer's own money—gift money is not allowed—but buyers can finance all of their nonrecurring closing costs. Loan limits vary depending on the county where the property is located. Recently, the FHA loan limit was increased to $151,725, from $124,750, but only in high cost areas such as San Francisco and Los Angeles. Each community has a different loan limit; some community limits remain at $124,750. For more information, call (916) 551-1351 for Sacramento, (213) 251-7122 for Los Angeles, (619) 557-5310 for San Diego, and (415) 556-5900 for San Francisco.

7. Cal-Vet. Eligible California veterans can apply for a Cal-Vet low-interest rate home loan program. Loans are available for up to 95 percent of the appraised value with a maximum loan amount of $170,000 or 90 percent of the county's median home price, whichever is higher. For example, in 1992, the Cal-Vet loan limit in pricey Alameda and Contra Costa counties was $242,100. The maximum loan amounts are adjusted each year. For more information, call (800) 952-5626.

8. California Housing Finance Agency (CHFA). This state-sponsored agency has first-time buyer programs available at below-market interest rates and with as little as a 5 percent cash down payment. CHFA allows higher housing-to-income and overall debt-to-income ratios than are allowed on conventional loans. This enables first-timers to buy more house for their money. Income and purchase price restrictions apply, and funds are not always available. For more information, call (916) 322-3991 in Sacramento, or (213) 735-2355 in Los Angeles.

9. Community Home Buyer Programs. These Fannie Mae loans require less income to qualify and less cash to close. They are available through major lenders including Countrywide Funding Corporation, American Savings Bank, First Interstate Bank, World Savings and Loan, and California Federal Bank, to name a few. These loans require a 5 percent cash down payment, of which 2 percent can be a gift, a loan from a relative, or a grant from a government agency or nonprofit organization. Income restrictions apply and the borrower must attend a seminar on the home buying process and home ownership. The maximum loan amount is $203,150 and PMI is required, but no additional cash reserves are required. Fannie Mae has a similar loan program, called the MAGNET program, that permits an employer to give grants for closing costs and part of the down payment. For more information about these Fannie Mae programs, call (202) 752-3421. Or, for the Community Home Buyer Program, contact a local participating lender. Bank of America, Wells Fargo Bank, and other large banks offer programs similar to the Community Home Buyer Program.

10. Local city and county programs. Many cities and counties throughout the state have down payment and mortgage assistance programs for first-time buyers. The Mortgage Credit Certificate Program is one example. This program allows buyers credit in qualifying for the tax advantage they'll receive after they purchase the home. This makes qualifying easier. Income, loan amount, and purchase price restrictions usually apply, and these programs are subject to the availability of funds. Call your local housing or redevelopment agency to find out what programs are available in your area.

11. B, C, and D loans. All of the above loan programs require that you have good credit. Prospective buyers whose credit is less than noteworthy can often get a loan if they have the cash down payment and adequate income, and if they're willing to pay a premium price for the loan. Loans that have the best interest rates and terms are called "A" loans. "A" loans are made to the most qualified borrowers. "B, C, and D" loans are for borrowers who can't qualify for a loan under conventional guidelines. You'll probably have to use a mortgage broker who will place the loan directly with an investor. Expect to pay a higher interest rate, higher loan origination fee, and a higher margin on an ARM. The loan could have a prepayment penalty. The reason that the rates and terms are so exorbitant on B,C, and D loans is to compensate the investor for the increased risk involved because the borrower is not A-rated.

12. Cosigner. A cosigner is someone, usually a relative, who's financially qualified to buy a home, who will apply for the loan with you, but won't occupy the home. A cosigner must also take title to the house with you and will be liable for making the loan payments if you go into default.

194

13. Relocating double-income couples. Relocating couples find it difficult to qualify for a new home mortgage when one spouse is transferred but the other spouse has not yet lined up a job. Some lenders will make exceptions for double income transferring couples. These lenders recognize the likelihood that the unemployed spouse will be able to find work in the new location and will take the spouse's past income into account in qualifying the couple for the new loan. A condition of approval on such a loan might be that the buyers put an amount in escrow sufficient to cover six months' mortgage payments until they can provide proof that the unemployed spouse has a job. Also, these lenders will probably only count 50 to 75 percent of the unemployed spouse's former income in qualifying the couple for a loan.

Submitting the Loan Application

Completing the residential loan application and submitting it to your lender as soon as possible after you enter into a purchase agreement is critical to speedy loan approval. A sample Freddie Mac/Fannie Mae Uniform Residential Loan Application is included in this chapter; this is the standard form used by most residential lenders in California.

The first page of the form asks for the loan terms you're applying for, the source of your cash down payment and settlement costs, your address, and your employer. The next page asks for your gross monthly income, your present and proposed housing expense information, and an itemization of your assets and liabilities (including all checking, savings, and credit account numbers). Page 3 of the application asks for information about real estate that you already own and the financial details of the pending transaction (which your real estate agent can help you with). In addition, you're asked various questions regarding your financial history. If you or your co-borrower will be answering "yes" to any of these questions, let your loan representative know before you submit the application. A "yes" answer to one of the questions could preclude loan approval; falsifying an application can have more serious consequences. The information requested at the bottom of this page helps the government monitor the lender's compliance with the equal credit opportunity act; supplying this information is optional. The form must be signed and dated at the bottom. The final page is a continuation sheet if you need more space to complete other sections of the application.

The loan application package will also include forms authorizing the lender to verify the source of the cash down payment and employment. The verification of the cash required for the down payment and closing costs must be one or more of the following: evidence of account balances from financial institutions; a certified copy of a final closing statement if the source is the proceeds from the sale of another property; or a gift letter. A gift letter must state that the gift is to be used for the purchase of the specific property and that no repayment is required. Most lenders will accept a gift letter only if it's from an immediate relative and will require that the borrowers contribute to the cash down payment (usually at least

195

Uniform Residential Loan Application

This application is designed to be completed by the applicant(s) with the lender's assistance. Applicants should complete this form as "Borrower" or "Co-Borrower", as applicable. Co-Borrower information must also be provided (and the appropriate box checked) when ☐ the income or assets of a person other than the "Borrower" (including the Borrower's spouse) will be used as a basis for loan qualification or ☐ the income or assets of the Borrower's spouse will not be used as a basis for loan qualification, but his or her liabilities must be considered because the Borrower resides in a community property state, the security property is located in a community property state, or the Borrower is relying on other property located in a community property state as a basis for repayment of the loan.

I. TYPE OF MORTGAGE AND TERMS OF LOAN

Mortgage Applied for:	☐ VA ☐ FHA	☐ Conventional ☐ FmHA	☐ Other:	Agency Case Number		Lender Case No.
Amount $	Interest Rate %	No. of Months	Amortization Type:	☐ Fixed Rate ☐ GPM	☐ Other (explain): ☐ ARM (type):	

II. PROPERTY INFORMATION AND PURPOSE OF LOAN

Subject Property Address (street, city, state, & ZIP)	No. of Units

Legal Description of Subject Property (attach description if necessary)	Year Built

Purpose of Loan	☐ Purchase ☐ Refinance	☐ Construction ☐ Construction-Permanent	☐ Other (explain):	Property will be: ☐ Primary Residence	☐ Secondary Residence	☐ Investment

Complete this line if construction or construction-permanent loan.

Year Lot Acquired	Original Cost $	Amount Existing Liens $	(a) Present Value of Lot $	(b) Cost of Improvements $	Total (a + b) $

Complete this line if this is a refinance loan.

Year Acquired	Original Cost $	Amount Existing Liens $	Purpose of Refinance	Describe Improvements ☐ made ☐ to be made Cost: $

Title will be held in what Name(s)	Manner in which Title will be held	Estate will be held in: ☐ Fee Simple ☐ Leasehold (show expiration date)
Source of Down Payment, Settlement Charges and/or Subordinate Financing (explain)		

III. BORROWER INFORMATION

Borrower	Co-Borrower
Borrower's Name (include Jr. or Sr. if applicable)	Co-Borrower's Name (include Jr. or Sr. if applicable)
Social Security Number / Home Phone (incl. area code) / Age / Yrs. School	Social Security Number / Home Phone (incl. area code) / Age / Yrs. School
☐ Married ☐ Unmarried (include single, divorced, widowed) ☐ Separated / Dependents (not listed by Co-Borrower) no. ages	☐ Married ☐ Unmarried (include single, divorced, widowed) ☐ Separated / Dependents (not listed by Borrower) no. ages
Present Address (street, city, state, ZIP) ☐ Own ☐ Rent ___ No. Yrs.	Present Address (street, city, state, ZIP) ☐ Own ☐ Rent ___ No. Yrs.

If residing at present address for less than two years, complete the following:

Former Address (street, city, state, ZIP) ☐ Own ☐ Rent ___ No. Yrs.	Former Address (street, city, state, ZIP) ☐ Own ☐ Rent ___ No. Yrs.
...ate, ZIP) ☐	Yrs. Former Address

5 percent of the purchase price). If you're making a 20 percent cash down payment, the entire amount of the down can be a gift. Let your loan officer know at the time you make application for a loan if part of the cash down payment is a gift or if the cash is coming from a source other than savings.

Self-employed individuals and commissioned employees will need to provide the lender with copies of income tax returns for the last two years, as well as a current profit and loss statement. Be prepared to sign a form that allows the lender to send for actual copies of your tax returns if you're applying for a Fannie Mae loan. Borrowers who have partnership or corporation income will need to provide those additional tax returns as well. If you've been at your current job for less than two years, the lender will require that you verify your previous employment. Find out who should be contacted to verify employment and follow up to

Source of Down Payment	...or Subordinate Financing (exp...	Fee Sim...
		Leasehold
		(show expiration date)

III. BORROWER INFORMATION

Borrower					Co-Borrower				
Borrower's Name (include Jr. or Sr. if applicable)					Co-Borrower's Name (include Jr. or Sr. if applicable)				

Social Security Number	Home Phone (incl. area code)	Age	Yrs. School	Social Security Number	Home Phone (incl. area code)	Age	Yrs. School

☐ Married ☐ Unmarried (include single, divorced, widowed) ☐ Separated	Dependents (not listed by Co-Borrower) no. ages	☐ Married ☐ Unmarried (include single, divorced, widowed) ☐ Separated	Dependents (not listed by Borrower) no. ages

Present Address (street, city, state, ZIP) ☐ Own ☐ Rent _____ No. Yrs.	Present Address (street, city, state, ZIP) ☐ Own ☐ Rent _____ No. Yrs.

If residing at present address for less than two years, complete the following:

Former Address (street, city, state, ZIP) ☐ Own ☐ Rent _____ No. Yrs.	Former Address (street, city, state, ZIP) ☐ Own ☐ Rent _____ No. Yrs.

Former Address (street, city, state, ZIP) ☐ Own ☐ Rent _____ No. Yrs.	Former Address (street, city, state, ZIP) ☐ Own ☐ Rent _____ No. Yrs.

IV. EMPLOYMENT INFORMATION

Borrower		Co-Borrower	
Name & Address of Employer ☐ Self Employed	Yrs. on this job	Name & Address of Employer ☐ Self Employed	Yrs. on this job
	Yrs. employed in this line of work/profession		Yrs. employed in this line of work/profession
Position/Title/Type of Business	Business Phone (incl. area code)	Position/Title/Type of Business	Business Phone (incl. area code)

If employed in current position for less than two years or if currently employed in more than one position, complete the following:

Name & Address of Employer ☐ Self Employed	Dates (from - to)	Name & Address of Employer ☐ Self Employed	Dates (from - to)
	Monthly Income $		Monthly Income $
Position/Title/Type of Business	Business Phone (incl. area code)	Position/Title/Type of Business	Business Phone (incl. area code)
Name & Address of Employer ☐ Self Employed	Dates (from - to)	Name & Address of Employer ☐ Self Employed	Dates (from - to)
	Monthly Income $		Monthly Income $
Position/Title/Type of Business	Business Phone (incl. area code)	Position/Title/Type of Business	Business Phone (incl. area code)

Freddie Mac Form 65   10/92   Page 1 of 4   Fannie Mae Form 1003   10/92

197

make sure that the form has been returned to the lender. Misdirected verification forms or forms that sit unopened on someone's desk are a common cause of delayed loan approval.

Income reported by the borrower that is coming from sources such as rental property, alimony, or monthly payments on a note carried back on a property will require additional verification. Be aware that lenders will count only 75 percent of verifiable rental income in qualifying a borrower for a home loan to allow for unanticipated tenant vacancies. If you're divorced, the lender will want to see a copy of your divorce decree or separation agreement.

A copy of the purchase agreement, including counteroffers and addenda, should be included with your loan application and request for verification forms. Ask your real estate agent to provide you with an extra complete copy of the

V. MONTHLY INCOME AND COMBINED HOUSING EXPENSE INFORMATION

Gross Monthly Income	Borrower	Co-Borrower	Total	Combined Monthly Housing Expense	Present	Proposed
Base Empl. Income*	$	$	$	Rent	$	
Overtime				First Mortgage (P&I)		$
Bonuses				Other Financing (P&I)		
Commissions				Hazard Insurance		
Dividends/Interest				Real Estate Taxes		
Net Rental Income				Mortgage Insurance		
Other (before completing, see the notice in "describe other income," below)				Homeowner Assn. Dues		
				Other:		
Total	$	$	$	Total	$	$

* Self Employed Borrower(s) may be required to provide additional documentation such as tax returns and financial statements.

Describe Other Income *Notice:* Alimony, child support, or separate maintenance income need not be revealed if the Borrower (B) or Co-Borrower (C) does not choose to have it considered for repaying this loan.

B/C		Monthly Amount
		$

VI. ASSETS AND LIABILITIES

This Statement and any applicable supporting schedules may be completed jointly by both married and unmarried Co-Borrowers if their assets and liabilities are sufficiently joined so that the Statement can be meaningfully and fairly presented on a combined basis; otherwise separate Statements and Schedules are required. If the Co-Borrower section was completed about a spouse, this Statement and supporting schedules must be completed about that spouse also.

Completed ☐ Jointly ☐ Not Jointly

ASSETS Description	Cash or Market Value	Liabilities and Pledged Assets. List the creditor's name, address and account number for all outstanding debts, including automobile loans, revolving charge accounts, real estate loans, alimony, child support, stock pledges, etc. Use continuation sheet, if necessary. Indicate by (*) those liabilities which will be satisfied upon sale of real estate owned or upon refinancing of the subject property.		
Cash deposit toward purchase held by:	$	LIABILITIES	Monthly Payt. & Mos. Left to Pay	Unpaid Balance
		Name and address of Company	$ Payt./Mos.	$
List checking and savings accounts below				
Name and address of Bank, S&L, or Credit Union				
		Acct. no.		
		Name and address of Company	$ Payt./Mos.	$
Acct. no.	$			
Name and address of Bank, S&L, or Credit Union				
		Acct. no.		
		Name and address of Company	$ Payt./Mos.	$
Acct. no.	$			
Name and address of Bank, S&L, or Credit Union				
		Acct. no.		
		Name and address of Company	$ Payt./Mos.	$
Acct. no.	$			
Name and address of Bank, S&L, or Credit Union				

purchase contract. The lender will also need two copies of the preliminary title report on the property and may want a copy of the termite report. Your agent can instruct the title company to send the preliminary title reports to the lender when they're available, as well as provide the termite report if required. In most cases, you'll be required to pay for a credit report and property appraisal at the time you submit your loan application. Sometimes this is referred to as an application fee.

Some home buyers submit loan applications to more than one lender. For instance, one lender may offer a preferred program that the buyers aren't sure they'll qualify for; submitting double applications could maximize the buyers' ability to close the escrow. You're probably better off informing lenders if you're considering more than one. They're likely to find out anyway because inquiries

		Acct. no.		
		Name and address of Company	$ Payt./Mos.	$
Acct. no.	$			
Name and address of Bank, S&L, or Credit Union				
		Acct. no.		
		Name and address of Company	$ Payt./Mos.	$
Acct. no.	$			
Name and address of Bank, S&L, or Credit Union				
		Acct. no.		
		Name and address of Company	$ Payt./Mos.	$
Acct. no.	$			
Name and address of Bank, S&L, or Credit Union				
		Acct. no.		
		Name and address of Company	$ Payt./Mos.	$
Acct. no.	$			
Stocks & Bonds (Company name/number & description)	$			
		Acct. no.		
		Name and address of Company	$ Payt./Mos.	$
Life insurance net cash value	$			
Face amount: $				
Subtotal Liquid Assets	$			
Real estate owned (enter market value from schedule of real estate owned)	$			
		Acct. no.		
Vested interest in retirement fund	$	Name and address of Company	$ Payt./Mos.	$
Net worth of business(es) owned (attach financial statement)	$			
Automobiles owned (make and year)	$			
		Acct. no.		
		Alimony/Child Support/Separate Maintenance Payments Owed to:	$	
Other Assets (itemize)	$	Job Related Expense (child care, union dues, etc.)	$	
		Total Monthly Payments	$	
Total Assets a.	$	Net Worth (a minus b)	$	Total Liabilities b.	$

Freddie Mac Form 65   10/92   Page 2 of 4   Fannie Mae Form 1003   10/92

199

made about your credit are usually recorded automatically in your credit file. Since lenders will check your credit when processing your loan application, they may discover that other lenders have also recently inquired about your credit. Find out in advance if there are nonrefundable fees involved if you don't take a loan that's offered to you.

Within three days after a loan application is submitted, the lender, in most cases, is required to send the prospective borrower a Good Faith Estimate of settlement, or closing, costs and a Truth in Lending disclosure (also called a Reg Z disclosure). If you have any questions about these disclosures, ask your loan agent or mortgage broker for an explanation.

Be sure that your loan agent knows if you need a letter of lender prequalification within a certain number of days. Contact your lender at least once a

2

VI. ASSETS AND LIABILITIES (cont.)

Schedule of Real Estate Owned (If additional properties are owned, use continuation sheet.)

Property Address (enter S if sold, PS if pending sale or R if rental being held for income)	Type of Property	Present Market Value	Amount of Mortgages & Liens	Gross Rental Income	Mortgage Payments	Insurance, Maintenance, Taxes & Misc.	Net Rental Income
		$	$	$	$	$	$
Totals		$	$	$	$	$	$

List any additional names under which credit has previously been received and indicate appropriate creditor name(s) and account number(s):

Alternate Name	Creditor Name	Account Number

VII. DETAILS OF TRANSACTION

a. Purchase price	$
b. Alterations, improvements, repairs	
c. Land (if acquired separately)	
d. Refinance (incl. debts to be paid off)	
e. Estimated prepaid items	
f. Estimated closing costs	
g. PMI, MIP, Funding Fee	
h. Discount (if Borrower will pay)	
i. Total costs (add items a through h)	
j. Subordinate financing	
k. Borrower's closing costs paid by Seller	
l. Other Credits (explain)	
m. Loan amount (exclude PMI, MIP, Funding Fee financed)	
n. PMI, MIP, Funding Fee financed	
o. Loan amount (add m & n)	
p. Cash from/to Borrower (subtract j, k, l & o from i)	

VIII. DECLARATIONS

If you answer "yes" to any questions a through i, please use continuation sheet for explanation.

Borrower Yes No / Co-Borrower Yes No

a. Are there any outstanding judgments against you?

b. Have you been declared bankrupt within the past 7 years?

c. Have you had property foreclosed upon or given title or deed in lieu thereof in the last 7 years?

d. Are you a party to a lawsuit?

e. Have you directly or indirectly been obligated on any loan which resulted in foreclosure, transfer of title in lieu of foreclosure, or judgment? (This would include such loans as home mortgage loans, SBA loans, home improvement loans, educational loans, manufactured (mobile) home loans, any mortgage, financial obligation, bond, or loan guarantee. If "Yes," provide details, including date, name and address of Lender, FHA or VA case number, if any, and reasons for the action.)

f. Are you presently delinquent or in default on any Federal debt or any other loan, mortgage, financial obligation, bond, or loan guarantee? If "Yes," give details as described in the preceding question.

g. Are you obligated to pay alimony, child support, or separate maintenance?

h. Is any part of the down payment borrowed?

i. Are you a co-maker or endorser on a note?

j. Are you a U.S. citizen?

k. Are you a permanent resident alien?

l. Do you intend to occupy the property as your primary residence? If "Yes," complete question m below.

m. Have you had an ownership interest in a property in the last three years?

(1) What type of property did you own–principal residence (PR), second home (SH), or investment property (IP)?

(2) How did you hold title to the home–solely by yourself (S), jointly with your spouse (SP), or jointly with another person (O)?

IX. ACKNOWLEDGMENT AND AGREEMENT

The undersigned specifically acknowledge(s) and agree(s) that: (1) the loan requested by this application will be secured by a first mortgage or deed of trust on the property described herein; (2) the property will not be used for any illegal or prohibited purpose or use; (3) all statements made in this application are made for the purpose of obtaining the loan indicated herein; (4) occupation of the property will be as indicated above; (5) verification or reverification of any information contained in the application may be made at any time by the Lender, its agents, successors and assigns, either directly or through a credit reporting agency, from any source named in this application, and the original copy of ... application will be retained by the Lender, even if the ... is not approved; (6) the Lender, its agents, su... and assigns will rely on the inf... ...e contained

---

200

week to verify that the approval process is on schedule. In all of these matters you should feel free to seek the assistance of your real estate agent.

Property Appraisal

An appraisal is a professional, although somewhat subjective, opinion of the market value of a property. An appraisal is required before a lender will approve and fund a home loan. The lender or loan broker selects the appraiser, but the prospective borrower usually pays the fee. An appraisal fee will vary with the price of the home: the higher the price, the more expensive the appraisal. An appraisal on a $250,000 home will cost about $300 to $350.

The appraiser customarily examines the property and then compares it with three similar properties located nearby that have sold during the past six months.

otal costs

j. Subordinate financing

k. Borrower's closing costs paid by Seller

l. Other Credits (explain)

m. Loan amount
(exclude PMI, MIP, Funding Fee financed)

n. PMI, MIP, Funding Fee financed

o. Loan amount (add m & n)

p. Cash from/to Borrower
(subtract j, k, l & o from i)

...red (mobile) Home ... details, including date, name and ...ess of Lender, ... number, if any, and reasons for the action.)

f. Are you presently delinquent or in default on any Federal debt or any other loan, mortgage, financial obligation, bond, or loan guarantee? If "Yes," give details as described in the preceding question.

g. Are you obligated to pay alimony, child support, or separate maintenance?

h. Is any part of the down payment borrowed?

i. Are you a co-maker or endorser on a note?

j. Are you a U.S. citizen?

k. Are you a permanent resident alien?

l. Do you intend to occupy the property as your primary residence?
If "Yes," complete question m below.

m. Have you had an ownership interest in a property in the last three years?

(1) What type of property did you own–principal residence (PR), second home (SH), or investment property (IP)?

(2) How did you hold title to the home–solely by yourself (S), jointly with your spouse (SP), or jointly with another person (O)?

IX. ACKNOWLEDGMENT AND AGREEMENT

The undersigned specifically acknowledge(s) and agree(s) that: (1) the loan requested by this application will be secured by a first mortgage or deed of trust on the property described herein; (2) the property will not be used for any illegal or prohibited purpose or use; (3) all statements made in this application are made for the purpose of obtaining the loan indicated herein; (4) occupation of the property will be as indicated above; (5) verification or reverification of any information contained in the application may be made at any time by the Lender, its agents, successors and assigns, either directly or through a credit reporting agency, from any source named in this application, and the original copy of this application will be retained by the Lender, even if the loan is not approved; (6) the Lender, its agents, successors and assigns will rely on the information contained in the application and I/we have a continuing obligation to amend and/or supplement the information provided in this application if any of the material facts which I/we have represented herein should change prior to closing; (7) in the event my/our payments on the loan indicated in this application become delinquent, the Lender, its agents, successors and assigns, may, in addition to all their other rights and remedies, report my/our name(s) and account information to a credit reporting agency; (8) ownership of the loan may be transferred to successor or assign of the Lender without notice to me and/or the administration of the loan account may be transferred to an agent, successor or assign of the Lender with prior notice to me; (9) the Lender, its agents, successors and assigns make no representations or warranties, express or implied, to the Borrower(s) regarding the property, the condition of the property, or the value of the property.
Certification: I/We certify that the information provided in this application is true and correct as of the date set forth opposite my/our signature(s) on this application and acknowledge my/our understanding that any intentional or negligent misrepresentation(s) of the information contained in this application may result in civil liability and/or criminal penalties including, but not limited to, fine or imprisonment or both under the provisions of Title 18, United States Code, Section 1001, et seq. and liability for monetary damages to the Lender, its agents, successors and assigns, insurers and any other person who may suffer any loss due to reliance upon any misrepresentation which I/we have made on this application.

Borrower's Signature   Date   Co-Borrower's Signature   Date

X   X

X. INFORMATION FOR GOVERNMENT MONITORING PURPOSES

The following information is requested by the Federal Government for certain types of loans related to a dwelling, in order to monitor the Lender's compliance with equal credit opportunity, fair housing and home mortgage disclosure laws. You are not required to furnish this information, but are encouraged to do so. The law provides that a Lender may neither discriminate on the basis of this information, nor on whether you choose to furnish it. However, if you choose not to furnish it, under Federal regulations this Lender is required to note race and sex on the basis of visual observation or surname. If you do not wish to furnish the above information, please check the box below. (Lender must review the above material to assure that the disclosures satisfy all requirements to which the Lender is subject under applicable state law for the particular type of loan applied for.)

BORROWER
I do not wish to furnish this information
Race/National Origin: American Indian or Alaskan Native / Asian or Pacific Islander / White, not of Hispanic Origin / Black, not of Hispanic origin / Hispanic / Other (specify)
Sex: Female / Male

CO-BORROWER
I do not wish to furnish this information
Race/National Origin: American Indian or Alaskan Native / Asian or Pacific Islander / White, not of Hispanic Origin / Black, not of Hispanic origin / Hispanic / Other (specify)
Sex: Female / Male

To be Completed by Interviewer
This application was taken by:
face-to-face interview
by mail
by telephone

Interviewer's Name (print or type)
Interviewer's Signature   Date
Interviewer's Phone Number (incl. area code)
Name and Address of Interviewer's Employer

201

Freddie Mac Form 65 10/92   Page 3 of 4   Fannie Mae Form 1003 10/92

A dollar value is assigned to features on the subject property which the comparable properties lacked. Likewise, value is deducted from the property in question if the comparable properties featured amenities that it doesn't have.

It's important for the buyer's real estate agent to meet the appraiser at the property in order to make access easy and to provide the appraiser with recent comparable sales information. This will save the appraiser time, which is critical in busy real estate markets when appraisals can run as much as four to six weeks behind.

Appraisals are easier to do when prices are relatively stable. Difficulties with appraisals may arise in real estate markets with fast appreciation or depreciation. Escrows typically take approximately 60 days to close. If a house down the street sold two weeks ago for $25,000 more than anything else in the neighborhood, it may be difficult for the appraiser to justify the new market value until that escrow

Continuation Sheet/Residential Loan Application		
Use this continuation sheet if you need more space to complete the Residential Loan Application. Mark B for Borrower or C for Co-Borrower.	Borrower:	Agency Case Number:
	Co-Borrower:	Lender Case Number:

202

closes. On the other hand, if market values are dropping, a property could appraise for higher than current market value if very recent sales have not yet closed escrow. In slow markets or in areas with very low turnover, appraisals are tricky because of insufficient comparable home sales information. When there are few recent comparable sales, appraisers can sometimes use similar properties that sold in adjacent neighborhoods.

Establishing value is easier in tract developments where there's consistency in home size and amenities than in neighborhoods with lots of variability in home size, style, and age. Appraisals are ideally done by someone knowledgeable in the area who will know the subtle differences that can affect local values.

Another problem that has complicated appraisals recently is that appraisers often require proof that building permits were taken out for large additions and remodels made to the property. If this proof cannot be provided, the appraiser

I/We fully understand that it is a Federal crime punishable by fine or imprisonment, or both, to knowingly make any false statements concerning any of the above facts as applicable under the provisions of Title 18, United States Code, Section 1001, et seq.

Borrower's Signature:	Date	Co-Borrower's Signature:	Date
X		X	

Freddie Mac Form 65   10/92   Page 4 of 4   Fannie Mae Form 1003   10/92

might not count the additional square footage in the evaluation of property value. This could make a big difference if, for instance, the addition turned a small two-bedroom, one-bath home (with an approximate value of $175,000) into a three-bedroom, two-bath home (with a current market value of approximately $250,000). It's possible, in some instances, to obtain city building permits after the fact for a fee.

The appraisal is important because it helps to determine what size loan the lender will give you. Lenders will usually lend up to a certain percentage of the property's appraised value (typically 80, 90, or 95 percent). This percentage is called the loan-to-value ratio (LTV). Lenders are less concerned about granting a loan when the loan-to-value ratio is low than when the buyer is making a small cash down payment and the LTV is high. If the appraisal comes in a little low, the lender will usually be more lenient in approving the loan if the borrower has a large cash down, since the equity position of the lender in this case is relatively secure.

Sometimes a property will appraise for lower than fair market value because the appraiser is not familiar with the local neighborhood, in which case an appraisal review should be requested and the buyer's agent should provide the appraiser and the lender with comparable sales information. If the appraisal comes in low and the lender cannot be convinced to revise it upwards, there are several alternatives. Buyers who are convinced they're paying over fair market value for their home can terminate the contract and their deposit will be refunded if the low appraisal causes the lender to deny approval for the loan amount the buyers specified in their financing contingency. The buyers also have grounds for terminating the contract if it includes a contingency for the property to appraise for the purchase price. If, on the other hand, the buyers and sellers want to carry on with the transaction, either the buyers can make up the difference between the loan amount requested and the amount approved by the lender in cash, or the sellers can agree to lower the purchase price, or carry back a note for the buyers. Another alternative is to take the loan to another lender, such as a portfolio lender, who might be more flexible.

California Senate Bill 492, which took effect in January of 1993, requires lenders to notify borrowers that they're entitled to a copy of their appraisal if they have paid for it and if they make a written request for a copy. The request should be made to the lender, not to the appraiser. If you're having difficulty getting a copy of the appraisal on the home you're buying or refinancing, ask to speak to your loan agent's supervisor.

What to Do About a Bad Credit Report

A minor blemish on a credit report may require nothing more than a simple letter of explanation from the prospective borrower to the lender. For example, if a payment due on your department store charge card was late one month because you were out of town on business and your spouse forgot to pay the bill, a letter explaining this will probably suffice to clear up the problem as far as your loan approval is concerned.

There are sometimes mistakes in credit reports. One study showed that about 19 percent of all credit reports had errors that could keep borrowers from being approved for a loan. A late payment could show up if, for instance, your bank put a hold, or stop-payment, on a check in error. You're entitled to information about a negative entry in your credit file, and you have the right to challenge such an entry according to the National Foundation for Consumer Credit. Ask your loan agent whom to contact if you suspect there's a mistake on your credit report.

Lenders will usually run more than one credit report on a prospective

> *Borrowers are entitled to a copy of the appraisal on the property they're purchasing if they paid for it and they request a copy in writing.*

borrower. Don't assume that just because you have a clean TRW credit report that you'll have no credit problems. It's a good idea to obtain copies of your credit reports from the three major credit reporting agencies before applying for a loan. The three main national credit reporting agencies are: TRW (800) 392-1122, Equifax (800) 685-1111, and Trans Union (800) 582-0420. If you've been turned down for a loan because of bad credit, you're entitled to a free copy of your report. If you just want to check it, there will be a charge of about $20.

Good credit is impérative. Even a quick qualifier loan that requires a minimum of documentation will require good credit. But, don't assume a credit problem is insurmountable.

> **Sylvia and Robert Linquist thought their loan approval would be a breeze because they were buying a house for much less than they could afford. But, their hefty incomes didn't satisfy five lenders who all denied them a loan due to a credit report littered with late payments and tax liens. It turns out that most of the credit quirks were caused by their respective ex-spouses. The Linquists finally found a loan agent who spent hours showing them how to clean up their messy credit trail. Their application was then approved, although the lender required the Linquists to make an extra 5 percent cash down payment for security.**

205

A previous bankruptcy can remain in a credit file for up to ten years. There are lenders, however, who will consider an applicant who went through a bankruptcy as recently as two years ago, as long as good credit has been re-established. Foreclosures are normally reported by credit agencies for at least seven years. If your credit history was shaky in the past but has improved recently, ask previous creditors to remove disparaging comments from your credit record.

No credit can be as difficult to deal with as bad credit when applying for a home loan. To establish credit, get a credit card or two, charge a few items, and then pay the credit card balances off immediately when they're due.

There's really nothing you can do to fix bad credit (as opposed to correcting mistakes on a credit report). But, you can start to rebuild good credit by paying all installment debt payments on time. Borrowers with bad credit will have to work hard to get a loan. Be candid with your loan agent about your credit problems before you submit an application so that you can work together to get your loan approved. You may have to take a "B, C, or D" loan (usually available through a mortgage broker) if your credit history is weak, and this could mean paying a higher-than-market interest rate on the loan, or making a larger cash down payment. But, if you make your mortgage

Loan applicants are entitled to an explanation if they're denied a loan due to bad credit.

payments on time, the next time you apply for a home loan, the process will be much easier.

Final Loan Approval

Loan approval depends on three things: the prospective borrower's credit history, the loan application, and the property appraisal. After all these documents are assembled, including all verifications of employment, cash reserves, and assets and liabilities, the loan package is submitted to underwriting. The underwriter reviews the loan package of documents in order to determine the level of risk involved in approving the loan. After underwriting, the loan package is submitted for formal loan approval.

Having your new home loan approved should mean that you have an unconditional commitment from the lender to loan you the amount of money you requested on the loan application at the interest rate and terms you stipulated. The commitment should be in writing and will state a date by which the escrow must close. In periods of rising interest rates, the loan commitment may expire before the close of escrow date stated in your purchase agreement. If this occurs, have your agent contact the seller's agent and request an early close of escrow in order to protect your loan commitment. The sellers may need to keep possession of the property after close if they're unable to push their move date forward to coincide with the earlier close of escrow.

Make certain that the loan approval is firm, not conditional, before removing the financing contingency from the purchase agreement. For example, a lender might approve a loan conditioned upon approving additional documents such as: a copy of the maintenance agreement on a shared driveway or private road; a copy of a certified closing statement on the home you just sold; verification that you've paid down a charge card debt; a copy of a note that the seller has agreed to carry for you; confirmation that the seller has completed a repair on the property that you requested as part of the purchase agreement; a certified copy of your divorce decree; or even, as absurd as it may sound, a letter from you stating that you like your current job and don't anticipate making a job change in the near future.

Final approval may require an additional confirmation from an underwriter or a private mortgage insurance company. Again, make sure that the loan is fully approved before removing the loan contingency from the purchase contract.

Jack and Ginny Mason bought their first home with a contingency for them to obtain a loan commitment for 90 percent of the purchase price. The loan broker called three weeks later to tell them the loan had been approved. Based on this verbal communication, and without getting a written commitment from the lender, the Mason's removed their financing contingency from the contract. A week before closing, the loan broker called to say that the underwriter wanted to see copies of permits for an addition and kitchen remodel before the buyers' loan documents would be drawn. A previous owner had

completed this work on the house, and the current owners didn't
have copies of permits. An examination of the city building records
also failed to produce copies of any permits. The Masons were lucky
that the underwriter accepted a letter from a contractor that stated
that the work appeared to comply with building code requirements.
Otherwise, they might have had to default on the contract and forfeit
their deposit, or worse.

How to Finance a Home Purchase When Interest Rates Are High

When rates are high, the most attractive alternative to conventional financing,
aside from seller financing (which will be discussed in the next section of this
chapter), is a buyer takeover of an existing low-interest-rate assumable mortgage.
Most adjustable-rate mortgages are assumable. Sellers who agree to an assumption will want to be sure that they're relieved of future responsibility for loan
repayment. Buyers will want to read and review the existing loan documents
before committing to take on the responsibility of repayment. Check with the
lender to determine the fees charged for an assumption as well as the terms and
conditions of assumption.

Most assumable loans now require that the buyer be qualified to make the
loan payments. Therefore, a qualification procedure, similar to that required for
a new mortgage, will be necessary to secure approval. Be sure to allow at least
four to eight weeks for processing, since qualifying a buyer for an assumption is
likely to rank low on the lender's priority list. Lenders are understandably less
interested in facilitating assumptions of low-interest-rate loans than in originat-
ing new loans at higher rates.

When the amount of the remaining balance on the assumable loan is low in
relation to the purchase price, the seller may offer to carry back a second deed
of trust in order to make up the difference between the remaining balance on the
first loan and the amount of the buyer's cash down payment. For example, let's
say you agree to pay $300,000 for a house. You'll finance the purchase by putting
$60,000 down and assuming the seller's existing $200,000 loan. The seller will
carry a second loan for you secured by a deed of trust against the property for the
remaining $40,000.

Buyers and sellers are cautioned against entering into any agreement conditioned upon the buyers taking over the existing loan if that loan is not expressly
assumable. If the lender discovers that the nonassumable loan (which contains a
"due on sale clause") has been taken over by the buyers without permission, the
note is likely to be called immediately due and payable, which could put the buyers in a difficult position if affordable financing is not available.

The lease option is another possibility during periods of high interest rates
and low real estate sales activity. With this method of home purchase, the seller
retains title to the property, accepts an amount of money from the buyer (the

207

option money), and leases the property to the buyer for a specified period of time. When the term of the loan is up, the buyer either pays the balance agreed upon in the option agreement and completes the purchase, or forfeits the option money and the seller retains title to the property.

A lease option agreement works well for the buyer short on cash and the seller who is unable to sell. A seller should make any agreement to lease option a property conditioned upon approval of the potential buyer's financing statement and credit report within a specified number of days following acceptance of the lease option contract.

A contract of sale is a creative financing device similar to the lease option. Title to the property does not transfer to the buyer until certain terms and conditions are met. Usually the seller continues to make the existing mortgage payments, as is the case with the lease option arrangement. The buyer occupies the property and makes payments to the seller on a monthly basis until title to the property transfers to the buyer.

The buyer and seller both incur potential risks by entering into a lease option or a contract of sale arrangement. A buyer could end up with more debt than anticipated if the seller doesn't keep the existing mortgage payments current or if the seller further encumbers the property without the buyer's consent. On the other hand, the seller could find that the property is unsalable if the prospective buyer lets it fall into a state of disrepair and then doesn't follow through with the purchase. Before entering into a contract of sale agreement, seek the advice of a knowledgeable real estate attorney.

Seller Financing

Seller financing offers benefits to both buyers and sellers, but risks are involved that should be thoroughly understood. The benefits include tax relief for the seller, the ability to complete a sale transaction at times when conventional financing is not readily available or is prohibitively expensive, and good investment opportunities for both the buyer and seller.

A buyer should make sure that seller financing isn't being offered as a concession for an inflated price. This is especially important if the seller-carry loan has a short term. If the note is not fully amortized and comes due and payable in two or three years, the buyer will need to pay the remaining principal balance (the balloon payment) by selling or refinancing the property. Problems for the buyer may also arise if interest rates are exorbitantly high or housing values are deflated when the note comes due. The house might not sell or be appraised for enough to provide the buyer with funds sufficient to pay off the remaining loan balance. Whenever possible, buyers should negotiate an extension provision allowing for an automatic extension of the term of the loan if refinancing cannot be obtained at the time the note is due.

California Civil Code 2966 requires that the seller send a special notice to the buyer between 90 and 150 days before a balloon payment is due. This applies to residential property containing one to four units. Buyers and sellers should

208

also be aware that in cases when the seller is carrying a second mortgage for the buyer, most lenders will require that the due date of the loan be at least five years after the close of escrow. This is to help ensure that the buyer will not be caught short of funds when the balloon payment comes due.

Regardless of how creditworthy a buyer may appear to be, sellers are cautioned to avoid a "no-cash down deal." A "no-money down" transaction is one in which the buyers invest none of their own money. An example might work as follows: The buyers agree to purchase the seller's home at an inflated price, using a new first mortgage and a large second loan carried by the seller. The total of the two loans exceeds the current market value of the property, and the buyers walk away from the escrow with cash in hand. They may occupy the property for a period of time and make the mortgage payments, but when they disappear, the seller's only recourse is to foreclose. It's unlikely, however, that the seller will be able to recover the full amount of the seller-carry loan since the market value of the property will not be enough to cover the amount of both loans.

California Civil Code section 2956, which came into effect in 1983, requires detailed disclosure of the terms and conditions of seller financing when an arranger of credit is involved in the transaction. A real estate agent, acting either as an agent or as a principal in a transaction involving the sale of one-to-four residential units, is considered to be an arranger of credit under the provisions of this requirement. California Association of Realtors form SFD-14, a sample of which is included in this chapter, was developed to help real estate agents comply with this law. This form should be completed and signed by buyers, sellers, and their respective agents at the time the purchase agreement is negotiated.

Section A of the Seller Financing Disclosure Statement refers to the credit documents used to evidence the extension of credit. The note and deed of trust are the most commonly used credit documents. The note is an agreement that states the amount and terms of the loan. The deed of trust secures the note against the property. The installment land sale contract is the same as the contract of sale referred to in the previous section of this chapter.

An all-inclusive note and deed of trust, also called a wrap-around loan, is a second mortgage that the seller carries for an amount that includes both the existing first loan balance and the amount of the seller-carry second. The buyer makes one lump loan payment to the seller out of which the seller makes the payments on the underlying first loan. This method of seller financing is risky if the underlying first loan has a "due on sale" clause because the loan might be called due when the first lender becomes aware that the property has transferred title.

The credit terms itemized in the SFD-14 form (section B) should duplicate those agreed to by the buyer and seller in the financing section of the purchase agreement. The interest rate is negotiable but will undoubtedly be determined by current interest rates charged on conventional home loans, as well as by the interest the seller could earn if the money were placed in another form of investment. Sellers should be aware that the IRS requires that a minimum interest rate

209

SELLER FINANCING DISCLOSURE STATEMENT
(California Civil Code 2956-2967)
CALIFORNIA ASSOCIATION OF REALTORS' (CAR) STANDARD FORM

This two page disclosure statement from the Purchaser (Buyer) and Vendor (Seller) is prepared by an arranger of credit [defined in Civil Code 2957 (a)] and provided to **both** the Purchaser (Buyer) and Vendor (Seller) in a residential real estate transaction involving four or fewer units whenever the Seller has agreed to extend credit to the Buyer as part of the purchase price.

Buyer: _____

Seller: _____

Arranger of Credit: _____

Real Property: _____

A. Credit Documents: This extension of credit by the Seller is evidenced by ☐ note and deed of trust, ☐ all-inclusive note and deed of trust, ☐ installment land sale contract, ☐ lease/option (when parties intend transfer of equitable title), ☐ other (specify) _____ .

B. Credit Terms:
1. ☐ See attached copy of credit documents referred to in Section A above for description of credit terms; **or**
2. ☐ The terms of the credit documents referred to in Section A above are: Principal amount $_____ interest at _____% per annum payable at $_____ per _____ (month/year/etc.) with the entire unpaid principal and accrued interest of approximately $_____ due _____ 19____ (maturity date).

Late Charge: If any payment is not made within _____ days after it is due, a late charge of $_____ or _____% of the installment due may be charged to the Buyer.

Prepayment: If all or part of this loan is paid early, the Buyer ☐ will, ☐ will **not**, have to pay a prepayment penalty as follows: _____
_____ .

Due on Sale: If any interest in the property securing this obligation is sold or otherwise transferred, the Seller ☐ has, ☐ does **not** have, the option to require immediate payment of the entire unpaid balance and accrued interest.

Other Terms: _____
_____
_____ .

C. Available information on loans/encumbrances * that will be **senior** to the Seller's extension of credit:

	1st	2nd	3rd
1. Original Balance	$_____	$_____	$_____
2. Current Balance	$_____	$_____	$_____
3. Periodic Payment (e.g. $100/month)	$_____/_____	$_____/_____	$_____/_____
4. Amt. of Balloon Payment	$_____	$_____	$_____
5. Date of Balloon Payment	_____	_____	_____
6. Maturity Date	_____	_____	_____
7. Due On Sale ('Yes' or 'No')	_____	_____	_____
8. Interest Rate (per annum)	_____%	_____%	_____%
9. Fixed or Variable Rate: If Variable Rate:	☐ a copy of note attached ☐ variable provisions are explained on attached separate sheet	☐ a copy of note attached ☐ variable provisions are explained on attached separate sheet	☐ a copy of note attached ☐ variable provisions are explained on attached separate sheet
10. Is Payment Current?	_____	_____	_____

☐ SEPARATE SHEET WITH INFORMATION REGARDING OTHER SENIOR LOANS/ENCUMBRANCES IS ATTACHED.

*IMP___ _NOTE: Asterisk (*) denotes an e___ ___ obligation ___ ___ for a balloon paym___

be charged; otherwise interest is imputed at a specific rate and the sellers are taxed as if they had received the imputed rate.

A seller will usually want to incorporate a late charge to encourage the buyer to make monthly loan payments on time. A customary late charge is $5, or 6 percent of the payment, whichever is more, if it isn't made within 10 days of coming due.

A buyer will probably want to stipulate that prepayment of the loan be without penalty. This should not cause a problem unless the loan payments are a source of retirement income or part of an installment sale, in which case early prepayment could have negative financial repercussions for the seller.

Most sellers prefer to have a due on sale provision included in the note, but this can be a negotiable item. Buyers who are concerned that they might be forced to sell during a period of high interest rates can request that the note be

2. Current Ba...					
3. Periodic Payment					
(e.g. $100/month)	$ _____ / _____		$ _____ / _____		$ _____ / _____
4. Amt. of Balloon Payment	$ _____		$ _____		$ _____
5. Date of Balloon Payment					
6. Maturity Date					
7. Due On Sale ('Yes' or 'No')					
8. Interest Rate (per annum)	_____%		_____%		_____%
9. Fixed or Variable Rate:					

If Variable Rate:

☐ a copy of note attached   ☐ a copy of note attached   ☐ a copy of note attached
☐ variable provisions are   ☐ variable provisions are   ☐ variable provisions are
    explained on attached   explained on attached   explained on attached
    separate sheet   separate sheet   separate sheet

10. Is Payment Current? _____

☐ SEPARATE SHEET WITH INFORMATION REGARDING OTHER SENIOR LOANS/ENCUMBRANCES IS ATTACHED.

*IMPORTANT NOTE: Asterisk (*) denotes an estimate.

D. **Caution:** If any of the obligations secured by the property calls for a balloon payment, then Seller and Buyer are aware that refinancing of the balloon payment at maturity may be difficult or impossible depending on the conditions in the mortgage marketplace at that time. There are no assurances that new financing or a loan extension will be available when the balloon payment is due.

E. **Deferred Interest:**

"Deferred interest" results when the Buyer's periodic payments are less than the amount of interest earned on the obligation, or when the obligation does not require periodic payments. This accrued interest will have to be paid by the Buyer at a later time and may result in the Buyer owing more on the obligation than at origination.

☐ The credit being extended to the Buyer by the Seller does **not** provide for "deferred interest," **or**
☐ The credit being extended to the Buyer by the Seller does provide for "deferred interest."

    The credit documents provide the following regarding deferred interest:

    ☐ All deferred interest shall be due and payable along with the principal at maturity (simple interest); **or**
    ☐ The deferred interest shall be added to the principal _____ (e.g., annually, monthly, etc.) and thereafter shall bear interest at the rate specified in the credit documents (compound interest); **or**
    ☐ Other (specify) _____

F. **All-Inclusive Deed of Trust or Installment Land Sale Contract:**

☐ This transaction does **not** involve the use of an all-inclusive (or wraparound) deed of trust or an installment land sale contract; **or**
☐ This transaction **does** involve the use of either an all-inclusive (or wraparound) deed of trust or an installment land sale contract which provides as follows:

    1) In the event of an acceleration of any senior encumbrance, the responsibility for payment or for legal defense is:
       ☐ **Not** specified in the credit or security documents; **or**
       ☐ Specified in the credit or security documents as follows:

_____
_____

211

Buyer and Seller acknowledge receipt of copy of this page, which constitutes Page 1 of 2 Pages.
Buyer's Initials (_____) (_____) Seller's Initials (_____) (_____)

BROKER'S COPY

--- OFFICE USE ONLY ---
Reviewed by Broker or Designee _____
Date _____

EQUAL HOUSING OPPORTUNITY
M-SC-FEB-91

SELLER FINANCING DISCLOSURE STATEMENT (SFD-14 PAGE 1 OF 2)

assumable by a future buyer, and sellers might find this provision agreeable as long as they have the right to approve the future buyer's credit report and financial statement.

Section C provides for disclosure of all loans or encumbrances secured against the property that will be senior to the seller financing. If the buyer is assuming an existing loan, the particulars of the loan need to be provided, and copies of any notes and variable interest rate disclosures should be attached and initialed by the buyer and seller. When the buyer is obtaining new financing as part of the transaction, all particulars should be provided along with copies of any notes and adjustable-rate mortgage disclosures.

Sellers should be wary of carrying back a second for a buyer who makes a small cash down payment and obtains a large adjustable-rate first mortgage (ARM) that allows negative amortization. If interest rates rise dramatically, the

☐   —

2) In the event of the prepayment of a senior encumbrance, the responsibilities and rights of Seller and Buyer regarding refinancing, prepayment penalties, and any prepayment discounts are:
☐ **Not** specified in the credit or security documents; **or**
☐ Specified in the credit or security documents as follows:

_____
_____

3) The financing provided that the Buyer will make periodic payments to _____
[e.g., a collection agent (such as a bank or savings and loan); Seller; etc.] and that _____
will be responsible for disbursing payments to the payee(s) on the senior encumbrance(s) and to the Seller.

CAUTION: The parties are advised to consider designating a neutral third party as the collection agent for receiving Buyer's payments and disbursing them to the payee(s) on the senior encumbrance(s) and to the Seller.

G. Buyer's Creditworthiness: Section 580(b) of the California Code of Civil Procedure generally limits a Seller's rights in the event of a default by the Buyer in the financing extended by the Seller, to a foreclosure of the property.
☐ No disclosure concerning the Buyer's creditworthiness has been made to the Seller; **or**
☐ The following representations concerning the Buyer's creditworthiness have been made by the Buyer(s) to the Seller:

1. Occupation: _____	1. Occupation: _____
2. Employer: _____	2. Employer: _____
3. Length of Employment: _____	3. Length of Employment: _____
4. Monthly Gross Income: _____	4. Monthly Gross Income: _____
5. Buyer ☐ has, ☐ has **not**, provided Seller a current credit report issued by: _____	5. Buyer ☐ has, ☐ has **not**, provided Seller a current credit report issued by: _____
6. Buyer ☐ has, ☐ has **not**, provided Seller a completed loan application.	6. Buyer ☐ has, ☐ has **not**, provided Seller a completed loan application.
7. Other (specify): _____	7. Other (specify): _____

H. Insurance:
☐ The parties' escrow holder or insurance carrier has been or will be directed to add a loss payee clause to the property insurance protecting the Seller; **or**
☐ No provision has been made for adding a loss payee clause to the property insurance protecting the Seller. Seller is advised to secure such clauses or acquire a separate insurance policy.

I. Request for Notice:
☐ A Request for Notice of Default under Section 2924(b) of the California Civil Code has been or will be recorded; **or**
☐ No provision for recording a Request for Notice of Default has been made. Seller is advised to consider recording a Request for Notice of Default.

J. Title Insurance:
☐ Title insurance coverage will be provided to **both** Seller and Buyer insuring their respective interests in the property; **or**
☐ No provision for title insurance coverage of **both** Seller and Buyer has been made. Seller and Buyer are advised to consider securing such title insurance coverage.

K. Tax Service:
☐ A tax service has been arranged to report to Seller whether property taxes have been paid on the property. _____ (e.g., Seller, Buyer, etc.) will be responsible for the continued retention and payment of such tax service; **or**
☐ No provision has been made for a tax service. Seller should consider retaining a tax service or otherwise determine that the property taxes are paid.

L. Recording:
☐ The security documents (e.g., deed of trust, installment land contract, etc.) will be recorded with the county recorder where the property is located; **or**
☐ The security documents will **not** be recorded with the county recorder. Seller and Buyer are advised that their respective interests in the property ...ardized by intervening liens ... subsequent transfers which a...

remaining principal balance on the first loan could rise to a point where it jeopardizes the seller's equity.

Section G contains an important disclosure that sellers should note. California Civil Code section 580(b) protects buyers from personal liability in the event that they default on a seller financed arrangement, leaving foreclosure—even if the foreclosure sale proceeds are not sufficient to pay off the debt—as the seller's only remedy.

It's wise for sellers who are carrying financing for a buyer to include a contingency in their purchase contract for the sellers to approve a financial statement (or a completed lender loan application) and credit report from the buyer. You'll need written permission from a buyer to check his or her credit. If you feel you're

☐ A Req~~uest~~ ~~ion 292~~ ~~een or w~~
☐ No provision for ~~~~ ~~equest for Notice of Default has~~ ~~advised to consider recording a Request for Notice of Default.~~

J. Title Insurance:
☐ Title insurance coverage will be provided to **both** Seller and Buyer insuring their respective interests in the property; **or**
☐ No provision for title insurance coverage of **both** Seller and Buyer has been made. Seller and Buyer are advised to consider securing such title insurance coverage.

K. Tax Service:
☐ A tax service has been arranged to report to Seller whether property taxes have been paid on the property. _____ (e.g., Seller, Buyer, etc.) will be responsible for the continued retention and payment of such tax service; **or**
☐ No provision has been made for a tax service. Seller should consider retaining a tax service or otherwise determine that the property taxes are paid.

L. Recording:
☐ The security documents (e.g., deed of trust, installment land contract, etc.) will be recorded with the county recorder where the property is located; **or**
☐ The security documents will **not** be recorded with the county recorder. Seller and Buyer are advised that their respective interests in the property may be jeopardized by intervening liens, judgments or subsequent transfers which are recorded.

M. Proceeds to Buyer:
☐ Buyer will **NOT** receive any cash proceeds at the close of the sale transaction; **or**
☐ Buyer will receive approximately $_____ from _____ (indicate source from the sale transaction proceeds of such funds). Buyer represents that the purpose of such disbursement is as follows:_____
_____

N. Notice of Delinquency:
☐ A Request for Notice of Delinquency under Section 2924(e) of the California Civil Code has been or will be made to the Senior lienholder(s); **or**
☐ No provision for making a Request for Notice of Delinquency has been made. Seller should consider making a Request for Notice of Delinquency.

The above information has been provided to: (a) the Buyer, by the arranger of credit and the Seller (with respect to information within the knowledge of the Seller); (b) the Seller, by the arranger of credit and the Buyer (with respect to information within the knowledge of the Buyer).

Arranger of Credit _____
Date _____ , 19____   By _____

Buyer and Seller acknowledge that the information each has provided to the arranger of credit for inclusion in this disclosure form is accurate to the best of their knowledge.

Buyer and Seller hereby acknowledge receipt of a completed copy of this disclosure form.

Date _____ , 19____   Date _____ , 19____

Buyer _____   Seller _____

Buyer _____   Seller _____

213

THIS STANDARD DOCUMENT HAS BEEN APPROVED BY THE CALIFORNIA ASSOCIATION OF REALTORS¹ IN FORM ONLY. NO REPRESENTATION IS MADE AS TO THE LEGAL VALIDITY OF ANY PROVISION OR THE ADEQUACY OF ANY PROVISION IN ANY SPECIFIC TRANSACTION.
A REAL ESTATE BROKER IS THE PERSON QUALIFIED TO ADVISE ON REAL ESTATE TRANSACTIONS. IF YOU DESIRE LEGAL OR TAX ADVICE, CONSULT AN APPROPRIATE PROFESSIONAL.
This form is available for use by the entire real estate industry. The use of this form is not intended to identify the user as a REALTOR®. REALTOR® is a registered collective membership mark which may be used only by real estate licensees who are members of the NATIONAL ASSOCIATION OF REALTORS® and who subscribe to its Code of Ethics.

BROKER'S COPY

— OFFICE USE ONLY —
Reviewed by Broker or Designee _____
Date _____

EQUAL HOUSING OPPORTUNITY
M-SC-FEB-91

Page 2 of _____ Pages.

SELLER FINANCING DISCLOSURE STATEMENT (SFD-14 PAGE 2 OF 2)

not qualified to evaluate the buyer's financial documents, take them to your banker, accountant, or financial advisor to review.

A seller should require the buyer to carry hazard (fire) insurance naming the seller as the loss payee. A Request for Notice of Default should be recorded so that the seller is notified if the buyer goes into default on any senior loans. Most sellers and buyers will want title insurance to protect their respective interests and a tax service to monitor the payment of property taxes. Who pays for the Request for Notice of Default, title insurance, and tax service is negotiable, but it's often the buyer.

The security document should be recorded to ensure that the buyer's or seller's interest in the property is not jeopardized by intervening liens, judgments, or subsequent transfers of title. With a land contract of sale, for instance, title remains in the seller's name; this means that the seller could further encumber the property and jeopardize the buyer's interest.

A simple seller-carry note is often drawn up by the escrow company. However, if the note is complex or if the rate is adjustable, the escrow officer will usually require that the principals engage the services of a real estate attorney. A seller who plans to sell the note after the close of escrow should use Fannie Mae forms. Fannie Mae will buy private notes, at a discount, if they meet certain credit and appraisal standards, are on standard approved forms, and are serviced by an approved lender (who will charge a servicing fee).

Seller-carry loans are normally treated as installment sales for income tax purposes, which means that the seller's gain is taxed over the period that principal payments on the note are received. IRS rules regarding installment sales have changed several times in recent years, so be sure to consult with your tax advisor for more information about the tax ramifications of an installment sale before entering into a binding agreement with a buyer.

CHAPTER 11

The *ESCROW* *and* CLOSING

What Is an Escrow?

Buyers, sellers, and real estate agents throw the term "escrow" around loosely. "The house is in escrow; we hope nothing goes wrong"; or "we finally closed escrow; the house is ours"; or "the house fell out of escrow; boy, are we upset."

Technically an escrow is an agreement between the buyer and seller to let a neutral party, usually an escrow or title company, prepare and hold documents and funds until the terms of the purchase agreement have been fulfilled.

Typically, an escrow is "opened" by the buyer, seller, or their agent within a day of the final acceptance of the purchase contract. How long an escrow lasts is negotiable—whatever length the buyers and sellers agree to in their contract. An average length from an opening of escrow to closing is 45 to 60 days.

It is during the escrow that the buyers remove any contingencies they have in the contract. Most buyers will at least have an inspection and a financing contingency. After the buyer's contingencies are satisfied and the loan is approved, the buyer's lender delivers the new loan papers to the escrow officer who then prepares all the additional documents necessary to complete the sale. The escrow officer also orders all the paperwork needed for the sellers to pay off any existing liens against the property so that clear title can be passed to the buyer.

The escrow officer acts as a limited dual agent for both parties in a transaction but cannot advise either party and acts only on instructions from the buyer and seller. The escrow instructions, which restate the terms of the real estate purchase agreement, delineate the escrow officer's responsibilities. In Southern California, escrows are usually handled by escrow companies, and escrow instructions are given to the escrow holder soon after the purchase agreement is accepted. They are signed by the buyers and sellers at that time. In Northern California, escrows are usually handled by title companies. A copy of the purchase agreement may or may not be sent to the escrow holder upon opening escrow, but the actual escrow instructions are prepared and signed by the buyers and sellers in Northern California toward the end of the escrow period.

Since most buyers don't have an established working relationship with an escrow officer, your agent can recommend someone. There is an advantage to working with an escrow officer who has worked extensively with your agent and who wants your agent's repeat business.

RECEIPT FOR INCREASED DEPOSIT/LIQUIDATED DAMAGES
THIS IS INTENDED TO BE A LEGALLY BINDING CONTRACT. READ IT CAREFULLY.
CALIFORNIA ASSOCIATION OF REALTORS® (CAR) STANDARD FORM

This Receipt for Increased Deposit relates to the ☐ Real Estate Purchase Contract and Receipt for Deposit, or

☐ _____ , dated _____ on property known as

_____

in which _____ is referred to as Buyer

and _____ is referred to as Seller.

Received from_____ ,

the sum of _____

Dollars ($_____) evidenced by ☐ cash, ☐ cashier's check, ☐ personal check, or ☐ _____ ,

payable to _____ as additional deposit for the purchase of the above described property.

Buyer hereby increases the total deposit to_____

_____ Dollars ($_____).

Date _____

Real Estate Broker _____ By _____

THE FOLLOWING LIQUIDATED DAMAGES PROVISION WHEN INITIALLED BY BOTH BUYER AND SELLER IS HEREBY INCORPORATED IN AND MADE A PART OF THE ABOVE REFERENCED AGREEMENT.

Seller's Initial

Many buyers and sellers operate under the misconception that the escrow holder is responsible for the closing. It's important to understand that nothing happens automatically in escrow, nor should it. The escrow officer acts on your instructions; without those instructions, the escrow officer has authority to do nothing. Your real estate agent can give your escrow instructions to the escrow holder for you.

The mutual efforts of a good escrow officer, conscientious real estate agents, and cooperative buyers and sellers can make the difference between an escrow that proceeds smoothly and one that doesn't. After your escrow is opened, obtain your escrow officer's name, address, and phone number, and get your escrow number. Check in with your escrow officer once a week. When you call, you'll get faster service if you identify yourself by your name and escrow number because escrow officers keep track of their files this way. Let your escrow officer know that you're available to help if necessary and that you want to be kept informed of the progress of the escrow, especially if a problem arises.

The escrow is said to be "closed" when title to the property passes from the seller to the buyer. The escrow officer takes care of this by recording the grant deed, which is the document that transfers title, at the county recorder's office.

The Deposit Money

The buyer's deposit check is usually held by the escrow holder and is applied toward the purchase price at closing. Some brokers have trust accounts set up for the purpose of holding the buyer's deposit money. In the case of a probate sale, the buyer's deposit could be held by the executor or attorney for the estate.

THE FOLLOWING LIQUIDATED DAMAGES PROVISION WHEN INITIALLED BY BOTH BUYER AND SELLER IS HEREBY INCORPORATED IN AND MADE A PART OF THE ABOVE REFERENCED AGREEMENT.

Buyer's Initials   Seller's Initials

_____/_____ _____/_____ **LIQUIDATED DAMAGES:** If Buyer fails to complete said purchase as herein provided by reason of any default of Buyer, Seller shall be released from obligation to sell the property to Buyer and may proceed against Buyer upon any claim or remedy which he/she may have in law or equity; provided, however, that by initialling this provision Buyer and Seller agree that Seller shall retain the original and increased deposit as liquidated damages. If the described property is a dwelling with no more than four units, one of which the Buyer intends to occupy as his/her residence, Seller shall retain as liquidated damages the total deposit actually paid, or an amount therefrom, not more than 3% of the purchase price and promptly return any excess to Buyer.

(Funds deposited in trust accounts or in escrow are not released automatically in the event of a dispute. Release of funds requires written agreement of the parties, judicial decision or arbitration.)

The undersigned have read and acknowledge receipt of a copy of this agreement.

Date _____ Date _____

BUYER _____ SELLER _____

BUYER _____ SELLER _____

FORM RID-11

EQUAL HOUSING OPPORTUNITY
M-SC-MAR-92

The buyer should be aware that once there's an accepted purchase contract, the deposit check will be cashed unless other provisions have been specified in the contract.

The escrow holder is not permitted to collect interest on the deposit money. Unless instructed otherwise, the escrow officer will place the buyer's deposit check into a non-interest-bearing account, although it can usually be placed in an interest-bearing account if the buyer requests this and the seller has no objection. Determining who is entitled to the interest on the buyer's deposit money can become a subject of some debate. In a probate sale, for instance, the buyer is required to make a cash deposit to the estate equal to 10 percent of the purchase price. Some attorneys who handle probate sales require that any interest earned on the buyer's deposit money during escrow go to the estate. To avoid confusion, an agreement should be made in writing between buyer and seller in advance. In a conventional sale, the interest earned on the buyer's deposit money usually goes to the buyer. The party to benefit fills out a form giving the escrow holder relevant tax information.

Don't expect your money to earn any more than passbook account interest rates. Also, keep in mind that the escrow holder will need to withdraw your deposit money from the interest-bearing account before close of escrow in order to have good funds available for closing. For a short escrow period, an interest-bearing account may not merit the time and effort, but it's definitely worth pursuing if the deposit is large and the escrow period long.

When a purchase agreement calls for an increased deposit during the escrow period and the buyer and seller have initialed the liquidated damages clause, a

217

Receipt for Increased Deposit/Liquidated Damages form must be filled out and signed by both parties. A sample of this form is included. Sellers should make certain that this form accompanies the buyer's deposit check if liquidated damages are part of the contract. This simple but critical bit of paperwork is often overlooked by real estate agents.

Also, make certain that your agent or escrow officer provides you with copies of receipts for your deposit checks. The seller should also receive copies of these receipts.

Don't make the mistake made by Candice and Kevin Carpenter. The Carpenters sold their home to a buyer who removed contract contingencies in a timely fashion, but when their real estate agent instructed the escrow officer to prepare the final closing papers, the officer responded that the buyer's deposit check had never been received. The Carpenters' agent called the buyer's agent, who said that the buyer was planning to close the escrow and that the missing check was simply an oversight. The buyer ended up defaulting and the Carpenters had to hire an attorney to sue for damages. If the parties involved had made sure the buyer's check was received the day after acceptance of the contract, the buyer might have been less likely to default knowing that the sellers could tie up the deposit money in escrow until they received satisfactory compensation for their damages.

218

How to Read a Preliminary Title Report

The buyer, seller, and their real estate agents should receive a copy of a preliminary title report (commonly known as the "prelim") within five days after escrow is opened. The preliminary title report is a statement regarding the present condition of the title to the property. It shows who owns the property and details any liens and encumbrances affecting the title. The report also delineates the terms and conditions under which the title company will issue a policy of title insurance.

The title company's name and address, the title officer's name, and a reference number appear at the top of the report, followed by the address of the subject property and the buyer's name. A narrative statement from the title company outlining the scope and terms of the preliminary title report usually appears next.

Examine the exceptions or exclusions to the preliminary title report carefully; direct any questions to your title or escrow officer.

Then comes a statement regarding the estate or interest covered by the report, followed by the name of the vested owner and the manner in which title is currently held. A fee is the highest type of interest that a property owner can have; a fee interest or estate is freely transferable by the owner of record.

A list of exceptions and exclusions will follow. These will appear as exceptions to the policy of title insurance unless they are paid, released, or otherwise eliminated from the public record before the close of escrow. Exceptions include property taxes (the amounts due and current status), tax delinquencies, easements (rights of others to use a portion of the property), CC&Rs (Covenants, Conditions, and Restrictions), deeds of trust securing indebtedness against the property, tax liens, mechanics' liens, and judgments. The preliminary title report will also include a legal description of the property and a statement indicating whether there were any transfers of record during the six months preceding the date of the report.

The title company may require the sellers or buyers to provide a statement of identification (or identity) before a policy of title insurance will be issued. This requirement enables the title company to determine if there are any other liens or judgments that might affect title to the property and is almost always required when buyers or sellers have relatively common names.

A plat map is usually included with the preliminary title report for informational purposes only. The map is a reduced copy of the county assessor's map or the recorded subdivision map but is not a survey of the property boundary lines and is not a part of the report.

Paragraph 6 of the Real Estate Purchase Contract and Receipt for Deposit allows the buyer to review the preliminary title report, and to disapprove any item contained in it within the time frame specified in paragraph 24 of the contract. This paragraph further states that the seller will deliver the property with title free of liens, encumbrances, easements, restrictions, rights and conditions of record known to seller, except for matters shown in the preliminary title report which are not disapproved in writing by the buyer. The burden is on the buyer to reasonably disapprove, in writing, any title matter contained within the preliminary title report within the specified time period. If the seller is unwilling or unable to remedy the title matter disapproved by the buyer, the buyer may terminate the purchase agreement and the buyer's deposit will be returned.

219

> **Brian and Shelley Green examined the preliminary title report of the home they were buying and thought it was odd that there were two sewer easements on the property (usually there's only one). They didn't object to this in writing during the time period provided in their purchase contract. Instead, they accepted the preliminary report as it was. After close of escrow, they had the property surveyed and discovered that one of the sewer easements ran underneath the house, which is a violation of the city building ordinance. They were understandably upset, mostly at themselves for not raising the issue before they closed escrow.**

A buyer should request that the title company provide complete copies of all easements (particularly those involving shared driveways and access easements) and CC&Rs. The prelim will list only the easements and CC&Rs, so the buyer should review the complete documents, which the title company will make available upon request, to make sure they don't contain an unacceptable restriction. Some CC&Rs that are listed in the prelim may contain expiration dates and may no longer be applicable.

Both the buyers and sellers need to verify that the vesting (ownership) indicated on the preliminary title report is accurate. Buyers should make sure that the owner of record shown on the prelim is the same person who signed, as the seller, on the purchase agreement. A problem could arise if only one seller signed the purchase agreement and there are multiple owners of record. When a vesting is in the name of a deceased owner, an heir may not have the legal capacity to transfer the property.

Sellers are advised to examine carefully the list of liens and encumbrances, particularly deeds of trust, securing indebtedness against the property. Sometimes an old debt, paid off long ago, will appear as a current lien on the property. This could indicate that the title company's search of the county records was incomplete, or it could mean that the deed of reconveyance (which is issued when the debt is paid in full) was never recorded. A seller can assist in clearing up this sort of title matter by providing the escrow officer with a copy of the recorded deed of reconveyance. When title matters are cleared up, make sure the title company issues an amended preliminary title report reflecting the corrections.

220

Ensuring Good Title

Title insurance protects the buyer from problems that might arise due to defects in the title. The title insurance policy is paid once, at close of escrow, and it remains in force during the buyer's period of ownership. The policy is not transferable to a subsequent owner.

The coverage that most buyers take is the California Land Title Association Standard Coverage Policy (commonly referred to as a CLTA Standard Coverage Policy), which protects against defects discoverable through an examination of the public records. A CLTA policy will not, however, protect the buyer from title risks discernible only from a physical inspection of the property. Boundary disputes and encroachments, unrecorded easements, and rights of persons in possession of the property are not covered under the CLTA Standard Coverage Policy.

More extensive title protection is provided under the American Land Title Association Owner's Policy (commonly referred to as an ALTA Owner's Policy), which does cover defects that can only be discovered from a physical inspection of the property. A buyer will usually have to pay the cost of a survey before a title company will issue an ALTA Owner's policy.

The only way to accurately determine where the property lines are is to have a survey done.

Many title companies issue an ALTA Residential policy which provides broader coverage than the CLTA coverage, but does not involve the cost of a survey. An ALTA Residential policy will cover off-record matters such as unrecorded easements but it normally excludes from coverage fences and boundary walls and in-law units (which are often built without permits and are nonconforming with respect to zoning use). The title company will send a representative out to examine the property for irregularities. If any are found, such as a corner of the house that appears to be built over the property line, this could be made an exception to the ALTA Residential coverage. If a title company doesn't offer an ALTA Residential policy, ask if they offer a Homeowner's Endorsement to their CLTA policy (also referred to as a CLTA policy with a 126 endorsement). This endorsement provides protection for encroachments, easements not of record, some zoning issues, and mechanics' liens. The ALTA Residential policy, and the CLTA Standard policy with the Homeowner's Endorsement, shouldn't cost any more than the standard CLTA policy.

A lender will normally require that the buyer purchase an ALTA Loan policy. In addition to protecting the lender from "off the record" title defects, the ALTA Loan policy will ensure that the lender's deed of trust takes precedence over unrecorded claims against the property. A title company insuring the lender, but not the buyer, with an ALTA policy will usually issue a separate policy to the lender covering the deed of trust only.

Many purchase agreements require the seller to provide the buyer with a CLTA policy of title insurance. This should not be construed as a guarantee that a CLTA policy is the title insurance of preference for your transaction. If you have any reservations about exceptions from the CLTA policy coverage, particularly where boundary lines are concerned, it may be worthwhile to pay for a survey and obtain an extended coverage policy. In addition, be aware that special endorsements are obtainable from the title company to cover specific problem situations. Don't hesitate to ask your escrow or title officer to explain the different title insurance policies, and consult a real estate attorney if you have any questions regarding which type of title insurance you should purchase to protect your interests. At close of escrow, make sure that you have received the kind of title insurance you ordered.

221

Title insurance is commonly paid for by the buyer in Northern California and by the seller in Southern California. If the title record of a property has been searched within the past two years, either due to a transfer of ownership or a lender refinance, a discounted short-term title insurance rate usually applies.

All modifications to the purchase agreement should be written.

CONTRACT SUPPLEMENT/ADDENDUM
THIS IS INTENDED TO BE A LEGALLY BINDING CONTRACT. READ IT CAREFULLY.
CALIFORNIA ASSOCIATION OF REALTORS® (CAR) STANDARD FORM

The following terms and conditions are hereby incorporated in and made a part of the: ☐ Real Estate Purchase Contract and Receipt for Deposit, ☐ Mobile Home Purchase Contract and Receipt for Deposit, ☐ Business Purchase Contract and Receipt for Deposit, ☐ other _____
dated _____ , 19_____ , on property known as: _____
in which_____ is referred to as Buyer
and _____ is referred to as Seller.

222

Addenda to the Purchase Agreement

Rarely does a purchase agreement remain unchanged during the term of the escrow period. When modifications are made to the original purchase contract, it's important that they be agreed to in writing by both buyer and seller on a Contract Supplement/Addendum form. Let's say, for instance, that you'd like to move up the close date, and the sellers verbally agree that an earlier close sounds fine to them. Based on this, you rearrange all your moving plans around what you assume will be the new close of escrow. Without having the modification in writing, however, the date is unenforceable, and you may find yourself unhappily surprised to discover that you can't move in when you wanted to.

In periods of rising interest rates and short loan commitments, the lender may require the buyer to close escrow early. If the seller can't vacate early, the

The undersigned acknowledge receipt of a copy of this page, which constitutes Page _____ of _____ Pages.

Date _____   Date _____

Buyer _____   Seller _____

Buyer _____   Seller _____

OFFICE USE ONLY
Reviewed by Broker or Designee _____
Date _____

BROKER'S COPY
DS-14

M-MO-May 92

223

buyer and seller can agree to an early close but retain the occupancy date they agreed to in the original purchase agreement. The seller in this situation may rent back the house from the buyer, after the closing, at a per diem rate that is mutually agreeable. This sort of a modification should include an Interim Occupancy Agreement that permits the seller to remain in possession for a specified period of time after the close of escrow.

Terminating a Purchase Agreement

Once in a while, irreconcilable differences will occur during the escrow period. The inspection reports might reveal property defects that the seller is unable or unwilling to repair. If the buyer won't purchase the property unless the defects are remedied, a Release of Contract form, signed by buyer and seller, is usually

---

RELEASE OF CONTRACT

THIS IS INTENDED TO BE A LEGALLY BINDING CONTRACT. READ IT CAREFULLY.
CALIFORNIA ASSOCIATION OF REALTORS® (CAR) STANDARD FORM

☐

The undersigned Buyer and Seller (or exchange party(ies), if applicable), the parties to that certain:
(Check all that apply):

☐ Real Estate Purchase Contract and Receipt for Deposit
☐ Mobile Home Purchase Contract and Receipt for Deposit
☐ Business Purchase Contract and Receipt for Deposit
☐ Escrow instructions
☐ Other _____,
(hereinafter, "Contract"), covering the following described property:

_____

_____

_____

_____

_____

_____

hereby mutually release each other from all further obligation to buy, sell, or exchange under the Contract and all related documents, and from all claims, actions, and demands which each may have against the other(s) by reason of said Contract. It is the intent of this Agreement that all rights and obligations arising out of said Contract are null and void.

_____ is hereby instructed to cancel Escrow Number _____.
(Name of Escrow Holder)

, holder of the _____

---

sufficient to cancel the escrow and release both parties from their respective responsibilities. A less clear-cut situation exists when the buyer or seller has failed to remove a contingency within the requisite time period and a formal written request for an extension of the contingency time period has not been made. A real estate purchase contract cannot be declared null and void by one party without the written consent and approval of the other party. This means that neither the escrow, nor the purchase contract, will be automatically canceled if a contingency is not removed within the time frame specified in the purchase agreement.

What do you, as a buyer or seller, do if a contingency has not been removed, an extension has not been requested, and the time period for performance has passed? The first step is to ask your agent to put a request in writing that the other party perform within a reasonable time period: 24 to 48 hours should be sufficient. If the other party fails to respond to your inquiry or does not remove the contingency in question within that time period, consult with a real estate attorney to determine the next appropriate course of action.

In this situation, the seller should be careful not to elevate a backup offer into primary position without receiving a signed Release of Contract form from the first buyer. Make certain that you don't sell one property to two eager buyers. If both parties make a legal claim to your home, you could end up unable to convey free and clear title to either of them.

224

_____ is hereby instructed to cancel Escrow Number _____.
(Name of Escrow Holder)

_____, holder of the deposit under the terms of said Contract, is hereby
(Name of Broker or Escrow Holder)

instructed to disburse said deposit in the following manner:

$ _____ TO _____
$ _____ TO _____
$ _____ TO _____
$ _____ TO _____

Dated _____   Dated _____

Buyer _____   Seller _____

Buyer _____   Seller _____

Dated _____   Dated _____

Broker _____   Broker _____

By_____   By_____

Payoff Demands and Beneficiary Statements

225

The escrow officer orders payoff demands from the existing lenders when loans secured against the property need to be paid off in order to close escrow. The payoff demand indicates how much money the seller owes to pay the loan off in full. The cost of a payoff demand, or statement fee, varies from one lender to the next, but it should not exceed $65. The timing involved in ordering a payoff demand is important. If it's ordered too late in the escrow period and the precise figures aren't available in time, closing could be delayed unless the seller is willing to leave excess funds in escrow to protect the escrow company in case the payoff demand includes unanticipated charges such as late fees, delinquent payments, or prepayment penalties. A payoff demand that's ordered too early may necessitate an update during the escrow (often done only for an additional fee) if the lender will not give revised figures to the escrow officer over the phone. Ideally, the payoff demand should be ordered approximately 30 days before closing.

The seller should keep loan payments current during the escrow period in order to avoid having to pay late fees. Be aware, however, that a loan payment will usually not be credited to your account until the check has cleared. It might be worth your while to make a payment that's due just before the closing in person and with a cashier's check. Get a receipt from the lender so you can verify to the escrow officer that you made the payment. Another alternative is to make your last payment well in advance so that you're sure the check will clear by closing. Any overpayments to the lender will be credited back to the seller after the close of escrow. The lender usually sends a check covering the overpayment amount to the seller in care of the escrow company.

A beneficiary statement is ordered when the buyer intends to take over the existing loan on the property. Like the payoff demand, it is a request for information on the condition of the loan. It asks, for instance, if the payments are current, whether there are any fees or delinquent payments the seller owes, and the remaining principal balance due.

A seller should request a copy of the payoff demand or beneficiary statement as soon as the escrow officer receives it. Call the lender directly if you think a billing error has been made, and don't be surprised if you're charged a corrected statement fee even though the lender made the mistake. Sellers who discover at the last minute, when closing documents are being signed, that an unanticipated prepayment penalty is due, may have no alternative but to pay it or risk a delayed closing. A prepayment penalty, by the way, can cost thousands of dollars, so it makes sense to confirm the lender's closing charges in advance. Buyers who are assuming an existing loan will want to review the beneficiary statement in advance of the closing and should request that any late charges or delinquent payments be brought current by the sellers at or before close of escrow.

Don't Wait Until the Last Minute

Certain documents that are occasionally involved in home sales require special approval from the legal department of the title company before closing. Let's say, for instance, that your spouse is planning to be out of the country when the closing papers are signed and gives you a power of attorney to sign for both of you. The power of attorney must be in a legal form acceptable to both the title company and the new lender, and it must be notarized.

A quitclaim deed is another document that needs title company approval before closing. This document relinquishes any interest that the grantor might have in the property. It's common, in a divorce situation, for one party to quitclaim interest in a property to the other party at the time of a formal property settlement. The title company might request a copy of the divorce decree if the divorce is not final or if the decree has not been recorded.

The title company will want to approve a financing statement from the builder before transferring title to a new home if the lien period has not passed by the close of escrow. During the 60-day lien period, which begins after the notice of completion is recorded, contractors who worked on the project can file mechanics' liens against the property. In addition to a satisfactory financial statement, the title company may require that the builder enter into an

226

Ask your escrow officer to send you copies of payoff demands so you can check them for accuracy.

indemnity agreement stating that the title company will not be responsible for future liens recorded against the property.

Contact your escrow officer as soon as possible after the escrow is opened if you suspect that any aspect of the property transfer will require title company approval.

Shop Carefully for Homeowner's Insurance

Insurance rates can vary by as much as 100 percent from one company to the next, so it pays to shop around before making a choice. Be sure, when making comparisons, that you receive quotes for equivalent coverage. In addition to cost, you'll want to know whether the insurance carrier has a reputation for prompt and dependable claims service, so it's a good idea to check references.

Until recently, most lenders required that the borrower carry insurance at least in the amount of the loan. California law now prohibits a lender from requiring the borrower to carry fire insurance in excess of the replacement value of the improvements on the property, even if this amount is less than the loan amount. The borrower's property insurer, however, must establish the replacement value.

Overinsuring a property results in wasted dollars. Underinsuring can have more serious consequences. Guaranteed replacement cost coverage provides the broadest coverage and is available if the home is insured for 100 percent of the cost to replace the structure. With guaranteed replacement cost coverage, the entire structure will be replaced at the insurance company's expense, even if the actual cost to rebuild is more than the coverage amount. If you don't have guaranteed replacement cost coverage and your house burns to the ground, the insurance company will pay only up to the coverage amount, even if it ends up costing more to rebuild. Be wary of policies that offer guaranteed replacement cost coverage but put a cap on the amount paid out on a single loss.

227

> **Beth and Ted Singer lost their home in the 1991 Oakland firestorm. They felt they had more than adequate coverage since their policy limit was $500,000 and the value of their home was about $350,000. Building costs soared after the Oakland fire due to the demand for labor and materials so the actual cost to rebuild the Singers' home came in at about $400,000. The remaining $100,000 didn't cover the cost of replacing their personal belongings and their interim living expenses for the year and a half it took to rebuild.**

Insurance in the amount of the purchase price is probably not necessary, because even when a house burns to the ground, a concrete foundation and the land usually remain. An older foundation could need upgrading though in order to meet modern building code requirements, so make sure your policy includes a rider that provides coverage for any upgrades that might be required in order to comply with current code requirements.

Insuring for adequate protection, but not more than you need, is one way to save money. Another is to select a policy with a larger deductible amount. The deductible is the amount the homeowner pays on any given claim. The amount you save by taking a $500 or $1,000 deductible amount, rather than a $250 deductible, will vary from one company to the next, so shop around.

Even if you're in the fortunate position of paying all cash for your home, it's advisable to insure the property for its replacement value at the close of escrow. Buyers who take out a loan will be required to cover the house with a fire insurance policy that names the lender as loss payee. In addition to fire insurance, you'll want to consider personal property coverage to protect against loss of your personal possessions and liability coverage to protect against claims for injury or damage. Many policies have a cap on the amount they'll pay to replace personal property (often 50 to 75 percent of the value of the home). It's usually preferable to carry coverage to guarantee full replacement of your belongings.

Earthquake insurance is available as an additional rider to a homeowner's insurance policy, but it usually has a very large deductible (as much as 5 to 10 percent of the replacement cost). If you live in an older home, the insurer may require that the home be secured to the foundation with anchor bolts, which can be installed by a contractor or structural pest control company. Flood insurance is customarily required by lenders in areas designated as "flood prone" under the National Flood Insurance Program. Purchasers of condominiums need insurance in addition to the general policy provided through membership in the homeowners' association which, in most cases, covers losses sustained to common areas but not damage to the inside of individual units or loss of personal possessions. The general homeowners' association policy also doesn't cover personal liability.

After you've selected insurance coverage for your new home, ask the insurance agent to contact your escrow officer to arrange for delivery of a policy or binder before closing. Most lenders will want the buyer to prepay the cost of the first year of coverage at the time of closing, although you may be able to arrange to pay semiannually or quarterly, depending on the lender and the insurance carrier.

The insurance agent will want specific information about the property being covered before issuing the insurance policy. Some agents will want to physically inspect the property. Since insurance premium discounts are available if the home is new or remodeled, has a smoke or security alarm, or is located close to a fire hydrant, make sure that your insurance agent has all the necessary information about the property before the policy is written.

When sellers hold title in the name of a trust, the title company must approve the trust agreement.

After you close escrow, talk to your insurance agent each year to make sure your policy is kept up to date. Building costs vary. Many of the Oakland firestorm victims were insured based on a cost to rebuild of $100 per square foot. The actual cost to rebuild ranged from about $150 to $300 per square foot, depending on the uniqueness and architectural detailing of the home that was destroyed. If you're underinsured, your policy may provide enough to rebuild a house, but not enough to duplicate the custom details, such as hardwood floors and handcrafted moldings, that attracted you to your home in the first place.

How to Take Title to Your New Home

The manner in which you take title to property is an important consideration and shouldn't be treated lightly. All too often, buyers give no consideration to this part of buying a home until they walk into the escrow office to sign the final closing papers.

Taking title as a single person is simple; there are no decisions to make because it's sole ownership. California is a community property state, so if you're married and are purchasing property that is to belong to you only, the title company will require a quitclaim deed in which your spouse relinquishes any interest in the property.

Two or more related or unrelated persons purchasing real property together have different options. How title is held between co-owners has legal, tax, and estate planning ramifications. Co-owners should consult with their legal or tax advisors before instructing the escrow officer how they want title to vest. The following is a brief summary of the three most common kinds of joint ownership used in California.

Unmarried co-owners can hold title with one another as joint tenants or as tenants in common. Joint tenancy provides for equal ownership interests and the right of survivorship, which means that at the death of one co-owner, that person's interest in the property passes to the remaining co-owner.

Tenants in common need not have equal interests in the property. Upon the death of one co-tenant, the decedent's interest in the property will pass to the heirs and not to the remaining co-tenants (unless they happen to be named as heirs under the will). In other words, the right of survivorship does not apply.

Married co-owners can hold title as tenants in common or as joint tenants. In California, married individuals can also take title to real property as community property. Under community property ownership, the interests of the co-owners are equal, and each has the right to dispose of his or her one-half interest by will. In the absence of a will, the decedent's interest goes to the remaining spouse by right of succession.

The tax consequences of joint tenancy and community property ownership differ significantly when one spouse dies before the other. With community property, the entire tax basis of the property is stepped up to the fair market value at the date of the spouse's death. If the surviving spouse then sells the property for that fair market value, the taxable gain is zero. With joint tenancy, only one half

229

of the tax basis is stepped up to fair market value at the date of the spouse's death, which makes taxable gain at the time of sale a greater likelihood.

The estate of a deceased homeowner may need to be probated by the court, depending on how title was held during that person's lifetime. Consult your legal and tax advisors regarding which method of holding title is best for you and your family.

Ordering and Reviewing the Loan Documents

Approximately two weeks before the close of escrow, the buyer's loan officer should order loan documents from the buyer's new lender. The timing is important because loan papers usually contain an expiration date. Papers that are drawn too early may expire before closing; redrawing them usually involves an additional charge and can delay the closing. There is also a risk that the note could be redrawn at a higher rate if interest rates move upwards in the meantime.

It's not the escrow officer's responsibility to monitor the loan approval process; this should be taken care of by the real estate agent, the loan representative, and the buyers. But once the loan is approved, the escrow officer needs to be in contact with the individual processing the loan for the lender (called a loan processor) in order to ensure a smooth closing.

Ask your escrow officer to provide you with a copy of the note to review in advance of signing the final closing papers. A fixed-rate note is fairly straightforward; you'll want to verify that the interest rate, monthly payment, and term of the loan are correct. An ARM note is much more complicated, and you won't be able to read and understand it in the half hour or so that you spend at the escrow company signing the final papers. Take time beforehand to study the way your ARM loan will work, making certain that the index, margin, periodic and lifetime caps, adjustment period, payment cap (if applicable), as well as the initial interest rate, monthly payment, and term of the loan are accurate on the note itself. Direct any questions you have to your loan agent, and if the lender has made an error on the note, have it corrected at the lender's expense.

Settling Up: Who Pays for What?

Before an escrow is closed, a final accounting of what charges the buyers and sellers owe is prepared by the escrow officer. If time permits, ask for a copy of the settlement statement (see sample form included) so you can review the itemization of charges in advance. At the very least, have your agent review the settlement sheet with the escrow officer to make sure that there are no mistakes.

Your closing costs shouldn't come as a surprise to you. Under the Real Estate Settlement Procedures Act, the lender is required to provide the buyers with an estimate of closing costs within three days of receiving a residential loan application. In addition, your real estate agent should have prepared an approximate buyer's or seller's cost sheet at the time you negotiated the purchase agreement. Who pays which closing costs isn't set by law and varies somewhat from one county to the next. Local custom usually prevails.

Buyers' closing costs usually include: loan fees (points), appraisal and credit report fees, proration of interest on the new loan, all or part of a local transfer tax (where applicable), inspection fees, title insurance (in some counties), escrow fees (in some counties), document preparation fees, recording and notary fees, property tax proration, the fire insurance premium, Property Mortgage Insurance premium (if the buyer is putting less than 20 percent down), impounds (if required by the lender), and a tax service (if required by the lender). Buyers have the option of purchasing a home protection plan at the close of escrow if the seller doesn't offer one; sometimes this expense is shared between the buyers and sellers.

Proration of interest is a charge collected by the lender at closing if your first loan payment is not due exactly 30 days following the date of recordation. For instance, let's say escrow closes on May 15, and your first loan payment is due July 1; this payment will include interest owed for the month of June. The lender will collect at closing a sum equal to the interest owed from May 15 to June 1; this is referred to as prorated interest. Since interest paid on your home mortgage is tax deductible, make certain that the statement you receive from your lender indicating interest paid in your first year of ownership includes this prorated interest amount.

The IRS will generally consider the loan origination fee, or points, paid on your new home loan to be tax deductible in the year of purchase if payment is made directly from the borrower's own funds. If this fee is merely subtracted from the loan proceeds, however, the deduction might have to be taken over the loan term. Check with you tax advisor if you plan to deduct the points in the year of purchase. You may want to make arrangements to pay for the points separately.

231

Prorations are usually based on a 30-day month and on a 360-day year. Property taxes will be prorated at the day escrow closes. If the seller has prepaid property taxes, the buyer credits the seller for any overpayment in escrow; if taxes have been accruing but are not yet due, the amount owed by the seller is credited to the buyer, who then takes responsibility for the future tax bill when it becomes due. If escrow is to close several days before taxes are due, the escrow officer will often arrange to pay the bill through the escrow. Property taxes in California are paid in two installments. The first, which covers the period of ownership from July 1 through December 31, is due November 1 and becomes delinquent December 10; the second is due February 1, becomes delinquent April 10, and covers from January 1 through June 30.

Following close of escrow, the property is reassessed and a supplemental tax bill is issued which becomes a lien against the property. How soon the supplemental bill will arrive after the close varies from several weeks to six months or longer, depending on the county in which the property is located. If the sellers have recently acquired title to the property (through inheritance, for instance), their supplemental tax figures might not be available at the time of closing. In this case, the buyer should make sure that an agreement is drawn up stating that

A. Settlement Statement

U.S. Department of Housing
and Urban Development

OMB Approval No. 2502-0265

B. Type of Loan

1. ☐ FHA 2. ☐ FmHA 3. ☐ ,Conv. Unins.
4. ☐ VA 5. ☐ Conv. Ins.

6. File Number	7. Loan Number	8. Mortgage Insurance Case Number

C. Note: This form is furnished to give you a statement of actual settlement costs. Amounts paid to and by the settlement agent are shown. Items marked "(p.o.c.)" were paid outside the closing; they are shown here for informational purposes and are not included in the totals.

D. Name and Address of Borrower	E. Name and Address of Seller	F. Name and Address of Lender

G. Property Location	H. Settlement Agent	
	Place of Settlement	I. Settlement Date

J. Summary of Borrower's Transaction		K. Summary of Seller's Transaction	
100. Gross Amount Due From Borrower		**400. Gross Amount Due To Seller**	
101. Contract sales price		401. Contract sales price	
102. Personal property		402. Personal property	
103. Settlement charges to borrower (line 1400)		403.	
104.		404.	
105.		405.	
Adjustments for items paid by seller in advance		Adjustments for items paid by seller in advance	
106. City/town taxes to		406. City/town taxes to	
107. County taxes to		407. County taxes to	
108. Assessments to		408. Assessments to	
109.		409.	
110.		410.	
111.		411.	
112.		412.	
120. Gross Amount Due From Borrower		**420. Gross Amount Due To Seller**	
200. Amounts Paid By Or In Behalf Of Borrower		**500. Reductions In Amount Due To Seller**	
201. Deposit or earnest money		501. Excess deposit (see instructions)	
202. Principal amount of new loan(s)		502. Settlement charges to seller (line 1400)	
203. Existing loan(s) taken subject to		503. Existing loan(s) taken subject to	
204.		504. Payoff of first mortgage loan	
205.		505. Payoff of second mortgage loan	
206.		506.	
207.		507.	
208.		508.	
209.		509.	
...ments for items unpaid by seller		Adjustments for ite... seller	
		510. City/tow...	

the sellers will pay for their supplemental tax bill when it becomes available. This also applies to a new construction which will be reassessed when the home is completed and again when it's sold to the buyer. The builder should be responsible for the supplemental tax bill for the period from date of completion until title transfers into the buyer's name.

A buyer is responsible for the payment of property taxes and monthly loan payments regardless of whether or not a tax bill or payment coupon is received. Mark the due dates of your first loan and property tax payments on your calendar as a reminder. If you haven't received the appropriate bills in time, call the escrow officer who can tell you where to make the loan payment and the account number that should appear on the check. The escrow officer can also find out the amount of property tax owed, the reference number to include on your check, and where you need to send the payment. Remember, lenders charge late fees that

103. Settle... ...400)			405.			
104.						
105.						

Adjustments for items paid by seller in advance			Adjustments for items paid by seller in advance		
106. City/town taxes	to		406. City/town taxes	to	
107. County taxes	to		407. County taxes	to	
108. Assessments	to		408. Assessments	to	
109.			409.		
110.			410.		
111.			411.		
112.			412.		

120. Gross Amount Due From Borrower		420. Gross Amount Due To Seller	

200. Amounts Paid By Or In Behalf Of Borrower		500. Reductions In Amount Due To Seller	
201. Deposit or earnest money		501. Excess deposit (see instructions)	
202. Principal amount of new loan(s)		502. Settlement charges to seller (line 1400)	
203. Existing loan(s) taken subject to		503. Existing loan(s) taken subject to	
204.		504. Payoff of first mortgage loan	
205.		505. Payoff of second mortgage loan	
206.		506.	
207.		507.	
208.		508.	
209.		509.	

Adjustments for items unpaid by seller			Adjustments for items unpaid by seller		
210. City/town taxes	to		510. City/town taxes	to	
211. County taxes	to		511. County taxes	to	
212. Assessments	to		512. Assessments	to	
213.			513.		
214.			514.		
215.			515.		
216.			516.		
217.			517.		
218.			518.		
219.			519.		

220. Total Paid By/For Borrower		520. Total Reduction Amount Due Seller	

300. Cash At Settlement From/To Borrower		600. Cash At Settlement To/From Seller	
301. Gross Amount due from borrower (line 120)		601. Gross amount due to seller (line 420)	
302. Less amounts paid by/for borrower (line 220)	( )	602. Less reductions in amt. due seller (line 520)	( )
303. Cash ☐ From ☐ To Borrower		603. Cash ☐ To ☐ From Seller	

233

will probably be reflected on your credit record, and there are penalties for delinquent property taxes.

Sellers' costs customarily include payoffs of existing loans, prepayment penalties and late charges, accrued interest on existing loans, property tax proration, the documentary transfer tax ($1.10 per thousand dollars), all or a portion of a local transfer tax (where applicable), a home protection plan (optional and sometimes a shared expense), structural pest control work (if negotiated as a part of the sale), real estate commission, document preparation, title insurance (in some counties), escrow fees (in some counties), recording and notary fees, and a credit for the buyer's nonrecurring closing costs (if negotiated as part of the sale).

A seller is always one month behind on interest payments owed to the lender because interest is paid at the end, not the beginning, of each month. For example, the loan payment for May will include interest for the month of April.

L. Settlement Charges

		Paid From Borrowers Funds at Settlement	Paid From Seller's Funds at Settlement
700. Total Sales/Broker's Commission based on price $ @ % =			
Division of Commission (line 700) as follows:			
701. $ to			
702. $ to			
703. Commission paid at Settlement			
704.			
800. Items Payable In Connection With Loan			
801. Loan Origination Fee %			
802. Loan Discount %			
803. Appraisal Fee to			
804. Credit Report to			
805. Lender's Inspection Fee			
806. Mortgage Insurance Application Fee to			
807. Assumption Fee			
808.			
809.			
810.			
811.			
900. Items Required By Lender To Be Paid In Advance			
901. Interest from to @$ /day			
902. Mortgage Insurance Premium for months to			
903. Hazard Insurance Premium for years to			
904. years to			
905.			
1000. Reserves Deposited With Lender			
1001. Hazard insurance months@$ per month			
1002. Mortgage insurance months@$ per month			
1003. City property taxes months@$ per month			
1004. County property taxes months@$ per month			
1005. Annual assessments months@$ per month			
1006. months@$ per month			
1007. months@$ per month			
1008. months@$ per month			
1100. Title Charges			
1101. Settlement or closing fee to			
1102. Abstract or title search to			
1103. Title examination to			
1104. Title insurance binder to			
1105. Document preparation to			
1106. Notary fees to			
1107. Attorney's fees to			
(includes above items numbers:)			
1108. Title insurance to			
(includes above items numbers:)			
1109. Lender's coverage $			
1110. Owner's coverage $			
1111.			
1112.			
1113.			
1200. Government Recording and Transfer Charges			
...ing fees: Deed $; Releases $			

When a seller pays a loan off in full, the lender collects any remaining interest owed, which is usually at least one month's worth. This is referred to as accrued interest. In addition to this, the seller's lender charges interest until they receive the loan payoff check, which could be several days following the close date if the lender isn't local. Ask the escrow officer to send the loan payoff check by express mail if your daily interest charge is more than the cost of express mail. If you have an FHA loan, you could be charged an extra 30 days' interest at loan payoff because a loan payment on an FHA loan can usually only be made once a month.

Rents are prorated to the close of escrow if the property is tenant occupied, and any deposits the seller is holding are transferred to the buyer at closing. If a seller is staying in possession after the close and is paying rent to the buyer, the

1004.	months@$			
1005. Annual assessments	months@$			
1006.	months@$	per month		
1007.	months@$	per month		
1008.	months@$	per month		
1100. Title Charges				
1101. Settlement or closing fee	to			
1102. Abstract or title search	to			
1103. Title examination	to			
1104. Title insurance binder	to			
1105. Document preparation	to			
1106. Notary fees	to			
1107. Attorney's fees	to			
(includes above items numbers:		)		
1108. Title insurance	to			
(includes above items numbers:		)		
1109. Lender's coverage	$			
1110. Owner's coverage	$			
1111.				
1112.				
1113.				
1200. Government Recording and Transfer Charges				
1201. Recording fees: Deed $	; Mortgage $	; Releases $		
1202. City/county tax/stamps: Deed $	; Mortgage $			
1203. State tax/stamps: Deed $	; Mortgage $			
1204.				
1205.				
1300. Additional Settlement Charges				
1301. Survey to				
1302. Pest inspection to				
1303.				
1304.				
1305.				
1400. Total Settlement Charges (enter on lines 103, Section J and 502, Section K)				

235

Public Reporting Burden for this collection of information is estimated to average 0.25 hours per response, including the time for reviewing instructions, searching existing data sources, gathering and maintaining the data needed, and completing and reviewing the collection of information. Send comments regarding this burden estimate or any other aspect of this collection of information, including suggestions for reducing this burden, to the Reports Management Officer, Office of Information Policies and Systems, U.S. Department of Housing and Urban Development, Washington, D.C. 20410-3600; and to the Office of Management and Budget, Paperwork Reduction Project (2502-0265), Washington, D.C. 20503

U.S. GOVERNMENT PRINTING OFFICE: 1989 O—944-345

rent money can either be credited to the buyer at closing or it can be held by the escrow holder until the seller vacates the property. When funds are held, prorated rent is released to the buyer at the time the seller vacates, and any unused portion is returned to the seller. Likewise, if the buyer moved into the property before transfer of title and agreed to pay rent to the seller, this would appear as a credit to the seller on the settlement sheet unless the buyer paid the rent money directly to the seller in advance.

Signing the Closing Documents

The closing papers are ideally signed at the escrow or title company, where a notary is available and last minute changes to documents are made if necessary.

In California, the buyer and seller usually don't sign papers at the same time, and papers must be signed several days before the actual close date.

A buyer can expect to sign the escrow instructions and settlement sheet; the note and deed of trust from the lender; miscellaneous additional paperwork from the lender; an affidavit of vendor and vendee (if required); copies of termite and other reports pertaining to the property (including the preliminary title report); a change of ownership form for the county tax assessor; and any special instructions to the escrow holder regarding such items as holdbacks for work to be completed after the close or seller rent-back agreements. The seller's papers are usually less cumbersome and include the settlement sheet and escrow instructions; the grant deed; an affidavit of vendor and vendee (if required); copies of relevant reports pertaining to the property; any special instructions to the escrow holder; and IRS and state tax reporting forms. Be sure to take your driver's license or a valid passport with you when you sign closing papers. The escrow officer will need identification in order to notarize documents for you.

An affidavit of vendor and vendee is a form often required by the lender, particularly if the buyers are putting less than 20 percent cash down, which specifies the purchase price and the amount of the new loan. The buyer and seller disclose any additional financing that the seller is providing for the buyer. Signatures on this form must be notarized; providing false information can result in serious consequences.

236

Buyers and sellers are cautioned that they should not sign reports pertaining to the property if they have not received and read copies of the reports beforehand. If you find yourself being asked to sign for receipt of documents you're unsure about, tell the escrow officer you'd like the opportunity to read them and return the reports to escrow later. If this is not possible, you can sign all documents and instruct the officer not to close the escrow until you give final authorization to do so.

Sellers need to tell the escrow holder what to do with the sale proceeds check when it becomes available. This will usually be sometime during the day that the grant deed is recorded and title transfers to the buyer. If the sale proceeds are not going immediately toward the purchase of a new home, the sellers can either pick up the proceeds check, have it delivered to their real estate agent, or have it wired into their bank account, which will require a deposit slip or bank branch, account number, and routing instructions. Wired funds are immediately good when they're received by your bank; a several-day hold could be imposed on a title company check.

To reduce closing costs, close escrow late in the month which decreases the prorated interest owed to the lender at closing.

Sellers should keep their homeowner's insurance in effect on the property until confirmation is received that the escrow has closed and title is transferred to the new owner's name.

Coordinating Two or More Escrows

Many people who are buying are also selling. A seller who is transferring the proceeds from the sale of one property to an escrow for the purpose of buying another should let both escrow officers know about the other escrow as soon as possible after they're opened. If you're buying and selling properties located in different counties, it may be necessary to have both escrows handled by the same title company in order to close the escrows simultaneously. A safer strategy is to stagger the close dates so that the home you're selling will close a day or two before the home you're buying. In any event, cooperation and timely communication are necessary to ensure that multiple escrow closings are coordinated satisfactorily.

The Final Walk-Through Inspection

Your contract may provide you a walk-through inspection of the home you're buying before close of escrow. Sometimes the walk-through is worded as a contingency in your contract, in which case the contingency will need to be removed from the contract in writing after you complete the inspection. For instance, let's say you're buying a new construction that wasn't finished at the time your offer was accepted. The walk-through contingency gives you the opportunity to confirm that the house is completed before you close escrow. If finishing details remain, you can either delay closing until they're done or ask the builder to leave money from his proceeds in the escrow account until the items are completed. It's wise to ask the builder to leave more than enough money in the escrow account, say one and a half to two times the cost of completing the work. If the lender won't allow any money to be left in the escrow account after closing, the buyer and the builder can agree to have a check cut from the builder's proceeds in an amount that more than covers the cost of the remaining work. The check can be made payable to both the buyer and the builder and the buyer can hold it until the work is completed at which time the check can be endorsed over to the builder.

237

Frequently the buyer's final walk-through is a far more informal event. It's not a contingency of the purchase contract; it's merely an opportunity for the buyer to come through the house before closing to make sure that everything is as it was when the purchase agreement was entered into. If the sellers are home during the walk-through, they can answer the buyer's questions about the idiosyncrasies of the house, such as how to operate the security alarm or how to program the automatic sprinkler system.

Regardless of the reasons for a buyer's final walk-through, the buyer's approval of the final inspection should not be unreasonably withheld. Any problems that are discovered during the final walk-through should be resolved between the buyer and seller before close of escrow.

The buyer's walk-through should address the following issues: Is the property, including the grounds, in the same condition it was when the purchase contract was ratified? Have any repairs that the seller agreed to complete by close of escrow been done? If the sellers agreed to leave appliances or items of personal property, are they still in the house or were they moved out by accident? Have the tenants (if there were any) vacated the property?

Funding the Purchase and Closing the Escrow

Collected (negotiable) funds are required to close an escrow in California. This means that the funding check from the lender plus the check covering the buyer's cash down payment and all closing costs must both be deposited into the escrow trust account before escrow can close. Additionally, closing funds must be in the form of either a cashier's check drawn on a California bank, wired funds (which are negotiable upon receipt), or personal checks deposited into escrow far enough in advance so that they clear by the closing date. Out-of-state buyers who are purchasing homes in California commonly pay with wired funds.

A buyer who is providing a separate check to pay for loan points should make sure that this is a cashier's check unless a personal check was deposited to escrow early enough to have cleared before the projected close date. Many buyers make the mistake of assuming that their money market account checks constitute collected funds. Many money market account funds are drawn on out-of-state banks, so make arrangements with your local account representative well ahead of time.

When wiring funds, get the appropriate information from the escrow holder regarding how and where funds are to be wired. There are usually special bank routing requirements, and you should follow up to make certain that the funds are received. Plan ahead to avoid an awkward or costly last minute foul-up.

After the closing papers are signed, the buyer's loan documents and settlement papers (referred to as the funding package) are returned to the lender for final approval. This is to verify that all the loan documents have been properly signed and that any additional documentation required by the lender is included with the signed documents. Funding packages are usually approved by the lending institution in the order they are received. A delay at your end will undoubtedly cause a delay for the lender. (Some lenders don't need to approve their loan packages before funding their loans, but most do.)

When the funding package is finally approved, the buyer's lender issues a check for the loan amount (called the funding check). The escrow holder should volunteer to pick up the check to facilitate a speedy closing. According to California state law, the check for the loan amount, as well as the remainder of the buyer's funds required for closing, must be in the escrow holder's trust account the day before the close date. The escrow holder arranges for the grant deed to be recorded at the county recorder's office on the day of closing, thereby transferring title to the property from the seller to the buyer.

Closing monies (wired funds or a cashier's check drawn on a California bank) need to be in escrow the day before closing.

238

What to Do If Your Escrow Doesn't Close on Time

The following items typically cause a delayed close of escrow:

1. The homeowner's insurance policy is not ordered far enough in advance of closing, or it is not received by the escrow holder in time.
2. The buyer's funds don't arrive in time. This could happen if wired funds are accidentally misdirected, or if the buyer provides the escrow holder with a personal check rather than a cashier's check drawn on a California bank.
3. The funding check from the buyer's lender is not issued on time, or the lender funds with a cashier's check drawn on an out-of-state bank.
4. A notice of completion is required from a structural pest control (termite) company, or some other work is required by the lender, before the escrow can close and the work is delayed.
5. The home being purchased is a new construction and the work required to finish the home isn't complete enough for a Certificate of Occupancy to be issued.
6. Two escrows are closing concurrently or sequentially and a delay in one ties up funds needed to close the other.
7. The lender imposes last minute additional requirements, such as a review appraisal or a further explanation of a credit defect.

239

The first thing to do when you hear that your escrow is not going to close as scheduled is to stay calm. Be sure that your agent informs all other parties involved in the transaction that there is an unavoidable delay. Get a written extension of the close of escrow if the closing will be postponed for longer than 24 hours. The last thing you should do, no matter how frustrated you may feel, is to call the loan processor directly to complain. Let your escrow officer and loan agent handle the problem if it's related to your new loan.

Normally, escrows handled by title and escrow companies are recorded at the county recorder's office once daily. In some counties, it's possible for the escrow holder to arrange for a "special" recording later in the day. Ask your escrow officer or real estate agent to set up a special recording if the cause of the delay is resolved quickly.

Ideally, buyers shouldn't take possession of their new homes until the escrow has closed. Whenever possible, postpone the move until the last-minute problem has been sorted out. In busy real estate markets, it may not be possible to reschedule professional movers late in the game. As a last resort, the buyer can ask the seller for permission to occupy the property before the closing and, if the seller is agreeable, an addendum should be drawn up indicating the terms and conditions under which the buyer can move in early. An Interim Occupancy Agreement should also be signed by the buyer and seller, and the buyer's personal property and liability insurance must be in effect as of the date of occupancy.

CALIFORNIA ASSOCIATION OF REALTORS®

☐

INTERIM OCCUPANCY AGREEMENT
(Buyer in Possession)
THIS IS INTENDED TO BE A LEGALLY BINDING AGREEMENT — READ IT CAREFULLY.
CALIFORNIA ASSOCIATION OF REALTORS® (CAR) STANDARD FORM

_____, California _____, 19____.

_____, "LESSOR" and

_____, "LESSEE" agree:

1. On _____, 19____, LESSOR as SELLER and LESSEE as BUYER entered into an agreement for the sale and purchase of the real property commonly known as _____,
_____, California ("Premises") and the escrow thereof is scheduled to close on or before
_____, 19____.

2. Pending completion of sale and close of escrow, LESSEE is to be given immediate occupancy of the premises in accordance with the terms of this agreement.

3. LESSEE acknowledges an inspection of, and has found the premises in satisfactory condition and ready for occupancy, except as follows: _____
_____
_____
_____ .

4. LESSEE shall pay to LESSOR for the occupancy of said premises the sum of $_____ per _____

day/week/month

   commencing _____, 19____, to and including _____

specific date/other

   _____. Said sum shall be paid _____ in advance.

weekly/monthly

   Prorations, if any, shall be predicated upon a 30 day month. As additional consideration, LESSEE shall pay for all utilities and services based upon occupancy of the premises and the following charges: _____
   except _____ which shall be paid by LESSOR.

5. If the purchase and sale agreement between LESSOR and LESSEE is not completed within its designated term, or any written extension thereof through no fault of LESSOR, LESSEE agrees to vacate the premises upon service of a written notice in the form and manner provided by law. Any holding over thereafter shall create a day-to-day tenancy with a fair rental value of $_____ per day. Except as to daily rent and tenancy, all other covenants and conditions herein contained shall remain in full force and effect.

6. Except as provided by law LESSEE shall keep the premises and yards clean, sanitary, and in good order and repair during the term hereof and shall surrender the same in like condition if the said sale is not completed, reasonable wear and tear excepted. Additionally, LESSEE shall save and hold LESSOR harmless from any and all claims, demands, damages or liabilities arising out of LESSEE's occupancy of the premises caused or permitted by LESSEE, LESSEE'S family, agents, servants, employees, guests and invitees.

7. As additional consideration passing from LESSEE to LESSOR, LESSEE shall obtain and maintain during the term of this agreement public liability insurance naming both LESSOR and LESSEE as co-insureds in the amount of not less than $_____ for injury to one person; $_____ for injury to a group; and $_____ for property damage. If permitted, LESSOR agrees to retain his fire insurance on the premises until close of escrow. Otherwise, LESSEE shall obtain fire insurance on the premises in a sum of not less than that designated as the sales price of the subject property.

8. The premises are to be used as a residence only by LESSEE and his immediate family and no animal, bird or pet except _____ shall be kept on or about the premises without LESSOR'S prior written c_____. LESSEE shall not violate any law or ordinance in the use of the premises, nor permit waste or nuisance upon or about ___ except as pr____ ____ all not make any ad____

240

Whom to Call If You Have a Question

Buyers and sellers often wonder whom to call when they have questions about their escrow. Questions pertaining to the terms of your purchase contract; personal property included in the sale; the closing and possession; time periods for removing your contract contingencies; getting the keys to the house; and transferring utilities into or out of your name should be directed to your real estate agent. Call your escrow officer for answers to questions about the funds needed to close; how much you'll net from the sale; your settlement sheet and closing papers; the preliminary title report; property taxes; and title insurance. Your loan agent can answer questions about loan qualification; impound accounts and PMI; holdback restrictions; and the loan approval process. Call your insurance agent for informa-

5. If the purcha~~...~~ ~~...between LESSO~~ ~~...~~ ~~...~~pleted within its ~~...~~ ~~...~~erm, or any wr~~...~~ extension thereof through no fault of LESSOR, LESSEE agre~~...~~ ~~...~~ate the premises upon service of a written notice in the form and manner provided by law. Any holding over thereafter shall create a day-to-day tenancy with a fair rental value of $_____ per day. Except as to daily rent and tenancy, all other covenants and conditions herein contained shall remain in full force and effect.

6. Except as provided by law LESSEE shall keep the premises and yards clean, sanitary, and in good order and repair during the term hereof and shall surrender the same in like condition if the said sale is not completed, reasonable wear and tear excepted. Additionally, LESSEE shall save and hold LESSOR harmless from any and all claims, demands, damages or liabilities arising out of LESSEE's occupancy of the premises caused or permitted by LESSEE, LESSEE'S family, agents, servants, employees, guests and invitees.

7. As additional consideration passing from LESSEE to LESSOR, LESSEE shall obtain and maintain during the term of this agreement public liability insurance naming both LESSOR and LESSEE as co-insureds in the amount of not less than $_____ for injury to one person; $_____ for injury to a group; and $_____ for property damage. If permitted, LESSOR agrees to retain his fire insurance on the premises until close of escrow. Otherwise, LESSEE shall obtain fire insurance on the premises in a sum of not less than that designated as the sales price of the subject property.

8. The premises are to be used as a residence only by LESSEE and his immediate family and no animal, bird or pet except _____ shall be kept on or about the premises without LESSOR'S prior written consent. LESSEE shall not violate any law or ordinance in the use of the premises, nor permit waste or nuisance upon or about the premises and, except as provided by law, LESSEE shall not make any additions, alterations, or repairs to the premises without the prior written consent of LESSOR.

9. $_____ as security has been deposited. LESSOR may use therefrom such amounts as are reasonably necessary to remedy LESSEE defaults in the payment of rent, to repair damages caused by LESSEE, or to clean the premises if necessary upon the termination of tenancy. If used toward rent or damages during the term of this agreement, LESSEE agrees to reinstate said total security deposit upon 5 days written notice delivered to LESSEE in person or by mail. The balance of the security deposit, if any, shall be mailed to LESSEE'S last known address within 14 days of surrender of premises. Alternatively, and upon completion of sale, said security deposit shall be mailed to LESSEE at the subject premises within 10 days of close of escrow.

10. In the event of any action or proceeding between LESSOR and LESSEE under this agreement, the prevailing party shall be entitled to recover reasonable attorney's fees and costs.

11. The right to occupy the premises as granted LESSEE herein is personal to LESSEE and any attempt to assign, transfer, or hypothecate the same shall be null and void.

12. The undersigned LESSEE acknowledges having read the foregoing and receipt of a copy.

LESSOR and LESSEE have executed this agreement on the day and year above written.

Lessor _____   Lessee _____

Lessor _____   Lessee _____

241

FORM IOA-14

OFFICE USE ONLY
Reviewed by Broker or Designee _____
Date _____

EQUAL HOUSING OPPORTUNITY
M-SC-JUN-92

tion about hazard and earthquake insurance. Finally, an attorney and/or tax advisor can advise you on how to take title to your new home. It's a good idea to keep a written record of phone conversations you have with the various professionals you're working with during your real estate transaction.

CHAPTER 12

FINISHING UP

Settlement Papers

Soon after closing you will receive various documents from your escrow holder. Buyers should expect a copy of the final settlement sheet, the title insurance policy, a homeowner's insurance policy, and usually a small refund check. The escrow holder will estimate closing costs (particularly interest and property tax prorations) on the high side to cover for the possibility that the closing will be delayed several days. The settlement sheet is adjusted as of the close date to reflect prorations, and the excess funds are returned to the buyer.

Sellers will receive a copy of the final settlement statement, which may or may not accompany the proceeds check. The escrow holder will usually prepare the checks first and copies of the final paperwork later. If the proceeds are not to be transferred immediately to another escrow, the seller should arrange to deposit the funds into an interest-bearing account as soon as possible. Sellers who carry financing for the buyer will also receive the note, a recorded deed of trust in favor of the sellers, a copy of the title insurance policy, and a fire insurance policy to cover the seller as loss payee. Recorded documents, including recorded reconveyances of loans that were paid off at closing, will usually be sent to the sellers separately.

Keep your settlement papers in a safe place. Some of the expenses associated with buying and selling a home are tax deductible; other expenses adjust your cost basis for the purposes of calculating your capital gains liability. Consult your tax advisor if you have any questions about the tax consequences of buying and selling.

Selecting a Mover

Buyers and sellers should start planning the move no later than the date escrow is opened. A seller who is transferring across the country should begin even sooner. Ask your real estate agent and friends who've moved recently to recommend movers to you.

Obtain written estimates from several movers in advance and check to make sure that the moving companies have been licensed by the Public Utilities Commission (PUC). Without a license, it's illegal to take money to move someone.

Also, a PUC-licensed mover must carry adequate insurance for breakage, and the actual cost to move can't exceed the estimate by more than 10 percent. Have the movers visit your home and survey the contents before giving you a bid; over-the-phone estimates aren't binding. Find out in advance what the payment options are. Some movers won't unload you at your new home until they have received cash to cover the cost of the move.

One way to save money moving, if you have the time, is to pack yourself. Be aware that a new PUC ruling makes the moving company liable only for damage done to boxes packed by the mover. Boxes you pack yourself will only be covered if the mover determines in advance that they are packed correctly. If you're undecided about whether you'll be doing the packing, ask each moving company representative to give you two estimates: one for moving and the other for both packing and moving.

Movers' rates are based on weight and distance. A surefire way to save on moving expenses is to throw out, sell, or donate surplus possessions before you move. Arrange to make donations in advance, and obtain a receipt for the approximate value of your donated items. This amount can be deducted from your gross income at tax time if you itemize deductions. Having a garage sale is another way to save on moving costs. This is best done before movers give you estimates.

Your homeowner's insurance usually won't cover insuring your possessions while they're in transit. Find out what the moving company's maximum liability is for loss or damage to your possessions. Arrange for additional insurance coverage if necessary.

Select a mover, and set the move date 30 to 60 days in advance. During periods of peak real estate activity, it may be necessary to schedule the move farther ahead. Many moving companies have free literature that can be helpful in planning and making your move. Ask each representative to provide you with whatever informational material they have available.

Getting Ready to Move

Once you've eliminated everything you're not moving, prepare an inventory of the possessions you're taking with you. Start packing possessions you're not currently using and list the contents of each box on two sides. If labeling doesn't appeal to you, you can number each box and keep a list of the contents to simplify unloading and unpacking at the new home. It helps to decide in advance where your possessions will be placed in your new house. Use colored labels, a different color for each room, to designate where each item is to

Get written estimates from two or three movers licensed by the PUC.

243

go. Also, sturdy boxes suitable for packing are hard to find; they can be purchased directly from moving companies if necessary.

At least two weeks before the move, call the gas, electric, phone, water, garbage collection, and cable television companies in the new and old locations and arrange for the services to be transferred out of your name at the old house and into your name at the new house. It's preferable to have utilities transferred rather than shut off. This way you will avoid reconnect fees and the inconvenience of waiting for installers. Also, shutting the gas off completely can result in irreparable damage to a gas furnace. Buyers who aren't taking possession as soon as the seller vacates should make sure that utilities are transferred into their names so that lights can be left on and the yard watered.

> *Use colored labels to designate where your possessions will be placed in your new home: a different color for each room.*

Arrange to sell or transfer any club memberships if you're moving out of the area. Notify the post office of your new address and send change of address cards to magazine publishers, credit card companies, your present employer, banks, friends, and relatives. Don't forget to notify important business contacts, the Department of Motor Vehicles, and your insurance carriers.

Stop services at the old location such as the gardener, housekeeper, and newspaper delivery. If the buyer is not immediately taking possession of the property, make arrangements for someone to water the yard.

Ask your dentist, doctor, lawyer, investment broker, and tax advisor for recommendations of professionals to work with in your new community. Transfer important documents such as school and medical records. Open a bank checking account convenient to your new home, and transfer funds in advance so that you have a source of cash when you arrive. If this isn't possible, at least purchase a good supply of traveler's checks to tide you over.

Have rugs and draperies you're taking with you professionally cleaned and packed for moving during the last week before the move. If you'll be driving a long distance to your new location, have the car serviced. Take care of overdue doctor or dentist appointments before you go. Moving companies usually won't move pets and sometimes won't move houseplants, so make separate arrangements for both. Carry jewelry and valuables with you, or mail them registered to yourself at your new address.

> *Don't have utilities shut off; have them transferred into the buyer's name.*

Your purchase contract will usually specify that you remove all your possessions and debris from the property and that the house be left broom clean. Hire a cleaning person or crew to come in and

244

clean up after you move out if you're making a long-distance move or you're short on time.

Sellers are responsible for maintaining the property until they deliver possession to the buyer. This usually means replacing cracked and broken glass and fixing anything that has broken since the time you accepted the buyer's offer. Make sure to line up the appropriate tradespeople well in advance of moving day to take care of these items.

Ask the buyers if they want you to leave surplus paint for them. If you have old paint containers that the buyers don't want, arrange to dispose of them at a household hazardous waste center. Call your local fire department for the location of the center closest to you. The same goes for disposing of other hazardous household products such as bleach and ammonia-based cleaners. These products should not be poured down the drain.

Learning the Idiosyncracies of Your New Home in Advance

Ask your real estate agent to arra˙ ge for a meeting with the sellers to learn the intricacies of the home. It saves the buyer time and frustration if the locations of outdoor lights, sprinkler system valves, and electrical panels are known in advance. Automatic sprinkler and security systems may require special instructions.

The buyer should inquire if there are any specific routine maintenance items required to keep the house in top condition. How often do gutters need cleaning? Are there any drains that need to be cleaned out periodically? Are there areas of the roof or around the foundation that require caulking? Ask the sellers to leave you the names and phone numbers of the tradespeople they have used to maintain the house in the past. Such recommendations are valuable because these people have worked on the house and are familiar with it. If you're moving into a completely new community, ask the sellers to give you a rundown of the neighborhood and to introduce you to a few of your new neighbors.

245

Your agent should accompany you on this final meeting with the sellers. If you meet alone with the sellers and they disclose a material defect previously undisclosed, you must get the information in writing. This information should have been included on the Real Estate Transfer Disclosure statement; if it wasn't, it needs to be in writing at this point.

A disclosure of a material fact affecting a residential property automatically institutes a three-day right of rescission period, during which time the buyer can terminate the contract and the deposit money will be returned. At this late date, the last thing the buyer will want is to rescind the contract. But full disclosure is required by California law, and the disclosure at least gives the

> *For information on disposing of hazardous household products, call the California Integrated Waste Management Board (CIWMB) Recycling Hotline at (800) 553-2062.*

buyer the opportunity to negotiate satisfactory compensation for a previously undisclosed problem. Failing to deal with the problem before the closing could result in more time-consuming and costly attempts at reconciliation after the close.

When buyers and sellers don't have the opportunity to conduct a walk-through before the buyers take possession of the home, the sellers should leave a note detailing any relevant information, along with any operating manuals the sellers have in their possession.

On Moving Day

Before the movers arrive, you should have packed a survival kit of clothes, toys for children, toilet articles, and food: everything you'll need until the remainder of your possessions arrive at your new home. You'll also want your driver's license, car registration, credit cards, checkbook and traveler's checks, pertinent addresses and phone numbers, and maps. Also take a phone book from your old house with you in case you need to reach someone in your former location.

You should be on hand to supervise the move and packing if the movers are also packing your possessions.

Ross Sutter had a pressing problem at work and wasn't home the day the movers came to pack his belongings and move them to his new home. The movers packed a number of items that were to remain in the house for the new buyers including the automatic garage door openers. This presented a considerable problem when the buyers attempted to move in, since the only way to move large pieces of furniture into the house was through the garage.

Leave the house keys with your real estate agent or a neighbor, and make sure the buyers are informed about when and where the keys can be picked up. Extra keys should be left in the house along with automatic garage door openers. Make sure to leave your new mailing address at your old home, so the mail can be forwarded. If your house will be left vacant for some time before the buyers move in, notify the police and let your neighbors know.

Be available to supervise the unloading when the movers arrive at your new home. Make sure that your possessions are intact and that nothing is missing. Report any damage or suspected theft to the moving company immediately. The unloading will proceed quickly if you know in advance where you want your possessions placed.

Make Home Maintenance a Top Priority

One of the first things you should do after you unpack and settle into your new home is to set up a home maintenance routine. Before each rainy season, carefully inspect your home for needed repairs. All holes and voids in the exterior

246

should be patched and sealed to keep moisture out. Have the roof checked each year or so and clean gutters and downspouts as necessary. Replace missing roof shingles, flashing, and caulking. Make sure all roof water is directed away from the foundation. Check underneath your house after a heavy rain to see if there's any excessive moisture and look for signs of standing water around the property. Consult a drainage expert if necessary to see if there's anything you can do to improve on the drainage in and around your home; one of the biggest causes of damage to houses is water. Have your fireplace and furnace checked and cleaned regularly. Make sure doors and windows are watertight. Also, you can lower your energy bills by weatherstripping doors and windows and adding insulation.

Review the inspection reports that were completed at the time you purchased the home. Make arrangements to correct any defects you agreed to take care of after close of escrow. All too often buyers take a credit from the seller for repairs, they use the money to offset their closing costs, and then fail to have the repairs done. This is a mistake as little problems can turn into bigger ones that will be more expensive to fix later. One way to protect your investment is to remedy problems as they appear and to keep your home well maintained.

Interest Rate Factor Chart

Interest Rate %	15-Year Term	30-Year Term	Interest Rate %	15-Year Term	30-Year Term
4.00	7.40	4.77	10.00	10.75	8.78
4.25	7.52	4.92	10.25	10.90	8.96
4.50	7.65	5.07	10.50	11.05	9.15
4.75	7.78	5.22	10.75	11.21	9.33
5.00	7.91	5.37	11.00	11.37	9.52
5.25	8.04	5.52	11.25	11.52	9.71
5.50	8.17	5.68	11.50	11.68	9.90
5.75	8.30	5.84	11.75	11.84	10.09
6.00	8.44	6.00	12.00	12.00	10.29
6.25	8.57	6.16	12.25	12.16	10.48
6.50	8.71	6.32	12.50	12.33	10.67
6.75	8.85	6.49	12.75	12.49	10.87
7.00	8.99	6.65	13.00	12.65	11.06
7.25	9.13	6.82	13.25	12.82	11.26
7.50	9.27	6.99	13.50	12.99	11.45
7.75	9.41	7.16	13.75	13.15	11.65
8.00	9.56	7.34	14.00	13.32	11.84
8.25	9.70	7.51	14.25	13.49	12.05
8.50	9.85	7.69	14.50	13.66	12.25
8.75	10.00	7.87	14.75	13.83	12.44
9.00	10.14	8.05	15.00	14.00	12.64
9.25	10.29	8.23	15.25	14.17	12.84
9.50	10.44	8.41	15.50	14.34	13.05
9.75	10.59	8.59	15.75	14.51	13.25

This chart indicates *the monthly dollar amount required to amortize a loan of $1,000. Divide your Affordable Mortgage Payment (see Chapter 1) by the appropriate factor and multiply by $1,000 to determine your Affordable Loan Amount. For example, if your Affordable Mortgage Payment is $1,020 and you want to know what size loan you can afford if you apply for a home loan with a 7% interest rate (30-year term), divide $1,020 by 6.65 and multiply by $1,000. Your Affordable Loan Amount is approximately $153,383.*

To determine the monthly payment (principal and interest only) on any loan amount, divide the loan amount by 1,000 and multiply by the appropriate factor. For instance, a $150,000 loan with an 8% interest rate and a 30-year term will have a monthly payment of $1,101. (Divide $150,000 by 1,000 and multiply by 7.34.)

To calculate your Approximate Affordable Purchase Price, once you know your Affordable Loan Amount, divide the loan amount by 80% (.80) or 90% (.90), depending on how much cash you have available. For example, if you can afford a $150,000 loan amount, your Approximate Affordable Purchase Price will be $187,500 if you obtain an 80% loan ($150,000 divided by .80). Buyers who are well-qualified but short on cash may need to apply for 90% financing, in which case your Approximate Affordable Purchase Price will be $166,667 ($150,000 divided by .90). Subtract the Affordable Loan Amount from the Approximate Affordable Purchase Price to determine the amount of your cash down payment. Don't forget to multiply the Affordable Loan Amount by 4% (.04) to determine your approximate closing costs and add this figure to your down payment to arrive at the approximate cash required to buy your new home.

The figures contained in the tables in this book are believed to be accurate but cannot be guaranteed.

Amortization Schedule

How to Use the Amortization Schedule

The amortization schedule is used to determine the monthly principal and interest payment for any loan amount, given an interest rate and term. Read down the far left column until you reach the loan amount in question, then read across the page to the appropriate interest rate and select a 15-year or 30-year amortization period. Monthly principal and interest payments for loan amounts not provided on the chart are computed by looking at smaller loan amounts and adding their corresponding monthly payment figures together. For example, to find the monthly principal and interest payment on a $92,000 30-year loan with an interest rate of 7.75%, add $644.77 (the monthly payment on a $90,000 loan with a 7.75% interest rate and a 30-year due date) to $14.33 (the monthly payment on a $2,000 loan with a 7.75% interest rate and a 30-year due date) for a total of $659.10. Likewise, the monthly principal and interest payment on a $150,000 loan with a 9% interest rate and a 15-year due date is $1,521.40 and is calculated by adding $1,014.27 (the monthly payment on a $100,000 loan with a 9% interest rate and a 15-year due date) to $507.13 (the monthly payment on a $50,000 loan with a 9% interest rate and a 15-year due date).

250

Amortization Tables (Monthly Payments)

Interest Rate	4.00%		4.25%		4.50%		4.75%	
Terms (Years) Loan Amount	15	30	15	30	15	30	15	30
1,000	7.40	4.77	7.52	4.92	7.65	5.07	7.78	5.22
2,000	14.79	9.55	15.05	9.84	15.30	10.13	15.56	10.43
3,000	22.19	14.32	22.57	14.76	22.95	15.20	23.33	15.65
4,000	29.59	19.10	30.09	19.68	30.60	20.27	31.11	20.87
5,000	36.98	23.87	37.61	24.60	38.25	25.33	38.89	26.08
6,000	44.38	28.64	45.14	29.52	45.90	30.40	46.67	31.30
7,000	51.78	33.42	52.66	34.44	53.55	35.47	54.45	36.52
8,000	59.18	38.19	60.18	39.36	61.20	40.53	62.23	41.73
9,000	66.57	42.97	67.71	44.27	68.85	45.60	70.00	46.95
10,000	73.97	47.74	75.23	49.19	76.50	50.67	77.78	52.16
20,000	147.94	95.48	150.46	98.39	153.00	101.34	155.57	104.33
30,000	221.91	143.22	225.68	147.58	229.50	152.01	233.35	156.49
40,000	295.88	190.97	300.91	196.78	306.00	202.67	311.13	208.66
50,000	369.84	238.71	376.14	245.97	382.50	253.34	388.92	260.82
60,000	443.81	286.45	451.37	295.16	459.00	304.01	466.70	312.99
70,000	517.78	334.19	526.59	344.36	535.50	354.68	544.48	365.15
80,000	591.75	381.93	601.82	393.55	611.99	405.35	622.27	417.32
90,000	665.72	429.67	677.05	442.75	688.49	456.02	700.05	469.48
100,000	739.69	477.42	752.28	491.94	764.99	506.69	777.83	521.65

Interest Rate	5.00%		5.25%		5.50%		5.75%	
Term (Years) Loan Amount	15	30	15	30	15	30	15	30
1,000	7.91	5.37	8.04	5.52	8.17	5.68	8.30	5.84
2,000	15.82	10.74	16.08	11.04	16.34	11.36	16.61	11.67
3,000	23.72	16.10	24.12	16.57	24.51	17.03	24.91	17.51
4,000	31.63	21.47	32.16	22.09	32.68	22.71	33.22	23.34
5,000	39.54	26.84	40.19	27.61	40.85	28.39	41.52	29.18
6,000	47.45	32.21	48.23	33.13	49.03	34.07	49.82	35.01
7,000	55.36	37.58	56.27	38.65	57.20	39.75	58.13	40.85
8,000	63.26	42.95	64.31	44.18	65.37	45.42	66.43	46.69
9,000	71.17	48.31	72.35	49.70	73.54	51.10	74.74	52.52
10,000	79.08	53.68	80.39	55.22	81.71	56.78	83.04	58.36
20,000	158.16	107.36	160.78	110.44	163.42	113.56	166.08	116.71
30,000	237.24	161.05	241.16	165.66	245.13	170.34	249.12	175.07
40,000	316.32	214.73	321.55	220.88	326.83	227.12	332.16	233.43
50,000	395.40	268.41	401.94	276.10	408.54	283.89	415.21	291.79
60,000	474.48	322.09	482.33	331.32	490.25	340.67	498.25	350.14
70,000	553.56	375.78	562.71	386.54	571.96	397.45	581.29	408.50
80,000	632.63	429.46	643.10	441.76	653.67	454.23	664.33	466.86
90,000	711.71	483.14	723.49	496.98	735.38	511.01	747.37	525.22
100,000	790.79	536.82	803.88	552.20	817.08	567.79	830.41	583.57

Interest Rate	6.00%		6.25%		6.50%		6.75%	
Term (Years) Loan Amount	15	30	15	30	15	30	15	30
1,000	8.44	6.00	8.57	6.16	8.71	6.32	8.85	6.49
2,000	16.88	11.99	17.15	12.31	17.42	12.64	17.70	12.97
3,000	25.32	17.99	25.72	18.47	26.13	18.96	26.55	19.46
4,000	33.75	23.98	34.30	24.63	34.84	25.28	35.40	25.94
5,000	42.19	29.98	42.87	30.79	43.56	31.60	44.25	32.43
6,000	50.63	35.97	51.45	36.94	52.27	37.92	53.09	38.92
7,000	59.07	41.97	60.02	43.10	60.98	44.24	61.94	45.40
8,000	67.51	47.96	68.59	49.26	69.69	50.57	70.79	51.89
9,000	75.95	53.96	77.17	55.41	78.40	56.89	79.64	58.37
10,000	84.39	59.96	85.74	61.57	87.11	63.21	88.49	64.86
20,000	168.77	119.91	171.48	123.14	174.22	126.41	176.98	129.72
30,000	253.16	179.87	257.23	184.72	261.33	189.62	265.47	194.58
40,000	337.54	239.82	342.97	246.29	348.44	252.83	353.96	259.44
50,000	421.93	299.78	428.71	307.86	435.55	316.03	442.45	324.30
60,000	506.31	359.73	514.45	369.43	522.66	379.24	530.95	389.16
70,000	590.70	419.69	600.20	431.00	609.78	442.45	619.44	454.02
80,000	675.09	479.64	685.94	492.57	696.89	505.65	707.93	518.88
90,000	759.47	539.60	771.68	554.15	784.00	568.86	796.42	583.74
100,000	843.86	599.55	857.42	615.72	871.11	632.07	884.91	648.60

Interest Rate	7.00%		7.25%		7.50%		7.75%	
Term (Years) Loan Amount	15	30	15	30	15	30	15	30
1,000	8.99	6.65	9.13	6.82	9.27	6.99	9.41	7.16
2,000	17.98	13.31	18.26	13.64	18.54	13.98	18.83	14.33
3,000	26.96	19.96	27.39	20.47	27.81	20.98	28.24	21.49
4,000	35.95	26.61	36.51	27.29	37.08	27.97	37.65	28.66
5,000	44.94	33.27	45.64	34.11	46.35	34.96	47.06	35.82
6,000	53.93	39.92	54.77	40.93	55.62	41.95	56.48	42.98
7,000	62.92	46.57	63.90	47.75	64.89	48.95	65.89	50.15
8,000	71.91	53.22	73.03	54.57	74.16	55.94	75.30	57.31
9,000	80.89	59.88	82.16	61.40	83.43	62.93	84.71	64.48
10,000	89.88	66.53	91.29	68.22	92.70	69.92	94.13	71.64
20,000	179.77	133.06	182.57	136.44	185.40	139.84	188.26	143.28
30,000	269.65	199.59	273.86	204.65	278.10	209.76	282.38	214.92
40,000	359.53	266.12	365.15	272.87	370.80	279.69	376.51	286.56
50,000	449.41	332.65	456.43	341.09	463.51	349.61	470.64	358.21
60,000	539.30	399.18	547.72	409.31	556.21	419.53	564.77	429.85
70,000	629.18	465.71	639.00	477.52	648.91	489.45	658.89	501.49
80,000	719.06	532.24	730.29	545.74	741.61	559.37	753.02	573.13
90,000	808.95	598.77	821.58	613.96	834.31	629.29	847.15	644.77
100,000	898.83	665.30	912.86	682.18	927.01	699.21	941.28	716.41

Interest Rate	8.00%		8.25%		8.50%		8.75%	
Term (Years) Loan Amount	15	30	15	30	15	30	15	30
1,000	9.56	7.34	9.70	7.51	9.85	7.69	9.99	7.87
2,000	19.11	14.68	19.40	15.03	19.69	15.38	19.99	15.73
3,000	28.67	22.01	29.10	22.54	29.54	23.07	29.98	23.60
4,000	38.23	29.35	38.81	30.05	39.39	30.76	39.98	31.47
5,000	47.78	36.69	48.51	37.56	49.24	38.45	49.97	39.34
6,000	57.34	44.03	58.21	45.08	59.08	46.13	59.97	47.20
7,000	66.90	51.36	67.91	52.59	68.93	53.82	69.96	55.07
8,000	76.45	58.70	77.61	60.10	78.78	61.51	79.96	62.94
9,000	86.01	66.04	87.31	67.61	88.63	69.20	89.95	70.80
10,000	95.57	73.38	97.01	75.13	98.47	76.89	99.94	78.67
20,000	191.13	146.75	194.03	150.25	196.95	153.78	199.89	157.34
30,000	286.70	220.13	291.04	225.38	295.42	230.67	299.83	236.01
40,000	382.26	293.51	388.06	300.51	393.90	307.57	399.78	314.68
50,000	477.83	366.88	485.07	375.63	492.37	384.46	499.72	393.35
60,000	573.39	440.26	582.08	450.76	590.84	461.35	599.67	472.02
70,000	668.96	513.64	679.10	525.89	689.32	538.24	699.61	550.69
80,000	764.52	587.01	776.11	601.01	787.79	615.13	799.56	629.36
90,000	860.09	660.39	873.13	676.14	886.27	692.02	899.50	708.03
100,000	955.65	733.76	970.14	751.27	984.74	768.91	999.45	786.70

Interest Rate	9.00%		9.25%		9.50%		9.75%	
Term (Years) Loan Amount	15	30	15	30	15	30	15	30
1,000	10.14	8.05	10.29	8.23	10.44	8.41	10.59	8.59
2,000	20.29	16.09	20.58	16.45	20.88	16.82	21.19	17.18
3,000	30.43	24.14	30.88	24.68	31.33	25.23	31.78	25.77
4,000	40.57	32.18	41.17	32.91	41.77	33.63	42.37	34.37
5,000	50.71	40.23	51.46	41.13	52.21	42.04	52.97	42.96
6,000	60.86	48.28	61.75	49.36	62.65	50.45	63.56	51.55
7,000	71.00	56.32	72.04	57.59	73.10	58.86	74.16	60.14
8,000	81.14	64.37	82.34	65.81	83.54	67.27	84.75	68.73
9,000	91.28	72.42	92.63	74.04	93.98	75.68	95.34	77.32
10,000	101.43	80.46	102.92	82.27	104.42	84.09	105.94	85.92
20,000	202.85	160.92	205.84	164.54	208.84	168.17	211.87	171.83
30,000	304.28	241.39	308.76	246.80	313.27	252.26	317.81	257.75
40,000	405.71	321.85	411.68	329.07	417.69	336.34	423.75	343.66
50,000	507.13	402.31	514.60	411.34	522.11	420.43	529.68	429.58
60,000	608.56	482.77	617.52	493.61	626.53	504.51	635.62	515.49
70,000	709.99	563.24	720.43	575.87	730.96	588.60	741.55	601.41
80,000	811.41	643.70	823.35	658.14	835.38	672.68	847.49	687.32
90,000	912.84	724.16	926.27	740.41	939.80	756.77	953.43	773.24
100,000	1014.27	804.62	1029.19	822.68	1044.22	840.85	1059.36	859.15

Interest Rate	10.00%		10.25%		10.50%		10.75%	
Term (Years) Loan Amount	15	30	15	30	15	30	15	30
1,000	10.75	8.78	10.90	8.96	11.05	9.15	11.21	9.33
2,000	21.49	17.55	21.80	17.92	22.11	18.29	22.42	18.67
3,000	32.24	26.33	32.70	26.88	33.16	27.44	33.63	28.00
4,000	42.98	35.10	43.60	35.84	44.22	36.59	44.84	37.34
5,000	53.73	43.88	54.50	44.81	55.27	45.74	56.05	46.67
6,000	64.48	52.65	65.40	53.77	66.32	54.88	67.26	56.01
7,000	75.22	61.43	76.30	62.73	77.38	64.03	78.47	65.34
8,000	85.97	70.21	87.20	71.69	88.43	73.18	89.68	74.68
9,000	96.71	78.98	98.10	80.65	99.49	82.33	100.89	84.01
10,000	107.46	87.76	109.00	89.61	110.54	91.47	112.09	93.35
20,000	214.92	175.51	217.99	179.22	221.08	182.95	224.19	186.70
30,000	322.38	263.27	326.99	268.83	331.62	274.42	336.28	280.04
40,000	429.84	351.03	435.98	358.44	442.16	365.90	448.38	373.39
50,000	537.30	438.79	544.98	448.05	552.70	457.37	560.47	466.74
60,000	644.76	526.54	653.97	537.66	663.24	548.84	672.57	560.09
70,000	752.22	614.30	762.97	627.27	773.78	640.32	784.66	653.44
80,000	859.68	702.06	871.96	716.88	884.32	731.79	896.76	746.79
90,000	967.14	789.81	980.96	806.49	994.86	823.27	1008.85	840.13
100,000	1074.61	877.57	1089.95	896.10	1105.40	914.74	1120.95	933.48

Interest Rate	11.00%		11.25%		11.50%		11.75%	
Term (Years) Loan Amount	15	30	15	30	15	30	15	30
1,000	11.37	9.52	11.52	9.71	11.68	9.90	11.84	10.09
2,000	22.73	19.05	23.05	19.43	23.36	19.81	23.68	20.19
3,000	34.10	28.57	34.57	29.14	35.05	29.71	35.52	30.28
4,000	45.46	38.09	46.09	38.85	46.73	39.61	47.37	40.38
5,000	56.83	47.62	57.62	48.56	58.41	49.51	59.21	50.47
6,000	68.20	57.14	69.14	58.28	70.09	59.42	71.05	60.56
7,000	79.56	66.66	80.66	67.99	81.77	69.32	82.89	70.66
8,000	90.93	76.19	92.19	77.70	93.46	79.22	94.73	80.75
9,000	102.29	85.71	103.71	87.41	105.14	89.13	106.57	90.85
10,000	113.66	95.23	115.23	97.13	116.82	99.03	118.41	100.94
20,000	227.32	190.46	230.47	194.25	233.64	198.06	236.83	201.88
30,000	340.98	285.70	345.70	291.38	350.46	297.09	355.24	302.82
40,000	454.64	380.93	460.94	388.50	467.28	396.12	473.65	403.76
50,000	568.30	476.16	576.17	485.63	584.09	495.15	592.07	504.70
60,000	681.96	571.39	691.41	582.76	700.91	594.17	710.48	605.65
70,000	795.62	666.63	806.64	679.88	817.73	693.20	828.89	706.59
80,000	909.28	761.86	921.88	777.01	934.55	792.23	947.31	807.53
90,000	1022.94	857.09	1037.11	874.14	1051.37	891.26	1065.72	908.47
100,000	1136.60	952.32	1152.34	971.26	1168.19	990.29	1184.13	1009.41

Interest Rate	12.00%		12.25%		12.50%		12.75%	
Term (Years) Loan Amount	15	30	15	30	15	30	15	30
1,000	12.00	10.29	12.16	10.48	12.33	10.67	12.49	10.87
2,000	24.00	20.57	24.33	20.96	24.65	21.35	24.98	21.73
3,000	36.01	30.86	36.49	31.44	36.98	32.02	37.47	32.60
4,000	48.01	41.14	48.65	41.92	49.30	42.69	49.95	43.47
5,000	60.01	51.43	60.81	52.39	61.63	53.36	62.44	54.33
6,000	72.01	61.72	72.98	62.87	73.95	64.04	74.93	65.20
7,000	84.01	72.00	85.14	73.35	86.28	74.71	87.42	76.07
8,000	96.01	82.29	97.30	83.83	98.60	85.38	99.91	86.94
9,000	108.02	92.58	109.47	94.31	110.93	96.05	112.40	97.80
10,000	120.02	102.86	121.63	104.79	123.25	106.73	124.88	108.67
20,000	240.03	205.72	243.26	209.58	246.50	213.45	249.77	217.34
30,000	360.05	308.58	364.89	314.37	369.76	320.18	374.65	326.01
40,000	480.07	411.45	486.52	419.16	493.01	426.90	499.53	434.68
50,000	600.08	514.31	608.15	523.95	616.26	533.63	624.42	543.35
60,000	720.10	617.17	729.78	628.74	739.51	640.35	749.30	652.02
70,000	840.12	720.03	851.41	733.53	862.77	747.08	874.19	760.69
80,000	960.13	822.89	973.04	838.32	986.02	853.81	999.07	869.35
90,000	1080.15	925.75	1094.67	943.11	1109.27	960.53	1123.95	978.02
100,000	1200.17	1028.61	1216.30	1047.90	1232.52	1067.26	1248.84	1086.69

Interest Rate	13.00%		13.25%		13.50%		13.75%	
Term (Years) Loan Amount	15	30	15	30	15	30	15	30
1,000	12.65	11.06	12.82	11.26	12.98	11.45	13.15	11.65
2,000	25.30	22.12	25.63	22.52	25.97	22.91	26.30	23.30
3,000	37.96	33.19	38.45	33.77	38.95	34.36	39.45	34.95
4,000	50.61	44.25	51.27	45.03	51.93	45.82	52.60	46.60
5,000	63.26	55.31	64.09	56.29	64.92	57.27	65.75	58.26
6,000	75.91	66.37	76.90	67.55	77.90	68.72	78.90	69.91
7,000	88.57	77.43	89.72	78.80	90.88	80.18	92.05	81.56
8,000	101.22	88.50	102.54	90.06	103.87	91.63	105.20	93.21
9,000	113.87	99.56	115.36	101.32	116.85	103.09	118.35	104.86
10,000	126.52	110.62	128.17	112.58	129.83	114.54	131.50	116.51
20,000	253.05	221.24	256.35	225.15	259.66	229.08	263.00	233.02
30,000	379.57	331.86	384.52	337.73	389.50	343.62	394.50	349.53
40,000	506.10	442.48	512.69	450.31	519.33	458.16	525.99	466.05
50,000	632.62	553.10	640.87	562.89	649.16	572.71	657.49	582.56
60,000	759.15	663.72	769.04	675.46	778.99	687.25	788.99	699.07
70,000	885.67	774.34	897.22	788.04	908.82	801.79	920.49	815.58
80,000	1012.19	884.96	1025.39	900.62	1038.65	916.33	1051.99	932.09
90,000	1138.72	995.58	1153.56	1013.20	1168.49	1030.87	1183.49	1048.60
100,000	1265.24	1106.20	1281.74	1125.77	1298.32	1145.41	1314.99	1165.11

Interest Rate	14.00%		14.25%		14.50%		14.75%	
Term (Years) Loan Amount	15	30	15	30	15	30	15	30
1,000	13.32	11.85	13.49	12.05	13.66	12.25	13.83	12.44
2,000	26.63	23.70	26.97	24.09	27.31	24.49	27.65	24.89
3,000	39.95	35.55	40.46	36.14	40.97	36.74	41.48	37.33
4,000	53.27	47.39	53.94	48.19	54.62	48.98	55.30	49.78
5,000	66.59	59.24	67.43	60.23	68.28	61.23	69.13	62.22
6,000	79.90	71.09	80.91	72.28	81.93	73.47	82.95	74.67
7,000	93.22	82.94	94.40	84.33	95.59	85.72	96.78	87.11
8,000	106.54	94.79	107.89	96.37	109.24	97.96	110.60	99.56
9,000	119.86	106.64	121.37	108.42	122.90	110.21	124.43	112.00
10,000	133.17	118.49	134.86	120.47	136.55	122.46	138.25	124.45
20,000	266.35	236.97	269.72	240.94	273.10	244.91	276.50	248.90
30,000	399.52	355.46	404.57	361.41	409.65	367.37	414.75	373.34
40,000	532.70	473.95	539.43	481.87	546.20	489.82	553.00	497.79
50,000	665.87	592.44	674.29	602.34	682.75	612.28	691.25	622.24
60,000	799.04	710.92	809.15	722.81	819.30	734.73	829.50	746.69
70,000	932.22	829.41	944.01	843.28	955.85	857.19	967.75	871.13
80,000	1065.39	947.90	1078.86	963.75	1092.40	979.64	1106.00	995.58
90,000	1198.57	1066.38	1213.72	1084.22	1228.95	1102.10	1244.25	1120.03
100,000	1331.74	1184.87	1348.58	1204.69	1365.50	1224.56	1382.50	1244.48

Interest Rate	15.00%		15.25%		15.50%		15.75%	
Term (Years) Loan Amount	15	30	15	30	15	30	15	30
1,000	14.00	12.64	14.17	12.84	14.34	13.05	14.51	13.25
2,000	27.99	25.29	28.33	25.69	28.68	26.09	29.03	26.49
3,000	41.99	37.93	42.50	38.53	43.02	39.14	43.54	39.74
4,000	55.98	50.58	56.67	51.38	57.36	52.18	58.05	52.98
5,000	69.98	63.22	70.84	64.22	71.70	65.23	72.57	66.23
6,000	83.98	75.87	85.00	77.07	86.04	78.27	87.08	79.48
7,000	97.97	88.51	99.17	89.91	100.38	91.32	101.59	92.72
8,000	111.97	101.16	113.34	102.76	114.72	104.36	116.10	105.97
9,000	125.96	113.80	127.51	115.60	129.06	117.41	130.62	119.22
10,000	139.96	126.44	141.67	128.45	143.40	130.45	145.13	132.46
20,000	279.92	252.89	283.35	256.89	286.80	260.90	290.26	264.92
30,000	419.88	379.33	425.02	385.34	430.20	391.36	435.39	397.39
40,000	559.83	505.78	566.70	513.78	573.60	521.81	580.52	529.85
50,000	699.79	632.22	708.37	642.23	717.00	652.26	725.65	662.31
60,000	839.75	758.67	850.05	770.68	860.39	782.71	870.78	794.77
70,000	979.71	885.11	991.72	899.12	1003.79	913.16	1015.92	927.23
80,000	1119.67	1011.56	1133.40	1027.57	1147.19	1043.61	1161.05	1059.69
90,000	1259.63	1138.00	1275.07	1156.01	1290.59	1174.07	1306.18	1192.16
100,000	1399.59	1264.44	1416.75	1284.46	1433.99	1304.52	1451.31	1324.62

GLOSSARY

Acceleration Clause: Gives the lender the right to call immediately due and payable all sums owed to the lender upon the occurrence of a specific event, such as sale of the property or delinquent repayment.

Acquisition Indebtedness: Used by the IRS to indicate the initial debt incurred to purchase a primary residence or second home.

Addendum: A list of items to be added to a purchase contract or escrow instructions.

All-Inclusive Deed of Trust: A second deed of trust with a face value equal to the amount of a first loan plus a second loan. The borrower pays the second lender one payment from which the second lender makes a payment to the first lender. Also called a wrap-around mortgage.

Amortized Loan: A loan that is paid off in full with equal periodic payments of principal and interest over a fixed period of time.

Appraisal: An opinion about the value of a property based on a factual analysis.

Assumption: An agreement whereby the buyer takes on the liability for repayment of an existing loan on a property. Usually requires the lender's approval. The seller is not automatically relieved of liability.

Attorney-in-Fact: Someone who is authorized to act as an agent for another person under a power of attorney.

Backup Offer: An offer to buy a property that's accepted in secondary position, subject to the collapse of the primary offer.

Balloon Payment: A payment on an installment debt that is significantly larger than the other payments, usually the final payment. Loans with interest-only payments, rather than amortized payments, will have a balloon payment due at maturity.

Beneficiary Statement: A statement issued by the lender stipulating pertinent information about the loan such as the remaining loan balance, interest rate, and monthly payment. Requested from the lender when a buyer is assuming the loan.

Buy-Down: A payment made to the buyer's lender, usually by the seller, in order to reduce the buyer's interest rate on a new loan for a specified period of time.

Capital Gain: Generally the difference between the original cost and the selling price of a capital asset, such as real property, adjusted to allow for deductible expenses. Capital gain is currently taxed as ordinary income.

CC&Rs: Abbreviation for "Covenants, Conditions, and Restrictions," which describe restrictive limitations that apply to a property. Usually found in planned community developments.

Closing: The successful completion of a real estate transaction or refinance, including the transfer of documents and disbursement of funds.

Closing Costs: Miscellaneous fees and expenses that buyers and sellers incur in a real estate sale.

Conforming Loan: A loan in an amount that doesn't exceed the Fannie Mae/Freddie Mac limit. This limit changes annually and was $203,150 in 1993. Conforming loans usually carry the best interest rates and terms. A conforming loan is a loan that is packaged for sale on the secondary mortgage market.

Contingency: A condition that must be met before a contract becomes binding, e.g., an inspection of the property.

Contingent Sale: An offer to purchase a property that is dependent upon the sale of another property.

Contract of Sale: A real property sales contract that provides for title to remain in the seller's name until a prescribed portion of the purchase price is paid by the buyer.

Cosigner: A second person who signs a note with the primary borrower and is thereby equally responsible for repaying the loan.

Counteroffer: An offer in response to an offer (as opposed to an acceptance).

Deed of Trust: A legal document, used instead of a mortgage in California, by which the borrower pledges a piece of real property as a guarantee for repayment of a loan.

Default: Failure to fulfill a promise or perform a legal duty.

Dual Agency: One broker representing both the buyer and seller in a real estate transaction. Dual agency exists if two agents working for the same broker represent the buyer and seller in a transaction.

Due on Sale Clause: A clause in a real estate loan stating that the amount owed to the lender is all due and payable when title to the property is transferred to a new owner.

Easement: A right, privilege, or interest which one party has pertaining to land that belongs to another party.

Encroachment: Building improvements that are wholly or partly on another's adjacent property.

Encumbrance: Anything that limits the title to real property, including liens, easements, or restrictions of any kind.

Equity: The current value of a property, less any liens secured against it.

Escape Clause: A clause in a purchase contract that allows one party to withdraw from the contract under certain terms and conditions. Also called a Release Clause.

Escrow: The deposit of the funds, documents, and instructions required to complete a real estate purchase with a neutral third party until all the terms of the purchase contract have been mutually fulfilled, at which time title to the property is transferred and the escrow is said to be closed.

Exclusion: An item of real property that is not included in the sale (such as a dining room light fixture). Also, an individual who is an exception from the listing agreement. If the owners sell to the exclusion, a real estate commission is not owed to the real estate broker.

Fannie Mae: Federal National Mortgage Association (FNMA). A private corporation that buys and sells mortgages at a discount.

Fiduciary: A person acting in a relationship of trust and confidence, as between principal and broker.

First Deed of Trust: A deed of trust that has priority over all other voluntary liens secured against a property.

Fixture: Personal property that is attached to real property and is therefore treated as real property, such as plumbing and light fixtures. Fixtures transfer with real property, unless specifically excluded from the sale.

Foreclosure: A procedure whereby a property that is pledged as collateral for a debt is sold to pay that debt in the event the borrower defaults on payments or terms.

Freddie Mac: Federal Home Loan Mortgage Corporation (FHLMC). An organization that purchases loans from banks and savings and loans.

FSBO: (pronounced Fisbo) For Sale by Owner. A property offered for sale without the assistance of a real estate broker.

Grant Deed: A type of deed, used to transfer real property, that contains an implied warranty that the property has not already been conveyed to another person and that the property is free from encumbrances placed by the person granting the deed.

Homeowner's Policy: An insurance policy available to homeowners for a premium that provides coverage for the home and its contents in the case of damage or loss due to fire. Lenders almost always require that a homeowner's policy be in effect.

Home Protection Plan: An insurance policy to insure buyers and sellers against defects in a home they're buying or selling (usually in heating, electrical, and plumbing systems).

Impounds: An account set up by a lender for the collection of funds to pay for future property taxes, mortgage insurance, and homeowner's insurance premiums. These funds are usually collected with the note payment. Often required when the buyer is putting less than 20 percent cash down.

In-House Sale: A sale of a property in which the buyer's and seller's agents both work for the same broker.

Installment Sale: A tax term used to refer to a sale in which the seller carries financing for the buyer to spread capital gain liability over a number of years.

Interim Loan: Also called a Swing or Bridge Loan. A temporary, short-term loan that enables a homeowner to liquidate the equity in one home, before it's sold, in order to make a cash down payment on another home. Also refers to a construction loan.

Jumbo Loan: A loan in an amount that exceeds the conforming loan limit which, in 1993, was $203,150. The conforming loan limit is adjusted annually for Fannie Mae and Freddie Mac. Jumbo loans usually have higher interest rates than conforming loans.

Junior Loan (or Lien): Any mortgage, deed of trust, or other lien against a property that is of lesser priority than the first mortgage or deed of trust. For instance, a second deed of trust.

Keybox: Also called lockbox. A metal box, hung on, or close to, the front door, containing the house key. It is opened by special keys issued only to member agents of the Multiple Listing Service.

Lease Option: A lease giving the lessee the option to purchase the property at the specific price and terms set forth in the option agreement.

Lessee: One who contracts to rent a property; a tenant.

Lessor: An owner who enters into an agreement to rent to a tenant; a landlord.

Leverage: The use of borrowed money and a small amount of cash to purchase a property or investment in order to maximize the return per dollar of equity invested.

Lien: A type of encumbrance that makes a property the security for a debt or obligation.

Liquidated Damages: A predetermined sum, agreed to by the parties in a contract, to be considered as full damages if a certain event occurs, e.g., a breach.

Listing Agreement: An employment contract between a property owner and an agent authorizing the agent to perform certain services involving the property.

Loan-to-Value (LTV) Ratio: The percentage of a property's appraised value that a lender may be willing to loan to a borrower. Usually the higher the ratio, the higher the interest rate charged on the loan.

Lockbox: See keybox.

Lock-In: A guarantee from a lender to a borrower who's submitting an application that a specified interest rate will be held for a specified period of time.

Loss Payee: A clause in a homeowner's policy stating the priority of claims in the event the property is destroyed. Lenders and sellers carrying financing for the buyer will usually be named as loss payees and will be paid the amounts owing to them before the buyer is paid.

Market Value: The highest price a willing buyer would pay and a willing seller would accept for a property that is exposed to the open market for a reasonable period of time, and with both buyer and seller being well informed and neither party acting under undue pressure.

Material Fact: A fact that is not known to or readily observable by the buyer that materially affects the value or desirability of a property.

Mechanic's Lien: A lien created by statute that exists against real property in favor of persons who have performed work or provided materials for the purpose of improving that property.

Mortgage: Technically, a legal document by which property is hypothecated to secure payment of a debt or obligation. The term is commonly used to refer to a home loan, and it is often used interchangeably with "deed of trust" (although a mortgage and a deed of trust are different legal instruments).

Multiple Listing: A listing, usually an exclusive right to sell, taken by a member of an organization of real estate brokers with a provision that all members will have an opportunity to find a buyer for the property, thus ensuring wider market exposure for the seller.

Negative Amortization: A condition that occurs when the monthly payments on a loan are insufficient to pay the interest accruing on the principal balance. The unpaid interest is added to the remaining principal due.

Nonrecurring Closing Costs: Closing costs that are paid on a one-time-only basis such as title insurance or points.

Notary Public: One who has the authority to take the acknowledgments of persons signing documents and to affix an official seal.

Note: A signed written document acknowledging a debt and promising repayment on specific terms and conditions. When concerning real property, the note is secured by a deed of trust or mortgage.

Notice of Default: A notice filed to show that a borrower is behind in payments due.

Notice of Delinquency: A notice filed to show that a borrower's payment is past due.

260

Payoff Demand: A written request for a lender to provide exact figures of the amount owed by the borrower in order to pay the loan off in full.

PITI: Abbreviation for Principal, Interest, Taxes, and Insurance. Prorated on a monthly basis; the monthly housing expense.

Points: The origination fee charged by the lender. One point is equal to 1 percent of the loan amount.

Portfolio Lender: A lender that originates loans for its own portfolio, as opposed to a lender that packages loans to be sold on the secondary money market (to Freddie Mac or Fannie Mae).

Power of Attorney: A legal document authorizing a person to act as an agent for the person granting it. A power of attorney can be general or specific.

Preliminary Title Report: Also called a prelim. A report issued before the completion of a real estate sale or loan transaction indicating the condition of the title.

Prepayment Penalty: A charge paid by a borrower to a lender if the loan is paid off before its maturity and if the loan agreement contains a provision stating that such a charge applies.

Private Mortgage Insurance (PMI): Insurance that a borrower pays to protect the lender in case of default. Usually required with high-risk home loans.

Proration: To divide property taxes, insurance premiums, interest, rental amounts, etc., between buyer and seller according to proportionate use as of the closing or an agreed-upon date.

Purchase Contract: An agreement between the buyer and seller that sets forth the terms and conditions of the sale.

Quitclaim Deed: A deed that relinquishes, without warranty, any interest in a property that the grantor may have.

Reconveyance: A legal document commonly used when a debt is satisfied or paid in full under the terms of a deed of trust. Also called a deed of reconveyance or release.

Recording: Placing a document on file with a designated public official (usually the County Recorder) for everyone to see. Recording is governed by statute, and signatures on legal documents usually must be notarized before the documents can be recorded.

Recurring Closing Costs: Costs paid at escrow closing that will be paid again on an on-going basis, such as hazard insurance or PMI (Property Mortgage Insurance).

Red Flag: Anything a real estate agent sees while completing a diligent visual inspection of a property that might indicate that a problem exists.

Refinance: To pay off an existing loan on a property and replace it with another loan.

Seller Financing: A loan on real property, secured either by a first (or junior) deed of trust that a seller carries for a buyer. The seller is the lender rather than a bank or savings and loan.

Single Agency: One real estate broker representing one principal: buyer or seller, but not both.

Specific Performance: A legal action to compel the performance of a contract requirement.

Statement of Identity: Also called Statement of Identification. A confidential form that a title company requires the buyer and seller to complete as a condition of issuing title insurance to ensure that liens and judgments of record do not apply to the individuals in question.

Statute of Limitation: A legal limit on the time period within which a court action must be initiated.

Subject to: Taking over an existing loan on a property without going through a formal assumption process. The original borrower is not released from responsibility for repayment of a loan.

Tax Lien: A lien that attaches to real property if the property owner fails to pay property or income taxes when they are due.

261

Termite Report: A Wood Destroying Pests and Organisms Inspection Report which covers active infection and infestation by wood destroying organisms, damage from such organisms, conditions that resulted in current structural pest control problems, and conditions that are deemed likely to lead to such problems in the future.

Title: Evidence of ownership and right to real property.

Title Insurance: Insurance issued by a title company to protect a property owner from loss due to imperfect title.

Underwriting: The technical analysis completed by a lender to ensure that a contemplated loan is a sound investment.

Vesting: The manner in which title of ownership to a particular property is held, including the names and status of the owners.

Waiver: To abandon or release a right to enforce or require something.

Zoning: The act of a governing authority specifying how property in specific areas can be used.

APPENDIX

□

RESIDENTIAL LEASE WITH PURCHASE OPTION
THIS IS INTENDED TO BE A LEGALLY BINDING CONTRACT. READ IT CAREFULLY.
CALIFORNIA ASSOCIATION OF REALTORS® (CAR) STANDARD FORM

_____, California _____ 19____
_____, Landlord,
and _____, Tenant, agree as follows:

1. **PROPERTY:** Landlord leases to Tenant and Tenant leases from Landlord the real property and improvements described as:
_____
(Street address or other description)
_____ ("Premises"). Inventory of personal
(City, County, State)
property, if any, is attached as Exhibit "A."

2. **TERM:** The term of this lease shall be for a period of _____ commencing
(years, months, days)
_____, 19____ and terminating _____, 19____, at 11:59 p.m.

3. **RENT:** Tenant agrees to pay a total rent of $_____, payable as follows:_____
_____
_____ .
$_____ upon the signing of this Agreement, as prorated rent from _____ 19___ to
_____ 19___.
$_____ per month commencing on the _____ day of _____ 19___, and on
the same day of each calendar month thereafter until the expiration of this Agreement. Rent installments are payable in advance. Rent
will be accepted from the named Tenant only.

4. **LATE CHARGE:** Tenant acknowledges that late payment of rent may cause Landlord to incur costs and expenses, the exact amount of
such costs being extremely difficult and impractical to fix. Such costs may include, but are not limited to, processing and accounting expenses,
late charges that may be imposed on Landlord by terms of any loan secured by the property, costs for additional attempts to collect rent,
and preparation of notices. Therefore, if any installment of rent due from Tenant is not received by Landlord within _____ calendar
days after date due, Tenant shall pay to Landlord an additional sum of $_____ as a late charge, which shall be deemed
additional rent. The Parties agree that this late charge represents a fair and reasonable estimate of the costs that Landlord may incur by
reason of Tenant's late payments. Acceptance of any late charge shall not constitute a waiver of Tenant's default with respect to the past
due amount, or prevent Landlord from exercising any other rights and remedies under this agreement, and as provided by law.

5. **PAYMENT:** The rent shall be paid at _____ .
or at any other location specified by Landlord.
(Address, City, State, Zip)

6. **SECURITY DEPOSIT:** $_____ has been received as a security deposit. Landlord may use therefrom such amounts
as are reasonably necessary to remedy Tenant's default in the payment of rent, to repair damages caused by Tenant, or by a guest or a
licensee of Tenant, to clean the premises, if necessary, upon termination of tenancy, and to replace or repair personal property, fixtures,
and appurtenances exclusive of ordinary wear and tear. If used toward rent or damages during the term of tenancy, Tenant agrees to reinstate
said total security deposit upon five calendar days written notice delivered to Tenant in person or by mail. Within two weeks after Tenant
has vacated the premises, Landlord shall furnish to Tenant an itemized written statement of the amount of any security received, the amount
of and basis for any deductions, and the disposition of the security, and shall return any remaining portion of the security to Tenant. **Broker(s)
will disburse to Landlord or Landlord's successor, upon request, any security deposit held in trust by broker(s). Thereafter, return
of any portion of security deposit due upon termination of tenancy will be handled directly between Landlord or Landlord's successor
and Tenant without involvement by broker(s).**

7. **UTILITIES:** Tenant agrees to pay for all utilities and services based upon occupancy of the premises and the following charges:
_____ ;
except _____ which shall be paid for by
(Specify exceptions or write "none")

___ utilities are not separ___ Ten___ ___nt's proport___ ___ of as

Appendix

or at any other lo.......... ..by Landlord.   ....y, State, Zip)

6. SECURITY DEPOSIT: $_____ has been rece.......... ..o a security deposit. Landlord may use therefrom such amounts as are reasonably necessary to remedy Tenant's default in the payment of rent, to repair damages caused by Tenant, or by a guest or a licensee of Tenant, to clean the premises, if necessary, upon termination of tenancy, and to replace or repair personal property, fixtures, and appurtenances exclusive of ordinary wear and tear. If used toward rent or damages during the term of tenancy, Tenant agrees to reinstate said total security deposit upon five calendar days written notice delivered to Tenant in person or by mail. Within two weeks after Tenant has vacated the premises, Landlord shall furnish to Tenant an itemized written statement of the amount of any security received, the amount of and basis for any deductions, and the disposition of the security, and shall return any remaining portion of the security to Tenant. **Broker(s) will disburse to Landlord or Landlord's successor, upon request, any security deposit held in trust by broker(s). Thereafter, return of any portion of security deposit due upon termination of tenancy will be handled directly between Landlord or Landlord's successor and Tenant without involvement by broker(s).**

7. UTILITIES: Tenant agrees to pay for all utilities and services based upon occupancy of the premises and the following charges: _____ ;
except _____ which shall be paid for by
(Specify exceptions or write "none")
Landlord. If any utilities are not separately metered, _____ Tenant shall pay Tenant's proportional share thereof as reasonably determined by Landlord.

8. CONDITION: Tenant has examined the premises and all furniture, furnishings, and appliances, if any, and fixtures, including smoke detector(s) contained therein, and accepts the same as being clean, and in operative condition, with the following exceptions: _____ .

9. OCCUPANTS: The premises are for the sole use as a residence by the following named persons **only:** _____ .

10. PETS: No animal, bird or pet shall be kept on or about the premises without Landlord's prior written consent, except_____ .

11. USE: Tenant shall not disturb, annoy, endanger, or interfere with other tenants of the building or neighbors, nor use the premises for any unlawful purposes, nor violate any law or ordinance, nor commit waste or nuisance upon or about the premises.

12. RULES AND REGULATIONS: Tenant agrees (a) to comply with all covenants, conditions, and restrictions, bylaws, regulations, and decisions of owners' association, which are at any time posted on the premises or delivered to Tenant, and (b) to be liable for any fines, assessments and charges levied due to violation(s).

13. MAINTENANCE: Tenant shall properly use and operate all furniture, furnishings and appliances, electrical, gas, and plumbing fixtures and keep them as clean and sanitary as their condition permits. Excluding ordinary wear and tear, Tenant shall notify Landlord and pay for all repairs or replacements caused by Tenant or Tenant's invitees. **Tenant's personal property is not insured by Landlord.**

14. ALTERATIONS: Except as provided by law, Tenant shall not paint, wallpaper, add or change locks, or make alterations to the property without Landlord's prior written consent.

263

Tenant and Landlord acknowledge receipt of copy of this page, which constitutes Page 1 of _____ Pages.
Tenant's Initials (_____) (_____)   Landlord's Initials (_____) (_____)

----- OFFICE USE ONLY -----
Reviewed by Broker or Designee _____
Date _____

☐

Subject Property Address: _____ _____, 19_____

15. KEYS: Tenant acknowledges receipt of:
☐ _____ key(s) to premises,
☐ _____ key(s) to mailbox,
☐ _____ remote control device(s) for garage door opener(s),
☐ _____ .
At Tenant's expense, Tenant may re-key existing locks and shall deliver copies of all new keys to Landlord upon installation.

16. ENTRY: Upon not less than 24 hours notice, Tenant shall make the premises available during normal business hours to Landlord, authorized agent, or representative, for the purpose of entering to (a) make necessary or agreed repairs, decorations, alterations, or improvements or supply necessary or agreed services, or (b) show the premises to prospective or actual purchasers, mortgagees, tenants, or contractors. In an emergency, Landlord, authorized agent, or representative may enter the premises, at any time, without prior permission from Tenant.

17. POSSESSION: Possession of the Premises shall be delivered to Tenant:
☐ upon execution of this lease, or
☐ _____ .
If Tenant abandons or vacates the Premises, Landlord may terminate this lease and regain lawful possession. If Landlord is unable to deliver possession of the Premises on the Commencement Date, the Commencement Date shall be extended to the date on which possession is made available to Tenant. If Landlord is unable to deliver possession for a period of more than _____ days from the original Commencement Date, Tenant may terminate this Agreement by giving written notice to Landlord, and shall receive a refund of all rent, security deposit, and option consideration paid.

18. HOLD OVER: Any holding over at the expiration of this lease shall create a month to month tenancy at a monthly rent of $_____ payable in advance. All other terms and conditions herein shall remain in full force and effect.

19. OPTION TO PURCHASE: In consideration of the payment of $_____ as option consideration,
☐ receipt of $_____ of which is acknowledged by Landlord, evidenced by ☐ cash, ☐ cashier's check, ☐ personal check, or ☐ _____
☐ payable as follows:_____ ,

Landlord grants to Tenant the option to purchase the Premises on the terms and conditions set forth in the attached:
☐ Real Estate Purchase Contract and Receipt for Deposit,
☐ Mobile Home Purchase Contract and Receipt for Deposit,
☐ Other _____
which are incorporated by this reference as a part of this Agreement. All of the time limits contained in the attached agreement shall begin to run on the date the option is exercised. Rent shall continue to be payable as above, after the option is exercised, until the close of the sale. If any contingency in the attached agreement, including but not limited to any right of inspection or financing provision, is not satisfied or is disapproved by Tenant at any time, all option consideration paid, rent paid, services rendered to Landlord, and improvements to the Premises, if any, by Tenant, shall be retained by Landlord in consideration of the granting of the option.

20. SUPPLEMENTS: The ATTACHED supplements below are incorporated as part of this Agreement:
☐ _____ ☐ _____
☐ _____ ☐ _____
☐ _____ ☐ _____

21. TERM OF OPTION: The Option shall begin on _____, 19_____, and shall end at 11:59 p.m. on _____, 19_____.

22. MANNER OF EXERCISE: Tenant may exercise the Option **only** by:
(a) delivering to Landlord, no earlier than _____ and no later than _____, a written, unconditional notice of exercise, signed by Tenant, **and**
(b) ☐ [If checked] opening escrow with the escrow holder named in the attached agreement, **and**

264

the close of the _____ ...ngency in the attached a... _____ ...g but not limited to any right of inspection or financing provision, is not satisfied or is disapproved by Tenant at any time, all option consideration paid, rent paid, services rendered to Landlord, and improvements to the Premises, if any, by Tenant, shall be retained by Landlord in consideration of the granting of the option.

20. SUPPLEMENTS: The ATTACHED supplements below are incorporated as part of this Agreement:

☐ _____ ☐ _____
☐ _____ ☐ _____
☐ _____ ☐ _____

21. TERM OF OPTION: The Option shall begin on _____, 19____, and shall end at 11:59 p.m. on _____, 19____.

22. MANNER OF EXERCISE: Tenant may exercise the Option **only** by:
(a) delivering to Landlord, no earlier than _____ and no later than _____, a written, unconditional notice of exercise, signed by Tenant, <u>and</u>
(b) ☐ [If checked] opening escrow with the escrow holder named in the attached agreement, <u>and</u>
(c) ☐ [If checked] delivering
   ☐ a copy of the notice of exercise,
   ☐ signed escrow instructions, to the named escrow holder, <u>and</u>
(d) ☐ [If checked] Other: _____.

23. EFFECT OF DEFAULT ON OPTION:
(a) Tenant shall have no right to exercise the Option (i) during the time period any monetary or non-monetary obligation of Tenant then due is unpaid or unperformed (whether or not notice of default is given to Tenant), or (ii) if Landlord has given to Tenant three or more notices of default under this Agreement during the immediately preceding 12 month period, whether or not the defaults are cured.
(b) All of Tenant's rights under the Option shall terminate, even if the Option is timely exercised if, after exercise and before the close of the sale, (i) Tenant fails to pay or perform any monetary or non-monetary obligation under the terms of this Agreement, for a period of 30 days after the obligation becomes due or before the scheduled close of the sale, whichever occurs first (whether or not Landlord gives notice of default to Tenant), or (ii) Landlord gives to Tenant three or more notices of default during any 12 month period, whether or not the defaults are cured.

24. NON-EXERCISE: If the Option is not exercised in the manner specified, within the option period or any written extension thereof, or if it is terminated under any provision of this Agreement, then:
(a) The Option and all rights of Tenant to purchase the property shall immediately terminate without notice.
(b) All Option consideration paid, rent paid, services rendered to Landlord, and improvements to the Premises, if any, by Tenant, shall be retained by Landlord in consideration of the granting of the Option.
(c) Any security deposit shall be disbursed as provided by law.
(d) If requested by Landlord, Tenant shall execute, acknowledge, and deliver to Landlord within _____ calendar days of Landlord's request, a release, quitclaim deed, or any other document reasonably required by Landlord or a title insurance company to verify the termination of the Option.

25. ASSIGNMENT OF LEASE AND OPTION; SUBLETTING: Tenant shall not let or sublet all or any part of the Premises nor assign the lease or the Option or any interest therein
☐ [If checked] except upon Landlord's review and approval of financial statements, tax returns, and credit history of the proposed sublessee(s) or assignee(s). Any assignment or subletting in violation of this paragraph shall be void.

265

Tenant and Landlord acknowledge receipt of copy of this page, which constitutes Page 2 of _____ Pages.
Tenant's Initials (_____) (_____) Landlord's Initials (_____) (_____)

— OFFICE USE ONLY —
Reviewed by Broker or Designee _____
Date _____

BROKER'S COPY

RESIDENTIAL LEASE WITH PURCHASE OPTION (LRO-14 PAGE 2 OF 4)

☐

Subject Property Address: _____ _____, 19____

26. **NOTICES:** Unless otherwise provided in this Agreement, any notice, tender, or delivery to be given by either party to the other may be effected by personal delivery, or by registered or certified mail, postage prepaid, return receipt requested, and shall be deemed delivered when mailed (except for acceptance of the offer to enter into this Agreement, which must be done in the manner specified in paragraph 38). Mailed notices shall be addressed as shown below, but each party may designate a new address by written notice to the other.

27. **TRANSFER DISCLOSURE STATEMENT:** Unless exempt, if the Premises contain one-to-four residential dwelling units, Landlord must comply with Civil Code §§1102 et seq., by providing Tenant with a Real Estate Transfer Disclosure Statement. **Unless exempt, Tenant has received and read a Real Estate Transfer Disclosure Statement.**

28. **TAX WITHHOLDING:** (a) Under the Foreign Investment in Real Property Tax Act (FIRPTA), IRC §1445, every Buyer of U.S. real property must, unless an exemption applies, deduct and withhold from Seller's proceeds 10% of the gross sales price. The primary FIRPTA exemptions are: No withholding is required if (i) Seller provides Buyer an affidavit under penalty of perjury, that Seller is not a "foreign person," or (ii) Seller provides Buyer a "qualifying statement" issued by the Internal Revenue Service, or (iii) Buyer purchases real property for use as a residence and the purchase price is $300,000 or less and Buyer or a member of Buyer's family has definite plans to reside at the Property for at least 50% of the number of days it is in use during each of the first two 12-month periods after transfer. (b) In addition, under California Revenue and Taxation Code §§18805 and 26131, every Buyer must, unless an exemption applies, deduct and withhold from the Seller's proceeds 3⅓% of the gross sales price if the Seller has a last known address outside of California, or if the Seller's proceeds will be paid to a financial intermediary of the Seller. The primary exemptions are: No withholding is required if (i) the Property is Seller's principal residence, under specified conditions, or (ii) the Property is selling for $100,000 or less, or (iii) the Franchise Tax Board issues a certificate authorizing a lower amount or no withholding, or (iv) the Seller signs an affidavit stating that the Seller is a California resident or a corporation qualified to do business in California. (c) Seller and Buyer agree to execute and deliver as directed any instrument, affidavit, or statement reasonably necessary to carry out those statutes and regulations promulgated thereunder. (CAR FORM AS-14, SELLER'S AFFIDAVIT OF NON-FOREIGN STATUS AND/OR CALIFORNIA RESIDENCY, OR CAR FORM AB-11, BUYER'S AFFIDAVIT, OR SIMILAR FORMS, IF APPLICABLE, SHALL SATISFY THESE REQUIREMENTS.)

29. **ARBITRATION OF DISPUTES: Any dispute or claim in law or equity arising out of this contract or any resulting transaction shall be decided by neutral binding arbitration in accordance with the rules of the American Arbitration Association, and not by court action except as provided by California law for judicial review of arbitration proceedings. Judgment upon the award rendered by the arbitrator(s) may be entered in any court having jurisdiction thereof. The parties shall have the right to discovery in accordance with Code of Civil Procedure §1283.05. The following matters are excluded from arbitration hereunder: (a) a judicial or non-judicial foreclosure or other action or proceeding to enforce a deed of trust, mortgage, or real property sales contract as defined in Civil Code §2985, (b) an unlawful detainer action, (c) the filing or enforcement of a mechanic's lien, (d) any matter which is within the jurisdiction of a probate or small claims court, or (e) an action for bodily injury or wrongful death, or for latent or patent defects to which Code of Civil Procedure §337.1 or §337.15 applies. The filing of a judicial action to enable the recording of a notice of pending action, for order of attachment, receivership, injunction, or other provisional remedies, shall not constitute a waiver of the right to arbitrate under this provision.**

Any dispute or claim by or against broker(s) and/or associate licensee(s) participating in this transaction shall be submitted to arbitration consistent with the provision above only if the broker(s) and/or associate licensee(s) making the claim or against whom the claim is made shall have agreed to submit it to arbitration consistent with this provision.

"NOTICE: BY INITIALLING IN THE SPACE BELOW YOU ARE AGREEING TO HAVE ANY DISPUTE ARISING OUT OF THE MATTERS INCLUDED IN THE 'ARBITRATION OF DISPUTES' PROVISION DECIDED BY NEUTRAL ARBITRATION AS PROVIDED BY CALIFORNIA LAW AND YOU ARE GIVING UP ANY RIGHTS YOU MIGHT POSSESS TO HAVE THE DISPUTE LITIGATED IN A COURT OR JURY TRIAL. BY INITIALLING IN THE SPACE BELOW YOU ARE GIVING UP YOUR JUDICIAL RIGHTS TO DISCOVERY AND APPEAL, UNLESS THOSE RIGHTS ARE SPECIFICALLY INCLUDED IN THE 'ARBITRATION OF DISPUTES' PROVISION. IF YOU REFUSE TO SUBMIT TO ARBITRATION AFTER AGREEING TO THIS PROVISION, YOU MAY BE COMPELLED TO ARBITRATE UNDER THE AUTHORITY OF THE CALIFORNIA CODE OF CIVIL PROCEDURE. YOUR AGREEMENT TO THIS ARBITRATION PROVISION IS VOLUNTARY."

"WE HAVE READ AND UNDERSTAND THE FOREGOING AND AGREE TO SUBMIT DISPUTES ARISING OUT OF THE MATTERS INCLUDED IN THE 'ARBITRATION OF DISPUTES' PROVISION TO NEUTRAL ARBITRATION."

Landlord's (Seller's)

266

which a ....ng o~

action, for order ....., receivership, injunction, ... remedies, shall not co...... a waiver of the rig... to arbitrate under this provision.

Any dispute or claim by or against broker(s) and/or associate licensee(s) participating in this transaction shall be submitted to arbitration consistent with the provision above only if the broker(s) and/or associate licensee(s) making the claim or against whom the claim is made shall have agreed to submit it to arbitration consistent with this provision.

"NOTICE: BY INITIALLING IN THE SPACE BELOW YOU ARE AGREEING TO HAVE ANY DISPUTE ARISING OUT OF THE MATTERS INCLUDED IN THE 'ARBITRATION OF DISPUTES' PROVISION DECIDED BY NEUTRAL ARBITRATION AS PROVIDED BY CALIFORNIA LAW AND YOU ARE GIVING UP ANY RIGHTS YOU MIGHT POSSESS TO HAVE THE DISPUTE LITIGATED IN A COURT OR JURY TRIAL. BY INITIALLING IN THE SPACE BELOW YOU ARE GIVING UP YOUR JUDICIAL RIGHTS TO DISCOVERY AND APPEAL, UNLESS THOSE RIGHTS ARE SPECIFICALLY INCLUDED IN THE 'ARBITRATION OF DISPUTES' PROVISION. IF YOU REFUSE TO SUBMIT TO ARBITRATION AFTER AGREEING TO THIS PROVISION, YOU MAY BE COMPELLED TO ARBITRATE UNDER THE AUTHORITY OF THE CALIFORNIA CODE OF CIVIL PROCEDURE. YOUR AGREEMENT TO THIS ARBITRATION PROVISION IS VOLUNTARY."

"WE HAVE READ AND UNDERSTAND THE FOREGOING AND AGREE TO SUBMIT DISPUTES ARISING OUT OF THE MATTERS INCLUDED IN THE 'ARBITRATION OF DISPUTES' PROVISION TO NEUTRAL ARBITRATION."

Tenant's (Buyer's) Initials _____ / _____   Landlord's (Seller's) Initials _____ / _____

30. OTHER TERMS AND CONDITIONS: _____

_____
_____
_____
_____
_____
_____
_____
_____
_____
_____
_____
_____
_____
_____
_____
_____

267

31. ATTORNEY'S FEES: In any judicial, arbitration, or other proceeding arising out of this Agreement, the prevailing party shall be entitled to reasonable attorney's fees and costs.

32. RECORDING: Landlord or Tenant shall, upon request, execute, acknowledge, and deliver to the other a memorandum of this Agreement for recording purposes. All resulting fees and taxes shall be paid by the party requesting recordation.

Tenant and Landlord acknowledge receipt of copy of this page, which constitutes Page 3 of _____ Pages.

Tenant's Initials (_____) (_____)   Landlord's Initials (_____) (_____)

OFFICE USE ONLY
Reviewed by Broker or Designee _____
Date _____

BROKER'S COPY

EQUAL HOUSING OPPORTUNITY
M-SC-MAR-92

RESIDENTIAL LEASE WITH PURCHASE OPTION (LRO-14 PAGE 3 OF 4)

☐

Subject Property Address: _____ _____, 19____

33. ENTIRE CONTRACT: Time is of the essence. All prior agreements between the parties are incorporated in this Agreement which constitutes the entire contract. Its terms are intended by the parties as a final expression of their agreement with respect to such terms as are included herein and may not be contradicted by evidence of any prior agreement or contemporaneous oral agreement. The parties further intend that this Agreement constitutes the complete and exclusive statement of its terms and that no extrinsic evidence whatsoever may be introduced in any judicial or arbitration proceeding, if any, involving this Agreement.

34. WAIVER: The waiver of any breach shall not be construed to be a continuing waiver of the same or any subsequent breach.

35. CAPTIONS: The captions in this Agreement are for convenience of reference only and are not intended as part of this Agreement.

36. AGENCY CONFIRMATION: The following agency relationship(s) are hereby confirmed for this transaction:

Listing Agent: _____ is the agent of (check one):
(Print Firm Name)

☐ the Landlord (Seller) exclusively; or
☐ both the Tenant (Buyer) and Landlord (Seller).

Selling Agent: _____ (if not same as Listing Agent) is the agent of (check one):
(Print Firm Name)

☐ the Tenant (Buyer) exclusively; or
☐ the Landlord (Seller) exclusively; or
☐ both the Tenant (Buyer) and Landlord (Seller).

37. AMENDMENTS: This Agreement may not be amended, modified, altered or changed in any respect whatsoever except by a further agreement in writing executed by Tenant and Landlord.

38. OFFER: This constitutes an offer to acquire a lease with an option to purchase the described property. Unless acceptance is signed by Landlord and a signed copy delivered in person, by mail, or by facsimile, and received by Tenant at the address below, or by _____ who is authorized to receive it on behalf of Tenant, within _____ calendar days of the date hereof, this offer shall be deemed revoked and Tenant's deposit shall be returned. Tenant has read and acknowledges receipt of a copy of this offer. This Agreement and any supplement, addendum, or modification relating hereto, including any photocopy or facsimile thereof, may be executed in two or more counterparts, all of which shall constitute one and the same writing.

REAL ESTATE BROKER_____ TENANT_____
By_____ TENANT_____
Address _____ Address _____
_____ _____
Telephone _____ Fax _____ Telephone _____ Fax _____

ACCEPTANCE

The undersigned Landlord accepts and agrees to lease and to grant an option to purchase the property on the above terms and conditions and agrees to the above confirmation of agency relationships (☐ subject to attached counter offer).

Landlord agrees to pay to Broker(s) _____

compensation for services as follows: (1) _____ upon execution of this Agreement; and (2) _____ upon close of a sale if the Option is exercised, payable: (a) On recordation of the deed or other evidence of title, or (b) if completion of sale is prevented by default of Landlord, upon Landlord's default, or (c) if completion of sale is prevented by default of Tenant, only if and when Landlord collects damages from Tenant, by suit or otherwise, and then in an amount not less than one-half of the damages recovered, but not to exceed the above fee, after deducting title and escrow expenses and the expenses of collection, if any. Landlord shall execute and deliver an escrow instruction

Appendix

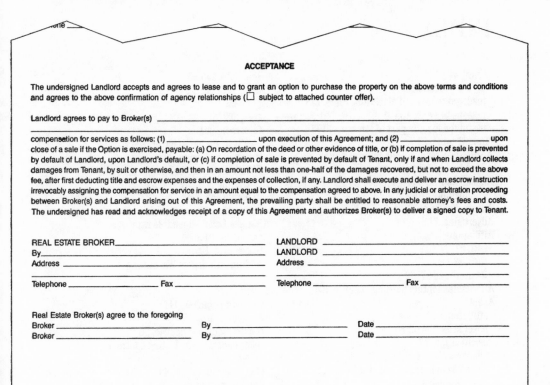

ACCEPTANCE

The undersigned Landlord accepts and agrees to lease and to grant an option to purchase the property on the above terms and conditions and agrees to the above confirmation of agency relationships (☐ subject to attached counter offer).

Landlord agrees to pay to Broker(s) _____

_____
compensation for services as follows: (1) _____ upon execution of this Agreement; and (2) _____ upon close of a sale if the Option is exercised, payable: (a) On recordation of the deed or other evidence of title, or (b) if completion of sale is prevented by default of Landlord, upon Landlord's default, or (c) if completion of sale is prevented by default of Tenant, only if and when Landlord collects damages from Tenant, by suit or otherwise, and then in an amount not less than one-half of the damages recovered, but not to exceed the above fee, after first deducting title and escrow expenses and the expenses of collection, if any. Landlord shall execute and deliver an escrow instruction irrevocably assigning the compensation for service in an amount equal to the compensation agreed to above. In any judicial or arbitration proceeding between Broker(s) and Landlord arising out of this Agreement, the prevailing party shall be entitled to reasonable attorney's fees and costs. The undersigned has read and acknowledges receipt of a copy of this Agreement and authorizes Broker(s) to deliver a signed copy to Tenant.

REAL ESTATE BROKER_____ LANDLORD _____
By_____ LANDLORD _____
Address _____ Address _____

Telephone _____ Fax _____ Telephone _____ Fax _____

Real Estate Broker(s) agree to the foregoing
Broker _____ By _____ Date _____
Broker _____ By _____ Date _____

269

BROKER'S COPY
Page 4 of _____ Pages.

OFFICE USE ONLY
Reviewed by Broker or Designee _____
Date _____

RESIDENTIAL LEASE WITH PURCHASE OPTION (LRO-14 PAGE 4 OF 4)

INDEX

273

274

275

278